# BACK TO SQUARE ONE

Also by Joyce Goldstein

*The Mediterranean Kitchen*

JOYCE GOLDSTEIN

# BACK TO SQUARE ONE

## OLD-WORLD FOOD IN A NEW-WORLD KITCHEN

WILLIAM MORROW AND COMPANY, INC.
NEW YORK

It is the policy of William Morrow and Company, Inc., and its imprints and affiliates recognizing the importance of preserving what has been written, to print the books we publish on acid-free paper, and we exert our best efforts to that end.

Library of Congress Cataloging-in-Publication Data

Goldstein, Joyce Esersky.
    Back to square one : old-world food in a new-world kitchen / Joyce
Goldstein.
        p.        cm.
    Includes index.
    ISBN 0-688-10122-4
    1. Cookery, International.     I. Title.
TX725.A1G475        1992
641.59—dc20                                                    92-8366
                                                              CIP

Printed in the United States of America

First Edition

1 2 3 4 5 6 7 8 9 10

BOOK DESIGN BY PENTAGRAM DESIGNS INC.

ILLUSTRATIONS © 1992 BY RACHEL GOLDSTEIN

In memory of Mo Bernstein and Jim Daneu

We miss their critical presence at Square One

# ACKNOWLEDGMENTS

When running a busy restaurant, if you want to set aside time to write, you need an extraordinary staff. I have one at Square One, and I want to thank them for helping to make this book possible. I appreciate their attention to detail and their keeping the restaurant running smoothly while all this writing was going on.

A Giant Thank You To: Paul Buscemi, Gerald Gass, and Gary Woo for running the kitchen, interpreting my recipes and cooking great food, day in and day out. And tasting . . . and tasting . . . and tasting.

Jennifer Millar and Jerry Tewell for creating elegant desserts and giving me extra cookies.

Julia Drori, Michael Levitan, Leslie Carman, and all the other warriors on the line who helped transcribe the recipes and cooked the food over and over to test recipe accuracy.

Tom Benthin, Frank Everett, and our floor staff for making sure that our guests were happy and well cared for.

Peter Granoff for picking the perfect wines to serve with our food.

I Also Want To Say Thank You To: Evan, "my son the sommelier," for his excellent wine commentary, his expertise, and his endless enthusiasm.

My daughter Rachel for her beautiful illustrations and creative energy. And to my son-in-law Barney Baker for testing some of the recipes and letting me know how they worked for the non-professional cook.

Kit Hinrichs of Pentagram who was one of the first supporters of Square One and whose impeccable graphic skills and good taste has shaped this book and many of our anniversary posters.

My editor Ann Bramson who allowed me freedom of expression that enabled me to write more than just recipes.

My agents Maureen and Eric Lasher for encouragement, support, and the voice of reality.

Stephanie Lyness for asking all the right recipe questions.

Chet Lieb for his opinions, critical eye, and friendship.

Barry Reder and Chuck Frank for good advice and perspective.

And to my much loved regular customers for their feedback, enthusiasm, and support. Thanks for coming Back to Square One!

# C O N T E N T S

# INTRODUCTION

Recipes are the artifacts of a people's culture. They are a country's ethnic identity transcribed in food. Traditional classic dishes have slight variations that differentiate one township from another, one family from another, one person from another. Recipes tell you about people, how they lived, what they grew, what was deemed special for holidays and festivals, what was readily available to them for everyday sustenance.

Most home cooks don't have the time for extensive recipe research and experimentation. However, this culinary exploration keeps my creative energy flowing. I enjoy the challenge of discovering and mastering a dish, of finding and experimenting with new ingredients. I consider myself very fortunate to be a chef, as I can be an artist, interpreter, and caretaker of cultural artworks we call recipes. I love them all. To me they are as precious as Russian icons, Greek sculptures, Japanese prints, or Italian primitive panel paintings. I can discover the history of a dish and its variations, and then select one to cook. I try to find out about the people who cooked this food—when, why, how. What were the different interpretations of the recipe? How did it change as it crossed national and regional boundaries?

From Iran to Turkey. From Turkey to Russia. From Greece to Sicily. From Catalan Spain to Sardinia. From Portugal to Brazil, from China to Cuba. Immigration has not been confined to America. Tribes and peoples have been in motion for generations, for one reason or another, and the food moved with them and influenced the cuisine of the country where they stopped. The melting pot has been around for a long time, and not just here!

### Food and Tradition

When people leave their homeland to immigrate to another country, they make great sacrifices. They give up their homes, they give up their language, they sacrifice many of their social customs, but they do not give up their food. Food is the tie that binds the family together. It connects people to their cultural roots.

As a chef, cooking for people every day, I am very much aware of the power of food memory. I know how comforting a familiar taste is to the diner who hungers for recognizable flavors in a world that seems to be in a state of constant culinary titillation. I have seen how evocative a dish can be to the person who hasn't tasted it in a long while. When we serve a traditionally inspired classic dish, we can give the diner a present of his past and an enduring symbol of love and happy times.

I remember an elderly woman who tasted one of my pastas, closed her eyes for a moment, then wiped her plate clean with some bread. Later her daughter took me aside and told me that her mother hadn't eaten that pasta since she left Italy and thanked me for giving her mother such pleasure. A man from Romania stopped me in the dining room to talk about the mushroom stuffed quail he ate that evening. It was a specialty of his village and he wondered how I knew about it. The food connection was so strong, he could have talked for hours. At a Jewish Community Center benefit I served chopped liver and gribines. People's eyes misted over as they reminisced about eating chopped liver and gribines at their grandmothers' houses. That evening, despite good intentions, out of the power of memory and sentiment, they went off their low-fat diets.

The great grandmothers and grandmothers (and a few grandfathers too) who used to cook the traditional foods are gone. Unfortunately many family recipes have vanished with them. Little did we know when we followed these women and men around the kitchen, licking the spoons, listening to their stories, that we ought to be taking notes about how to prepare our family's favorites. Years later, when we tried to re-create these recipes, there was always something missing. It never dawned on us that Aunt Ida's recipe for dumplings was not just like any one we read in the newspaper. Or Zio Tony's hot fennel sausage. Or cousin Helen's almond cake. Only after tasting it did we realize that Grandma's recipe for stuffed cabbage was not the recipe in Aunt Florence's files.

Most cooks in our grandparents' and great grandparents' generation didn't work from written recipes. They cooked from habit and from memory. They rarely measured, used a pinch of this, a pinch of that, stopped kneading the bread when it felt right, or took the stew out of the oven when it smelled a certain way. They just knew when it was done and when to stop. The dishes they cooked were based on a limited set of local ingredients and traditional ethnic food themes. Now, granted, their culinary repertoire wasn't vast. But what they knew, they knew. They knew it by feel, by smell, by taste memory. The recipe was visceral and a part of them. Unlike our generation, they didn't collect and read cookbooks. There weren't glossy food magazines to tempt them with the food of other cultures, other lands. They knew what they grew up with and that was enough. And it was good and comforting and a part of life.

### Recipe Evolution: Closing the Circle

Today things change so fast, many of us are starting to feel a special need to be connected to our past. While constant change can be stimulating and exciting, it's impossible to keep up. We're bewildered by too many options. It's no wonder that there are moments when we reflect on how nice it would be to have established traditions, live a simpler life, and reduce stress by reducing choices. We look with nostalgia at the lives of our grandparents. Maybe life was harder for them physically, but emotionally it seemed clearer and less confusing.

If we look at the evolution of ethnic recipes and food in our country, we can see a circular pattern emerging. Immigrants came to America bringing their recipes with them, their food history, and taste memories. In the old country they were mostly agrarian people and lived off seasonal local produce and livestock. In their new country, however, not all of the ingredients were the same as back home. Or even to be found. The recipes had to be modified. They evolved. They kept some tastes of the past, dropped some ingredients and procedures, and added new elements. Not only did they transform the recipe but even may have changed the sequence of the dish in the meal and the occasion on which it was served.

For example, look what happened to pasta. In Italian restaurants it was a first course, savored in small portions, by and for itself. It was then followed by a small meat or fish course, then the vegetables or salad. Then cheese and maybe fruit. At home, many families dined mostly on pasta, soups and salads, with meat reserved for special feast days. When the Italians came to America they found that meat was cheap and plentiful. Pasta represented the poorer past. It thus became the accompaniment to a meat entree and appeared on the same plate, with vegetables. The American way! The desire for large entree portions, symbolic of American abundance and richness, affected pasta's place on the table. For most other Americans not of Italian descent, pasta became an economical meal in itself, a big heaping bowl as dinner with salad first. So when American tourists traveled to Italy they wondered why the pasta portion was so small!

Some variation of this scenario can be repeated whether our ancestors came from Russia or Poland, from Greece or Turkey or Albania, from Mexico or Brazil, Thailand or China, Japan or India. Over time the clarity of our family's recipes became obscured as one nationality's cuisine was combined with aspects of another or several others. With travel giving us greater exposure to the traditional foods in their original environment, we can return to the source and taste the food in its homeland. We can import ethnic ingredients or learn to grow the ingredients in America. Today we can buy tamarind, turmeric, lemongrass, galangal, endless chiles, arugula, radicchio, blood oranges, romanesco broccoli, Charentaise melons, French haricots verts, favas, daikon, and broccoli rape. We import parmigiano reggiano, prosciutto di Parma, French lentils, basmati rice, saffron, Thai fish sauce, oyster sauce, balsamic vinegar, and olive oils from all over the Mediterranean. The tastes of our ancestors are at our local markets. We can cook Italian one night and Greek the next. We can follow our Russian roots for one dinner and our French roots at the next.

Today, at holidays and family get-togethers the traditional family recipes are culled from dusty files. Fewer and fewer people seem to remember how they were supposed to be prepared or what they tasted like. The great grandchildren and grandchildren haven't really known the food of their ethnic heritage or their family, except in watered-down and distorted forms. The ties that bind are getting loose. We need to keep these traditional foods alive. It's all well and good to try the latest melting pot combination of Cal-Ital or Franco-Asian or American melange cooking. But we need to keep in touch with our own food history, before our taste memories are lost forever. For our family's sake and for our stomachs. And for our souls.

This book is a personal collection of some of my favorite recipes from cultures whose food is of special interest to me. When you cook these recipes you bring them to life, you share the food and "art" created by people like yourself, and you help close the recipe circle and get Back to Square One.

## A Few Thoughts About Food, Health, and Heritage

Every day the newspaper reports on yet another study that shows us that butter is bad, that butter may be better for you than margarine, that chicken skin should be removed, that leaving the skin on chicken doesn't add any additional fat to the meat, that wine is bad, that a glass of red wine each day will help clear the plaque from your arteries, that drinking milk will prevent osteoporosis, that drinking milk won't help increase body calcium in middle years, that shellfish is high in cholesterol, that some shellfish has the good kind of cholesterol, that calories should be counted, that carbohydrates are high in calories but they are burned up easily so they don't count. I could go on and on. It's no wonder that we're confused about what is "healthy." By the time we combine all this conflicting information with reports on pesticide residues, polluted waters, radiation, salmonella, parasites and botulism, and horror stories about the effects of weird food additives, we are scared to death. Takes the joy out of eating, doesn't it?

Our grandparents didn't ever think about these things. Even our parents' generation sat down at the table with cheerful anticipation, without worrying that every bite might be potentially dangerous. Of course, ignorance is not bliss, but too much information can be dangerous for dining pleasure. Health cannot be guaranteed by following set regimes and advice from the FDA or AMA or

NIH or the Surgeon General. Or your guru. Or your Aunt Mabel who is 89. We cannot enjoy eating if every bite invokes feelings of fear, depriva- tion, punishment, or cheating. These are emotional judgments and have noth- ing to do with nutrition or health. If food can represent love, community, and sensuous pleasure as well as survival, we must learn to keep the positive parts of the dining experience as alive as we hope to be.

Wouldn't it be easy if there were a perfect diet that worked for everyone? If we all processed foods the same way? If we all liked the same foods and had the same life-style, the same agriculture, the same food traditions? But that is not the case. Genetic programming has a great deal to do with how we metabolize foods; what is good for our particular ethnic heritage may not be good for another's. Our bodies are tailored to respond well to the diets of our ancestors. Even if we are immigrants living in another country, or "natives" living an- other life-style that is supposed to be modern and healthy, our genes and chromosomes have been very slow to process all the new information. Take the Pima Indians who gave up their native diet of beans, grains, vegetables, and fruits and berries and started eating the contemporary All American diet, filled with fats, sugars, and processed foods. They grew obese and developed diabe- tes. Put back on a native diet, fried bread and sweets removed, the diabetes retreated and the weight gain disappeared.

But native diets are not always perfect either. The Japanese eat lots of rice, vegetables, seaweed, and fish; it is supposed to be the ideal healthy diet. Yet they still have a high incidence of stroke. Eskimos eat a rich diet of whale meat and fatty fish, yet they have a low incidence of heart disease as these fats are monosaturates that lower cholesterol. The French eat a diet laden with butter, cream, foie gras, cheese, and croissants. They smoke a lot, don't exercise much, and outlast us by quite a few years. They've learned to relax over a glass of red wine and eat what they like. The magic "Mediterranean diet" includes cream, cheese, and butter as well as olive oil. But due to more varied and sensible eating patterns, most Mediterranean peoples eat less saturated fat and processed food than we do. (Alas, even this is changing as "progress" and fast food come to Europe.)

I'm sure we all know people who can eat the richest, fattiest food and are blessed with a cholesterol level that ignores their saturated fat intake. Others eat simply and their body manufactures the stuff. Anatomy is destiny and it doesn't seem quite fair. If you could stay close to the diet of your ancestors, you'd probably be on a safe road, but that is not always possible or likely. Many of us have strayed too far from our roots. We're now Americans. We're assimilated and out of touch with what our ancestors' native diet was. So we need to take a different path and that path is known as . . . moderation. The M word. You can have your cake and eat it too. Just not so much all the time. If we eat a very rich meal one day, we ought to eat simply for a few days after. A piece of steak is not a death sentence but pasta with vegetables or grilled fish and salads should be on our personal menu plan for the next few days to balance excess. Excess is not bad in moderation either!

Variety in the diet, moderate exercise, and use of fresh, quality ingredients are all contributing factors to a healthy life-style. What is equally important is that food taste good and be well prepared. Who cares if it's good for you if it tastes terrible or boring? Why would you want to eat that way? How could you stay on such a regimen? What we can do is use first-rate ingredients from healthy sources, handle food with care, and store it properly to reduce spreading food-borne illnesses. We can cut down on fat and only use it where it is essential for the flavor and texture of the food. Use low-fat milk, or nonfat yogurt whenever possible, but if you need a tablespoon of sour cream to hold a sauce together, it's okay. The Fat Police won't come to take you away. Just remember that citrus juices, fresh herbs, garlic, and onions are flavor enhancers that will help compensate for reduced fats and sugars in our food. And don't worry that you will be constantly hungry. Small portions are not necessary when you are eating pasta, grains, vegetables, and fruits. Eat lots. Moderation should be the word with meats, poultry, fish, shellfish, cheeses, and other sources of heavily saturated fats. Once you get out of the habit of eating rich cream sauces, foods floating in butter, and excessively sweet desserts, you'll probably feel queasy if you overindulge in them later on. Your body doesn't need them in quantity. A small scoop of ice cream can be as satisfying as a pint, once your body is attuned to balance, variety, and fresh well-prepared foods. If you dine for pleasure and cook interesting recipes with good ingredients, you'll feel richer than when you dine on empty calories of junk.

In this book you will find recipes that are models for a sensible diet, and surprise! they still taste wonderful. You will also find some that are rich, designed for an occasional indulgence. If your doctor has prescribed a certain diet for you, follow it as faithfully as possible. And if you stray, don't beat yourself up. Stress is still one of the major causes of heart disease, so a long walk after dinner might be more conducive to good health and stress reduction than self-flagellation and weeks of punitive deprivation. I know it sounds trite to preach moderation, but given the mixed messages on health and nutrition, the stress in everyday life, and our lack of connections to genetic dietary roots, moderation is the best answer to dietary imponderables at this time.

Working full-time, marketing, and cooking dinner can put pressure on our ability to eat well at home. We can't perform culinary miracles every day. That's why most of the recipes in this book are easy to prepare. Many require only a good marinade and the simplest cooking techniques. A stove with oven and broiler, a few pots and pans, and some sharp knives will get you what you want. We have tested these recipes many times. We have shared them with friends who report success.

It is with all this in mind that we invite you to come Back to Square One, where we prepare old-world food for a new-world kitchen. Most of the recipes in this book are ethnic classics. They never go out of style but they will profit from a fresh contemporary eye and your personal palate to infuse them with new vitality and culinary excitement. Enjoy cooking!

# WINE NOTES BY EVAN GOLDSTEIN

While most of the recipes in my mother's book *The Mediterranean Kitchen* are from countries with a strong wine tradition, many of the recipes in *Back to Square One* are from places that not only don't cultivate wine, they don't even serve it! Even when a country does produce some wine, such as Romania, Brazil, or Russia, the wines are next to impossible to locate in our local wine shops, and they rarely travel well.

Pairing regional food with regional wine is usually a safe bet. But in a culture that is not wine based, how can you determine which wine will go well with the food? When the formula of local food, local wine won't work, it's best to concentrate on the ingredients in the dish and select a wine to match the ingredients rather than the ethnicity. In fact, many of the most successful food and wine combinations I've tasted have been with wines that are not "regionally correct." With a northern Italian veal chop, a Petite Sirah from California can work just as well as an untamed Barolo. Sauvignon Blancs from America, France, and New Zealand are for the most part interchangeable, regardless of the food's country of origin.

So let's relax, possibly over a glass of wine, and consider how to select wines to go with the recipes in this book.

*Temperature:* How often have we been served white wine that's so cold that it could double as a Slurpee? Not only does this mask the wine's inherent flavors, it also distorts the food and wine flavor combinations. In fact cold wine can be absolutely flavorless; it has to warm up to unravel. This doesn't mean that white wine shouldn't be chilled at all—many, such as sparkling wines and the lighter alcohol whites of Germany, northeastern Italy, and South America, are at their best when chilled. Chilled wines provide a lovely and refreshing contrast to hot and spicy foods.

When red wines are too cold their flavors are deadened and they need sufficient time at room temperature to come back to life. And when they are served too warm, the bitter tannins are accentuated, a feature that is not friendly to food.

Your own personal taste should prevail, but here are some starting points from which you can begin experimenting.

*White Wines:* Ideal range:    45–57 degrees
Stay at the warmer end of the temperature spectrum for more complex, dry whites like Chardonnay.

Rosés and medium-light wines:  45–50 degrees

Dessert wines:      40–45 degrees

Sparkling wines:                          45–50 degrees

**Red Wines:** Ideal range:               55–65 degrees

Ideal temperature will vary with the weight and structure of the wine.

Light reds (fruity with low tannin) 50–57 degrees

Fuller-bodied reds                        55–62 degrees

**Alcohol:** Alcohol is a critical element of wine. It plays an important role in determining the weight and flavor of the wine. The less alcohol in the wine, the lighter it will feel on your palate. A delicate 8 percent alcohol wine from Germany is significantly lighter in weight than a generous California Chardonnay at 13 percent. You will find that a rich flavorful dish will generally show better with a medium to full-bodied wine.

As for flavor, alcohol in small percentages colors your perception of the wine's sweetness. For example, a 13½ percent California chardonnay will taste perceptibly sweeter than a 12 percent Sauvignon Blanc. Alcohol also can exaggerate the heat in spicy foods, so with chili pepper or cayenne heat, opt for lighter wines.

**Complement and Contrast:** Wines and foods work best with flavors, tastes, and textural components that are either similar (complementing) or opposite (contrasting). An example of a food and wine match that works on similarity would be spicy marinated grilled fillet of lamb, served with a bold flavorful sauce, and accompanied by a strong Zinfandel, Cabernet Sauvignon, or Rhône blend. A contrast would be a hot and spicy lamb curry paired with an off-dry white wine, the slight sweetness of the wine serving as a delicious and refreshing foil for the spice of the stew.

I've offered wine recommendations with most of the recipes in *Back to Square One*. If you understand the general principles behind these choices, you'll be able to make more informed decisions on your own.

### Appetizers and First Courses

In putting together a meal, we usually build from lighter to heavier in the progression of dishes. To be consistent with this, wines should be selected so as not to peak too early and satiate the palate. Wines to be served with appetizers and salads will almost always be lighter in alcohol, fresh, clean, and flavorful. They can be sparkling wine or Champagne (an often overlooked first course wine), or youthful, simple whites or reds.

There are a few simple guidelines for pairing wine with vinaigrettes, a major part of many salads and appetizers. A few involve the vinaigrette itself: Opt for a citrus vinaigrette based on lemon or lime juice instead of the standard vinegar, and keep the sour component down to a minimum in the vinaigrette; the acid in the wine will more than compensate for the loss in the actual vinaigrette. If possible, use a bit of the wine that will be accompanying the food in place of the vinegar.

The critical wine elements are forward flavor, lighter alcohol, and clean, almost mouth-watering, acidity so the wine doesn't get lost behind the array of flavors. If your dining group is large, or your selection of appetizers varied, I recommend having several choices of wine, say a white and a red, open and available. Don't overlook the flexibility of dry rosé wines with many salads and first courses. They can be lovely.

## Soups

There are essentially three forms of soup: simple broth or bouillon; a puréed soup, which is denser in texture; and a combination—for example, a broth with pasta, mushrooms, meat, or shellfish that add texture and usually are the primary flavors, or a thickened soup that may have nonpuréed elements, such as some chowders, or a puréed bean soup that has partially whole beans. All three kinds require different wine approaches.

Selecting wine for a broth or bouillon is tricky as there is nothing for the wine to cling to. The clue here is to have a wine that is more viscous in body than the soup, so it does not get lost. This is why fortified wines such as sherry or Madeira are often recommended for consommés.

With puréed soup, choose wines that will stand up to the thicker texture. The richer the soup, generally the richer the wine, although using a very tart austere wine to cut through the soup's richness works, too.

In case of a combination soup, match your wine to the elements other than the broth. For example, in a classic minestrone that has a rich broth but also vegetables, pasta, and perhaps some pancetta or prosciutto, make your wine selection based on the pasta, vegetables, or pancetta—a medium full-bodied white such as a Vernaccia, for example, or a medium-bodied red, like a Chianti, Merlot, or country French red from the Midi. If these meal-in-a-bowl soups are all one is having for lunch or dinner, the wine should certainly be hearty.

### Pasta and Rice Dishes

Pasta has always been regionally pigeonholed. We think pasta and the Pavlovian response is either Chianti, Soave, or Valpolicella. While it is true that most Italian wines do work splendidly with pasta, there are many other options as well. Focus on the accompanying ingredients or sauce.

While a full-bodied Cabernet Sauvignon or Syrah is appropriate when risotto is the main course, a delicate Bardolino or supple Pinot Noir would work better for a dinner when pasta is only a small part of a seven-course extravaganza. Lighter course, lighter wine. Heavier wine when pasta is the whole meal.

When selecting wine for pasta we need to pay close attention to the degree of refinement. The Italian love for the rustic and the simple is manifested in the wholesomeness of the noodle. As most pasta is in the comfort food category, one need not use overkill in the wine and food match. While a Grand Cru red Burgundy will taste good with Persian Aushak (page 150), one doesn't really need so pedigreed a wine to enjoy the dish.

Light and crisp whites are especially good with simple pastas and risottos that accent the bounty of fresh produce or shellfish. Select Pinot Grigio, Tocai, and other northeastern Italian whites, Frascati, Soave, and simple Trebbiano from Italy. Or light examples of Sauvignon Blanc, South American Chardonnay, and clean zesty Chardonnay from the Mâconnais in France.

Slightly richer pasta and rice dishes—perhaps with cream added—call for light medium-bodied to medium-bodied whites. Go for Vernaccia and Greco di Tufo from Italy, Chardonnay from America or Australia, or "new wave" Tuscany, Rueda and richer white wines from Spain, and fuller-bodied French

Chardonnays, such as those from the Côte Chalonnaise or village level from the Côte d'Or.

Light-bodied nontannic red wines are best with shellfish and poultry in a light or spicy tomato-based sauce, and plain pastas with meat, either with or without sauce. Try Dolcetto, Valpolicella, Bardolino, or reds from Italy's northeast, Gamay from France, Gamay Beaujolais and Napa Gamay from California, a supple Pinot Noir from just about anywhere, or simple tasty reds from Spain or France's south and southwest.

Medium full-bodied red wines are excellent with richer pasta and risottos that include meat or poultry, or those that are heavily spiced. Look for Chianti, Barbera, Nebbiolo, or similar Italian choices; lighter-styled Cabernet Sauvignon from America, South America, or Bordeaux; Rioja from Spain; medium-power reds from France's Rhône and Midi; and once again, many a Pinot Noir.

Full-bodied powerful reds are ideal with very rustic pastas and risottos that include meat, sausage, pungent wild mushrooms, and hot pepper spice. Barolo, Barbaresco, Brunello, and many of the "super Tuscans" work well, as do American Pinot Noir or those more generous examples from France, American Syrah, and wines such as Côte Rôtie and Châteauneuf-du-Pape from France's Rhône Valley, Bordeaux, and other similar Cabernet Sauvignon-based wines.

### Fish and Shellfish

In matching fish with wine, both flavor and texture should be considered. Some fish are inherently sweet, particularly if they are very fresh—sole, trout, turbot, and angler to name a few. These need wines with youthful zip, and perhaps the lightest snap of sweetness, to show them off: Muscadet, Chablis, and Pinot Blanc from France or Germany, and Washington State Riesling at trocken or halbtrocken kabinett level are all well paired. Stronger, fairly "fishy" fish such as anchovy, mackerel, and sardines go better with earthier wines like Vernaccia, bold Chardonnays, or white wines from Spain or Portugal.

While some fish flake, like cod and snapper, others are almost meatlike in consistency, such as shark, tuna, and halibut. Meaty fish require full-bodied wines—whites like Chardonnay, Rhône varietals and rich Sauvignon Blanc, and even soft and nontannic reds. With more delicate flaking fish, clean fruity reds can work, like Beaujolais, although medium-bodied whites with ample flavor and structure are best.

The preparation of the fish and its sauce is also crucial in determining your wine selection. Is it served hot or cold? Grilled, sautéed, or steamed? Grilled tuna with an Asian soy-based sauce requires a more substantive wine than a simple baked tuna served with a wedge of lemon.

Salmon is unique in that it possesses qualities that can show equally well with either red or white wines. Simple fruity reds, free of astringent tannins, such as Pinot Noir or Dolcetto, can be very nice. Rich white wines, like pedigreed Chardonnay from Burgundy, are often a sublime balance for the oily texture of the salmon.

With shellfish, full-bodied, complex, and regal white wines are generally the rule. As with any fish, the preparation is critical. While we often prepare shellfish simply—broiled lobster, steamed clams, or fresh cracked crab—if there is a sauce the same factors in highlighting the sweet fillet fish apply, but bump up the richness and complexity just a notch.

### Poultry

Chicken has a very understated flavor, so wine to accompany it should be chosen according to how the dish is prepared rather than the taste of the chicken itself. While simple sautéed chicken with garlic and herbs served with mashed potatoes may be best with a young lemony Chardonnay from France, California, or Australia, a grilled marinated chicken with a spicy Moroccan charmoula wants a red wine full of exuberant fruit and ample tannin.

Since so many other fowl are like chicken in flavor (quail, poussin, Cornish hen, and even turkey), pay close attention to those other factors like spices, herbs, marinades, sauces, and accompanying side dishes (often stronger in flavor than the fowl itself), in addition to the method of cooking. A bird served at room temperature calls for different wine from one served warm. Cold roast chicken and a bottle of Vouvray are harmonious, while the same chicken served warm may be better with a fragrant Pinot Noir.

I associate the flavors and fatty texture of duck more with meat than with poultry. Because of this, I feel duck requires wines that are rich and generously structured. For a complementary white wine, full-bodied Chardonnays, Alsatian Pinot Gris, Rhône valley whites, and richer Semillon from the Pacific northwest are my recommendations. An austere white can provide a tasty and refreshing contrast if the duck is very rich—say with nuts and a thick sauce. Once again, focus on the method of preparation and sauce.

I also believe squab and game birds should really be placed in the meat family as their flesh is rich and gamy. There are at least as many red wines that work as white. I find that Pinot Noir, as with duck, is a natural match as are other wines with inherently spicy characteristics: Rhônes, Zinfandel, Syrah for reds, and Pinot Gris; for whites the cooler climate Gewürztraminer and earthy Chardonnays. A more gutsy red wine, say Barbaresco, cru bourgeois Bordeaux, or American Cabernet Sauvignon can be well matched if the birds are grilled or in a strong marinade.

### Meats

While I am a self-professed food and wine liberal, there are instances when I admit to siding with the "right" when it comes to meat dishes and wine. There are few natural food and wine affinities more sublime than a perfectly cooked steak with a glass of aged Cabernet Sauvignon or roast leg of lamb with Pinot Noir. In those situations, a white wine, regardless of its remarkable innate qualities, just won't show at its best. However, just as a tuna isn't a snapper and a duck isn't a chicken, veal and pork aren't the same as lamb or beef.

Meat can be divided into two categories, red and white. Red meats include beef, lamb, game, and some offal (liver, kidneys). They are red due to the physical presence of blood and are inherently stronger in flavor. One can adjust the meatiness through aging, by longer cooking methods, such as stewing or slow baking/roasting, or by trimming off fat. Fat, as we know, provides a tremendous amount of the flavor. Such meats require wines that are firm and robust. The classics—Bordeaux and other Cabernet Sauvignons, red Burgundy and other Pinot Noirs, Barolo or the noble Syrah-based wines of the world—are generally sure bets with these meats.

White meats—veal, pork, rabbit (I place it here rather than in poultry), and again some offal (tripe, sweetbreads)—are far more delicate and sweet. Their more subtle flavors call out just as often for white wines as they do for red. If you choose a red, choose a softer one: Pinot Noir, Chianti, Merlot. I personally prefer white wines like a full-bodied Chardonnay, rich white Rhônes, or waxy Semillon from Australia with many white meat dishes.

As with poultry and fish, the method of preparation, the sauce, and the temperature at which the dish is served are all important factors in choosing a wine. A veal stew with lemon, potatoes, and herbs will be lovely with a light Chardonnay or Sauvignon Blanc, but a thick grilled veal chop with a sauce of tomatoes, hot pepper, and mushrooms needs a young Brunello or Cabernet Sauvignon. And while a cold marinated steak with a rice and wild rice salad wants a soft juicy red wine, that same steak served warm off the broiler with grilled eggplant and zucchini does not.

In general, the simpler the preparation of meat, the greater the range of wines to choose from. When you visit a great château in Bordeaux, they invariably serve a simple aged roast beef to accompany their older vintages. If you want to show off a younger, less refined wine, serve it instead with a dish that has a gutsier preparation.

### Desserts

Most Americans don't have much experience with dessert wines and therefore are missing a treat. Dessert wines can add a sublime note to the end of a meal. In pairing dessert wines and desserts, there is one critical guideline: The level of sweetness in the wine must exceed the perceived level of sweetness in the dessert, or the wine will taste sour. This can be a little tricky as we all have different thresholds for sweetness.

If someone suggests a flute of Champagne or sparkling wine with dessert, remember that while sparkling wine can be both a light and special climax to a meal, all too often it's a dry one at brut level, as opposed to an extra dry or demi-sec style, both sweeter and designed with desserts in mind. Unless your dessert isn't at all sweet, a brut style wine will taste sour and harsh.

Balance is important in dessert wines. Those that are lacking in acid will taste both flabby and, more important, cloyingly sweet. These are not enjoyable by themselves and certainly will not be good accompaniments to dessert.

Although purists could argue that dessert wine is best on its own and not in the presence of any food, I believe that there are wines that work better with food than others. Some wines have flavors reminiscent of pear and honey (Sauternes), lychee (Beaumes-de-Venise), chocolate (port), nuts (sherry and Madeira), and apricots (German late-harvests), and can be ideal with desserts accenting or featuring those same flavors.

There are many categories of dessert wines ranging from those affected by botrytis cinerea (the "noble rot") such as Sauternes, German late-harvest wines, and many of the New World bottlings to fortified ports, sherries, and Madeiras. I encourage you to experiment.

# SALADS AND APPETIZERS

INDONESIAN HOT AND SWEET FRUIT SALAD • BELGIAN ENDIVE, RADICCHIO, MINT, AND BLOOD ORANGE SALAD • MOROCCAN ORANGE, ROMAINE, WALNUT, AND WATERCRESS SALAD • ENSALADA ANDALUZ • CARROT, APPLE, AND RED CABBAGE SALAD • RUSSIAN GARDEN SALAD WITH SOUR CREAM MUSTARD VINAIGRETTE • ARUGULA, BASIL, AND MINT SALAD WITH SUN-DRIED TOMATO VINAIGRETTE • BULGARIAN SALAD OF ROASTED PEPPERS, ONIONS, AND WALNUTS • SPINACH SALAD WITH WARM PANCETTA VINAIGRETTE • THREE SEPHARDIC SALADS: MUSHROOMS WITH PEPPERS AND PARSLEY VINAIGRETTE

◆ ARTICHOKES, CARROTS, AND ZUCCHINI WITH LEMON AND DILL

◆ LEEKS WITH TOMATO OLIVE VINAIGRETTE ◆ STEAK HOUSE TOMATO SALAD ◆ SQUARE ONE COLESLAW ◆ CURRIED RICE SALAD ◆ THAI-INSPIRED SHRIMP SALAD WITH SPICY PEANUT VINAIGRETTE ◆ SHRIMP AND AVOCADO ''COCKTAIL'' ◆ SHRIMP AND AVOCADO SALAD WITH TOMATO GINGER VINAIGRETTE ◆ SCALLOP SEVICHE ◆ BALKAN CRAB SALAD WITH WALNUT AND LEMON MAYONNAISE ◆ MOROCCAN TUNA AND FRISÉE SALAD ◆ TONNO TONNATO ◆ SMOKED TROUT, CARROTS, AND CUCUMBERS ◆ SMOKED TROUT WITH HORSERADISH APPLE CREAM ◆ PICKLED SALMON ◆ POLENTA WITH SMOKED FISH AND CRÈME FRAÎCHE ◆ GEFILTE FISH FOR PASSOVER ◆ SMOKED TROUT PÂTÉ ◆ TWO RECIPES FOR CURED FISH: SCOTCH GRAVLAX ◆ ORIENTAL ''GRAVLAX'' ◆ DUCK LIVER PÂTÉ WITH JUNIPER AND ALLSPICE ◆ HARD-BOILED EGGS WITH TAPENADE ◆ HUEVOS HAMINADOS ◆ DEEP-FRIED STUFFED OLIVES ◆

## INDONESIAN HOT AND SWEET FRUIT SALAD

♦ *Serves 8 to 10*

*1 cup brown sugar*

*3 cups water*

*2 teaspoons dried red pepper
flakes*

*3 tablespoons fresh lemon juice*

*3 large oranges*

*2 large grapefruit*

*2 mangoes, peeled and cut into
slices or chunks*

*1 medium pineapple, peeled,
cored, and cut into chunks*

*2 sliced cucumbers, preferably
Japanese or English (see note)*

*3 tablespoons chopped fresh
Thai basil or a combination of
basil and mint*

This fruit salad is a great accompaniment to Indonesian-Style Roast Duck with Coconut (page 254) or Indonesian Chicken Saté (page 231). It's also wonderful tossed with a little watercress or other greens.

### Procedure

In a small saucepan, boil the sugar and water over medium-high heat for 5 minutes. Add the pepper flakes and lemon juice. Let cool a bit.

Cut off all the white pith from the oranges and grapefruit with a small knife. Then remove the segments by cutting between the membranes. Place the segments in a large bowl and add all the remaining ingredients except the syrup. Toss well to combine. Pour the cooled sugar mixture over the fruits and chill well. Toss with greens, if desired.

**Note:** Japanese cucumbers are very small and need not be peeled or seeded. If you are using English cucumbers, seed them but do not bother to peel them. Regular American cucumbers must be both peeled and seeded.

**Wine Notes:** White wine is the answer: light, young, with zippy acidity and a snap of residual sugar. Try a Riesling at kabinett level from Germany's Mosel or Nahe regions, or a California Riesling in an off-dry style. For a fun variation, try a frizzante Moscato from Italy.

## BELGIAN ENDIVE, RADICCHIO, MINT, AND BLOOD ORANGE SALAD

♦ *Serves 6*

### Mint Vinaigrette

♦ *1½ cups infusion*

¼ cup fresh lemon juice

¼ cup chopped mint

1¼ cups mild olive oil

2 tablespoons fresh orange juice

¼ cup red wine vinegar

½ cup firmly packed chopped
  fresh mint

1 teaspoon sugar

½ teaspoon salt

1 tablespoon grated orange zest


3 blood or regular oranges

2 medium or 3 small heads of
  radicchio (leaves separated)

3 Belgian endive, red or white
  (leaves separated)

½ cup mint leaves

Chopped fresh mint (optional),
  for garnish

It's too bad that blood oranges are not readily available at every American market. In California, both the Sicilian Torrocco and the Spanish Morro are under cultivation and we are delighted to have them, both for their tart flavor and jewellike appearance. Regular oranges work well here but don't look quite as dramatic on the plate. This Italian salad is light and refreshing and makes a wonderful starter to a robust meal, or a perfect substitute for both salad and dessert after a big dinner.

### Procedure

For the mint vinaigrette, combine the lemon juice and mint in a small saucepan and heat to boiling. Remove from the heat and let steep 10 minutes. Strain into a small mixing bowl (there should be about ¼ cup). Whisk in the remaining vinaigrette ingredients. Cut off both ends of the oranges and then cut off the peel and all the bitter white pith. Cut the oranges crosswise into ¼-inch-thick slices and remove the seeds. Or cut between the membrane and flesh to remove the orange "fillets."

To serve, toss the radicchio, endive, and mint leaves with the vinaigrette and divide among 6 salad plates. Top with orange slices or fillets. Sprinkle with a little chopped mint, if desired.

*Wine Notes:* This salad is an interesting juxtaposition of bitter (the endive) and sweet (the orange). Try white wines with zesty acidity, such as a light fragrant Sauvignon Blanc, a Frascati, a Verdicchio, or a more austere Chablis-style Chardonnay.

# MOROCCAN ORANGE, ROMAINE, WALNUT, AND WATERCRESS SALAD

♦ *Serves 6*

### Citrus Cinnamon Vinaigrette

*2 tablespoons plus 1 teaspoon
   fresh lemon juice*

*3 tablespoons fresh orange juice*

*½ teaspoon cinnamon*

*2 teaspoons grated orange zest*

*1 teaspoon grated lemon zest*

*1 tablespoon confectioner's
   sugar*

*½ teaspoon salt*

*¾ cup mild olive oil*

*3 oranges*

*3 heads romaine, torn into
   2-inch pieces*

*1 large bunch watercress, stems
   trimmed*

*½ cup toasted walnuts, coarsely
   chopped*

This light and refreshing salad is a hybrid from the Morocco of my mind: California cuisine meets North Africa, felicitously. Try adding a few whole mint leaves to the greens as well.

### Procedure

For the vinaigrette, whisk together all the ingredients in a small bowl.

Cut off both ends of the oranges and then cut off the peel and all of the bitter white pith. Cut between the membrane and flesh to remove the orange segments.

To serve, toss the romaine, watercress, and walnuts with most of the vinaigrette and divide among 6 salad plates. Place the orange segments on top and drizzle with the remaining vinaigrette.

*Wine Notes:* Uncomplicated young whites with high acidity are the lone call here—youthful Sauvignon, dry Chenin Blanc, and German kabinett-style Riesling—even an intense California Chardonnay.

# ENSALADA ANDALUZ

◆ *Serves 6*

### Tomato Vinaigrette

1¼ *cups mild olive oil*

½ *cup diced plum tomatoes*
   *(canned are acceptable)*

¼ *cup fresh orange juice*

1 *tablespoon grated orange zest*

¼ *cup sherry wine vinegar*

*Salt and freshly ground pepper*

*Sugar (optional)*

2 *tablespoons tomato purée*
   *(optional)*


6 *oranges*

12 *cups spinach leaves, well*
   *washed and dried*

12 *small new potatoes, roasted*
   *or boiled and then sliced or*
   *quartered*

1½ *cups sliced (¼-inch) celery*

¾ *cup finely diced red onion*

1½ *cups toasted slivered*
   *almonds*

The inspiration for this salad is a Spanish salad that combines potatoes, oranges, and almonds with a very rich mayonnaise. In it, the celery and onions are dressed with a second vinaigrette, and the spinach with yet another. It all seemed like too many steps and too many flavors, so here is my streamlined version. Simple to prepare and only two tosses!

## Procedure

For the tomato vinaigrette; whisk together all the ingredients in a bowl, seasoning to taste with salt and pepper. Add a pinch of sugar and the tomato purée if the tomatoes are very acidic or have little flavor.

Cut off both ends of the oranges and then cut off the peel and all of the bitter white pith. Cut between the membranes and flesh to remove the orange segments.

To serve, toss the spinach leaves with some of the vinaigrette and divide them among 6 salad plates. Combine the rest of the ingredients and toss with the remaining vinaigrette. Place on top of the spinach.

***Wine Notes:*** I like whites here in a greener, earthy style—fragrant young Sauvignon Blanc (especially Italian and Chilean), bone-dry Chenin Blanc, and a Chardonnay-based sparkling wine are my best choices.

# CARROT, APPLE, AND RED CABBAGE SALAD

◆ *Serves 6*

**Horseradish Vinaigrette**

½ cup sliced, peeled fresh
   horseradish

¼ cup white vinegar

½ teaspoon salt

1 tablespoon sugar

½ teaspoon freshly ground
   pepper

¾ cup mild olive oil

3 cups peeled, thinly sliced
   carrots

3 tart apples (Pippin or Granny
   Smith), thinly sliced

7½ cups cored and thinly sliced
   red cabbage

1½ cups toasted walnuts,
   coarsely chopped

This tangy Russian salad makes a very colorful presentation. For a more substantial plate, serve with Smoked Trout Pâté (page 62) on croutons if desired.

**Procedure**

For the horseradish vinaigrette, purée the horseradish with the vinegar in a food processor or blender. Transfer to a bowl and whisk in the remaining ingredients.

To serve, toss the carrots, apples, cabbage, and walnuts with enough vinaigrette to coat.

*Wine Notes:* Wines do not really go well with this salad. If you must, go with fresh, tangy whites that emphasize spice—a young dry German (kabinett level) Riesling, or Chenin Blanc from the Loire Valley—or a nonvintage Champagne that is current stock.

## RUSSIAN GARDEN SALAD WITH SOUR CREAM MUSTARD VINAIGRETTE

♦ *Serves 6*

**Sour Cream Mustard Vinaigrette**

*2 teaspoons sugar*

*½ teaspoon salt*

*¼ cup fresh lemon juice*

*2 tablespoons Dijon mustard*

*1 tablespoon Square One Hot Mustard (page 348)*

*1½ cups sour cream*

*½ teaspoon freshly ground pepper*

*12 cups romaine lettuce, cut into 2-inch-pieces*

*3 cups diced, peeled cucumbers (½ inch)*

*1½ cups paper thin radish slices*

*¾ cup finely chopped green onions*

My grandmother loved this kind of salad. The tangy vinaigrette makes a nice counterpoint to the mild romaine and cucumbers, and picks up the zip of the radishes as well. For a more filling dish, serve with Potato Knishes (page 97) or Smoked Trout Pâté (page 62) on rye bread.

### Procedure

For the vinaigrette, combine the sugar, salt, and lemon juice in a bowl. Whisk in the mustards, sour cream, and pepper. Adjust the salt, pepper, and sugar to taste.

To serve, combine the romaine, cucumber, radish, and onion in a bowl and toss with enough vinaigrette to coat.

# ARUGULA, BASIL, AND MINT SALAD WITH SUN-DRIED TOMATO VINAIGRETTE

♦ *Serves 4*

### Sun-Dried Tomato Vinaigrette

¼ *cup mild olive oil such as*
  *Sasso*

¼ *cup virgin olive oil*

¼ *cup sun-dried tomato infused*
  *oil* (*see note*)

2 *tablespoons red wine vinegar,*
  *or 3 tablespoons fresh lemon*
  *juice*

2 *tablespoons chopped sun-dried*
  *tomatoes*

2 *tablespoons finely chopped*
  *basil or mint*

*Salt and freshly ground pepper*

6 *cups arugula*

2 *cups mixed whole basil and*
  *mint leaves*

6 *tablespoons sun-dried*
  *tomatoes, cut into thin strips*
  (*optional*)

1 *cup thinly sliced fennel*
  (*optional*)

24 *thin strips pecorino cheese*
  (*removed with a potato*
  *peeler*)

This salad is an ideal first course, but can make a lovely light lunch if you omit the pecorino, add some sliced fennel, and serve with a thick round of goat cheese that has been dipped in a coating of bread crumbs and chopped mint and baked at 350 degrees until hot and creamy, 8 to 10 minutes.

## Procedure

For the vinaigrette, whisk together the oils, vinegar, tomatoes, and herbs in a bowl. Season to taste with salt and pepper. To serve, combine the arugula, herbs, tomatoes, and fennel, if using, in a bowl, and toss with enough vinaigrette to coat. Top with the pecorino cheese.

*Note:* Sun-dried tomato infused oil is the oil in which the tomatoes are packed. If you do not have enough for this recipe, warm ⅓ cup virgin olive oil in a small saucepan over low heat. Remove from the heat, add 2 tablespoons chopped sun-dried tomatoes and allow to steep for a few hours until flavorful.

*Wine Notes:* Serve regional wines—Italian Vernaccia, Greco di Tufo, and a more sophisticated Soave—or earthy young whites with some spice, minerally Montagny or Rully Blanc from Burgundy, a Spanish white from Rioja or the Rueda, or an exuberant Vinho Verde from Portugal.

# BULGARIAN SALAD OF ROASTED PEPPERS, ONIONS, AND WALNUTS

◆ *Serves 4*

### Garlic Vinaigrette

⅓ cup virgin olive oil

⅓ cup mild olive oil

2 tablespoons red wine vinegar

½ tablespoon finely chopped
   garlic

1 teaspoon salt

1 teaspoon freshly ground
   pepper


2 medium unpeeled red onions

Olive oil for roasting the onions

2 large red bell peppers

1 cup walnuts

4 small handfuls of arugula

1 cup feta cheese, crumbled

Well, maybe the Bulgarians don't serve it exactly this way, but we think the arugula adds a certain tart and peppery contrast to the voluptuous fleshy peppers, the crunchy walnuts, the creamy feta, and the garlicky vinaigrette. Actually this salad is a composite of a few recipes from Bulgaria tempered with a contemporary salad sensibility. Bulgarians would eat some variation of this as a meal with bread, while we eat it as a salad course. You, of course, can do as you like.

### Procedure

Preheat the oven to 400 degrees. Rub the onions with olive oil and roast in a baking dish until tender, but not mushy, 45 minutes to 1 hour. Let stand until cool enough to handle. Then peel and cut into ½-inch strips.

Char the peppers in a broiler or over direct flame, turning often with tongs until they are blackened on all sides. Transfer to a plastic container with a lid, or a paper or plastic bag. Cover the container or close the bag and let the peppers steam for about 15 minutes. Then peel off the skins with your fingers, scraping off any stubborn pieces of peel with a knife blade. (If possible, do not wash the peppers; a few flakes of peel are acceptable.) Cut the peppers in half, remove the stems, seeds, and ribs, and cut the peppers into strips about ½-inch wide.

Place the walnuts on a baking sheet and toast in a 400-degree oven until fragrant, 7 to 10 minutes. Then coarsely chop.

For the garlic vinaigrette, whisk together all the ingredients in a bowl.

To serve, toss the arugula with about one third of the vinaigrette and place it on a platter or on individual serving plates. Toss the roasted peppers and onions with some of the remaining vinaigrette and place on top of the arugula. Top with toasted walnuts and crumbled feta cheese. Drizzle with the rest of the vinaigrette. You can make this salad without the arugula if you like.

*Wine Notes:* A generous and fairly full-bodied white is called for—try to pick up on the sweet-roasted qualities with wines like barrel-fermented Chardonnay from Australia, California, or even Burgundy; a white Hermitage or Châteauneuf-du-Pape; or a Pinot Gris from Oregon, Italy's northeast, or Alsace.

# SPINACH SALAD WITH WARM PANCETTA VINAIGRETTE

◆ *Serves 4*

**Pancetta Vinaigrette**

*4 ounces pancetta, sliced ¼ inch thick and then cut crosswise into ¼-inch strips*

*¾ cup mild olive oil*

*2 tablespoons red or sherry wine vinegar*

*1 tablespoon balsamic vinegar*

*Freshly ground pepper*

*1½ cups sliced white or brown mushrooms (⅛ inch thick)*

*8 cups stemmed spinach (smallest leaves preferred), carefully washed and dried*

*1 cup thinly sliced green onions (green and white parts)*

*Freshly ground black pepper*

*2 hard-boiled eggs, finely chopped*

This simple and pretty salad is a variation of the classic warm French salad of bitter greens with bacon. Try to use very young spinach—the leaves will be tender and will look better on the plate. Be sure to wash the spinach well so that it's grit free; the only crunch you want is the pancetta in the warm vinaigrette.

## Procedure

For the pancetta vinaigrette, cook the pancetta in a small sauté pan or skillet over medium heat until the fat is rendered and the pancetta is slightly crisp. Do not drain. (There won't be much fat in the pan.) Whisk in the remaining ingredients.

To serve, rewarm the vinaigrette over low heat, if necessary. Then toss the mushrooms with half the warm vinaigrette in a large salad bowl. Add the spinach and green onions to the bowl along with the remaining vinaigrette and toss to coat. Season to taste with pepper. Divide the salad among 4 salad plates and top with the chopped hard-boiled egg. Serve at once.

*Wine Notes:* Waxy Semillons, textured Chardonnays, and muscular southern French whites from the lower Rhône and Provence marry well with this rich vinaigrette. A leafy light red is not out of the question; France's Chinon or Bourgueil are examples.

## THREE SEPHARDIC SALADS

♦ *Serves 4*

The Sephardic Jews roamed so far from their home base that these salads taste more of the Middle East and Mitteleuropa than of Spain. With the contrasts of sweet and sour, the complex textures, and the interplay of two kinds of olives, these make a very colorful first course.

## MUSHROOMS WITH PEPPERS AND PARSLEY VINAIGRETTE

*2 tablespoons olive oil*

*2 red bell peppers, cored and seeded, cut into rough dice*

*3 cups quartered mushrooms*

*¼ cup finely diced red onion*

*½ cup finely chopped parsley*

*½ cup mild olive oil*

*¼ cup virgin olive oil*

*⅓ cup red wine vinegar*

*Salt and freshly ground pepper*

*Small handful of niçoise olives*

Warm the 2 tablespoons of olive oil in a small sauté pan or skillet over medium heat. Add the peppers and sauté until softened, 1 or 2 minutes. Transfer the peppers to a serving bowl with a slotted spoon and let cool. Then add the mushrooms, onion, and parsley to the bowl. Whisk together the olive oils and vinegar in a cup and season to taste with salt and pepper. Toss the vegetables with the vinaigrette and scatter the olives over the top.

## ARTICHOKES, CARROTS, AND ZUCCHINI WITH LEMON AND DILL

2 artichokes

3 tablespoons plus 1 cup olive
   oil

2 carrots, peeled and sliced
   about ¼ inch thick

1 zucchini, cut in half
   lengthwise and then into
   ½-inch rounds

⅓ cup fresh lemon juice

¼ cup chopped fresh dill

Salt and freshly ground pepper

Remove all the leaves from the artichokes. Trim the stems and pare the hearts until smooth. Remove the fuzzy choke with a sharp spoon. Cut the hearts into ¼-inch slices. Warm the 3 tablespoons of olive oil in a small sauté pan or skillet. Add the artichoke slices and ¼ cup water and cook until the artichokes are tender but still firm. (All the water should have been absorbed.)

Blanch the carrots in lightly salted water for a minute or two until crisp-tender. Refresh in cold water. Drain well.

Blanch the zucchini in a saucepan of lightly salted water until just tender, about 1 minute. Drain and refresh in cold water. Drain well.

Combine the cooked vegetables in a serving bowl. Whisk together the 1 cup olive oil, the lemon juice, and dill and toss with the vegetables. Let the salad rest for an hour or two before serving to allow for the flavors to develop.

## LEEKS WITH TOMATO OLIVE VINAIGRETTE

*24 small, slender leeks, or 16
  medium leeks*

*1 cup olive oil*

*¼ cup fresh lemon juice*

*3 tablespoons tomato purée*

*¼ cup drained chopped canned
  plum tomatoes*

*1 tablespoon honey*

*3 tablespoons pitted and
  quartered kalamata olives*

*Salt and freshly ground pepper*

Carefully trim the stringy roots from the leeks, leaving the tip of the bulb intact. Trim the green tops. Then split each leek down the middle almost to the root end. Wash them well (leeks are very sandy) in a large bowl of cold water, changing the water until clear.

Bring a large saucepan of lightly salted water to a boil. Add the leeks and simmer gently until tender and the bulb end of the leeks cracks slightly when pinched between your fingers. Drain and refresh in cold water. Transfer to a serving bowl.

Stir together the remaining ingredients in a bowl, adding salt and pepper to taste. Pour the mixture over the leeks and allow to marinate for an hour or two to develop the flavors.

***Wine Notes:*** All three salads are better with whites than reds: Pinot Grigio from Italy, Vinho Verde from Portugal, whites from Spain's Rueda, American Sauvignon Blanc.

## STEAK HOUSE TOMATO SALAD

♦ *Serves 8*

***Spicy Vinaigrette***

*1 egg yolk*

*½ teaspoon puréed garlic*

*5 tablespoons tomato purée*

*½ teaspoon turmeric*

*1 teaspoon salt*

*2½ teaspoons freshly ground pepper*

*3 tablespoons sugar*

*2 tablespoons puréed fresh horseradish*

*⅓ cup red wine vinegar*

*1¾ cups olive oil*

*4 to 6 large beefsteak tomatoes, cut crosswise into ¼-inch-thick slices*

*1 red onion, thinly sliced*

*2 small cucumbers, peeled, seeded, and thinly sliced*

Classics don't have to be many generations old to invoke powerful food memories. When I was little, my family used to go to a steak house called Peter Luger's. The steak was wonderful, but what I really remember is a great salad of flavorful beefsteak tomatoes topped with a spicy dressing. This is an approximation from the old taste memory bank.

### Procedure

For the vinaigrette, whisk together all the ingredients except the olive oil. Then gradually whisk in the oil to emulsify. The mixture should have the consistency of heavy cream. (You could also prepare this in a blender or food processor.)

Divide the tomato, onion, and cucumber slices among 8 serving plates and drizzle the vinaigrette over.

## SQUARE ONE COLESLAW

♦ *Serves 6*

*1 large head green cabbage*

*3 carrots*

*1 tablespoon dry mustard*

*1½ tablespoons sugar*

*1 teaspoon salt*

*⅓ to ½ cup distilled white vinegar*

*1 cup mayonnaise*

*½ cup sour cream or plain yogurt*

*2 teaspoons freshly ground pepper*

O n the Fourth of July I revel in our classic American favorites, and coleslaw is part of our clambake and lobster platter. I've added sour cream to the basic mayonnaise dressing as I think it provides a nice tang.

### Procedure

Shred the cabbage with a knife or with the shredding blade of a grater or food processor. Grate the carrots into long shreds.

Combine the mustard, sugar, and salt in a large bowl and stir in enough vinegar to form a paste. Gently stir in the mayonnaise and sour cream or yogurt. Thin with remaining vinegar to taste. Season to taste with salt and pepper.

Fold the cabbage and carrots into the mayonnaise mixture and refrigerate for a few hours. Taste for seasoning before serving. It should be a bit peppery.

# CURRIED RICE SALAD

◆ *Serves 8*

**Curry Vinaigrette**

*½ cup fresh lemon juice, or to
   taste*

*2 tablespoons salt*

*½ teaspoon freshly ground
   pepper*

*1 tablespoon curry powder*

*1 teaspoon ground cumin*

*½ teaspoon ground coriander*

*Pinch of cayenne pepper*

*1 cup (or as needed) peanut oil*

**Rice Salad**

*½ cup shelled pistachio nuts*

*2 cups white rice, preferably
   basmati*

*½ cup currants, plumped for 10
   minutes in hot water to cover
   and then drained*

*4 to 6 green onions, thinly sliced*

I like to serve this Indian-inspired rice salad with Roast Loin of Pork in Ginger Marinade (page 288). It's a great crowd pleaser for buffets. To turn the salad into a meal, add pieces of cooked chicken or duck.

## *Procedure*

For the curry vinaigrette, combine the lemon juice with the salt, pepper, and spices and gradually whisk in the oil. Taste and adjust seasoning. Add more lemon, if you like.

Preheat the oven to 350 degrees. Spread the pistachios over a baking sheet and toast in the oven until fragrant, 4 to 6 minutes.

Combine rice with 4 cups water in a saucepan and bring to a boil. Reduce the heat and simmer, covered, until cooked through but still firm, about 25 minutes. (Test a kernel of rice between your teeth.) Toss the warm rice with the vinaigrette, then fold in the plumped currants, the pistachios, and the green onions.

**Wine Notes:** More important than matching a wine to this salad is to work with what you are serving the salad with. Reds and whites of light medium body and inherently spicy flavors work well with curry. Dry Gewürztraminer and Muscat from Alsace are good white selections while Pinot Noir, lighter Rhône styles and very light Zinfandels all are tasty red accompaniments.

# THAI-INSPIRED SHRIMP SALAD WITH SPICY PEANUT VINAIGRETTE

♦ *Serves 6*

**Spicy Peanut Vinaigrette**

*5 tablespoons rice wine vinegar*

*3 tablespoons sugar*

*1 teaspoon cayenne pepper or 2 to 3 jalapeño peppers, finely minced*

*2 to 3 tablespoons soy sauce*

*½ cup peanut oil or mild olive oil*

*Salt*

*½ cup toasted peanuts, coarsely chopped*

*30 medium to large shrimp, shelled and deveined*

*white wine for poaching*

*6 cups small spinach leaves, well washed and dried*

*1½ cups julienned (2 inches long and ¼ inch wide) carrots*

*2 cups diced (½ inch) cucumbers*

*1½ cups thinly sliced red cabbage*

It's hard to live in California without becoming addicted to Thai cuisine. These recent immigrants to our country have marked our palates in a most impressive way. Thai food has the flavors Americans love: sweet, tart, and hot. This shrimp salad is a perfect example.

## Procedure

For the peanut vinaigrette, whisk the vinegar, sugar, cayenne or jalapeño peppers, soy sauce, and oil together in a small bowl. Season to taste with salt and stir in the peanuts. Poach the shrimp in a large saucepan over low heat in white wine or water to cover until just cooked through, about 5 minutes. Remove from the poaching liquid and let cool. Then cut the shrimp in half lengthwise.

To serve, toss the spinach with enough vinaigrette to lightly coat and place a bed on each of 6 salad plates. Then toss the carrots, cucumbers, red cabbage, and shrimp with the remaining vinaigrette and arrange on top of the spinach.

**Note:** A pinch of anchovy paste may be added to the vinaigrette instead of the salt to produce the flavor of Thai fish sauce, which is not readily available in many American markets.

**Wine Notes:** White wines that are light in body, fragrant, and flavorful are best. Sauvignon Blanc from Italy, Chile, or California are excellent choices. You might also try a dry trocken or halbtrocken Riesling from Germany, a mild Chardonnay, or even a dry French or American rosé.

# SHRIMP AND AVOCADO "COCKTAIL"

◆ *Serves 6*

**Spicy Tomato Cocktail Sauce**

*1 teaspoon coarsely ground
dried red pepper flakes, or 1
tablespoon minced jalapeño
pepper*

*1½ cups canned plum tomatoes,
drained and pulsed in a food
processor*

*½ cup thick tomato purée*

*⅓ cup red wine vinegar*

*3 tablespoons puréed fresh or
prepared horseradish*

*½ teaspoon freshly ground
pepper*

*½ teaspoon salt*

*Grated lemon or lime zest, to
taste (optional)*

*1½ pounds large shrimp, shelled
and deveined or 1½ pound
cooked crabmeat, picked over
for cartilage or 3 cooked
lobsters, shelled and cut into
chunks*

A salad of shrimp and avocado usually makes me think of Latin America, but "cocktail sauce" is a classic American creation. I've never understood why a shrimp salad served at the beginning of a meal became known as a "cocktail," except perhaps that it is served in a coupe that resembles a cocktail glass. Here, that classic gets a contemporary look: The spicy tomato sauce becomes tomato salsa, and while horseradish is used to heat the traditional American cocktail sauce, there's no reason why you can't add minced jalapeños for a Latin touch. Shrimp are expected, but why not crab or lobster?

## Procedure

For the spicy tomato sauce, whisk all the sauce ingredients together in a bowl. (The sauce may be prepared several hours ahead of serving.)

Poach the shrimp in a large saucepan over low heat with wine or water to cover until just cooked through, about 5 minutes. Remove from the poaching liquid and let cool. Chill until needed. Cut the avocados in half. Remove the pits and the peels and cut the avocados into 1-inch cubes.

To serve, divide the lettuces among 6 salad plates. (You may want to toss the lettuces with a little olive oil and lime or lemon juice.) Toss the avocado cubes in some of the cocktail sauce and place on top of the lettuces. Then toss shrimp or other seafood with the rest of the sauce and arrange on top of the avocado.

Serve with lemon or lime wedges.

*White wine or water for*
*poaching*

*3 ripe avocados*

*3 cups assorted small lettuces*

*Lemon or lime wedges, for*
*garnish*

**Wine Notes:** Both reds and whites would work here. A simple Bourgogne Village with lively young Pinot fruit or a flavorful Pinot Noir from California or Oregon would be sublime. Or choose an earthy and slightly austere white: a simple Chardonnay, an herbaceous Verdicchio or Frascati, or an assertive Spanish white from Tarragona or the Penedès.

## SHRIMP AND AVOCADO SALAD WITH TOMATO GINGER VINAIGRETTE

◆ *Serves 6*

**Tomato Ginger Vinaigrette**

¾ *cup peanut oil*

¼ *cup fresh lemon juice*

2 *tablespoons red wine vinegar*

1 *heaping tablespoon grated*
   *fresh ginger*

¾ *teaspoon sugar*

¼ *teaspoon salt*

1 *tablespoon tomato purée*

3 *tablespoons finely diced*
   *canned plum tomatoes*

¼ *teaspoon cayenne pepper or*
   *to taste*

¼ *teaspoon ground star anise*
   *(see note)*

30 *medium or large shrimp,*
   *shelled and deveined*

*White wine, beer, or water for*
   *poaching*

3 *avocados, peeled, and cut into*
   *large dice or crescents*

6 *cups watercress or spinach*
   *leaves, well washed and dried*

1½ *cups julienned jicama*
   *(optional)*

ere is a variation on Shrimp and Avocado Cocktail (page 46) but with an Oriental tang to the vinaigrette. Try replacing the avocado with blanched asparagus when they are in season. For a more Latin accent, add diced chilies and omit the ginger and star anise.

### Procedure

For the vinaigrette, whisk all the ingredients together in a bowl.

In a large saucepan, poach the shrimp over low heat in white wine, beer, or water to cover for about 5 minutes. Remove from the poaching liquid and let cool.

To serve, toss the shrimp, avocado, watercress, or spinach, and jicama, if using, with vinaigrette to coat.

**Note:** Grind star anise in a small spice grinder or coffee mill. Two pods will yield about ¼ teaspoon ground. If necessary, you may substitute Chinese five spice powder.

**Wine Notes:** Light reds à la Gamay (Beaujolais or American), Dolcetto, or Loire Valley Cabernet Sauvignon are excellent, as are fruitier styles or Pinot Noir with minimal tannin. For whites, try Alsatian Pinot Gris or Riesling, less buttery styles of Chardonnay from the Côte d'Or, or a Semillon from Washington State. For a twist, try a sparkling Blanc de Noirs.

# SCALLOP SEVICHE

♦ *Serves 6*

*½ cup fresh orange juice*

*⅓ cup fresh lime juice*

*1½ pounds sea or bay scallops, muscles removed, sliced horizontally if they are thick (see note)*

*½ cup mild olive oil*

*2 teaspoons minced garlic*

*2 to 3 teaspoons minced jalapeño pepper, or to taste*

*¼ cup finely chopped fresh cilantro*

*1 cup thinly sliced or diced red onions*

*1 cup thinly sliced or diced red and green peppers*

*Salt and freshly ground pepper to taste*

Seviche originated in Peru but is now popular throughout Latin America. It is usually prepared with a firm white fish marinated in lime and lemon juice, with sliced onions, peppers, garlic, and sometimes tomatoes. The fish "cooks" in the citrus juices and becomes white and tender. This seviche is not inexpensive but it is easy to prepare and easier to eat. Of course, you can make this with snapper, cod, or flounder if you like. In the summer I like to add some diced tomato and a little orange zest.

## Procedure

Combine the citrus juices and pour over the scallops in a shallow nonaluminum pan. Let marinate in the refrigerator for an hour or two, until the scallops turn white. Then add the rest of the ingredients and marinate in the refrigerator for 1 hour longer, to allow the flavors to marry. Serve with slices of avocado or with guacamole and tortilla chips, if you like.

**Note:** If you are using the tiny bay scallops, it is best to cut the onions and bell peppers into small dice. If using the larger sea scallops, slice the vegetables.

**Wine Notes:** Try zesty and spicy whites; a light tart Sauvignon Blanc from Chile or Italy; or a herbaceous Chardonnay, an Alsatian or Oregon Pinot Gris, or a Tuscan white blend.

# BALKAN CRAB SALAD WITH WALNUT AND LEMON MAYONNAISE

♦ *Serves 4*

### Walnut Lemon Mayonnaise

*2 egg yolks*

*¼ cup fresh lemon juice, or to taste*

*1 teaspoon finely puréed garlic*

*1¼ cups mild olive oil*

*¼ cup walnut oil*

*2 tablespoons grated lemon zest*

*½ cup finely chopped toasted walnuts*

*Salt and freshly ground pepper to taste*

*2 large cucumbers seeded and cut into ½-inch dice (about 3 cups) (see note)*

*1 pound cooked crabmeat, picked over for cartilage*

*Lettuces or watercress to line plate*

*Walnut oil and lemon juice for greens*

The crunch of the walnuts in the walnut-flavored mayonnaise adds an interesting and unusual depth of flavor to the salad and plays up the sweetness of the crab. You can serve this simply, on a bed of lettuces, or expand it with cooked potatoes, asparagus, or green beans drizzled with some of the thinned mayonnaise.

## Procedure

For the walnut lemon mayonnaise, combine the yolks, some of the lemon juice, and the puréed garlic in a bowl or blender, or in the bowl of a food processor. Gradually whisk or process in the oils, drop by drop at first, until a smooth emulsion is formed, and then more rapidly until all the oil has been added. (Of course you may use prepared mayonnaise if you don't want to make your own.) Blend in the remaining lemon juice, the lemon zest, and the chopped walnuts. Add salt and pepper and more lemon juice, if desired, to taste.

To serve, combine the diced cucumbers and crabmeat with the mayonnaise. Toss lettuces or watercress with a little walnut oil and lemon juice. Divide the greens among 4 salad plates. Top with the crab and cucumber mixture. Sprinkle with the walnuts and chopped parsley or dill.

**Note:** If cucumbers are bitter, peel them. English or Japanese cucumbers need not be peeled. If using asparagus and potatoes instead of cucumbers, dress the crab alone with half the mayonnaise and place on the bed of greens. Arrange the asparagus and pota-

½ cup coarsely chopped toasted
walnuts

Chopped parsley or fresh dill for
garnish

16 blanched asparagus spears
plus 8 little new potatoes (red,
white, or yellow Finnish),
roasted or boiled and then
sliced or quartered (optional)

toes on the platter and drizzle with the remaining
mayonnaise, thinned with a little water if necessary.
Top with chopped walnuts and dill.

**Wine Notes:** Fairly vigorous Italian whites (Vernaccia), Australian Semillon, barrel-fermented Sauvignon Blancs, and dry, slightly green Chenin Blancs
are all well matched.

# MOROCCAN TUNA AND FRISÉE SALAD

♦ *Serves 4*

### Lemon Cumin Vinaigrette

¾ *cup mild olive oil*

½ *cup virgin olive oil*

¼ *cup fresh lemon juice*

*1 tablespoon grated lemon zest*

*2 tablespoons toasted ground*
  *cumin seed*

½ *teaspoon salt*

¼ *teaspoon freshly ground*
  *pepper*


*12 ounces skinned tuna fillet*

*Olive oil*

*Salt and freshly ground pepper*

*2 large red or yellow bell*
  *peppers*

*8 cups loosely packed curly*
  *endive (also sold as "frisée")*

*2 ripe avocados, cut into chunks*
  *(optional)*

*24 to 30 Moroccan olives*
  *(kalamata or niçoise are fine)*

This recipe seems surprisingly California, but I found it in a Moroccan cookbook. I added cumin to the vinaigrette for a more authentic North African flavor. The addition of avocado is strictly my idea—it fills out the salad to make it more of a meal. You can use canned tuna and sauté the peppers if you don't have the time to broil fresh tuna or roast the peppers; canned tuna is standard fare in Morocco as fresh is not readily available.

## Procedure

Preheat the broiler. Cut the tuna into 1-inch-thick slices. Brush lightly with olive oil, sprinkle on both sides with salt and pepper and grill to medium rare or medium, about 3 minutes per side. (Or sauté the tuna in a little olive oil, 3 to 4 minutes per side.) Cover the tuna and refrigerate until needed. (Bring to room temperature before serving.)

Char the peppers in a broiler or over a direct flame, turning often with tongs, until blackened on all sides. Transfer to a plastic container or paper or plastic bag. Cover the container or close the bag and let steam for about 15 minutes. Peel the skins from the peppers; then cut in half, remove the stems, and scrape out the seeds. Slice into ½-inch wide strips. (Or steam and seed the raw peppers, cut into strips, and sauté them.)

For the lemon cumin vinaigrette, whisk together all the ingredients in a bowl.

To serve, break the tuna into chunks. Toss the curly endive, tuna, peppers, and avocado chunks, if using, with the vinaigrette in a serving bowl. Sprinkle the salad with the olives.

# TONNO TONNATO

**Seared Tuna with Tuna Sauce**

♦ *Serves 6*

**Tonnato Sauce**

*1 piece tuna fillet, about 6 ounces and ½ to ¾ inch thick, cooked to medium (see note) or 6 ounces Italian canned tuna packed in olive oil*

*¼ cup fresh lemon juice*

*2 tablespoons wine vinegar*

*1½ tablespoons anchovy purée*

*¾ cup mild olive oil*

*2 teaspoons salt*

*1 teaspoon freshly ground pepper*

*¼ cup water, or as needed*

*6 3-ounce pieces (¼ inch thick) fresh tuna*

*Salt and freshly ground pepper*

*Olive oil*

*Capers, chopped parsley, and small black olives, for garnish*

In Italy I came to enjoy the classic dish known as "vitello tonnato," braised veal with tuna sauce. To the people of Lombardy, where this dish originates, and to the average Italian, this combination doesn't seem unusual, but to the average American, it sounds strange. Why a public that can embrace the concept of surf and turf hasn't been won over, I don't understand. Perhaps it is the association of tuna fish as a sandwich spread. On the other hand, tuna served raw as sashimi or grilled and served rare in the Japanese tradition has become popular with American diners. So I have taken inspiration from this Oriental style and combined tuna slices, rare in the middle and seared nicely on the outside, with the classic Italian creamy tuna sauce usually served with the veal. Some Italians would probably be scandalized by this interpretation of their dish, but it is truly delicious.

To turn this appetizer into a light lunch or dinner, add a few slices of roasted or steamed potatoes and some slices of raw fennel or carrots and celery and drizzle them with tonnato sauce.

## Procedure

For the tonnato sauce, pulse the tuna, lemon juice, vinegar, and anchovy purée in a food processor or blender until combined. Add the oil with the motor running gradually to emulsify the sauce. Add the salt and pepper, and water, as necessary, to thin the sauce to the consistency of heavy cream. Sprinkle the tuna slices on both sides with salt and pepper. Brush lightly with olive oil and grill 1 minute on each side,

*(continued)*

or sear in a hot sauté pan or skillet until charred on the outside but still rare in the center.

To serve, spoon the sauce over the seared tuna slices. Sprinkle with capers and chopped parsley, and garnish with a few small black olives. Serve hot.

*Note:* You can grill the tuna 4 to 5 minutes each side, or bake it at 450 degrees for 10 minutes. It should be cooked through, but not dry.

*Wine Notes:* Earthy, leafy red wines are a great match for this dish. Nothing with tannin, mind you, but a Chinon or Bourgueil from France, a light herbal Merlot (Italy, Sonoma County, and some from Washington State), or a supple Pinot Noir.

# SMOKED TROUT, CARROTS, AND CUCUMBERS

♦ *Serves 4*

**Fennel Orange Vinaigrette**

2 tablespoons finely chopped
   pitted niçoise olives

1 tablespoon grated orange zest

1 tablespoon toasted fennel seed,
   ground

3 tablespoons fresh lemon juice

3 tablespoons fresh orange juice

½ cup olive oil

¼ teaspoon freshly ground
   pepper

Pinch of salt


2 cups thinly sliced English or
   Japanese cucumbers
   (Japanese need not be peeled)

2 cups very thinly sliced carrots

8 smoked trout, filleted, skin and
   bones carefully removed

Fennel fronds or chopped
   parsley, for garnish

Growing up in New York, I always thought all smoked fish was Jewish, but one day an Italian friend served me a smoked trout salad and I thought I'd better do a little research on smoked fish in Italy. This recipe is from the Veneto, which used to have a very large Jewish population, so maybe my assumption was true after all. In this salad the flavors come together in a most amazing way. If fennel is in season, you can use it in place of the carrots or cucumbers. Soak the carrots in ice water if you want them to curl, or slice them not quite as thin, blanch for 2 minutes, and then refresh in a bowl of ice water.

## Procedure

For the fennel orange vinaigrette, whisk all the ingredients in a bowl.

To serve, toss the cucumbers and carrots with some of the vinaigrette and divide the mixture among 4 salad plates. Top each with 2 fillets of the smoked trout, arranged in any way you choose. Drizzle with the remaining vinaigrette. Sprinkle with fennel fronds or parsley.

**Wine Notes:** A white wine with good acidity, low alcohol, nice earthiness, and a slightly green or herbal flavor such as Sauvignon Blanc would work best. A villages-level white Burgundy or Alsatian or Oregon Pinot Gris would also work well.

## SMOKED TROUT WITH HORSERADISH APPLE CREAM

♦ *Serves 6 to 8*

**Horseradish Apple Cream**

1 cup sour cream

¼ cup heavy cream

¾ cup peeled and finely diced apple

¼ cup very finely minced white onion

2 tablespoons finely puréed fresh horseradish (*see note*)

¼ cup white vinegar

Salt and freshly ground pepper

2 smoked trout, heads and skin removed, fillets carefully boned and broken into pieces

8 little new potatoes, boiled or roasted

1 cup sliced fennel or cucumber

Watercress, for garnish

Another example of La Cucina Ebraica—Italian Jewish food. This variation on the basic horseradish cream is from Treviso in the Veneto. It is excellent on smoked trout, cooked salmon, or on potato pancakes.

### Procedure

To make the horseradish apple cream, use a large whisk to mix together all the ingredients in a bowl with salt and pepper to taste. (You may also add ¼ cup chopped, toasted walnuts to this sauce in place of or in addition to the apple chunks.)

To serve, arrange the smoked trout, sliced cooked potatoes, and sliced fennel or cucumber on each of 6 to 8 salad plates. Drizzle the horseradish apple cream over. Garnish with watercress sprigs.

**Note:** To obtain 2 tablespoons finely puréed horseradish, purée ¼ cup peeled, thinly sliced fresh horseradish in a food processor along with 2 tablespoons white vinegar. If you have a large processor, you may have to do a larger quantity to get the results. Masochists may grate the horseradish by hand with a fine grater.

**Wine Notes:** All the suggestions on page 55 would be fine here. So would a dry Chenin Blanc or kabinett-level Riesling. And a Beaujolais might make some people very happy.

## PICKLED SALMON

♦ *Serves 6 to 8*

*1¼ cups distilled white vinegar*

*1 cup water*

*¼ cup sugar*

*⅛ cup kosher salt*

*2 pounds salmon fillet, skin and
    bones removed*

*⅛ cup mixed pickling spices*

*6 bay leaves*

*2 onions, sliced ¼ inch thick*

This recipe is a reworking of a very old family recipe. My mother-in-law used to soak lox—also known as smoked salmon—in water for days to remove the salt, then put it in pickling brine. As we can get great local salmon, I tried it for this dish, and it has become a much-requested favorite. The onions are not just a visual garnish. They pick up the flavor of the marinade and are a delicious counterpoint to the salmon. Serve with rye bread or, at Passover, with matzo.

### Procedure

Combine the vinegar, water, sugar, and salt in a saucepan and bring to a boil. Remove from the heat and let cool completely. Cut the salmon into 1- by 2-inch pieces. Arrange a layer of salmon pieces over the bottom of a ceramic crock, glass bowl, or plastic container. Sprinkle with pickling spices and bay leaves and a layer of sliced onions. Arrange a second layer of salmon over the first and sprinkle again with spices and onions.

Continue the layering until you have used all the fish and spices. Pour the cooled pickling liquid over the fish. If the fish floats, weight it down with a ceramic plate. Cover the container and refrigerate for 3 to 5 days. Serve the salmon with rye bread along with its pickled onions. A sliced cucumber salad with a sour cream dressing also makes a nice accompaniment.

*Wine Notes:* This is a dish that really cries out for an off-dry white wine and pretty much little else. Try Chenin Blanc from America or Europe, Riesling from Washington State or Germany—as long as there's a hint of sweetness.

# POLENTA WITH SMOKED FISH AND CRÈME FRAÎCHE

♦ *Serves 4*

*2 ears fresh corn, kernels removed, or 1½ cups frozen corn kernels*

*1 cup coarse cornmeal for polenta*

*4 cups cold water*

*Salt and freshly ground pepper*

*8 to 12 ounces boned, skinned smoked trout fillet, broken into 2-inch pieces, or 8 to 12 ounces smoked salmon, cut into strips about 2 inches long and ½ inch wide*

*2 cups blanched French green beans or asparagus pieces, or 2 cups sautéed leeks*

*½ cup (or as needed) crème fraîche (see note)*

*¼ cup minced fresh chives*

This is a perfect appetizer to begin a fancy dinner, and it makes a surprisingly interesting brunch or breakfast item. The polenta can be prepared ahead and refrigerated, then cut and grilled, broiled, sautéed, or simply heated in the oven. Although polenta is a northern Italian staple, it is also served in Romania and some of the Balkan nations where it is known as mamaliga. Adding fresh corn when it is in season gives a sweetness to the dish that plays nicely off the smokiness of the fish.

With smoked salmon or smoked trout, a drizzle of crème fraîche, and a sprinkling of chopped chives, you have a wonderfully complex-tasting dish. The accompanying vegetable garnish can be green beans, asparagus, or sautéed leeks.

### Procedure

To make the polenta, cook the fresh or frozen corn kernels in a saucepan of boiling salted water until tender, 2 to 3 minutes. Drain well and pat dry on a clean dish towel. (If the corn is too wet it will weaken the final polenta.) Combine the cornmeal and cold water in a heavy-bottomed saucepan and bring to a boil over medium heat. Reduce the heat and simmer, stirring often, until the polenta has thickened, and is no longer grainy, about 30 minutes. Stir in the blanched and well-drained corn. Season to taste with salt and pepper. Pour into a small, lightly oiled baking dish, cover with plastic wrap, and refrigerate until firm.

Preheat the grill or broiler. Preheat the oven to 400 degrees. Cut the polenta into 8 triangles or strips and grill until lightly colored. Then place 2 pieces in each of 4 lightly oiled gratin dishes and bake until warmed through, about 10 minutes.

To serve, garnish the hot polenta with a combination of the smoked fish and vegetables, and the crème fraîche and chives. I like the leeks best with the trout and the asparagus best with the smoked salmon but you may have different ideas.

**Note:** For a low-fat variation, substitute yogurt thinned with a little buttermilk for the crème fraîche. It should be of a spoonable texture without being too runny.

**Wine Notes:** If ever a dish were created to show off Chardonnay, this appetizer is it. Choose one with richness and balance, complexity and body, and you can't go wrong. An Australian Semillon, white Rhône, or even a supple but rich Alsatian Pinot Gris can substitute with honors.

## GEFILTE FISH FOR PASSOVER

◆ *About 45 small pieces*

### Fish Stock

*Bones, heads, and skins from*
    *12 pounds whole pike and*
    *whitefish*
*4 onions, peeled and chopped*
*2 carrots, peeled and chopped*
*1 piece of celery root, peeled*
    *and chopped (about 1 cup)*
*Pinch of sugar*
*⅛ cup whole peppercorns*
*1 cinnamon stick*
*3½ quarts water*

### Fish Balls

*3 pounds each whitefish and*
    *pike fillets*
*6 medium onions, peeled and*
    *puréed in the food processor*
*6 eggs*
*¼ cup matzo meal*
*2 tablespoons kosher salt*
*1½ tablespoons sugar*
*1½ teaspoons white pepper*
*½ cup ice water*
*3½ tablespoons very finely*
    *ground almonds*

A few years ago at Passover, a friend of mine gave me a video entitled "Gefilte Fish: An Endangered Species." It was divided into three segments. In the first part an elderly Jewish woman talked about chopping the fish by hand, and she showed us her worn wooden bowl and chopper. (I still have one of those sets.) The second scene took place in a modern kitchen, where her daughter demonstrated the technique of making gefilte fish in the food processor. In the final scene we met the woman's granddaughter, who showed us how she opened a jar of prepared gefilte fish and decorated the plate with lettuce leaves!

Every Passover I make a monster batch of gefilte fish. I grind the fish twice through the fine holes of a grinder. I purée the onions in the food processor as a compromise with modernity, but I assemble the rest by hand, chopping with a giant chopper/cleaver and doing the final mixing with my fingers.

Most traditional recipes for gefilte fish have you simmer the fish for hours. Like other dishes in Jewish cooking, it's cooked way too long. I prefer to poach the fish balls for 25 minutes, as if they were quenelles, which they are. This recipe is Sephardic-inspired, with a cinnamon stick in the fish stock and ground almonds in the fish. It keeps well for about the one week of Passover.

### Procedure

For the fish stock, combine all the ingredients in a large saucepan and bring to a boil. Skim the foam that rises to the top, reduce the heat, and simmer for about 30 minutes. Strain and chill.

*4 large carrots, peeled and
thinly sliced on the diagonal
(about 45 oval slices)*
*Salt and freshly ground pepper*
*½ pound fresh horseradish*
*¼ cup white vinegar*
*¼ cup water*
*Sugar or salt*

Grind the fish twice through the fine blades of a meat grinder (your fishmonger can do this for you). Turn it out onto a plastic chopping board or into a large bowl. Add the onions and the eggs and mix well with a chopper or cleaver. Dissolve the salt with sugar and pepper in the ice water. Then work in the matzo meal, almonds, and ice water, a bit at a time, with the chopper or cleaver. Refrigerate until chilled. Test the seasoning by poaching a tiny sample fish ball in simmering fish broth. Adjust seasoning as necessary. Then, with wet hands to keep the mixture from sticking, form all the fish mixture into ovals 3 to 3½ inches long and 1½ to 2 inches wide. Place the fish balls on baking sheets lined with parchment paper. Cover and refrigerate until ready to poach.

To poach the fish ovals bring the stock to a boil in a large saucepan. Add the fish balls, reduce the heat, and simmer covered, for 25 minutes, turning or basting the fish occasionally with the broth. Remove the cooked fish with a slotted spoon and set aside in a large shallow container in the refrigerator. Add the carrot slices to the simmering stock and poach until tender, about 7 minutes. Remove with a slotted spoon and set aside in a second container. Reduce the fish stock in the pan until slightly thickened. Add salt and pepper to taste. Pour the reduced stock over the gefilte fish to cover and pour a little over the carrot slices. Refrigerate until serving time. (The fish stock will jell as it cools.)

Peel the horseradish and cut into small chunks. Purée in a processor or blender with the white vinegar and water. Add sugar or salt to taste. (When

*(continued)*

puréeing, open the lid with caution and turn your head away as the fumes will be quite volatile.) Transfer to a bowl and refrigerate tightly covered with plastic wrap, until ready to serve.

To serve, place the fish on serving plates and spoon a little of the jellied broth on top. Arrange a carrot slice on the fish and garnish with a dollop of the horseradish mixture. Serve with matzo, if you like.

**Wine Notes:** While relatively bland sans horseradish, the fish wants a wine with some flavor. Try a French Chablis, simple white Burgundy, bright Sauvignon Blanc, or light Italian whites like Tocai or Arneis. An off-dry rosé can work, and even white Zinfandel.

## SMOKED TROUT PÂTÉ

♦ *Makes about 2½ cups*

*1½ pounds smoked trout, heads and skin removed, fillets carefully boned (should yield ½ pound smoked trout fillets)*

*½ cup very finely diced onion*

*½ cup chopped fresh chives*

*1 cup mayonnaise*

*¼ teaspoon salt*

*¼ teaspoon freshly ground pepper*

*Fresh lemon juice to taste*

Most of us associate smoked fish with northern Europe and urban Jewish delicatessens although North American Indians have long prepared smoked fish. This pâté is wonderful spread on croutons, tastes good on avocado slices, and makes a rich sandwich filling when paired with sliced cucumbers and watercress on dark rye or pumpernickel bread. It can be prepared a day or so ahead without any loss of flavor.

### Procedure

Place the trout in the container of a food processor and pulse to chop. Transfer to a bowl and fold in remaining ingredients.

**Wine Notes:** Serve a lively white wine—a young Mâcon Villages or a German trocken or halbtrocken. A fino or Manzanilla sherry, a glass of dry Champagne, or a light crisp pilsner-styled beer makes a lovely pairing.

## TWO RECIPES FOR CURED FISH

## SCOTCH GRAVLAX

♦ *Serves 10 to 12*

*2 pounds boneless salmon fillet,*
  *skin on*

*3 tablespoons sugar*

*3 tablespoons kosher salt*

*½ teaspoon freshly ground*
  *pepper*

*½ teaspoon ground allspice*

*24 dill sprigs*

*6 tablespoons scotch whisky*

**Mustard-Dill Sauce**

*4 tablespoons Dijon mustard*

*1 teaspoon dry mustard*

*3 tablespoons sugar*

*2 tablespoons white vinegar*

*½ cup peanut oil*

*2 tablespoons chopped fresh dill*

Everyone seems to have a version of this Scandinavian recipe and most of them are about the same. Quality depends on the fattiness and freshness of the fish, the pungency of the herbs, and the choice of basting liquid in the cure. I used to make this with aquavit, the Scandinavian caraway-flavored liquor, and it produces a very tasty gravlax. One day I was thinking about scotch salmon, scotch on salmon, why not try scotch-cured gravlax? It was a surprise. This has become my favorite way of preparing gravlax. The scotch adds a depth of flavor and velvety texture. I hope those of Scandinavian descent will forgive me this liberty and will give this gravlax recipe a try.

### Procedure

Place the salmon, skin side down, in a nonaluminum container. Combine the sugar, salt, pepper, and allspice and rub over the salmon. Place the dill sprigs on top. Sprinkle with the scotch. Cover the salmon with plastic wrap, weight it, and refrigerate for 3 days, basting once or twice a day with the juices that accumulate in the pan.

For the mustard-dill sauce, place all ingredients except the oil and the dill in the container of a small processor or blender and pulse to combine. Gradually process in the oil to emulsify. Fold in the dill.

To serve, thinly slice the salmon across the grain and serve with mustard-dill sauce and rye bread.

*(continued)*

*Wine Notes:* A wine with a little sweetness plays to the cured quality of the salmon. However, with the gravlax, the balance of acidity is more important, so be sure the wine has tartness. A sparkling wine would be lovely, too, from either Champagne or California.

## ORIENTAL "GRAVLAX"

### Fish Cured with Gin, Juniper, Orange, and Black Pepper

♦ *Serves 10 to 12*

*2 pounds boneless Alaskan halibut or Hawaiian ono fillet, skin on*

*¼ cup sugar*

*2 tablespoons kosher salt*

*1 teaspoon freshly ground pepper*

*½ teaspoon ground allspice*

*1 tablespoon juniper berries, coarsely ground*

*Zest from 2 large oranges, removed with peeler, in strips about 3 inches long*

*3 tablespoons Bombay or Seasoned Gin (page 65 )*

I t is hard to ignore the influence of Asian immigrants on our tastebuds. While gravlax and sashimi are not the same, they have a similar texture and take to a pungent sauce with equal aplomb. Here's a classic preparation for cured and marinated fish but with an Oriental twist. You'll need a fatty white fish, like Alaskan halibut or Hawaiian ono.

### Procedure

Place the fish, skin side down, in a nonaluminum container. Combine the sugar, salt, pepper, allspice, and juniper berries and rub over the fish. Place the strips of orange peel on top and sprinkle with the gin. Cover the fish with plastic wrap, weight it, and refrigerate for 4 days, basting once a day with the juices that accumulate in the pan.

For the wasabi cream, mix the wasabi and the vinegar to a paste in a small bowl. Let rest for about 5 minutes. Then stir the paste into the sour cream. Fold in the whipping cream and season with salt, pepper, and sugar to taste. Thin, if necessary, with more cream or water.

To serve, slice the fish in paper thin slices and drizzle with wasabi cream. Serve with thinly sliced cucumbers.

**Wasabi Cream**

3 tablespoons wasabi powder

3 tablespoons white vinegar

½ cup sour cream

⅓ cup whipping cream, whisked
   until lightly thickened

Salt and freshly ground pepper

1 teaspoon sugar, or to taste
   (optional)

**Seasoned Gin**

1 cinnamon stick

1 tablespoon black peppercorns

3 allspice berries

6 whole coriander seeds

2 strips each lemon and orange
   zest

1 liter bottle Bombay gin

Add the spices and zests to the
   gin bottle and let steep about
   1 week. This keeps quite a
   while.

**Wine Notes:** A good choice is a muscular white wine with fruity flavors and perhaps that snap of sweetness. Also a possibility is a very ripe New World (America, Australia, New Zealand) white that stresses fruit rather than oak barrels, or a crisp Alsatian white. Reds just do not seem to work here, although a balanced sparkling wine definitely does.

## DUCK LIVER PÂTÉ WITH JUNIPER AND ALLSPICE

◆ *About 1¾ pounds pâté*

*10 tablespoons unsalted butter*

*1½ pounds duck livers, trimmed*

*¾ cup diced onion*

*1 teaspoon ground allspice*

*1 teaspoon ground juniper*
*  berries*

*¼ cup Cognac*

*1 teaspoon salt*

*½ teaspoon freshly ground*
*  pepper*

I know, I know. This is probably not "good for you," but it sure is delicious. Pâté is a retrograde food that some of us are loathe to give up entirely, even in our modern quest for healthful dining. Generations of French have survived cheerfully and with great longevity, on a pâté laden diet. Recent medical studies show that fat may be counteracted by the traditional glass of red wine. If you are able to enjoy pâtés as part of your regimen, be sure to try this recipe.

### Procedure

Melt 4 tablespoons of the butter in a sauté pan or skillet over medium heat. Add the livers and sauté quickly, until they are firm but still pink in the center, 5 to 7 minutes. Remove from the pan and set aside. Melt 2 more tablespoons butter in the pan. Add the onions and cook until translucent and tender, about 10 minutes. Add the spices and cognac and cook for a minute or two. Purée the mixture in a blender or food processor. Process or blend in the additional 4 tablespoons softened butter. Serve at room temperature on toast or croutons.

*Wine Notes:* Red, red, and more red. A medium-bodied Rhône, a Tuscan Rosso di Montalcino or Chianti, Barbera or Nebbiolo d'Alba from Piedmont are all excellent. A California claret-style Zinfandel or a wine from France's Midi are also good selections.

# HARD-BOILED EGGS WITH TAPENADE

◆ *Makes 12 filled egg halves*

**Tapenade**

*1 cup pitted niçoise olives*

*2 tablespoons rinsed and chopped capers*

*1 tablespoon finely minced garlic*

*2 teaspoons chopped anchovies (preferably salt-packed)*

*½ teaspoon freshly ground pepper*

*2 tablespoons Armagnac or Cognac (optional)*

*1 tablespoon grated orange or lemon zest (optional)*

*4 to 6 tablespoons virgin olive oil*

*6 eggs*

*2 tablespoons mayonnaise*

*Chopped parsley, for garnish*

A nice picnic food or an addition to a buffet lunch and a good excuse to use that provençal spread called tapenade.

## Procedure

For the tapenade, combine all the ingredients in a food processor and purée.

Cover the eggs with cold water in a saucepan. Bring just to the boil, reduce the heat to low, and simmer gently 8 to 9 minutes. Run the cooked eggs under cold water. Peel, and then cut in half lengthwise. Remove the yolks to the bowl of a food processor and reserve the whites. Pulse the yolks just to break them up. Add 5 tablespoons of the tapenade and the mayonnaise and pulse to combine. Spoon the tapenade mixture into the egg white halves. Sprinkle with chopped parsley.

**Note:** Any leftover tapenade may be served spread on warm toast or as a topping for roasted, halved tomatoes.

**Wine Notes:** Make it an outspoken white wine—an aggressive Sauvignon Blanc or more austere Chablis-styled Chardonnay such as Mâcon Villages, Montagny, etc. Work with the olivy flavors, either with a Vernaccia, Friulian, or southern Italian white. Of course, the local whites (provençal Cassis, etc.) are formidable choices.

# HUEVOS HAMINADOS

## Onion-Scented Eggs

♦ *Makes 8 eggs*

*3 cups skins from yellow onions*

*8 eggs (room temperature)*

*1½ cups coffee grounds*

*¼ cup olive oil*

Jews—Greek, Turkish, and Italian—traditionally serve these eggs at Passover. Hamin means oven and the eggs can be baked, covered, for up to 6–8 hours. You can also cook them over very low heat, covered, on top of the stove. There is just a faint oniony taste to the eggs, a pale brown color, and an incredibly creamy texture. I like to serve these at Passover with a salad of romaine, cucumbers, and radishes with Horseradish Vinaigrette (page 33).

### Procedure

Arrange half the onion skins over the bottom of a heavy kettle or casserole. Place the eggs on top of the skins and cover with the remaining onion skins. Sprinkle the coffee grounds over. Cover with cold water and add the olive oil. Cover the pot and simmer over very low heat or cook in a 250-degree oven for 6 hours. Then plunge the eggs into cold water and peel. Eat as is or serve with romaine salad, sliced cucumbers, and sliced radishes.

# DEEP-FRIED STUFFED OLIVES

*24 to 30 kalamata or large*
   *green olives*
*1 tablespoon finely minced garlic*
*1 tablespoon finely minced*
   *anchovies*
*2 tablespoons grated orange zest*
*¼ cup all-purpose flour*
*1 egg, lightly beaten*
*½ cup toasted bread crumbs*
*Peanut or vegetable oil, for*
   *frying*
*Lemon wedges, for garnish*

This recipe is a cross between two Italian classics, stuffed olives from Umbria and fried stuffed olives from the neighboring region of Marche. (The Umbrian olives are stuffed and marinated overnight, the ones from the Marche are stuffed with a spiced meat mixture.) I realize that this seems like a lot of work for such a very little tidbit, but if you eat one I think you will agree that these olives are worth the effort.

## Procedure

Pit the olives. Mash together the garlic, anchovy, and orange zest with a fork and stuff the mixture into the olives. (A pastry bag may make this task easier.) Roll the olives in the flour, then dip them in the egg and roll in the crumbs.

Heat 4 inches oil in a deep fryer or large saucepan to 325 degrees. Add as many olives as will fit without crowding and fry until golden, about 3 minutes. Drain on paper towels and eat as soon as you can or others will get there before you.

**Wine Notes:** A wide range of choices. Sparkling wines are always good with deep-fried foods. Wines stressing more green flavors are best; a very dry style is a must. Try a light tart white as well: Aligoté and Muscadet from France, California Chardonnays, and bone-dry Chenin Blanc. Also dry sherry.

# SANDWICHES, PIZZAS, AND SAVORY PIES

PERSIAN FETA CHEESE AND HERB SANDWICH ◆ ROMANIAN-STYLE HERBED CHEESE FOR SANDWICHES ◆ GREEK SALAD SANDWICH ◆ CAESAR SALAD SANDWICH ◆ WALDORF CHICKEN SALAD SANDWICH ◆ CHINESE CHICKEN SALAD SANDWICH ◆ BRAZILIAN CHURRASCO STEAK SANDWICH ◆ TWO SPICY MAYONNAISES FOR SANDWICHES: INDONESIAN PEANUT SAUCE MAYONNAISE ◆ CHARMOULA MAYONNAISE ◆ BEEF SANDWICHES WITH MUSTARD SOY MAYONNAISE ◆ "TOAST": ITALIAN BAR SANDWICH ◆ BASIC PIZZA DOUGH ◆ PANCETTA, LEEK, AND GRUYÈRE PIZZA ◆ PIZZA WITH FENNEL SAUSAGE AND HOT PEPPERS ◆ PIZZA WITH PANCETTA

AND SUN-DRIED TOMATOES ◆ RATATOUILLE PIZZA ◆ MUSHROOM

PIZZA ◆ ALBANIAN LEEK AND GOAT CHEESE PIE ◆ CARAMELIZED

ONION, GORGONZOLA, AND WALNUT PIZZA ◆ BUTTERNUT SQUASH

FILO PIE ◆ POTATO KNISHES ◆ PIROSHKI ◆

# PERSIAN FETA CHEESE AND HERB SANDWICH

♦ *Serves 4*

*4 pita rounds*

*16 slices (¼ inch) feta cheese, each about 3 inches long and 2 inches wide*

*32 to 48 basil leaves*

*32 to 48 mint leaves*

*2 cups watercress leaves, stems trimmed*

This is so simple you'll wonder why it needs a recipe. But if I don't tell you about it, you'll never know how really delicious this sandwich is. I first ate it at a picnic with some Persian friends. What a wonderful surprise! These are addictive.

## Procedure

Wrap the pita bread in foil and warm in a 350-degree oven. Or steam on top of a double boiler until the bread is warm and soft. Then cut each round into 2 half circles.

Place 2 slices of cheese, 4 to 6 leaves of basil and mint, and some watercress into each pita half and eat. (These can be prepared ahead but are best when the bread is still a little warm.)

**Wine Notes:** Whites that are high in acidity with herbal and earthy flavors and medium to light bodied on the tongue are best: Sauvignon Blanc from any country; Alsatian Pinot Blanc and Sylvaner; northeastern Italian Pinot Grigio and Tocai Friulano. You might also try a dry tart rosé, or a bone-dry glass of sparkling wine.

## ROMANIAN-STYLE HERBED CHEESE FOR SANDWICHES

♦ *About 4 cups, enough for*
  *8 sandwiches*

*2½ cups feta cheese*

*1½ cups ricotta cheese*

*¼ pound soft butter*

*3 tablespoons chopped parsley*

*2 tablespoons chopped fresh*
  *chives*

*1½ tablespoons coarsely ground,*
  *toasted fennel seed*

*1½ tablespoons coarsely ground,*
  *toasted caraway seed*

*1 tablespoon paprika*

*1 teaspoon freshly ground*
  *pepper*

*½ cup finely diced white onion*
  *(optional)*

This cheese spread is lovely as an hors d'oeuvre topping for crackers or croutons. Or it makes a great sandwich, with good rye bread, some sliced cucumbers, and a few leaves of watercress. The cheese mixture is also good mounded on polenta strips and baked in the oven. Incidentally, in northern Greece, especially in Salonika, there is a similar feta cheese spread called *htipiti;* it uses oregano and green hot and sweet peppers as the seasoning, and is bound with olive oil and lemon juice.

### Procedure

Combine all the ingredients in the container of a food processor and process until combined. Taste and adjust seasonings; if the feta cheese is a bit too salty, add a little more ricotta. If you are using onions, fold in at the end.

**Wine Notes:** The whites suggested for the Albanian Leek and Goat Cheese Pie (page 92) are best. Try to stay away from rosés and reds—they mostly taste disjointed with this dish.

# GREEK SALAD SANDWICH

• *Serves 4 generously*

*2 large garlic cloves, finely minced*

*1 tablespoon pan-toasted dried oregano (see note)*

*¾ cup olive oil*

*¼ cup red wine vinegar*

*½ teaspoon salt*

*Freshly ground pepper*

*1 small red onion, sliced paper thin*

*8 slices whole grain bread*

*4 large leaves romaine lettuce, cut into 2-inch pieces*

*1 cup sliced (⅛ inch) cucumber, (peeled and seeded if necessary)*

*1 small red bell pepper, seeded, cored, and sliced (⅛ inch) into rings*

*1 small green bell pepper, seeded, cored, and sliced (⅛ inch) into rings*

*2 small tomatoes, sliced ⅛ inch thick*

*8 kalamata olives, pitted and sliced*

*4 ounces feta cheese, coarsely crumbled*

Another salad to put between slices of bread. French or Italian bread, sesame seed, pita, or whole grain breads are best. Instead of using a mayonnaise, this sandwich gets an oregano garlic vinaigrette. A few slices of cooked leg of lamb added to this makes for a more complex and filling combination.

## Procedure

Whisk together the garlic, oregano, oil, and vinegar in a small bowl. Season to taste with salt and pepper.

Pour a little of the vinaigrette over the onion in a small bowl and let marinate for about 10 minutes.

For each sandwich, drizzle each of 2 slices of bread with a generous tablespoon of vinaigrette. Top 1 slice with romaine and then add some cucumbers, onion, peppers, tomato, olives, and finally some of the cheese. Drizzle with a little vinaigrette. Cover with the second slice of bread. Cut in half and serve.

**Note:** To toast oregano, warm it for a few minutes in a dry sauté pan or skillet to revive its flavor and aroma.

**Wine Notes:** Stick to the recommendations for the Persian Feta Cheese and Herb Sandwich (page 73).

# CAESAR SALAD SANDWICH

◆ *Serves 4*

*6 hard-boiled eggs*

*1 tablespoon finely puréed garlic*

*3 tablespoons chopped anchovies*
*(preferably salt packed)*

*1 tablespoon grated lemon zest*

*2 to 3 tablespoons fresh lemon*
*juice*

*¾ to 1 cup Basic Mayonnaise*
*(see below)*

*Salt and freshly ground pepper*

*8 slices whole grain bread, or 4*
*kaiser rolls*

*8 large romaine lettuce leaves,*
*cut into 1-inch-wide strips*

*2 ounces Parmesan cheese,*
*shaved with a potato peeler*
*into long strips*

## Basic Mayonnaise

◆ *2¼ cups*

*2 egg yolks*

*3 tablespoons fresh lemon juice*

*1 teaspoon Dijon mustard*
*(optional)*

*2 cups mild olive oil (or use*
*part peanut oil)*

*Salt*

Another salad that will have you looking at the old coffee shop egg salad sandwich in a new way. Whole grain bread or kaiser rolls are the breads of choice.

## Procedure

Slice the cooked eggs or cut them into small chunks. Combine the garlic, anchovy, lemon zest, juice, and mayonnaise in a bowl. Stir to blend. Season to taste with salt and pepper. Anchovies are salty—you may not need any additional salt.

For each sandwich, spread each of 2 slices of bread, or both sides of a roll, with the flavored mayonnaise. Top 1 piece of bread with romaine and the other with egg. Arrange shavings of cheese over the lettuce. Assemble the sandwich and cut in half.

To make the mayonnaise, whisk the egg yolks in a bowl with the lemon juice, the mustard, if using, and a little of the oil. Gradually beat in the remaining oil, very slowly at first and then more quickly, until a thick emulsion is achieved. Season to taste with salt. Or, place the yolks and lemon juice in the bowl of a food processor or in a blender. Add 1 to 2 tablespoons oil and turn on the machine. Then, with the motor running, slowly pour in the remaining oil until a thick emulsion is achieved. If the mayonnaise is very thick, thin with a little water.

*Note:* For a lemon mayonnaise, add 1 tablespoon grated lemon zest and increase the lemon juice by 1 tablespoon. For an orange mayonnaise, add 1 tablespoon grated orange zest and 3 tablespoons orange juice. For aioli, fold in 1 tablespoon of finely minced or puréed garlic.

# WALDORF CHICKEN SALAD SANDWICH

♦ *Serves 4*

*6 boneless, skinless chicken breasts halves*

*1 green apple, such as Granny Smith, cored, sliced, and then cut into ⅓-inch dice*

*8 tablespoons chopped, toasted walnuts*

*4 teaspoons chopped fresh chives*

*1 cup Lemon Mayonnaise (see note)*

*Salt and freshly ground pepper*

*8 slices semolina, white, or walnut bread*

*8 lettuce leaves or some watercress sprigs*

This used to be *the* salad for the ladies who lunch. When it was originally served at the Waldorf Astoria, it was just apples, celery, and mayonnaise atop a bed of lettuces. Walnuts were added later. I've added the chicken, although left-over cooked turkey works well, too. It's a recipe that follows my theory—good salad, great sandwich filling. It can be served on white bread, white toast, or walnut bread, if you can find an acceptable commercial loaf.

## Procedure

Grill or broil the chicken breasts 3 to 4 minutes each side, or poach 8 to 10 minutes in chicken stock until just cooked through, but not dry. Cut into large dice and mix in a bowl with the apples, walnuts, chives, and ¾ cup of the mayonnaise. Season to taste with salt and pepper.

For each sandwich, spread 1 slice of bread with a little of the remaining mayonnaise. Arrange lettuce leaves on the bread and top with the chicken salad. Cover with a second bread slice. Cut in half and serve.

*Note:* To make Lemon Mayonnaise, add 1 tablespoon grated lemon zest and 1 tablespoon fresh lemon juice to 1 cup Basic Mayonnaise (page 76) or prepared mayonnaise.

*Wine Notes:* The same rules apply as for Chinese Chicken Salad Sandwich (page 78): slightly sweeter rosés rather than those just off-dry.

## CHINESE CHICKEN SALAD SANDWICH

◆ *Serves 6*

*8 boneless, skinless chicken
  breasts halves, or 24 generous
  slices leftover roast chicken*

*12 slices bread (semolina,
  sesame seed, or pita bread)*

*1½ cups Sesame Ginger
  Mayonnaise (see below )*

*2 thinly sliced (about 1½ cups)
  cucumbers, peeled and seeded
  if necessary*

*Cilantro sprigs*

*12 medium romaine leaves,
  coarsely chopped*

### Sesame Ginger Mayonnaise

◆ *1¾ cups*

*2 garlic cloves, peeled and
  chopped*

*3 walnut-size pieces of fresh
  ginger, peeled and sliced
  across the grain*

*1 tablespoon prepared hot
  mustard or Square One Hot
  Mustard (page 348)*

*1 tablespoon sugar*

If it makes a great salad, it can become a wonderful sandwich. Sesame seed bread is an ideal container for this one, but pita bread works well, too.

### Procedure

Cook the chicken breasts until just cooked through but not dry: Poach 8 to 10 minutes in simmering chicken stock, sauté 4 to 5 minutes each side in olive oil over medium heat, or brush with olive oil and broil or grill 3 to 4 minutes each side. (If you broil or sauté them, do not let them color too much on the outside or they will toughen.) Cut the chicken breasts into large slices.

For each sandwich, lightly spread 2 slices of bread with mayonnaise. Arrange chicken slices over 1 of the bread slices and then top with some of the cucumber and cilantro. Add 2 leaves of romaine and cover with the second slice of bread. Cut each sandwich in half and serve. Or, lightly spread a pita pocket with the mayonnaise and stuff with the chicken, cucumber slices, cilantro, and romaine.

Pulse the garlic and ginger in a food processor until puréed. (Or grate the ginger and chop the garlic by hand until both are very finely puréed.) Add the mustard, sugar, soy sauce, vinegar, and sesame oil and process to mix well. Fold this paste into the mayonnaise. Taste and adjust seasonings. (You may want more vinegar, ginger, salt, or sesame.) This mayonnaise will keep, well covered, for a day or two in the refrigerator.

*1 tablespoon soy sauce*

*1½ to 2 tablespoons distilled white vinegar or rice wine vinegar*

*1 tablespoon sesame oil*

*1½ cups Basic Mayonnaise (page 76)*

**Note:** As a variation, dice the chicken and the cucumbers and mix well with some of the mayonnaise. Shred the romaine and mix it with chopped cilantro. Spread 4 slices of bread lightly with the mayonnaise, and place a mound of the romaine mixture on each. Top with the chicken mixture and the remaining bread slices, spread with mayonnaise.

**Wine Notes:** Whites and rosés are the best options. To pick up on the sweetness and the pungency of the mustard and ginger, a lighter style is called for—Rieslings like German Mosel kabinett and kabinett halbtrocken would be lovely, as would a dry Chenin Blanc, a fruitier Sauvignon Blanc, or Gewürztraminer. A shade-off-dry rosé—American Grenache type, most Rhône Tavel, and some Crignolino—are taste matches.

# BRAZILIAN CHURRASCO STEAK SANDWICH

◆ *Serves 6 to 8*

*1 large onion, coarsely chopped*

*2 garlic cloves, finely minced*

*½ cup fresh lemon juice*

*½ teaspoon salt*

*2 teaspoons freshly ground
  pepper*

*2 flank steaks, each about 1
  pound*

*Olive oil*

*3 to 4 ripe avocados*

*12 to 16 slices corn bread or
  light rye bread*

*Salsa Mayonnaise (see below)*

*12 to 16 medium romaine leaves
  (optional), cut into thin slices*

### Salsa Mayonnaise

*1 cup Basic Mayonnaise
  (page 76)*

*1 tablespoon grated lemon zest*

*1½ teaspoons finely minced
  garlic*

*1 tablespoon fresh lemon juice*

*1½ teaspoons freshly ground
  pepper*

This is undoubtedly unheard of in Brazil, but the flank steak from the Churrasco (page 297) is irresistible at room temperature, so why not put it between two slices of bread? The tangy salsa mayonnaise is the perfect liaison between the meat and the creamy avocado. Romaine is a nice neutral lettuce, and the choice of bread is yours— focaccia, pita, rye, or corn bread are all compatible.

### Procedure

Pulse the onion and garlic in the food processor until almost puréed. Add the lemon juice and pulse again. Add the salt and pepper. Pour this mixture over the flank steaks in a nonaluminum container and let marinate for an hour, turning steaks once or twice.

Preheat the broiler or light a charcoal fire. Remove steaks from marinade, brush lightly with olive oil, and grill until rare, 3 minutes a side. Let steaks rest a few minutes. Thinly slice across the grain.

Cut avocados in half and remove pits and peels. Thinly slice, allowing half an avocado per person.

For each sandwich spread 2 slices of bread with salsa mayonnaise. Top 1 slice with sliced steak and 1 with avocado. Add 2 leaves of romaine, if using. Assemble sandwich, halve and serve.

### Procedure

Stir all the ingredients together. Taste and adjust seasonings.

**Wine Notes:** Look for flavorful, uncomplicated reds:

3 tablespoons finely minced

onion

1 tablespoon finely minced

jalapeño peppers

Salt to taste

## TWO SPICY MAYONNAISES FOR SANDWICHES: INDONESIAN PEANUT AND CHARMOULA

## INDONESIAN PEANUT SAUCE MAYONNAISE

◆ *Makes about 2 cups*

*3 garlic cloves*

*3 1-inch chunks fresh ginger,*

*peeled*

*¼ cup soy sauce*

*4 tablespoons chunky peanut*

*butter*

*3 tablespoons sherry*

*2 tablespoons balsamic vinegar*

*1 tablespoon sugar*

*1 teaspoon ground cumin*

*1 tablespoon dried hot pepper*

*flakes, ground in a spice mill*

*1½ cups Basic Mayonnaise*

*(page 76)*

a simple Bordeaux or Rhône, a California Zinfandel or Petite Sirah or a Chianti or Barbera from Italy. For a pleasant contrast, try an off-dry, not cloying, white Zinfandel.

A good sandwich is a wonderful combination of flavors and textures, an essential ingredient of which is a sauce of some sort to marry the flavors and to keep the sandwich from being dry. Here are two of my favorite mayonnaise recipes with suggestions as to how to use them. Have fun!

Indonesian satés of beef or chicken usually are served with a spicy peanut sauce. This one can also be adapted to make a wonderful spread to put on sandwiches. It's particularly good with cooked beef, chicken, and pork (see Roast Loin of Pork in Ginger Marinade, page 288). Cucumbers are a traditional accompaniment. The choice of bread is yours.

### Procedure

Combine all the ingredients except the mayonnaise in the bowl of a food processor and process to blend. Stir into the mayonnaise.

## CHARMOULA MAYONNAISE

◆ *Makes 1⅓ cups*

*3 to 4 garlic cloves, finely
  minced*

*¼ cup fresh lemon juice*

*1 tablespoon paprika*

*2 teaspoons ground toasted
  cumin seed or ground cumin*

*½ teaspoon cayenne pepper*

*Salt and freshly ground pepper*

*1 cup Basic Mayonnaise
  (page 76)*

*¼ cup finely chopped parsley*

*¼ cup finely chopped fresh
  cilantro*

A great spread for cooked chicken, grilled or canned tuna, or leg of lamb. Combine with strips of roasted or uncooked sweet green or red peppers, a little thinly sliced red onion, some leaves of romaine. Whole grain bread or pita will work well.

### Procedure

Whisk together the garlic, lemon juice, paprika, cumin, cayenne, and a little salt and pepper, or grind in a mortar. Fold into the mayonnaise. Fold in the parsley and cilantro.

## BEEF SANDWICHES WITH MUSTARD SOY MAYONNAISE

◆ *Serves 6 to 8*

### Mustard Soy Mayonnaise

◆ *Makes 1½ cups*

*2 star anise*

*1 walnut-size piece of fresh
  ginger, smashed with a cleaver
  or meat pounder*

Cold brisket makes a great sandwich, as does any kind of steak. Instead of just plain mustard, try this Far Eastern approach to mustard sauce. Cucumbers, romaine, or watercress are harmonious with the sauce and the meat. Choice of bread is up to you.

### Procedure

For the mayonnaise, make a soy infusion by bringing the star anise, ginger, soy sauce, sugar, vinegar, and garlic to a boil in a small saucepan. Reduce the heat and simmer for about 2 minutes. Strain the liquid and cool. Discard the anise and the ginger. Put the

3 tablespoons soy sauce

1 tablespoon brown sugar

2 tablespoons rice wine vinegar
   or white vinegar

2 small garlic cloves, minced2
   eggs

¼ cup Dijon mustard

1¼ cups peanut oil

Salt and freshly ground pepper


2 flank steaks, about 1 pound
   each, or 2 pounds cooked
   Brisket of Beef (page 311),
   thinly sliced

Olive oil as needed

Salt and freshly ground pepper

12 to 16 slices of bread

12 to 14 romaine lettuce leaves,
   cut into small strips, or 24
   small watercress sprigs,
   trimmed of thick stems

2 cucumbers, seeded, peeled (if
   not English), and thinly sliced

eggs in the bowl of a food processor. Add the mustard and process to blend. Then gradually process in the peanut oil to form a mayonnaise. Add the cooled soy infusion. Season to taste with salt and pepper. (If you like, you may simply stir the soy infusion into 1½ cups prepared mayonnaise.)

Preheat the broiler or make a charcoal fire. Brush the flank steaks with a little olive oil and sprinkle with salt and pepper. Grill until rare, about 3 minutes per side. Let cool and then thinly slice across the grain.

Spread mayonnaise generously over 1 side of each slice of bread. Cover half the bread slices with meat. Place the romaine or watercress on the remaining bread slices. Top with cucumbers. Assemble the sandwiches and cut each in half.

**Note:** To accent the Oriental flavors of this dish, make a double batch of the infusion. Use half for the mayonnaise, as usual, but combine the remainder with about ¼ cup oil and marinate the flank steaks in this mixture for 1 to 2 hours before grilling.

**Wine Notes:** Try a simple red such as a California Zinfandel, a Barbera from Italy, or an Australian Shiraz. Don't get too serious . . . just enjoy.

## "TOAST": ITALIAN BAR SANDWICH

♦ *Serves 4*

*8 thin slices fontina cheese*
    (*4 ounces total*)

*8 slices white or semolina bread,*
    *cut about ⅓ inch thick*

*8 thin slices prosciutto (about*
    *8 ounces total*)

*Butter and olive oil for sautéing*
    (*optional*)

This sandwich is enormously popular in Italian caffès. It is related to the French *croque monsieur* and to our grilled ham and cheese, only here the ham is imported prosciutto di Parma and the cheese is fontina. If your toaster doesn't come with the traditional European drop-in cage attachment, or if you don't have an electric sandwich griddle, you can make this in a sauté pan or on a stovetop griddle. Weight it down with a lid to speed browning.

### Procedure

For each sandwich, place a slice of fontina on 1 slice of bread. Top with 2 slices of prosciutto and then a second slice of fontina. Cover with another slice of bread. Preheat the sandwich grill to 375 degrees, and toast the sandwich until golden, 3 to 4 minutes. Or, melt some butter and oil in a sauté pan or on a griddle. Brush the outside of the sandwich on both sides with a mixture of melted butter and olive oil. Place the sandwich in the pan or on the griddle and weight with a lid. Cook, turning once and adding more butter and oil as needed, until golden brown, about 4 minutes. Cut on the diagonal into 4 triangles.

*Note:* You may add thin slices of apple to this sandwich as a variation.

*Wine Notes:* A fairly robust and somewhat coarse red wine is ideal: Nebbiolo-based wines (not as big as Barolo or Barbaresco) from Piedmont, youthful Spanish Riojas, a provençal or Midi red from France, or American Barbera or Charbono.

## PIZZA

Afew words about pizza. I am not a practitioner of froufrou designer pizza. As in most things having to do with food, I am a traditionalist. So you won't find pizza with caviar or flowers here. I also don't like pizzas that weigh two hundred pounds. The architectural adage that less is more is apropos, if you want a crisp pizza crust and no food on your shirt front.

Precise measurements for the dough are important, but for toppings, a handful, a sprinkle, and common sense are your best measures for success.

## BASIC PIZZA DOUGH

◆ *Makes 1 11- by 17-inch or 2 9-inch pizzas*

**Sponge**

*2 teaspoons dry yeast*

*½ cup warm water*

*½ cup unbleached all-purpose
   flour*

**Dough**

*¾ cup water*

*3 tablespoons olive oil*

*⅓ cup rye flour*

*3 cups unbleached all-purpose
   flour*

*1½ teaspoons salt*

You can assemble the dough by hand and knead by hand. It's fun and relaxing. Or you can use the electric mixer with a dough hook. The dough can also be assembled in a food processor, in which case some meditative hand kneading would not be a bad idea.

I use the sponge method as I find it relatively foolproof. This gives the yeast a head start.

### Procedure

For the sponge, dissolve the yeast in the warm water in a mixing bowl. Stir in the flour and let the sponge stand, covered, for about 30 minutes. Then add the dough ingredients and mix on low speed with a dough hook for about 10 minutes, or until the dough no longer sticks to the side of the bowl. Transfer the dough to a mixing bowl, cover with plastic wrap, and let rise in a warm place until almost doubled, about 1 hour. Punch down on a lightly floured surface and

(*continued*)

shape into 1 or 2 balls. Place the dough balls on a floured baking sheet, cover, and let rest for 30 minutes. Then stretch the dough into rounds or rectangles on a lightly floured surface and cover with topping.

Preheat the oven to 475 degrees. If you are using tiles or a pizza stone, heat them in the oven for about 30 minutes before baking the pizza. Then lightly dust with cornmeal, transfer the pizza from a wooden peel to the stone or tiles, and bake the pizza until golden brown, 12 to 15 minutes. Or you may bake the pizza directly on a well-seasoned baking sheet; the more seasoned the sheet, the better the crust.

*Variation:* To make a rosemary crust, warm 3 tablespoons chopped fresh rosemary in the 3 tablespoons olive oil to release its flavor. Then add the rosemary to the dough along with the oil. You may also substitute buckwheat flour for the rye flour.

# PANCETTA, LEEK, AND GRUYÈRE PIZZA

♦ *Makes 1 11- by 17-inch or 2 9-inch pizzas*

*Basic Pizza Dough (page 85)*

*2 tablespoons unsalted butter*

*3 cups chopped leeks, white and green parts, well washed and drained*

*Salt and freshly ground pepper*

*Grated nutmeg*

*6 ounces pancetta, cut into julienne*

*½ pound grated Gruyère cheese, or a combination of half mozzarella and half Gruyère cheeses*

*Virgin olive oil*

*2 to 3 tablespoons grated Parmesan cheese*

A northern Italian pizza with French overtones. This should not come as a big surprise as Piemonte was once ruled by France. Gruyère, a Swiss cheese, is as popular in Italy as it is in France.

### Procedure

Make the pizza dough. Preheat the oven to 475 degrees.

Melt the butter in a heavy skillet. Add the leeks and cook, stirring occasionally, until tender, about 10 minutes. Drain and season to taste with salt, pepper, and a little grated nutmeg.

Partially render the chopped pancetta in its own fat in a sauté pan or skillet, cooking it until almost cooked through but not crisp.

Prepare 2 9-inch round pizza crusts or 1 11- by 17-inch rectangular crust. Cover with the Gruyère or Gruyère and mozzarella cheeses and then top with the rendered pancetta and the leeks. Transfer the pizza to the oven and bake until the crust is golden and well puffed, about 15 minutes. Brush the edges with a little virgin olive oil and sprinkle with the grated Parmesan cheese.

*Wine Notes:* Both white and red wines go well with this dish. Italian whites are natural and Sauvignon Blanc from France or California is very good, too. Light nontannic reds such as Dolcetto, Beaujolais, or light rustic Pinot Noirs are lovely. Even red wines of a bit more strength—Chianti, some California Zinfandel and Syrah, certain Rhône wines, and many of the simpler Ghemme and Spanna of Piedmont—are also quite a match.

## PIZZA WITH FENNEL SAUSAGE AND HOT PEPPERS

♦ *Makes 1 11- by 17-inch or 2 9-inch pizzas*

*Basic Pizza Dough (page 85)*

*8 ounces fennel sausage*

*4 to 5 tablespoons olive oil*

*3 cups escarole, cut into ½-inch strips, well washed and drained*

*2 tablespoons red wine vinegar*

*Salt and freshly ground pepper*

*2 cups sliced (¼ inch) red onions*

*1 tablespoon dried red pepper flakes*

*1 tablespoon finely minced garlic, steeped in virgin olive oil for about 1 hour*

*1½ cups grated mozzarella cheese*

Make the pizza dough. Remove the casings from the sausage and break up the meat into 1-inch pieces. Set aside.

Heat 2 tablespoons of the olive oil in a sauté pan or skillet over high heat. Add the escarole and cook, stirring often, until partly wilted, about 2 minutes. Then add the vinegar and cook until the greens are tender but not mushy, about 3 more minutes. Drain the greens in a colander; there should be about 1 cup cooked greens. Season to taste with salt and pepper. Heat 2 to 3 tablespoons more olive oil in the sauté pan or skillet over medium heat. Add the onions and cook until tender, about 5 minutes. Add the red pepper flakes and cook 1 more minute.

Preheat the oven to 475 degrees. Prepare an 11- by 17-inch rectangular crust or 2 9-inch round crusts. Brush with the garlic oil. Sprinkle with about 1 cup grated cheese. Top with the onions, escarole, and sausage chunks. Sprinkle the top with the remaining cheese. Transfer to the oven and bake until the crust is golden and the cheese is bubbly, about 15 minutes.

**Wine Notes:** Best here are reds of medium to medium-full body—classics such as Chianti, Montepulciano d'Abruzzi, Nebbiolo d'Alba, Valpolicella, and Bardolino. In addition, non-Italian reds like Zinfandel, robust Pinot Noir, and Spanish or Portuguese table wines are quite nice.

# PIZZA WITH PANCETTA AND SUN-DRIED TOMATOES

♦ *Makes 1 11- by 17-inch or 2 9-inch pizzas*

*Basic Pizza Dough (page 85)*

*6 ounces pancetta, sliced ¼ inch thick*

*2 tablespoons olive oil*

*2 red onions, sliced ¼ inch thick*

*½ cup sun-dried tomatoes, cut into thin strips, oil reserved*

*1 tablespoon finely minced garlic, steeped in virgin olive oil for about 1 hour*

*3 to 5 ounces fresh mozzarella cheese, grated (optional)*

*½ cup grated pecorino cheese*

*¼ cup fresh basil, cut into very fine strips*

Instead of the basic tomato sauce, try sun-dried tomatoes.

## Procedure

Make the pizza dough.

Cut the sliced pancetta into small strips about ¼ inch wide. Place in a large sauté pan or skillet and cook over medium heat until almost crisp. Remove from the pan with a slotted spoon and set aside, reserving any fat that remains in the pan. Add the oil and onions to the pan and cook over medium heat until the onions are tender, about 10 minutes.

Preheat the oven to 475 degrees. Prepare a large rectangular crust or 2 round crusts. Brush with the sun-dried tomato oil and minced garlic. Sprinkle with the mozzarella cheese, if using. Then top with the onions, pancetta, and sun-dried tomato strips. Transfer to the oven and bake until golden, 12 to 15 minutes.

Sprinkle with the pecorino and basil before serving.

**Wine Notes:** Rich red wines, muscular and fairly robust, are the most harmonious with this pizza— Valpolicella or Barbera, Côtes du Rhône or Chianti, for example. Make certain that there is enough overt fruit to match up with the sweetness of the pancetta. Keep the tannin levels in check as they wreak havoc with the saltiness of the dried tomatoes. Bold country whites from Italy, France, or Spain are good alternatives for non-red wine drinkers.

# RATATOUILLE PIZZA

♦ *Makes 1 11- by 17-inch or 2 9-inch pizzas*

*Basic Pizza Dough (page 85)*

*½ cup olive oil, or as needed*

*2 to 3 Japanese eggplant, sliced ½ inch thick, or 1 large regular eggplant, peeled and sliced ½ inch thick*

*2 small zucchini, sliced ½ inch thick*

*Salt and freshly ground pepper*

*2 bell peppers, red and/or green, cored, seeded, and sliced ¼ inch thick*

*2 small red onions, thinly sliced*

*1 cup sliced (¼ inch) mushrooms*

*1 tablespoon finely minced garlic, steeped in virgin olive oil for about 1 hour*

*½ cup tomato purée*

*1 cup grated mozzarella cheese*

*¼ cup fresh basil, cut into thin strips*

*2 teaspoons chopped fresh thyme*

*¼ cup grated Parmesan cheese*

The vegetarian pizza par excellence. I gave it a French name as most people recognize the classic provençal ratatouille. Provence and the Côte d'Azur merge into the Italian Riviera and share many similar flavors and food combinations. Bon appetit or buon appetito, you'll love it no matter what you call this pizza.

## Procedure

Make the pizza dough.

Preheat the oven to 375 degrees. Lightly brush 2 baking sheets with some of the oil. Place the eggplant and zucchini slices on the baking sheets and brush with oil. Sprinkle with salt and pepper and bake until tender, about 8 minutes. Set aside.

Heat 1 to 2 tablespoons of the oil in a large sauté pan or skillet over medium heat and cook the pepper strips until tender, about 5 minutes. Sprinkle with salt and pepper to taste and set aside. Add a bit more oil to the pan and cook the onions over medium heat until tender, about 10 minutes; set aside. Heat 2 more tablespoons oil in the pan, add the mushrooms and cook until tender, about 5 minutes. Sprinkle with salt and pepper to taste and set aside.

Raise the oven temperature to 475 degrees. Prepare 1 11- by 17-inch rectangular crust or 2 9-inch round crusts. Brush with garlic oil and spread with the tomato purée. Sprinkle with the mozzarella cheese and distribute the vegetables over the top. Transfer to the oven and bake until golden, 12 to 15 minutes. Sprinkle the pizza with the fresh herbs and Parmesan before serving.

# MUSHROOM PIZZA

♦ *Makes 1 11- by 17-inch or 2 9-inch pizzas*

*2 to 3 tablespoons olive oil, plus oil for brushing*

*2 to 3 cups sliced (¼ inch) chanterelle mushrooms, brushed clean of dirt, or ½ cup sliced chanterelle mushrooms plus ½ cup sliced (¼ inch) cultivated mushrooms*

*1 tablespoon finely minced garlic*

*2 teaspoons chopped fresh thyme*

*Salt and freshly ground pepper*

*1 red onion, sliced ¼ inch thick*

*Basic Pizza Dough (page 85)*

*½ cup grated mozzarella cheese*

*½ cup rendered pancetta or strips of prosciutto (optional)*

*2 to 3 tablespoons grated Parmesan cheese*

Whenwild mushrooms are in season, this is the pizza to serve. Porcini or chanterelles alone, or combined with our cultivated mushrooms, sautéed and seasoned with garlic and thyme, need very little in the way of adornment. You can add strips of prosciutto or rendered pancetta, some sautéed red onions and a little Parmesan, but be careful not to overpower the mushroom flavor.

### *Procedure*

Heat the olive oil in a large sauté pan or skillet over medium heat. Add the mushrooms and sauté quickly until tender, about 4 minutes. Lower heat and add about half of the garlic and all of the thyme. Cook 1 minute longer, season with salt and pepper, and then remove the mushrooms with a slotted spoon and set aside. Then quickly sauté the onion in the oil remaining in the pan until crisp-tender, 5 to 7 minutes.

Preheat the oven to 475 degrees. Prepare 1 11- by 17-inch rectangular crust or 2 9-inch round crusts. Mix the remaining garlic with a little oil, and brush over the crust(s). Sprinkle the mozzarella cheese over the crust to anchor the mushrooms. Then arrange the onion, mushrooms, and pancetta or prosciutto, if using, on top. Transfer to the oven and bake until golden brown, 12 to 15 minutes. Sprinkle with the Parmesan cheese and brush the crust with a little oil.

***Wine Notes:*** A bevy of reds are the tastiest pairings: Loire Valley reds (Chinon and Bourgueil), medium-bodied California and Washington State Merlot, and the selection of Italian red wines suggested throughout the recipes for pizza.

## ALBANIAN LEEK AND GOAT CHEESE PIE

◆ *Serves 8 to 10 as a main course, or 16 to 18 as a small appetizer*

*10 medium leeks, most of the green tops removed*

*4 tablespoons unsalted butter*

*1¾ pounds fresh goat cheese (not too sharp!)*

*4 eggs, lightly beaten with a fork*

*Freshly ground pepper*

*Nutmeg (optional)*

*½ pound unsalted butter, melted, or 1 cup mild olive oil*

*16 to 20 sheets filo dough*

My friend Helen talked about her mother's leek pie so often that I had to learn how to make it, but when we tried the family recipe it didn't seem right. When Helen's mother came for a visit, she showed us how her family had made this pie in Albania. The truth was that it was a good pie but had the potential to be a great one. Over time, something had gotten lost in translation: When Helen's mother first came to America, she had had to substitute cottage cheese for the tart Albanian fresh cheese curds, and in making the dough, Crisco had become the layering agent. I realized how lucky we were today. We can get fresh goat cheese. We can buy filo dough for a thin and flaky crust to replace the Albanian *peda*, sort of a rustic puff pastry. Olive oil or butter can be used in the filo layering process.

I have made this pie with leeks, spinach, and zucchini. All are excellent. Similar versions of this pie are prepared in Greece and Turkey. For a lovely meal, serve with a salad of endive, apple, and walnuts with a walnut vinaigrette. Or assorted bitter greens, fennel, and hazelnuts.

### *Procedure*

For the filling, cut the leeks in half lengthwise and thinly slice them. Wash well in a sink full of cold water to remove the sand. Drain. (You should have about 4 cups sliced leeks.) Melt the 4 tablespoons butter in a large high sided sauté pan over medium heat. Add the leeks and cook until tender, about 15 minutes. During the cooking you may add up to 4 tablespoons water as needed to help wilt the leeks. (If there is a lot of water clinging to the leeks, you may not need to add any extra water.) Break the goat cheese into small pieces with your fingers and add, along with the eggs, to the leeks. Season to taste with pepper and, if you like, a little ground nutmeg.

Lightly brush a 15-inch pizza pan with melted butter or olive oil. Working with 1 sheet at a time, brush 8 to 10 sheets of filo with the melted butter or oil and arrange them in the pan, in an overlapping circular fashion, letting the edges of the filo overhang the pan (butter or oil the overhang as well). Spread the filling over the dough. Fold up the overhanging filo. Again working with 1 filo sheet at a time and brushing each sheet with butter or oil, arrange 8 to 10 more sheets of filo over the filling in the same circular fashion. Tuck the overhanging pieces under the pie. At this point you may refrigerate the pie overnight, covered loosely with a foil tent.

Bring the pie to room temperature, if refrigerated. Preheat the oven to 400 degrees. Bake the pie until pale golden in color, about 15 minutes. Remove from the oven and carefully tilt the pan to drain the excess butter or oil. Place a second 15-inch pizza pan over the pie and invert, turning the pie into the second pan. Return to oven and bake until golden brown, about 10 minutes. Invert again onto the original pan.

To serve, cut into wedges with a serrated knife and eat warm; the pastry gets soggy when cold.

***Wine Notes:*** White is the choice here: Experiment with Sauvignon Blanc, bone-dry Chenin Blanc, or a green Chardonnay. A spicy dry rosé will work, too.

# CARAMELIZED ONION, GORGONZOLA, AND WALNUT PIZZA

♦ *Makes 1 11- by 17-inch or 2 9-inch pizzas*

*4 tablespoons unsalted butter*

*3 pounds red onions, sliced ¼ inch thick (about 3 large onions)*

*Salt and freshly ground pepper*

*½ cup walnuts*

*Basic Pizza Dough (page 85), either buckwheat or rosemary variation*

*1 cup Gorgonzola "dolce latte" cheese, crumbled*

*Olive oil*

This pizza is the ideal cocktail party snack as its Piemontese flavors are so harmonious with wine. While most pizza is best when piping hot, this can be served warm or at room temperature because it is not too cheesy. You can prepare this ahead and warm it just slightly before serving.

## Procedure

Melt the butter in a heavy-bottomed wide sauté pan or skillet over low heat. Add the onions and cook slowly, stirring occasionally, until they are quite soft, golden brown, and reduced. This could take as long as 30 minutes. Be patient; the sweeter the onions, the better the pizza. Season to taste with salt and pepper and set aside to drain.

Turn the oven to 475 degrees. Prepare 1 11- by 17-inch or 2 9-inch round crusts. Cover with the onions. Distribute little chunks of Gorgonzola over the onions and sprinkle with the chopped walnuts. Transfer to the oven and bake until the crust is puffed and golden and the walnuts are toasty, about 12 minutes. Brush the edge of the crust lightly with olive oil.

**Wine Notes:** A simple Bordeaux or Burgundy, a Shiraz from Australia, or lighter French Rhône or Cabernet Sauvignon from Chile would be tasty. If you prefer white, try a rich Tokay-Pinot Gris from Alsace.

# BUTTERNUT SQUASH FILO PIE

♦ *Serves 8 to 10*

*2 butternut squash, about 2*
  *pounds each*

*Salt and freshly ground pepper*

*¼ pound clarified unsalted*
  *butter, melted*

*3 tablespoons sugar*

*1 teaspoon cinnamon*

*16 sheets filo dough*

Of all of the many *pita* (filo pies) I tasted on my last trip to Greece, this was my very favorite. Naturally I asked the woman who made this for the recipe, and through a translator I was told that the pumpkin squash was grated and then cooked in butter and the layers of filo were sprinkled with a little cinnamon sugar. I tried this grating technique a few times but the texture of the squash was never what I remember. It was too fragmented whereas the squash in the pie I ate was dense and solid. So I baked the butternut squash, then sliced it, and then enclosed the sliced cooked squash in filo. Aha! More like it. You'll like it, too.

## Procedure

Preheat the oven to 350 degrees. Bake the squash until tender but not mushy, soft but firm enough to be sliced. Let stand until cool enough to handle, and then peel. Cut off the rounded bottom part that holds the seeds and discard. Slice the rest of the squash (the solid part) about ½ inch thick. Sprinkle with salt and pepper; set aside. Lightly brush a 15-inch pizza pan with melted butter. Toss together the sugar and cinnamon. Place 1 sheet of filo in the center of the prepared pan. Brush with melted butter and sprinkle with the sugar mixture. Place another sheet of filo on top of the first, at an angle. Brush with butter and sprinkle with the sugar mixture. Continue layering 6 more filo sheets in this overlapping circular fashion, letting the edges of the filo overhang the edge of the pan (butter the overhang as well). Then

(*continued*)

arrange a layer of sliced squash to fill the entire diameter of the pan. Fold up the overhanging filo. Again working with 1 filo sheet at a time and brushing each sheet with butter and sprinkling with the sugar mixture, arrange 8 to 10 more sheets of filo over the filling in the same circular fashion. Tuck the overhanging filo under the pie.

Preheat the oven to 350 degrees. Bake the pie until golden brown, about 25 minutes. Check to see that the pie is browning well on the bottom; if not, carefully tilt the pan to drain the excess butter, place a second 15-inch pizza pan over the pie and invert, turning the pie onto the second pan. Then bake 5 to 10 more minutes to brown, flip it back onto the original pan, and finish baking a few more minutes.

To serve, cut the pie into wedges with a serrated knife and eat warm with salad or as an accompaniment to roast chicken or duck or pork.

*Wine Notes:* This craves either a wine to complement its richness, such as a white Rhône (French or California clone), Alsatian varietals like Gewürztraminer, Riesling or Pinot Gris, or a tart foil to cut its full body, like an off-dry Riesling or Chenin Blanc.

## POTATO KNISHES

◆ *Makes about 4 dozen*

### Filling

6 large russet potatoes

6 tablespoons rendered chicken
   fat

3 large onions, chopped fine
   (about 3 cups)

2 egg yolks

2 teaspoons salt

1½ to 2 teaspoons freshly
   ground pepper

2 tablespoons chopped parsley

¾ cup diced smoked salmon
   (optional)

### Blitz Pastry

6 cups all-purpose flour

1½ teaspoons salt

1¾ pounds chilled, unsalted
   butter

¼ pound chilled, rendered
   chicken fat

2 cups ice water

1 egg yolk, lightly beaten, for
   glazing

When I was growing up in Brooklyn, I was addicted to street food, made all the more appealing because it was forbidden by my mother. To this day I can still taste the potato knishes that I'd buy after school as a secret snack. While the ones I remember were considerably heavier and larger than these, you can tailor their proportions to suit the occasion. If you are nostalgic for Brooklyn street life, make them big. In California, away from the New York hustle and bustle, I make petite knishes for hors d'oeuvres and larger ones for lunch—excellent with Russian Garden Salad (page 34). Knishes can be made ahead and frozen. If frozen, do not thaw to bake.

### Procedure

For the filling, preheat the oven to 450 degrees. Bake the potatoes until tender, about 1 hour. While still warm, cut the potatoes in half and work the flesh through a ricer or mash with a fork. Do not purée or overwhip; the texture should be rough. (You should have about 3 cups.) Melt the chicken fat in a sauté pan or skillet. Add the onions and cook until translucent and pale gold in color, 10 to 15 minutes. Fold the onions into the potatoes, stir in the yolks, salt, pepper, parsley, and the smoked salmon, if using. Taste and adjust seasoning. The filling may be made a day ahead.

For the pastry, sift the flour and salt into a mixing bowl. Cut in the butter until the mixture resembles coarse cornmeal. Cut in the chicken fat. Then, working the dough as little as possible so as not to melt the

(*continued*)

fat, work in the water with your fingers just until the dough comes together. Roll out the pastry to a 9- by 18-inch rectangle on a lightly floured surface. Then fold the pastry a "turn" as you would for puff pastry: Fold the bottom third of the rectangle up toward the center and then fold the top third down to overlap. Refrigerate 15 minutes. Return the pastry to the work surface and give it a quarter turn so that the fold is now at the side, rather than at the bottom. Repeat rolling, folding, and turning 4 more times, refrigerating 15 minutes between each "turn." Wrap and refrigerate the dough overnight.

Preheat the oven to 350 degrees. Lightly oil 2 baking sheets. To assemble the knishes, cut the chilled pastry into 4 pieces. Working with one piece of pastry at a time and refrigerating the rest until you are ready for them, roll out the pastry as thin as possible, to about a 4- by 16-inch rectangle. Cut into 4-inch squares. Place about 2 tablespoons of filling in a mound in the center of the pastry squares. Fold in the sides, then fold up the bottom edge and fold down the top edge to completely cover the filling. Turn the knishes seam sides down on the prepared baking sheets. (At this point, the knishes may be frozen, or refrigerated for a day.) Brush the knishes with the egg yolk. Bake until golden, 15 to 20 minutes.

*Note:* You may also shape the knishes into long thin rolls and cut into bite-size pieces for serving.

*Wine Notes:* Because of the richness of the knish, sparkling wine would be lovely. For whites, try a Mâcon or Arneis from Piedmont. And if you want red, a nontannic Italian Dolcetto or Gamay would work well.

# PIROSHKI

◆ *Makes about 30 2½-inch ovals*

**Yeast Dough**

¼ ounce dry yeast

2 tablespoons plus ½ teaspoon sugar

2 teaspoons warm water (about 100 degrees)

4 cups all-purpose flour

1½ teaspoons salt

1¾ cups warm milk (95 degrees)

3 eggs

6 tablespoons unsalted butter, melted and cooled to lukewarm

**Piroshki Filling**

8 tablespoons unsalted butter

2 medium onions, minced (about 1½ cups)

1 pound mushrooms, minced

2 hard-boiled eggs, minced

¼ cup raw rice, cooked (to make about ½ cup cooked rice)

1½ teaspoons salt

½ teaspoon freshly ground pepper

¼ cup each minced fresh dill and parsley

As I get older, I become more nostalgic for the foods of my past. My grown children are also nostalgic, and their pasts are shorter than mine. They still talk about piroshki they ate years ago in San Francisco Russian restaurants that used to be on Clement Street. Alas, these little Mom and Pop places are gone, but obviously not forgotten. The piroshki recipe that follows is worth the effort to prepare. There are many different fillings, some with meat, some with cabbage; my favorite is with mushrooms.

The filling for these Russian pastries can be made well ahead. While they don't freeze well in an unbaked state, you can bake them and hold them for quite a while, then reheat. They are also really good deep-fried. A few of these plus a salad can be lunch, or served as an accompaniment to a soup (how about borscht?) for a light supper.

## Procedure

For the dough, stir together the yeast, ½ teaspoon sugar, and the water in a mixing bowl and let stand until bubbly, about 5 minutes. Transfer the yeast mixture to the bowl of an electric mixer and add the 2 tablespoons sugar, 2½ cups of the flour, the salt, and 1½ cups of the milk. Use the dough hook to beat 1 minute on low speed. Beat the 3 eggs lightly with a fork to blend and add to the mixer bowl along with the remaining flour and milk. Beat 1 minute on low speed. Increase speed to medium and beat 2 more minutes. Then reduce speed again to low, add the

*(continued)*

*Egg Wash*

*2 eggs*

*2 tablespoons heavy cream*

butter and beat 2 minutes more. Finally, turn the mixer to medium-high speed and beat for 10 minutes. (If yours is not a heavy duty mixer, you will need to stop a few times for 2 minutes at a time during this final beating to allow the mixer to cool off.) The dough is ready when it no longer sticks to the side of the bowl.

Cover the dough loosely with a towel and let rise in a warm place until doubled, about 45 minutes; punch down.

Meanwhile, to make the filling, melt the butter in a large sauté pan or skillet over medium heat. Add the minced onions and cook until soft and golden, but not brown, about 10 minutes. Add the mushrooms and cook 5 minutes longer. Remove from the heat and stir in the remaining filling ingredients. Taste and adjust seasonings. Let cool.

Preheat the oven to 375 degrees. To assemble the piroshki, roll out the dough on a lightly floured surface to 1/16 inch thick. Cut out circles of dough with a 2½-inch round pastry cutter. Make the egg wash by beating together the eggs and cream and brush over the edges of the circles. Place 1 heaping tablespoon of filling in the center of each circle. Cover with another circle of dough. Pinch the edges together to seal and place on an oiled baking sheet. Repeat to make all of the piroshki. Let the piroshki rise in a warm place until they are about one quarter again as large, 20 to 30 minutes. Brush the piroshki with the remaining egg wash and bake until golden, 8 to 10 minutes. Or, you may omit the final glazing and deep-fry them in hot peanut oil for about 3 minutes.

*Wine Notes:* Try to find a red wine that will pick up on the earthiness of the mushrooms and the dill: Chinon, Bourgueil, or autumnal Pinot Noirs and racier cru Beaujolais, all low in tannin. Pungent Sauvignon Blancs, especially those like Pouilly Fumé, are also great.

# S O U P S

CUCUMBER AND ZUCCHINI SOUP ◆ FRENCH APPLE CIDER AND
CARROT SOUP ◆ MOROCCAN CARROT SOUP ◆ CREAM OF BEET
SOUP ◆ CREAM OF FIVE ONION SOUP ◆ MEXICAN CAULIFLOWER
SOUP ◆ HUNGARIAN CAULIFLOWER SOUP ◆ SPINACH AND PEA
SOUP ◆ GREEN PEA AND LETTUCE SOUP ◆ CURRIED BROCCOLI
AND SPINACH SOUP ◆ AVOCADO SOUP ◆ WHITE CORN SOUP ◆
BLACK BEAN SOUP ◆ YELLOW SPLIT PEA SOUP WITH RED ONION,
LEMON, AND VIRGIN OLIVE OIL ◆ ASHE MASTE ◆ SOPA DI LIMA
◆ AJIACO BOGOTANO ◆ BRAZILIAN CORN CHOWDER WITH SHRIMP
◆ BRAZILIAN SHELLFISH CHOWDER À LA VATAPÀ ◆ CATALAN

CHICK-PEA AND SPINACH SOUP WITH SHRIMP, ALMONDS, AND
GARLIC ◆ MINESTRA DI BROCCOLI E VONGOLE ALLA ROMANA ◆
MATZO BALL SOUP ◆

# CUCUMBER AND ZUCCHINI SOUP

♦ *Serves 6*

*4 tablespoons unsalted butter*

*4 cups diced or thinly sliced*
*    onions*

*1 cup peeled and very thinly*
*    sliced potato*

*3 cups Chicken Stock (page*
*    119), plus stock for thinning*

*5 cups sliced zucchini (1 inch)*

*2 cups sliced (1 inch) cucumbers*
*    (Japanese or English)*

*Salt and freshly ground pepper*

*Yogurt or sour cream*

*Chopped fresh chives, dill, or*
*    mint, for garnish*

I f the cucumbers are sweet, this can be the most refreshing soup. If in doubt, peel them and remove all the seeds with care. Do not overcook the vegetables or the soup will be watery. Good either hot or chilled.

## Procedure

Melt the butter in a medium saucepan over low heat. Add the chopped onions and cook until tender and translucent, about 10 minutes. Add the potato slices and enough stock to barely cover. Bring to a boil, reduce the heat, and simmer for 10 minutes. Add the zucchini and cook until just tender, 5 to 7 minutes. Then add the cucumbers and cook 3 to 5 minutes longer. Purée the soup and add stock as necessary to thin. Season to taste with salt and pepper. Ladle into bowls and serve with a dollop of yogurt or sour cream and the chopped herb of your choice.

**Wine Notes:** White is the choice here, one of light to light-medium body with a crisp finish and pronounced herbal flavors: Sauvignon Blanc from California, France's Loire Valley (Sancerre, Pouilly Fumé), or Italy's northeast (Alto Adige, Friuli) would serve well.

# FRENCH APPLE CIDER AND CARROT SOUP

♦ *Serves 6*

*2 tablespoons unsalted butter*

*2 medium onions, chopped*
  *(1½ to 2 cups)*

*1¼ pounds carrots, peeled and*
  *cut into 2-inch chunks (about*
  *4 cups)*

*4 cups Chicken Stock*
  *(page 119)*

*1 cup hard apple cider*

*1 cup heavy cream*

*Salt and freshly ground pepper*

*Sugar or nutmeg, as necessary,*
  *if the carrots lack flavor*

*3 carrots peeled and cut into*
  *fine julienne on a mandoline*
  *and blanched (see note) or*
  *12 thin slices unpeeled green*
  *apple for garnish (optional)*

Inspired by the cuisine of Normandy. If you can't find the French cider at your liquor store, American hard cider will do—if it's not too high in alcohol.

## Procedure

Melt the butter in a large heavy saucepan over medium heat. Add the onions and cook until translucent and sweet, 10 to 15 minutes. Add the carrot chunks and the chicken stock and bring to a boil. Then reduce the heat and simmer until the carrots are very tender.

Purée the soup in the blender or food processor, using only as much of the stock as necessary to purée the carrots. Transfer the purée to a clean saucepan and then add the apple cider, the cream, and as much of the remaining stock as necessary to thin the soup to the desired consistency. Season to taste with salt and pepper. Add a pinch of sugar or nutmeg if the soup needs sweetening.

To serve, reheat the soup and add the carrot julienne, if using. Ladle the soup into bowls and top with the apple slices, if using. (Or, for a very special garnish, top with a dollop of whipped cream flavored with a little Calvados.)

**Note:** Blanch the carrot julienne in a small pot of lightly salted water until al dente, 2 to 3 minutes. Then drain and refresh in cold water. Use either the carrots or apple as garnish, but not both.

# MOROCCAN CARROT SOUP

♦ *Serves 8*

*3 tablespoons unsalted butter*

*2 onions, chopped (1½ to 2*
*cups)*

*1 teaspoon cinnamon*

*½ teaspoon ground cumin*

*Pinch of cayenne pepper*

*½ teaspoon salt*

*½ teaspoon freshly ground*
*pepper*

*5 cups peeled carrots cut into*
*chunks*

*6 cups Chicken Stock*
*(page 119)*

*½ cup fresh orange juice*

*2 tablespoons (or to taste) sugar*

*1 cup julienne (2 inches long*
*and ¼ inch thick) of carrot*
*(optional)*

*3 tablespoons chopped fresh*
*cilantro or mint*

It's unlikely that this soup is served in Morocco. But the spices are those used in the classic Moroccan carrot salad, so why not change the format? Serve with carrot julienne and chopped mint.

## Procedure

Melt the butter in a large saucepan over low heat. Add the onions and cook until translucent and tender, about 15 minutes. Add the spices, salt, and pepper and cook 2 to 3 more minutes. Add the carrot chunks and the chicken stock and bring to a boil. Then reduce the heat and simmer until the carrots are tender. Purée the soup in a blender. Return to the saucepan and add the orange juice and a little sugar to sweeten the soup. If you are using the carrot julienne, blanch the carrots 2 to 3 minutes in lightly salted, boiling water until tender but still firm. Drain and refresh in cold water.

To serve, return the soup to a boil and add the carrot julienne, if using. Ladle into soup bowls and garnish with the chopped mint or cilantro.

**Wine Notes:** A spicy and aggressive Gewürztraminer would pair nicely, as would a dry styled Muscat from Alsace, Austria, or this country. You might also try a red in a lighter fruitier style such as Beaujolais, a simple Pinot Noir, an Australian Shiraz, or a blend such as Burgundy's *passe tout grains* (a blend of Gamay and Pinot Noir).

## CREAM OF BEET SOUP

♦ *Serves 6 to 8*

*6 medium beets (about 4*
   *pounds)*

*2 tablespoons unsalted butter*

*2 medium red onions, sliced*
   *(about 3 cups)*

*6 cups Chicken Stock*
   *(page 119)*

*¾ cup light cream*

*1 teaspoon salt*

*½ teaspoon freshly ground*
   *pepper*

*1 tablespoon (or to taste)*
   *raspberry or black currant*
   *vinegar, or 1 tablespoon*
   *lemon juice plus a little sugar*
   *for balance*

This soup is a most amazing shocking pink. It tastes sweet, with a little tart undertone from the fruit-based vinegar. This is a perfect way to display the earthy sweetness of beets. Occasionally, however, they can taste "dirty" and there is nothing you can do to make the soup right. Taste the beets first before puréeing the soup just to be on the safe side.

### Procedure

Trim the leaves off the beets but leave about 1 inch of stem attached. Rinse.

Cover the beets with water in a large saucepan. Bring to a boil, reduce the heat and simmer until the beets are tender, 40 to 60 minutes. Drain, cover with fresh warm water, and let stand until cool enough to handle. Then peel the beets and cut 4 of them into rough dice; set aside. Cut the remaining 2 beets into julienne; set aside.

Melt the butter in a 2-quart saucepan over medium heat. Add the onions and cook until tender and translucent, 15 to 20 minutes. Add enough stock to cover (1 to 2 cups) and bring to a boil. Transfer the onions to a blender with a slotted spoon and purée along with the diced beets. Add stock if necessary for a smooth purée. Return the purée to the saucepan. Add the cream and enough stock to thin the soup to the desired consistency. Add the salt, pepper, and vinegar or lemon juice and sugar. Taste and adjust seasonings so that you get a good balance of sweet and tart.

To serve, reheat the soup. Ladle into bowls, and garnish with the beet julienne. (You may also want to add a dollop of sour cream flavored with chopped fresh dill, or whipped cream flavored with orange and sherry.)

*Wine Notes:* Echo the earthy quality of the beets with medium-rich reds that emphasize that "goût de terroir": Chinon or any other Cabernet franc-based wine, an earthy Italian red like a simple ripe Montepulciano d'Abruzzi or similar vino di tavola. Or play off the gentle sweetness of the beets with something a bit fruitier: a Grenache-based Rhône-style red (from France or California), a Washington Merlot, or a simple, lighter California Zinfandel.

# CREAM OF FIVE ONION SOUP

◆ *Serves 8*

*8 tablespoons unsalted butter*

*4 cups sliced red onions*

*4 cups sliced yellow onions*

*4 cups sliced leeks, white part only (well washed)*

*1 cup sliced shallots*

*4 to 5 cups Chicken Stock (page 119)*

*1 teaspoon salt*

*½ teaspoon freshly ground pepper*

*½ teaspoon grated nutmeg*

*½ cup heavy cream (optional)*

*¼ cup minced fresh chives*

The sweetness of the onions paired with the nutmeg make this French-inspired soup rich and satisfying. Top with toasted croutons, chopped toasted hazelnuts, and/or diced small bits of prosciutto; chopped chives are the understated garnish. As an experiment one night I added toasted almonds, diced cooked shrimp, and some watercress to this soup—not authentic but very tasty.

### Procedure

Melt 4 tablespoons of the butter in a large heavy saucepan over low heat. Add the onions and cook, without coloring, until very tender and soft, 15 to 20 minutes. Melt the remaining 4 tablespoons butter in another saucepan over low heat. Add the leeks and shallots and cook until tender but not colored, 20 to 25 minutes.

Combine the cooked onions, shallots, and leeks in one pan, add the 4 cups chicken stock and bring to a boil. Then reduce the heat and simmer for about 10 minutes. Purée the soup in a blender, return it to the saucepan, and add the salt, pepper, and nutmeg. Taste and adjust seasonings. For a slightly sweeter and smoother soup, add the cream. If the soup is too thick, thin with additional chicken stock.

To serve, reheat the soup. Ladle into bowls and serve sprinkled with the chives.

**Wine Notes:** An off-dry Riesling would be very nice with this savory soup, as would a white Rhône or a full, rich Chardonnay from California, Australia, or Italy. Alsatian "local" wines and the lighter, almost rosé-like Pinot Noir from this region are a luscious match.

# MEXICAN CAULIFLOWER SOUP

♦ *Serves 6 to 8*

*4 tablespoons unsalted butter or olive oil*

*6 cups sliced onions*

*1 tablespoon chili powder*

*2 teaspoons ground cumin*

*2 medium heads cauliflower, cored and cut into small chunks (about 8 cups)*

*1 large russet potato, peeled and diced (about 1 cup)*

*6 cups Chicken Stock (page 119)*

*1 teaspoon salt*

*½ teaspoon freshly ground pepper*

*Diced tomatoes and chopped fresh cilantro,*
*    or diced avocado and grated Monterey jack or Cheddar cheese,*
*    or diced tomato and chopped, fresh oregano, for garnish*

One day I had extra cauliflower and needed a soup. Instead of a classic cream of cauliflower with pesto garnish or Hungarian Cauliflower Soup (page 112) I decided to take this soup in a Latin American direction. The result was this recipe, which evolved from a Mexican recipe for cooked cauliflower with diced avocado and tomatoes.

## Procedure

Melt the butter or warm the oil in a large saucepan over medium heat. Add the onions and cook until translucent, about 10 minutes. Stir in the chili powder and cumin and cook for 1 to 2 minutes, stirring constantly. Add the cauliflower, potato, and chicken stock and bring the mixture to a boil. Then reduce the heat and simmer until the vegetables are tender, 15 to 20 minutes. Purée the soup in a blender or food processor. Return to the saucepan and thin to the desired consistency with stock, if necessary. Add the salt and pepper. Taste and adjust seasonings.

Reheat the soup. Ladle into bowls and serve with any combination of garnishes.

***Wine Notes:*** A light amber-styled beer would be perfect, but for those of you who prefer wine, look for something earthy and simple—Chardonnays from France's Côte Chalonnaise, a Rully or Montagny, a Vernaccia from Italy, or an aromatic Catalan white from Spain. Some bone-dry rosés, like those from Provence, might be interesting as well.

# HUNGARIAN CAULIFLOWER SOUP

◆ *Serves 8*

*4 tablespoons unsalted butter*

*2 onions, diced (about 1½ cups)*

*1 tablespoon paprika*

*¼ to ½ teaspoon (or to taste)*
*    cayenne pepper*

*1 potato, cut into small cubes or*
*    thinly sliced (about 1 cup)*

*2 heads cauliflower, cut into*
*    florets (about 12 cups loosely*
*    packed)*

*7 to 7½ cups Chicken Stock*
*    (page 119)*

*½ to ¾ cup heavy cream*
*    (optional)*

*1 teaspoon salt*

*½ teaspoon freshly ground*
*    pepper*

*3 slices (1 inch thick) country*
*    bread, toasted and cut into*
*    1-inch cubes*

*1 cup grated Cheddar cheese*

What makes a soup Hungarian? Hot and sweet paprika, of course. Garnish with croutons and grated cheese, and a sprinkle of paprika.

## Procedure

Melt the butter in a large saucepan over medium heat. Add the onions and cook, stirring occasionally, until tender, about 10 minutes. Add the paprika and cayenne (go easy on the cayenne if you do not like spicy food) and cook, stirring, 1 to 2 minutes. Add the potato and cauliflower, then 7 cups of the stock and bring to a boil. Reduce the heat and simmer until the vegetables are tender, 15 to 20 minutes. Purée the soup in a blender or food mill. Return to the saucepan and add cream, if you like, to tone down the spiciness. Add the salt and pepper and the remaining stock, if necessary, to thin the soup. Taste and adjust seasonings.

Reheat the soup, ladle into bowls, and top with the toasted bread cubes and cheese.

***Wine Notes:*** The pungent combination of paprika, cayenne, Cheddar, and cauliflower requires a wine with full flavor and long finish. White wines from southern Italy work well here, as does a less grassy Sauvignon Blanc from anywhere. Somewhat coarse reds of a light to medium body show well, too: Chianti, Rossi di Montalcino or Valpolicella from Italy, a selection from France's Midi or a California Barbera.

# SPINACH AND PEA SOUP

♦ *Serves 6*

*1 pound spinach (about 6
bunches), trimmed, to yield 10
to 12 loosely packed cups of
leaves*

*4 tablespoons unsalted butter*

*2 onions, sliced (about 2 cups)*

*1 russet potato, peeled and
thinly sliced*

*2 cups shelled peas (about 3
pounds, in the pod)*

*3 to 5 cups Chicken Stock
(page 119)*

*Salt and freshly ground pepper*

*½ cup heavy cream (optional)*

*Chopped fresh mint, or whipped
cream flavored with either
chopped mint or grated lemon
zest and juice, for garnish
(optional)*

This is the soup you need when you're craving fresh pea soup but don't have the patience to shell a ton of them. The color is bright green, the combination of spinach and pea very subtle. And if the peas are not perfectly sweet, the spinach carries them beautifully. Garnish with lemon cream or little fried croutons.

## Procedure

Wash the spinach well in several changes of water and drain. Melt the butter in a wide, heavy saucepan over medium heat. Add the onions and sauté until translucent, 7 to 10 minutes. Add the potato slices, the peas, and chicken stock. Bring to a boil, reduce the heat, and simmer until the potato and peas are tender, 10 to 15 minutes. Then add the spinach leaves, a handful at a time, stirring after each addition and submerging the leaves in the hot stock to wilt the spinach. When all the spinach has been added, bring the soup just to a boil over high heat and then remove from the heat.

Remove the vegetables from the stock with a slotted spoon and purée with a little of the cooking liquid in a blender or food processor; reserve the cooking liquid. (This must be done immediately or the soup will lose its bright green color.) Transfer the purée to a clean saucepan and add the reserved cooking liquid. If necessary, thin the soup to the desired consistency with additional stock. Season to taste. Add the cream, if you like, to round out the flavor.

Reheat the soup. Ladle into bowls, and sprinkle with the chopped mint, or serve with a dollop of mint- or lemon-flavored whipped cream.

## GREEN PEA AND LETTUCE SOUP

♦ *Serves 4*

*2 tablespoons unsalted butter*

*1 cup diced onions*

*4 cups shelled peas (about 6*
  *pounds, in the pod)*

*2½ cups Chicken Stock*
  *(page 119)*

*3 tightly packed cups romaine,*
  *butter, or assorted mild*
  *lettuces cut into ½-inch strips*

*Salt and freshly ground pepper*

*Pinch of sugar (optional)*

As soon as the first English peas of the season appear, I rush to make this soup. I suppose you could use frozen peas, but the texture will be different and somewhat less rich. For the lettuce you can use romaine, butter, or an assortment of greens. You do not need very much stock because as the lettuce cooks, it gives off quite a bit of liquid. For a garnish, try a mint cream, or a lemon cream and diced prosciutto, or fried bread croutons.

### Procedure

Melt the butter in a medium saucepan over medium heat. Add the onions and cook until tender and translucent, 8 to 10 minutes. Add the peas and 2 cups of the stock and bring to a boil. Then reduce the heat and simmer until the peas are tender, 5 to 8 minutes. Add the lettuce strips and cook until wilted, about 2 minutes. Purée the soup in a blender or food processor and return to the saucepan. Thin to the desired consistency with the remaining stock.

Reheat the soup and season to taste with salt and pepper. Add a pinch of sugar for balance if the peas lack sweetness.

**Wine Notes:** Choose wines with sufficient fruit to pick up on the sweetness of the peas. A Graves-style or Sauvignon Blanc would work well. A waxy Washington State Semillon or a medium-bodied fresh white from Spain's Rueda or a fresh Vinho Verde from Portugal would be lovely, too.

## CURRIED BROCCOLI AND SPINACH SOUP

◆ *Serves 8*

*4 tablespoons unsalted butter*

*2 medium onions, chopped*
 *(about 2 cups)*

*1 tablespoon grated fresh ginger*
 *(see note)*

*2 tablespoons curry powder*

*1 russet potato, peeled and*
 *cubed*

*6 cups Chicken Stock*
 *(page 119)*

*1 large head broccoli, cut into*
 *florets (about 4 cups)*

*8 tightly packed cups stemmed*
 *spinach leaves, well washed*
 *and dried*

*1½ teaspoons salt*

*½ teaspoon freshly ground*
 *pepper*

*¾ cup coconut cream*

*¼ to ½ cup heavy cream*
 *(optional)*

*Plain yogurt, toasted coconut, or*
 *lemon-flavored whipped*
 *cream, for garnish (optional)*

A classic Indian vegetable dish called *sag*—a curried purée of spinach and broccoli—was the inspiration for this dish. Curried soups can be served hot or cold. A dollop of yogurt or lemon cream on top, some crispy pappadams, and you may not need a big dinner to follow this one.

### Procedure

Melt the butter in a large saucepan over medium heat. Add the onions and cook slowly until tender, about 10 minutes. Add the grated ginger and curry powder and cook 1 to 2 minutes. Add the potato and the chicken stock and simmer 5 minutes. Add the broccoli florets, bring to a boil, reduce the heat, and simmer until the broccoli is tender, about 10 minutes. Add the spinach all at once, stirring until all the leaves are wilted and submerged in the stock. Immediately remove from the heat to keep the bright green color. Purée in a blender or food processor. Return the soup to the saucepan and add the salt, pepper, and coconut cream. Taste and adjust seasonings: If the ginger is too hot, add the cream for balance.

Reheat the soup, ladle into bowls, and serve garnished with yogurt, toasted coconut, or lemon cream.

**Note:** As fresh ginger varies in heat, you may want to start with less. Or, you can add cream to mellow the heat.

**Wine Notes:** With curry spices, aromatic and more exotic white wines like Alsatian Riesling, Muscat, and Pinot Gris work well. White Rhône types à la Condrieu hold their own, as do some of the richer Australian whites. And simple fruity reds like Beaujolais nouveau or primeur will go nicely.

# AVOCADO SOUP

◆ *Serves 6 to 8*

*3 large ripe avocados, peeled*
*  and diced*

*1 to 1½ cups heavy cream*

*4 to 5 cups Chicken Stock*
*  (page 119)*

*Salt and freshly ground pepper*

*Fresh lemon juice*

*Lime cream (see note),*
*  deep-fried tortilla strips, or*
*  diced tomatoes and red onion*
*  and chopped cilantro, for*
*  garnish*

This Latin American soup usually is served cold, but on a San Francisco summer day, when the fog comes in earlier than expected, it's delicious heated up for dinner.

Garnish the soup with whipped cream flavored with grated lime zest and lime juice, or go for a more Mexican taste with fried tortilla strips, paper-thin tiny lime wedges and sour cream, or diced tomatoes and chopped cilantro with a sprinkling of finely minced sweet red onion.

## Procedure

Combine the avocado, cream, and stock in a blender and purée. Season to taste with salt and pepper and lemon juice. Chill soup if serving cold or heat soup over low heat if serving warm. Ladle into bowls and garnish with the lime cream, tortilla strips, or chopped vegetables and cilantro.

*Note:* For the lime cream, whip 1 cup heavy cream until soft peaks form. Fold in 1 tablespoon grated lime zest and 1 tablespoon fresh lime juice.

*Wine Notes:* Medium-bodied wines with pronounced herbal flavors and ample sharpness are called for—Sauvignon Blanc from California, France's Loire Valley (Sancerre, Pouilly Fumé), or Chile would be best—or a bright and lean Chardonnay.

# WHITE CORN SOUP

♦ *Serves 6 to 8*

*4 tablespoons unsalted butter*

*1 large onion, diced (about*
*1½ cups)*

*10 ears of corn, kernels removed*
*(about 10 cups kernels)*

*5 cups Chicken Stock*
*(page 119)*

*½ teaspoon salt, or to taste*

*½ teaspoon freshly ground*
*pepper*

*Sugar (optional)*

*2 roasted, puréed red bell*
*peppers, or 2 roasted, puréed*
*pasilla chilies, or 2 tomatoes,*
*peeled, seeded, and diced, for*
*garnish or 2 tablespoons finely*
*chopped fresh cilantro*

The quality of this soup depends less on the ability of the cook than on the flavor of the corn. Sometimes the early summer white corn is so sweet you think that sugar has been added to the soup. But midseason corn may taste thin and flat, so you may want to add a little yellow corn for body and a pinch or two of sugar to make up for what nature left out. This all-American dish can be made to taste Mexican with a garnish of roasted pasilla chilies or diced tomatoes and cilantro.

## Procedure

Melt the butter in a large saucepan over medium heat. Add the onion and cook until tender and translucent, about 10 minutes. Stir in the corn kernels and cook 2 minutes. Then add the chicken stock (it should just barely cover the corn). Bring to a boil, reduce the heat, and simmer 4 to 6 minutes. Purée the soup in a blender, then pass through the coarse disk of a food mill or through a medium coarse strainer, to obtain a smooth, but not overprocessed, purée. Season to taste with salt, pepper, and sugar. Thin with a little more stock if needed. Reheat, if necessary, ladle into bowls and garnish with the roasted pepper purée or tomato, and the chopped cilantro.

*Wine Notes:* An off-dry Riesling (German kabinett to spätlese level) from Washington State, California, or the Mosel; French white Rhône; or a big ripe Chardonnay from California, Australia, or Tuscany will complement the sweetness and richness of the corn.

## BLACK BEAN SOUP

♦ *Serves 8*

*4 cups black beans, soaked*
*overnight in cold water to*
*cover*

*9 cups Chicken Stock*
*(page 119) or water*

*Ham or prosciutto bone, or*
*1 cup ham scraps*

*2 large onions, diced (about*
*3 cups)*

*6 garlic cloves, peeled*

*6 whole cloves*

*1 cinnamon stick*

*½ cup scotch whisky or sherry*
*(optional)*

*1 tablespoon fresh lemon juice*
*(optional)*

*12 paper-thin lemon slices*

Classic American black bean soup is usually made with sherry and garnished with paper-thin slices of lemon. One evening, I substituted scotch for the sherry and found that it adds depth of flavor to the soup. Of course black bean soup is wonderful in its own right and needs no booze at all.

To take this soup south of the border, add some ground cumin and garnish with a dollop of sour cream, finely diced red onions, and little slivers of lime. Or some lightly whipped cream flavored with lime juice and zest, and a little diced avocado or Avocado Salsa (page 351).

If you make this soup ahead of time, you'll notice that it thickens quite a bit. Just thin with water or stock, so that is not like glue.

### Procedure

Drain and rinse the beans. Cover with the chicken stock or fresh water in a large saucepan. Add the ham or prosciutto bone or the ham scraps, diced onions, and garlic cloves. Wrap the whole cloves and the cinnamon stick in cheesecloth or enclose in a metal tea ball, and add to the beans. (Or, if you haven't the patience for cheesecloth, sauté diced onion in a little olive oil in a large sauté pan or skillet over medium heat until tender. Then stir in ¼ teaspoon ground cloves and 1 teaspoon ground cinnamon and add this mixture to the beans.) Bring the liquid to a boil, reduce the heat, and simmer uncovered until the beans are very soft, about 1½ hours. Purée the soup in a blender and then reheat, if necessary, before adding the scotch or sherry; the alcohol must be added when the soup is very hot. (If you make the soup ahead, do not add the scotch or sherry until just before serving—the flavor of the liquor is lost as the soup sits.) Add the lemon juice, if using. Ladle the soup into bowls and top with the lemon slices. Serve at once.

## Chicken Stock

♦ *Makes about 4 quarts*

*6 pounds chicken parts—necks, backs, carcasses, thighs*

*2 medium onions, coarsely chopped*

*2 small carrots, coarsely chopped*

*1 large celery rib, coarsely chopped*

*Green tops of 2 leeks, coarsely chopped (optional)*

*2 garlic cloves (optional)*

*Several parsley sprigs*

*About 6 peppercorns*

*1 or 2 thyme sprigs*

*2 small bay leaves*

### Procedure

Rinse the chicken parts, put them in a large stockpot, and cover with cold water. Bring to a boil, reduce the heat, and skim the scum from the surface. Simmer 1 hour. Then add the remaining ingredients and simmer gently uncovered, 4 to 5 hours.

Remove the solids with a slotted spoon or Chinese skimmer. Pour the stock through a cheesecloth-lined strainer. Let cool, then refrigerate until cold. Remove the layer of fat from the top.

For a richer stock, gently boil the stock uncovered until reduced by half. Let cool and refrigerate or freeze.

**Wine Notes:** Choose a flavorful, tasty, and somewhat robust red—a California Zinfandel, French Rhône (Crozes-Hermitage or lighter-styled Cornas), or Piemontese Nebbiolo-based wine. White wine is not the best of possibilities, but a full-flavored Madeira (Sercial or Verdelho) will work nicely.

## YELLOW SPLIT PEA SOUP WITH RED ONION, LEMON, AND VIRGIN OLIVE OIL

◆ *Serves 6 to 8*

*3 tablespoons unsalted butter or
    olive oil*

*2 cups coarsely diced onion*

*2 teaspoons ground cumin*

*3 cups split peas*

*6 cups Chicken Stock
    (page 119)*

*2 tablespoons fresh lemon juice*

*1 teaspoon grated lemon zest*

*¾ teaspoon salt*

*2 teaspoons freshly ground
    pepper*

*3 tablespoons virgin olive oil*

*3 tablespoons finely diced red
    onion*

*Medium grind black pepper for
    serving*

In a small taverna on the Greek island of Santorini I tasted an appetizer of puréed favas, spread on a plate and topped with a puddle of good olive oil, cracked black pepper, thinly sliced red onion, accompanied by a wedge of lemon and some good bread. The favas were not a familiar shade of pale green so I went to the local grocery to see what they looked like in their uncooked state. Much to my surprise, in the bag of dried beans labeled "favas" were little yellow split peas. That mystery solved, I returned to San Francisco and started to play with the recipe. Bean purées are not big with the American public but split pea soup is a winner in any country. This fava spread now has been transformed into a tasty soup. The lemon juice and zest are incorporated into the purée, and the soup is topped with cracked black pepper, finely diced red onion, and a drizzle of virgin olive oil.

### Procedure

Heat the butter or olive oil in a heavy saucepan over medium heat. Add the onion and cook until tender and translucent, about 10 minutes. Add the cumin and stir for a few minutes. Add the split peas and the chicken stock. Bring to a boil, reduce the heat, and simmer until the peas are falling apart. Transfer to a blender or food processor and purée. Season to taste with lemon juice, zest, salt, and pepper. Return to the saucepan and reheat. (You may make this soup ahead and refrigerate. When you reheat it, it will probably need to be thinned with a little water or stock.) Ladle into bowls. Top with a drizzle of olive oil, the diced red onion, and a nice sprinkling of medium grind black pepper.

## ASHE MASTE
### Persian Yogurt Soup
### with Meatballs

◆ *Serves 6 to 8*

½ cup dried chick-peas

½ cup brown or green lentils

1 small onion, chopped

2 eggs

½ pound ground beef

½ teaspoon salt

½ teaspoon freshly ground
  pepper

1 teaspoon (or a bit more to
  taste) ground cinnamon

4 cups plain or low-fat yogurt

1 tablespoon all-purpose flour

½ teaspoon turmeric

¼ cup basmati rice

5 cups Chicken Stock
  (page 119) or water

¼ cup chopped parsley

¼ cup chopped green onions

5 tablespoons chopped fresh
  mint

2 tablespoons unsalted butter

2 garlic cloves, very finely
  minced

Salt and freshly ground black
  pepper

Pomegranate seeds (optional)

This classic Middle Eastern yogurt soup is bound with egg and flour and must not boil or the yogurt will curdle. The turmeric tints the soup a lovely pale yellow, which is set off by the green of the mint and green onions and the brown of the meatballs. When pomegranates are in season I sprinkle a few of the jewellike red seeds on top. It makes a great presentation.

To make this soup your main meal, just add a few more meatballs, and serve with a salad and a little pita bread. Well, maybe dessert.

### Procedure

Rinse the chick-peas and soak overnight in 4 cups cold water in the refrigerator. Drain and rinse well.

Put the chick-peas in a saucepan with fresh cold water to cover and bring to a boil. Reduce the heat and simmer until the chick-peas are tender, about 50 minutes. Drain and set aside. Put the lentils in another saucepan with cold water to cover. Bring to a boil, reduce the heat, and simmer until tender but still firm, about 20 minutes for brown lentils, 30 to 35 minutes for green. Drain.

Combine the chopped onion with 1 of the eggs in the container of a food processor and process until almost puréed. (Or, grate the onion by hand and then mix with the egg.) Transfer to a bowl and add the ground beef, the salt and pepper, and ½ teaspoon of the cinnamon (or more if you like). Mix well with your hands. Form into tiny meatballs and refrigerate.

*(continued)*

Whisk together the yogurt, the remaining egg, the flour, the turmeric, and the remaining ½ teaspoon cinnamon in a large saucepan. Add the rice and 2 cups of the stock or water. Bring to a simmer and cook gently, over low heat, stirring occasionally, for 10 to 12 minutes. Add the cooked chick-peas and lentils, the parsley, green onions, 3 tablespoons of the chopped mint and the rest of the stock. Simmer 10 more minutes. Then add the meatballs and simmer 10 minutes longer.

Melt the butter in a small sauté pan or skillet over low heat. Add the garlic and cook until soft but not colored, about 2 minutes. Scrape the garlic into the pan with the soup. Taste and adjust seasonings and sprinkle with the remaining chopped mint and pomegranate seeds, if using.

***Wine Notes:*** An Australian Semillon, a California Chardonnay, a full-bodied Pinot Gris from Oregon or Alsace are powerful enough to stand up to this soup. You could also try a fragrant herbal wine— Sauvignon from Italy or Chile, Pinot Blanc from Alsace or Friuli. And some slightly tart reds of light-medium body would meld well: a simple Pinot Noir from Burgundy, California, or Oregon; a Rioja red from Spain; or northern Italian Barbera or Merlot.

# SOPA DI LIMA
### *Yucatecan Soup with Chicken, Tortillas, and Lime*

◆ *Serves 4*

*2 tablespoons mild olive oil*

*½ cup diced onion*

*1 tablespoon minced garlic*

*1 teaspoon finely minced jalapeño peppers*

*3 cups reduced Chicken Stock (page 119), plus stock for poaching the chicken*

*½ cup diced, peeled, fresh or canned tomatoes*

*2 tablespoons chopped fresh cilantro*

*2 tablespoons fresh lime juice*

*1 teaspoon (or to taste) salt*

*¼ teaspoon freshly ground pepper*

*1 whole boneless, skinless chicken breast, split, and cut into 1-inch chunks*

*8 paper-thin slices of lime, cut into quarters*

*2 corn tortillas, cut into strips, 2 inches long by ½ inch wide, and then deep-fried*

No matter how many tortilla soups you have eaten in Mexican restaurants in America, you will be impressed with this one—it's the best. The first time I tasted this classic soup from the Yucatán was at a small outdoor restaurant during a festival in Mérida. All the time I was eating I kept thinking, remember this soup so you can make it at home. I've tried one variation—substituting shellfish for chicken. Very good!

### *Procedure*

Heat the oil in a large saucepan over medium heat. Add the onion and cook until translucent, about 10 minutes. Add the garlic and jalapeño and cook for 1 to 2 minutes. Add the stock and bring to a boil. Then add the tomatoes, cilantro, lime juice, and salt and pepper. Taste and adjust seasonings. Poach the chicken chunks separately in a saucepan with chicken stock to cover until just cooked through. (The chicken is not cooked directly in the soup because this would cloud the soup.) Divide the chunks among 4 bowls and pour the hot soup over. Top with little pieces of lime and the deep-fried tortilla strips.

***Wine Notes:*** Not really a great soup for wine, but you can try some Chardonnays from America, rustic Italian wines (Vernaccia, Greco di Tufo), and some of the fuller whites from Spain (Rueda made from the Verdelho grape or wines made from the slightly more pungent Albariño).

## AJIACO BOGOTANO

### Cream of Potato Soup with Avocado, Chicken, and Corn

• *Serves 6*

*4 tablespoons unsalted butter*

*2 cups onions, chopped*

*2 tablespoons ground cumin*

*5 cups peeled and diced russet potatoes*

*5¾ to 6 cups Chicken Stock (page 119)*

*1 to 1½ cups (or to taste) heavy cream*

*1½ whole, boneless, skinless chicken breasts, cut into bite-size pieces*

*Salt and freshly ground pepper*

*3 avocados, seeded, peeled, and cut into ½-inch cubes*

*3 tablespoons minced fresh chives*

*2 ears of corn, kernels removed, blanched and drained (about 2 cups kernels)*

Rich, full-flavored, and creamy, this Latin American soup is a study in interesting textures. Chicken is the traditional garnish, though shellfish makes a nice alternative.

### Procedure

Melt the butter in a large saucepan. Add the onions and cook until translucent, 10 to 15 minutes. Stir in the cumin and cook for 1 to 2 minutes. Add the diced potatoes and 4 cups of the chicken stock and bring to a boil. Reduce the heat and simmer until potatoes are very tender, about 20 minutes. Purée in a blender. Return soup to the saucepan and return to a simmer. Add cream to taste.

Meanwhile, bring the remaining chicken stock to a simmer in a saucepan. Add the chicken pieces and poach until just cooked through but not dry. Divide among 6 soup bowls.

Thin the soup, as necessary, with the stock used to poach the chicken. Season with salt and pepper. Pour over the chicken in the bowls. Add the avocado, chives, and corn, and serve.

**Note:** The soup base can be made the day before.

**Wine Notes:** Lots of possibilities: whites such as American Sauvignon Blanc, a French white Graves, dry Alsatian Riesling or Pinot Gris, even Italian Verdicchio. A light fruity red could provide interesting contrast: a Beaujolais, a California Gamay, an Italian Dolcetto, or a Spanish or Portuguese red. A rosé could harmonize well here, too.

# BRAZILIAN CORN CHOWDER WITH SHRIMP

♦ *Serves 6*

*18 medium shrimp*

*White wine, chicken stock, or*
*    water, for poaching*

*2 tablespoons unsalted butter*

*2 large onions, diced (3 to 4*
*    cups)*

*1 tablespoon paprika*

*2 teaspoons finely minced garlic*

*6½ cups Chicken Stock*
*    (page 119)*

*2 cups shrimp stock (see note)*

*2½ cups corn kernels (from 8 to*
*    9 ears fresh corn)*

*Salt and freshly ground pepper*

*3 tablespoons fresh lemon juice*

*1 teaspoon finely minced*
*    stemmed and seeded jalapeño*
*    pepper*

*1 large avocado, seeded, peeled,*
*    and cut into 1-inch dice*

*2 tablespoons finely chopped*
*    fresh cilantro or green onions*

A festive and colorful soup. It has wonderful textures of crunchy corn and chewy shellfish and creamy avocado, bound in a rich and flavorful broth.

## Procedure

Shell and devein the shrimp. Reserve the shells for the stock (see note). Poach the shrimp in a large saucepan over low heat in white wine, chicken stock, or water to cover until cooked through, 4 to 6 minutes.

Melt the butter in a large saucepan over medium heat. Add the onions and cook until translucent, 10 to 15 minutes. Add the paprika and 1 teaspoon of the minced garlic and cook 1 to 2 minutes longer. Then add 4 cups of the chicken stock and the shrimp stock and bring to a boil. Reduce the heat, add the corn kernels, and simmer until tender, 2 to 4 minutes. Season to taste with salt and pepper.

About 20 minutes before serving, cut the poached shrimp into 1-inch chunks and marinate in the lemon juice, the minced jalapeño, and the remaining 1 teaspoon minced garlic. Add to the hot soup along with the diced avocado and cilantro or green onions and serve at once.

**Note:** To make the shrimp stock, heat 1 tablespoon olive oil in a saucepan over medium heat. Add the reserved shrimp shells from 18 medium shrimp and cook, stirring, until they turn pink, 2 to 3 minutes. Then add the remaining 2½ cups of chicken stock and bring to a boil. Reduce the heat and simmer until flavorful, about 20 minutes. Strain, pressing the shells against the strainer to extract all the flavor.

(*continued*)

*Wine Notes:* An off-dry Riesling, a rich ripe Chardonnay from anywhere, or even an exuberant off-dry Chenin Blanc from France's Loire Valley or California is called for. A light fruity red wine could be a crowd pleaser, too.

# BRAZILIAN SHELLFISH CHOWDER À LA VATAPÀ

◆ *Serves 8*

*4 tablespoons unsalted butter*

*6 cups diced onions*

*2 to 3 tablespoons grated fresh ginger*

*2 garlic cloves, finely minced*

*2 teaspoons (or to taste) chopped jalapeños*

*¼ cup chopped fresh cilantro*

*½ cup (or to taste) coconut cream (canned Coco Lopez is fine)*

*½ cup dry roasted peanuts, ground fine in the food processor*

*¼ cup toasted, unsweetened coconut, ground fine in the food processor*

This recipe came about because of a miracle called leftovers. I had some of the Vatapà base (page 204) in the refrigerator but not enough shrimp to make the dish again. So I poached what few shrimp I had left, cut them up and added them to the base, thinned it a bit, and voilà—chowder. It was so good that I retraced my steps to come up with this recipe for Vatapà chowder without having to make Vatapà. The shrimp stock gives the soup its distinctive flavor.

## Procedure

Melt the butter in a heavy-bottomed saucepan over medium heat. Add the onions and cook until translucent, about 7 minutes. Add the ginger, garlic, and jalapeños and sauté for about 3 more minutes. Add half the chopped cilantro, all of the coconut cream, the ground peanuts, the toasted coconut, the tomatoes, and the tomato liquid and bring to a boil. Reduce the heat and simmer 5 minutes. Add the stock and simmer 5 more minutes. Add the salt. Taste and adjust seasonings: If too tart, add more coconut cream. If too sweet, add a little lemon juice.

To serve, place ¼ cup chopped shrimp or crabmeat in each of 4 bowls. Pour the hot chowder over

*1 cup diced, canned Italian*
*plum tomatoes, 1 cup liquid*
*reserved*

*3 cups shrimp (page 204),*
*chicken (page 119), or*
*fish stock*

*1 teaspoon salt*

*Fresh lemon juice (optional)*

*2 cups cooked shrimp, cut into*
*½-inch dice or 2 cups cooked*
*crabmeat, well picked over*

the shellfish and sprinkle with the remaining chopped cilantro.

**Wine Notes:** This dish melds richness, spice, and sweetness in the vein of a mild Indian or east African curry. Go either with a young off-dry wine with very distinguished and pronounced flavor and youthful acidity, like many of the wines recommended for the corn soups, or with apparently sweet white wines: big-barrel fermented Chardonnays from California or Australia, generous northern Rhône whites, or even waxy Semillons from Washington State or Australia.

# CATALAN CHICK-PEA AND SPINACH SOUP WITH SHRIMP, ALMONDS, AND GARLIC

♦ *Serves 6 to 8*

*1¼ cups dried chick-peas (or 3 cups canned chick-peas, drained and rinsed)*

*Ham hock or ½ pound prosciutto (optional)*

*2 tablespoons olive oil*

*2 onions, coarsely chopped (about 2½ cups)*

*1 garlic clove, finely minced*

*1 small russet potato, peeled and sliced (⅔ to 1 cup)*

*5 to 6 cups Chicken Stock (page 119)*

*1 teaspoon salt*

*¼ teaspoon freshly ground pepper*

*4 tablespoons unsalted butter or olive oil*

*6 cups stemmed spinach leaves, cut into chiffonade and well washed*

*6 tablespoons toasted sliced almonds, coarsely chopped*

Your Spanish grandma will remember this soup. Traditionally served on Good Friday and other fast days, it is made with cod or salt cod. Shrimp are a fabulous festive substitute for the fish.

### Procedure

If using dried chick-peas, rinse them and soak overnight in cold water to cover in the refrigerator. Drain and rinse again. Put the chick-peas in a medium saucepan with fresh, cold water to cover and the ham hock or prosciutto, if using. Bring to a boil, reduce the heat, and simmer, covered, until tender, about 1 hour. Drain and set aside. Discard the ham hock or prosciutto.

Heat the olive oil in a large saucepan over medium heat. Add the chopped onions and cook until translucent, 10 to 15 minutes. Add the minced garlic clove and cook, stirring, for 1 to 2 more minutes. Then add the sliced potato, half the cooked chick-peas, and 5 cups of the chicken stock and bring to a boil. Reduce the heat and simmer until the potato and beans are falling apart, about 20 minutes. Purée the soup in a blender. Return to the saucepan and add the salt and pepper.

Melt 2 tablespoons of the butter or heat 2 tablespoons of the oil in a very large sauté pan or skillet over medium heat. Add the spinach and cook, stirring, until wilted, 3 to 5 minutes. Set aside. Melt the remaining 2 tablespoons of butter or warm the remaining 2 tablespoons oil in a small sauté pan or skillet over medium heat. Add the almonds along

*1 teaspoon finely minced garlic*

*18 medium shrimp, shelled and*
*deveined (see note)*

*White wine for poaching*

with the 1 teaspoon minced garlic and cook a few minutes until fragrant. Set aside with the spinach. Poach the shrimp in a large saucepan over low heat with white wine to cover until just cooked through, 4 to 6 minutes. Drain and cut into small chunks; set aside.

Just before serving, bring the soup to a simmer. It will be necessary to thin it with some of the remaining stock, or with water. Add the spinach and almond mixture to the soup, along with the remaining chick-peas and the shrimp. Taste and adjust seasonings. Ladle into bowls and serve.

**Note:** This would make a very good main course soup; just double the number of shrimp. You may also make this recipe with a firm, white-fleshed fish such as cod, or with chicken, in lieu of the shrimp.

**Wine Notes:** Both white or red wines from Spain match up: a light to medium-bodied red from Valdepenas or Rioja, other light fruity fare from Catalonia, or even the new Somontano, Portuguese reds à la Colares or Periquita. A white from Catalonia, dry and somewhat austere, a Loire Valley or Chilean Sauvignon with clean-scented flavors or even a tart dry Pinot Blanc from northeastern Italy, Germany, or Alsace would also work.

## MINESTRA DI BROCCOLI E VONGOLE ALLA ROMANA

*Roman Broccoli and Clam Soup*

♦ *Serves 6*

¼ *cup olive oil*

*2 cups diced onions*

*2 cups white wine*

*60 small manila clams or 36 larger clams, well washed*

*3 cups broccoli florets, cut small enough to fit on a soup spoon*

*Salt*

½ *pound spaghetti, broken into 2-inch lengths*

*6 to 7 cups Chicken Stock (page 119)*

1½ *cups diced plum tomatoes*

*Freshly ground pepper*

*Grated pecorino or Parmesan cheese, for garnish (optional)*

This classic Roman soup originally was prepared with broccoli romanesco, an antique varietal that has recently been cultivated in America and is starting to find its way into our markets. Romanesco broccoli is pale green and each head looks like a bouquet of miniature Turkish minarets. If you can't get the antique, the modern dark green version will still give you happy results.

### Procedure

Heat the olive oil in a medium sauté pan or skillet over medium heat. Add the onions and cook until tender and translucent, 10 to 15 minutes. Set aside.

Bring the wine to a boil in a large sauté pan or skillet and add the clams. Cover the pan and steam the clams, stirring occasionally until open. Remove the clams from their shells; discard the shells. Strain the cooking liquid and reserve. If the clams are large, coarsely chop them.

Blanch the broccoli florets in a large pot of salted water until tender but not mushy, about 5 minutes. Remove with a slotted spoon and transfer to a bowl of ice water. Drain and set aside. Bring the salted water back to a boil. Add the spaghetti and cook until al dente. Drain and set aside. (You should have about 3 cups of cooked pasta.)

Add enough chicken stock to the reserved clam cooking liquid to equal 7½ cups combined. Bring to a boil in a large saucepan. Add the cooked onions and the tomatoes, reduce the heat, and simmer 3 to 5 minutes. Add the cooked broccoli, clams, and spaghetti. Season to taste with salt and pepper and serve piping hot. Cheese is not traditionally served with this soup but you might add a sprinkling of pecorino or Parmesan.

*Note:* You may add cooked white beans to this soup, if you like.

*Wine Notes:* A full-bodied white wine, especially one emphasizing similar green flavors to the broccoli, is sublime. The clams, of course, provide a pungency and sweetness, so an American Chardonnay or Australian Semillon or Chardonnay, or a French white Burgundy or even some white Rhônes would pair nicely, too. A lighter zippy northern Italian white such as a Sauvignon or Pinot Grigio from Friuli or the Alto Adige would work well.

# MATZO BALL SOUP

♦ *Serves 12*

*6 eggs*

*¾ cup cold water*

*⅓ cup rendered chicken fat*

*1 teaspoon salt*

*½ teaspoon freshly ground white pepper*

*3 cups plus 3 tablespoons matzo meal*

*20 cups Chicken Stock (page 119) reduced to 10 cups*

*½ cup chopped parsley*

I t wouldn't be Passover without it. Everyone wants matzo balls that are "floaters," not "sinkers." Accomplishing this is sort of like making muffins. Just fold in the dry ingredients and be careful not to overmix. Also crucial is the cooking time. The longer you poach the matzo ball, the lighter it will be. It goes without saying that good chicken soup is essential. To serve, sprinkle the soup with chopped parsley and allow 2 to 3 dumplings per portion.

### Procedure

Lightly whisk the eggs with the cold water in a large bowl. Add the chicken fat and stir until the fat dissolves. Stir in the salt and pepper. With a few quick strokes, stir in the matzo meal with a spoon. Do not overbeat. Chill for 30 minutes.

Line 2 large baking sheets with parchment paper. Using a large soup spoon dipped in cold water to keep the balls from sticking, form the chilled matzo mixture into balls about 1½ inches in diameter. Place on the prepared baking sheets and refrigerate. Bring 2 large saucepans of salted water to a boil. Drop the matzo balls into the boiling water and bring the water back to a boil. Then cover the pans, reduce the heat and simmer the matzo balls until cooked all the way through (test by cutting 1 in half), 30 to 45 minutes. (The matzo balls will have doubled in size.) Drain and set aside.

To serve, bring the chicken stock to a boil in a large saucepan. Season to taste with salt and pepper. Add the matzo balls, reduce the heat, and simmer to heat through. Ladle into bowls and sprinkle generously with chopped parsley.

*Wine Notes:* Contrary to popular thought, Mani-schewitz concord and this Jewish classic are *not* a match made in heaven. Something honest like a simple Chardonnay from France's Mâconnais, a balanced Arneis from Piedmont, or Long Island whites are much better. For those who can't imagine anything but red, try a weighty nontannic Italian Dolcetto, California Gamay, or French Côtes du Rhône.

# PASTA, RICE, AND GRAINS

SPAGHETTI ALLA BAGNA CAUDA ◆ ORECCHIETTE WITH BROCCOLI, CHICK-PEAS, ONIONS, AND TOMATOES ◆ CAESAR SALAD PASTA ◆ SPAGHETTI WITH SAFFRONED ONIONS, GREENS, SUN-DRIED TOMATOES, AND CURRANTS ◆ FETTUCCINE WITH POTATOES AND TOMATOES ◆ LINGUINE WITH TUNA, POTATOES, AND GREENS ◆ CIRCASSIAN CHICKEN FETTUCCINE WITH SPICED ONIONS, NUTS, AND CREAM ◆ FETTUCCINE WITH SALMON, SPINACH, AND CREAM ◆ PENNE WITH SAUSAGE, BROCCOLI, RICOTTA, AND TOASTED BREAD CRUMBS ◆ PASTA WITH ARTICHOKES, PROSCIUTTO, AND PEAS ◆ AUSHAK ◆ CRABMEAT, CORN, AND

SPINACH RISOTTO ◆ PORTUGUESE-INSPIRED DUCK AND SAUSAGE RISOTTO ◆ JAMBALAYA RISOTTO ◆ RISOTTO WITH BUTTERNUT SQUASH, GREENS, AND PROSCIUTTO ◆ PERSIAN-STYLE RICE ◆ CRACKED WHEAT OR BULGUR PILAF ◆ POLENTA ◆

# SPAGHETTI ALLA BAGNA CAUDA

◆ *Serves 2*

*Salt*

*2 red bell peppers*

*2 green bell peppers*

*6 ounces spaghetti*

*½ cup extra-virgin olive oil*

*¼ cup finely chopped anchovies*

*2 tablespoons finely minced garlic*

*4 tablespoons finely chopped parsley*

*Freshly ground pepper*

*2 tablespoons grated Parmesan cheese*

Bagna cauda is a Piedmontese sauce or dip for vegetables made with good olive oil (sometimes butter), anchovies, and garlic. It is served warm (*bagna cauda* means warm bath). Why not turn these ingredients into a pasta sauce and add a few roasted peppers? A little grilled tuna will make this a full dinner. A small portion with just the peppers is a great first course.

## Procedure

Char the peppers in a broiler or over direct flame, turning often with tongs, until they are blackened on all sides. Transfer to a plastic container with a lid, or a paper or plastic bag. Cover the container or close the bag and let the peppers steam for about 15 minutes. Then peel off the skin with your fingers, scraping off only stubborn pieces of peel with a knife blade. Cut the peppers into ½-inch strips. (You should have 1½ cups total.)

Bring a large pot of salted water to a boil for the pasta. Cook the spaghetti until al dente.

Meanwhile, warm the olive oil in a small sauté pan or skillet over medium heat. Add the anchovy and garlic and cook 1 to 2 minutes. Add the pepper strips and 1 tablespoon of the parsley and cook, stirring, until heated through.

Transfer the sauce to a warmed pasta bowl. Drain the pasta and quickly toss with the sauce to combine. Season to taste with salt and freshly ground pepper. Top with the remaining parsley and the grated cheese.

**Wine Notes:** A difficult wine match. This dish has more affinity for reds than whites, and a high level of acidity is essential.

# ORECCHIETTE WITH BROCCOLI, CHICK-PEAS, ONIONS, AND TOMATOES

♦ *Serves 3 to 4*

*½ cup dried chick-peas, or 1½*
    *cups canned chick-peas,*
    *drained and rinsed*

*Salt*

*5 tablespoons fruity olive oil*

*1 large head broccoli, cut into*
    *small florets (about 3 cups)*

*½ pound orecchiette or rigatoni*

*1 small red onion, diced*
    *(1 scant cup)*

*2 tablespoons finely minced*
    *garlic*

*2 cups drained, diced canned*
    *plum tomatoes*

*Freshly ground pepper*

*½ cup grated pecorino cheese*
    *(optional)*

This southern Italian pasta is fun to eat. The name means "little ears." The central dimple in the noodle is a perfect trap for those chick-peas.

## Procedure

Soak the dried chick-peas in 2½ cups cold water and refrigerate overnight. Drain and rinse. Transfer the chick-peas to a small saucepan and add water to cover. Bring to a boil over medium heat, then reduce the heat and simmer, covered, until the chick-peas are tender but not mushy, about 1 hour. Add 2 teaspoons salt during the last 15 minutes of cooking time. Drain and transfer to a bowl. Dress with 1 tablespoon of the olive oil. Set aside to cool.

Blanch the broccoli florets in boiling salted water. Drain and refresh in ice water. Drain well.

Bring a large pot of salted water to a boil. Add the orecchiette and cook until al dente, about 12 minutes.

Meanwhile, heat the remaining ¼ cup olive oil in a large sauté pan or skillet over medium heat. Add the diced onion and cook until tender. Add the chick-peas and garlic and cook until warmed through. Add the tomatoes and broccoli and cook 2 to 3 minutes longer. Season to taste with salt and pepper.

Drain the pasta and transfer to a warmed pasta bowl. Add the sauce and quickly toss to combine.

Sprinkle with grated pecorino cheese, if desired, and serve immediately.

**Wine Notes:** Look for a light to medium-bodied, muscular white with leafy qualities and a hint of earthiness.

# CAESAR SALAD PASTA

◆ *Serves 2*

*Salt*

*6 ounces spaghetti*

*3 tablespoons olive oil*

*3 tablespoons virgin olive oil*

*2 tablespoons finely minced garlic*

*¼ cup finely chopped anchovies*

*6 cups romaine or escarole lettuce, cut into ½-inch strips*

*1 cup Toasted Bread Crumbs (page 189)*

*2 teaspoons grated lemon zest*

*6 tablespoons grated Parmesan cheese*

*1 teaspoon freshly ground pepper*

In Italy a simple pasta with field greens and garlic is a very common dish. It's one of my favorite pastas. But this combination doesn't seem to excite the American imagination. I was wondering how to do this when I thought of Caesar salad. I suspected that if people loved Caesar salad, they'd probably love it as a pasta too. They do. You can make this for yourself, as you would a salad, or cook it for two.

## Procedure

Bring a large pot of salted water to a boil. Add the spaghetti and cook until al dente.

Meanwhile, heat the oils in a medium sauté pan or skillet over low heat. Add the garlic and anchovy and cook 2 minutes. Add the lettuce and cook, turning often, until partly wilted, about 3 minutes. Add half the bread crumbs, the lemon zest, and 2 tablespoons of the grated Parmesan and cook, stirring, 1 more minute. Add the drained pasta and the pepper and toss well to combine. Transfer to a warmed pasta bowl and top with the rest of the bread crumbs and the remaining Parmesan. Serve at once.

**Wine Notes:** Search out light, structured white wines with some earthiness and underlining herbal green qualities—northern Italian whites such as Arneis, Pinot Grigio, Sauvignon, and Tocai Friulano are all excellent. A lean Chablis-like Chardonnay from France, America, or Italy would be lovely, as would a Sauvignon Blanc, especially one more varietal in nature.

# SPAGHETTI WITH SAFFRONED ONIONS, GREENS, SUN-DRIED TOMATOES, AND CURRANTS

♦ *Serves 2*

*Salt*

*½ pound spaghetti*

*⅓ cup olive oil*

*2½ cups sliced (¼ inch) onions*

*¼ teaspoon crushed saffron filaments, steeped 10 minutes in 2 tablespoons white wine*

*1 cup sliced (⅛ inch) fennel*

*2 teaspoons finely minced garlic*

*1 tablespoon finely minced anchovies*

*½ to ⅔ cup finely julienned sun-dried tomatoes (see note)*

*¼ cup currants, plumped in hot water, drained*

*5 to 6 cups fine chiffonnade (strips) of Swiss chard or escarole*

Sicilian in inspiration, this recipe shows Arabic influences with the saffroned onions and currants, combined with the indigenous Sicilian ingredients of fennel and sun-dried tomatoes. While this pasta is very rich and complex in flavor, it's inexpensive and easy to prepare.

As a variation, add grilled tuna chunks for an even more wonderful and filling pasta.

## Procedure

Bring a large pot of salted water to a boil. Add the spaghetti and cook until al dente.

Meanwhile, warm the olive oil in a large sauté pan or skillet over medium heat. Add the onions and cook until tender and translucent, 8 to 10 minutes. Add the saffron and cook 1 minute. Then add the fennel, garlic, anchovy, and sun-dried tomatoes and cook until the fennel is softened, 3 to 4 minutes. Add the currants and then the greens and stir until the greens are wilted, 1 to 2 minutes.

Drain the pasta and toss quickly with the sauce to combine. Serve immediately. No cheese, please.

**Note:** Sun-dried tomatoes vary in quality and saltiness. If the tomatoes are sweet, use ⅔ cup. If salty, cut back to ½ cup.

**Wine Notes:** The sweetness of the currants adds a twist to this pasta. I lean toward whites, crisp with ripe fruit or off-dry. A dry Savennières, steely northwestern Pinot Gris or Riesling, young Rhône whites or a selection of wines from Alsace including Riesling and Gewürztraminer would be lovely.

## FETTUCCINE WITH POTATOES AND TOMATOES

◆ *Serves 4*

*1½ pounds little new potatoes (yellow Finnish, bintji, or red creamers)*

*½ to ⅔ cup mild olive oil*

*Salt and freshly ground pepper*

*2 cups diced tomatoes, fresh or canned*

*¾ to 1 cup Basic Tomato Sauce (page 349)*

*2 teaspoons finely minced garlic*

*1 tablespoon plus 1 teaspoon finely chopped fresh sage*

*1 pound fresh fettuccine*

*Grated Parmesan cheese*

This is a fine example of rustic cooking from the province of Lombardy. Potatoes and pasta are a most satisfying combination, sparked by garlic and sage and bound with a mixture of chopped tomatoes and tomato sauce. In the summer you may want to add a few green beans. Sprinkle with a little Parmesan and you have a meal in a bowl.

### Procedure

Preheat the oven to 400 degrees. Wash the potatoes and dry in a towel. Place them on a baking sheet or in a shallow baking pan and rub well with a few tablespoons of the olive oil. Sprinkle with salt and pepper and bake until cooked through, 20 to 35 minutes, depending on the size of the potatoes. Cut into ¾-inch chunks.

Bring a large pot of salted water to a boil for the pasta.

Heat the remaining olive oil in a large sauté pan or skillet over high heat and sauté the potato chunks until lightly browned. Add the tomatoes, tomato sauce, garlic, and the sage and cook until warmed through. Season to taste with salt and pepper.

Cook the fettuccine in the boiling salted water until just tender, 1 to 2 minutes. Drain and transfer to a warmed pasta bowl. Add the sauce and toss quickly to combine. Sprinkle with Parmesan cheese and serve.

**Wine Notes:** Look for medium-bodied whites, green with a dash of "goût de terroir." An olive-scented Vernaccia, herbal Sauvignon Blanc from California, France, or Italy, or a more muscular white from Spain's Catalonia will all match well with this pasta.

# LINGUINE WITH TUNA, POTATOES, AND GREENS

◆ *Serves 2*

*6 to 8 small new potatoes (creamers, reds, or yellow Finnish)*

*6 tablespoons (or as needed) mild olive oil*

*Salt and freshly ground pepper*

*½ cup green bean pieces (2 inch)*

*1 6-ounce piece (about 1 inch thick) yellowfin tuna*

*6 to 8 ounces linguine or spaghetti*

*4 cups arugula*

*2 teaspoons finely minced garlic*

*2 teaspoons dried red pepper flakes*

New potatoes are sweet and have a wonderful texture when combined with pasta. Tomato chunks or sun-dried tomato strips would also be a fine addition. So would scallops. As a matter of fact you could make this without the tuna and enjoy every bite.

## Procedure

Preheat the oven to 400 degrees. Place the potatoes in a small baking pan. Rub lightly with some of the olive oil and sprinkle with salt and pepper. Bake until cooked through but still firm, about 25 minutes. Set aside. When cool, cut the potatoes into ¾-inch chunks.

Blanch the green beans in a large pot of boiling, salted water until just tender, 3 to 5 minutes. Drain and refresh in cold water. Drain well. Set aside.

Preheat the broiler. Brush the tuna with olive oil and sprinkle on both sides with salt and pepper. Broil until medium rare, 2 to 3 minutes on each side. (Or, sauté the tuna in a sauté pan or skillet over medium-high heat with 1 tablespoon olive oil until medium-rare, 2 to 3 minutes on each side.) Cut into 1½-inch chunks.

Bring a large pot of salted water to a boil. Add the pasta and cook until al dente.

Meanwhile, heat 3 tablespoons olive oil in a large sauté pan or skillet over high heat. Add the potato chunks and cook, turning, until lightly browned. Add the green beans, arugula, garlic, and red pepper flakes and cook, stirring often, until the arugula is wilted. Add the tuna and warm through. Season to taste with salt and pepper.

Drain the pasta and toss quickly with the sauce to combine. Serve immediately.

***Wine Notes:*** Both red and white wines are happy alongside this pasta. Tuna and spicy arugula have an affinity for light flavorful reds, with assertive flavor and low tannin: cru Beaujolais, Dolcetto d'Alba, Rioja Crianza (very young), and balanced Beaune-styled Pinot Noir from Oregon and France. In whites, look for spice and muscularity: Vernaccia, rustic Tuscan Chardonnay, Pouilly Fumé, and Menetou-Salon from France's Loire Valley, and American and French Chardonnay.

## CIRCASSIAN CHICKEN FETTUCCINE WITH SPICED ONIONS, NUTS, AND CREAM

♦ *Serves 4 to 6*

*3 whole chicken breasts, about*
*1 pound each*

*⅓ cup olive oil*

*2 cups diced onion*

*Salt and freshly ground pepper*

*¼ teaspoon (or to taste)*
*cayenne pepper*

*2 teaspoons ground coriander*

*¾ cup coarsely chopped*
*walnuts, toasted*

*½ cup chopped slivered*
*almonds, toasted*

*3 cups heavy cream, or 1½ cups*
*heavy cream plus 1½ cups*
*chicken stock*

*16 ounces fresh fettuccine*

*¼ cup chopped fresh dill*

*¼ cup chopped parsley*

The classic Turkish-Russian dish circassian chicken consists of cooked chicken in a dense sauce of ground nuts, bread, and onions, usually served at room temperature. It has great flavor but is pretty heavy and rich. My dilemma: I love the tastes of the dish but I don't love the textures. The solution: Americans love pasta. And Russians love noodles. So why not turn this into a pasta dish that combines the best of both worlds? To lighten this even further, dilute the cream with chicken stock.

### Procedure

Remove the bones and skin from the chicken breasts and cut the flesh into strips 1½ inches long and ½ inch wide. Set aside.

Heat 3 tablespoons of the olive oil in a medium sauté pan or skillet over medium heat. Add the diced onions and cook until translucent, about 7 minutes. Add 1 teaspoon salt and ¼ teaspoon pepper and cook 3 minutes longer. Add the cayenne and coriander and cook 3 minutes. Set aside. (You should have about 1 cup cooked onions.)

Bring a large pot of salted water to a boil for the pasta.

Toss the chicken pieces with just enough olive oil to coat. Sprinkle with salt and pepper. Heat the remaining oil in a large sauté pan or skillet over high heat. Add the chicken and cook, turning frequently, until golden brown on all sides, 3 to 5 minutes. Add the onions to the pan along with the nuts and the cream (or cream and stock) and simmer 1 to 2 minutes to reduce cream slightly and 5 to 6 minutes for cream and stock. Do not allow the cream to thicken too much; the nuts will absorb some of the cream as will the fresh pasta.

Cook the fettuccine in the boiling salted water until just tender, 1 to 2 minutes. Meanwhile, add the herbs to the pan with the sauce and taste and adjust seasonings. Transfer to a warmed pasta bowl. Drain the pasta in a colander and add to the bowl. Quickly toss to combine. Serve at once.

***Wine Notes:*** Although this can go with lighter red wines, I prefer whites and dry rosés: light to medium-bodied white wines with straightforward slightly spicy flavors—American Chardonnay, simpler Mâconnais or similar Burgundy from France, and other Italian wines from the Veneto, Friuli, and the southwest (Campania), for example. For a more ethnic flair, try a clean-perfumed Sauvignon Blanc from Bulgaria.

## FETTUCCINE WITH SALMON, SPINACH, AND CREAM

♦ *Serves 2*

*Salt*

*4 to 6 ounces boneless salmon fillet, cut into 1-inch cubes*

*¾ cup heavy cream*

*4 cups trimmed spinach leaves, well washed and cut into ½-inch strips*

*2 teaspoons grated lemon zest, covered with 1 tablespoon fresh lemon juice*

*Freshly ground pepper*

*⅓ pound fresh fettuccine*

*2 tablespoons pine nuts, toasted*

Want a little fish but not too much? Here's one way to eat royally but keep the costs down. Not on a budget? This pasta can also be prepared with scallops or crabmeat.

### Procedure

Bring a large pot of salted water to a boil for the pasta.

Sprinkle the salmon with salt. Heat the cream in a deep sauté pan or skillet. Add the salmon, and poach 1 minute. Add the spinach and stir well to wilt. Add the lemon zest and juice, and salt and pepper to taste, and continue cooking until the salmon is just slightly underdone in the center and the cream has reduced a bit, 3 to 4 minutes.

Meanwhile, cook the fettuccine in the boiling, salted water until tender, 1 to 2 minutes. Drain and transfer to a warmed pasta bowl. Toss quickly with the sauce to combine. Sprinkle with the pine nuts and serve immediately.

*Variation:* Blanch ½ pound thin asparagus in boiling salted water until tender, 3 minutes. Refresh in cold water and drain well. Cut into 2-inch lengths and add to the cream sauce.

*Wine Notes:* The inherent sweetness of the salmon and the cream call for a white wine. American Chardonnay in a more austere style, Puligny-Montrachet, or other pedigreed white Burgundy and complex Sauvignon from the Loire Valley are my preferences. A German Riesling at the kabinett level or a crisp Spanish Albariño would pair well, too. Even the most delicate of reds just don't work here.

# PENNE WITH SAUSAGE, BROCCOLI, RICOTTA, AND TOASTED BREAD CRUMBS

♦ *Serves 4*

*Salt*

*1 large head broccoli, cut into florets (about 2 cups)*

*1 pound penne, rigatoni, or shells*

*⅓ cup mild olive oil*

*¾ pound fennel-garlic sausage mixture (see note)*

*2 cups diced plum tomatoes (you may use part tomato sauce)*

*¾ cup fresh ricotta cheese*

*Freshly ground pepper*

*1 cup Toasted Bread Crumbs (page 189)*

The textures of this Sicilian pasta are wonderful: creamy ricotta, chewy sausage, tender broccoli, and the crunch of toasted bread crumbs. It also is a complete meal with meat protein, greens, dairy, and double starch (pasta and bread).

## Procedure

Bring a large pot of salted water to a boil. Add the broccoli and cook until tender but still firm, 4 to 5 minutes. Remove with a slotted spoon or strainer and refresh in cold water. Set aside. Return the water to a boil. Add the pasta and cook until al dente.

Meanwhile, heat the olive oil in a large sauté pan or skillet over high heat. Crumble the sausage (or you may shape it into small balls, if you like) into the pan and brown. Reduce heat, add the tomatoes, and cook until warmed through. Then add the broccoli and the ricotta and cook until the cheese is creamy, but still in small pieces. Season to taste.

Drain the pasta and toss quickly with the sauce to combine. Divide among 4 warmed pasta bowls and top each bowl with a generous handful of toasted bread crumbs. Serve immediately.

**Note:** Use store-bought sausages (remove mixture from casings) or try my recipe in *The Mediterranean Kitchen*.

**Wine Notes:** A medium-bodied red is best. Among the Italians, try a Chianti, Barbera d'Alba, Rosso di Montalcino, or Venetian Merlot. American Pinot Noir, lighter styles of Zinfandel, Syrah, and Merlot are very nice as are Spanish Rioja and the red wines of France's southwest (Minervois, Fitou, Faugères).

## PASTA WITH ARTICHOKES, PROSCIUTTO, AND PEAS

◆ *Serves 2*

*2 large artichokes*

*1 lemon, halved, for juice*

*¼ cup plus 6 tablespoons olive oil*

*Salt and freshly ground pepper*

*1 cup sliced (¼ inch) red onions*

*1 cup sliced (¼ inch) mushrooms (white, chanterelles, and/or cepes)*

*⅓ cup julienned prosciutto*

*2 teaspoons very finely minced garlic*

*½ cup peas, blanched in boiling, salted water*

*2 teaspoons chopped fresh thyme (optional)*

*½ cup chopped (2-inch pieces) asparagus, blanched in boiling, salted water (optional)*

*6 to 8 ounces fresh fettuccine, dried penne, or farfalle*

*2 tablespoons freshly grated Parmesan cheese*

*2 tablespoons chopped Italian parsley*

This pasta reminds me of springtime in Italy. Oh, those little sweet peas! If you can't wait for peas or can't find any really good ones, use asparagus. If available, you can even add both.

### Procedure

Break off all the large outer leaves from the artichokes. Pare the outside to expose the heart. Using a sharp spoon, remove the fuzzy chokes. Cut the artichokes into ¼-inch slices and drop them in water acidulated with 2 teaspoons lemon juice. Heat the ¼ cup olive oil in a sauté pan or skillet over medium heat. Drain the artichokes and add to the pan. Squeeze a little lemon juice over the artichokes, add ¼ cup water, and cook, covered, stirring occasionally, until crisp-tender, 5 to 7 minutes. Season with salt and pepper. (Artichokes can be prepared up to 6 hours in advance.)

Bring a large pot of salted water to a boil for the pasta.

Heat the remaining 6 tablespoons olive oil in a large skillet over medium heat. Add the onions and cook until tender, 10 minutes. Add the mushrooms and cook until slightly wilted. Then stir in the artichokes, prosciutto, garlic, peas and/or asparagus, and thyme, if using. Cook until heated through. Season to taste with salt and pepper.

Meanwhile add the pasta to the boiling water and cook until tender if using fresh pasta, or al dente if using dried. Drain the pasta and transfer to a pasta bowl. Add the artichoke mixture and quickly toss to combine. Sprinkle with Parmesan and parsley. Serve hot.

***Wine Notes:*** Because of the artichokes, this pasta is difficult to match with wine. It requires a full-flavored wine, preferably red, that will stand alongside, and not be made sweet by, the artichoke. Try Nebbiolo-based reds (Gattinara, Nebbiolo d'Alba, Barbaresco), well-made Tuscan reds of Sangiovese (Rosso and Brunello di Montalcino), or those more staunch reds from the south. Gutsy Pinot Noir from California, an earthy red Bordeaux or Syrah-based red from the northern Rhône Valley are all quite good.

# AUSHAK

### Persian Ravioli with Leeks and Two Sauces

◆ *Serves 6*

### Lamb Sauce

3 tablespoons olive oil

2 pounds ground lamb

3 cups diced onion

3 tablespoons finely minced
   garlic

2 teaspoons cinnamon

4 cups Basic Tomato Sauce
   (page 349)

1 cup Lamb Stock (page 265)
   or Chicken Stock (page 119)

1 teaspoon salt

1 teaspoon freshly ground
   pepper

### Filling

8 tablespoons unsalted butter

6 cups chopped, firmly packed,
   well-washed leeks

1 teaspoon paprika

1/2 teaspoon cayenne pepper

1 1/2 cups ricotta cheese

Salt and freshly ground pepper

There are Persian and Afghani versions of this recipe for ravioli with two sauces. Traditionally the pasta is filled with just spiced leeks, but leek-filled ravioli have a tendency to fall apart in the water. So I have added a little ricotta cheese to bind the filling, but not too much to detract from the original oniony taste. As these are very rich, you might want to serve them as an entrée rather than as a starter course.

### Procedure

For the lamb sauce, heat the olive oil in a large sauté pan or skillet over high heat. Add the ground lamb and break it up with a spoon. Cook, stirring occasionally, until browned. Remove the meat from the pan with a slotted spoon. In the fat remaining in the pan, cook the onions over medium heat until tender, about 10 minutes. Add the garlic and the cinnamon and cook a few minutes longer. Return the lamb to the pan and add the tomato sauce. Add the lamb or chicken stock, bring to a simmer, and cook about 25 minutes. Stir in the salt and pepper. Taste and adjust seasonings. (This sauce can be made 1 day ahead.)

For the filling, melt the butter in a large sauté pan or skillet over medium-low heat. Add the leeks and cook, stirring occasionally, until wilted and tender, 15 to 20 minutes. Add the paprika and cayenne and cook 1 to 2 minutes longer. Let cool. Then stir the cooled leeks into the ricotta and season the mixture with salt and pepper. (This filling may be made 1 day ahead.)

**Fresh Pasta**

*3 cups all-purpose flour*

*½ teaspoon salt*

*3 large eggs*

*2 tablespoons water, or more as
    needed*

**Yogurt Sauce**

*2 tablespoons unsalted butter*

*2 tablespoons finely minced
    garlic*

*2 cups plain yogurt*

*½ cup chopped fresh mint*

*Salt and freshly ground pepper*

For the pasta, mix together the flour and salt on a work surface. Shape into a mound and make a well in the center. Break the eggs into the center and add the water. Mix the egg and water with your hand and then gradually pull in the flour to make a rough dough. Knead the dough by hand until smooth and silky, 10 to 15 minutes. Or, mix the flour and salt in a food processor or mixer with the paddle. Add the eggs and water and process or mix about 1 minute (the dough will be crumbly). Then knead by hand 15 minutes or in the mixer with the dough hook, 8 to 10 minutes on low speed. Add a little water if the dough is very dry. Form into a large disc and place the dough in a plastic bag and let rest 1 hour at room temperature.

For the yogurt sauce, melt the butter over low heat in a small sauté pan or skillet. Add the garlic and cook 1 to 2 minutes without coloring. Cool for a few minutes and then add the yogurt. Stir in the chopped mint and season to taste with salt and pepper. (This sauce may be made a few hours ahead and refrigerated.)

Cut the pasta dough into 6 pieces and flatten into rectangles about the width of the rolling bars on the pasta machine. Roll each pasta rectangle through the machine, starting at the largest setting and then moving through all of the settings until the pasta has been rolled to thin rectangular sheets. Cover 5 of the pasta sheets with plastic wrap. Fold the remaining sheet in half lengthwise to mark it, and then unfold. Spoon small mounds of filling (1 heaping tablespoon

*(continued)*

each), 2 inches apart, on the bottom half of the dough. Use a plant mister to spray lightly with water, then fold the top half over the bottom. Press gently around the filling mounds to seal, but do not seal the bottom edge. Then cut the ravioli with a ravioli wheel, starting from the top, closed edge and running down to the bottom, pressing any trapped air out the unsealed bottom. Press the bottom edge closed and trim the excess with the ravioli cutter. Place the ravioli in a single layer, not touching one another, on a baking sheet lined with parchment paper or sprinkled with rice flour or Wondra. Sprinkle the tops with flour. Fill and roll the remaining pasta sheets in the same manner. Refrigerate the ravioli, uncovered, until serving time.

To serve, bring a large pot of salted water to a boil. Bring the yogurt sauce to room temperature, if refrigerated. Reheat the lamb sauce in a large saucepan. Drop the ravioli into the boiling water, reduce the heat, and simmer 4 minutes. Remove with a slotted spoon or large skimmer, shake off the excess water, and place on 6 serving plates. Spoon the warm lamb sauce over the ravioli, then drizzle with the yogurt sauce.

**Wine Notes:** Lighter-styled Rhône reds, firm Carignan-based reds from Corbières and Roussillon, earthier honest Pinot Noirs from California and France, and autumnal Italian reds, such as Barbaresco, Vino Nobile di Montepulciano, and Torgiano are all great choices. Zinfandel, Syrah, and California Rhône-clones are also well-suited American wines.

# CRABMEAT, CORN, AND SPINACH RISOTTO

♦ *Serves 6*

*5 to 6 cups Chicken Stock*
*(page 119)*

*4 tablespoons unsalted butter*

*4 tablespoons mild olive oil*

*2 cups diced onion*

*2 cups arborio rice*

*1½ cups corn kernels*

*3 to 4 cups tightly packed*
*spinach strips (½ inch wide)*

*1 pound crabmeat, picked over*
*for cartilage*

*1 tablespoon grated fresh ginger*
*and/or 1 teaspoon minced*
*garlic (optional)*

*Salt and freshly ground pepper*

The sweetness of the crabmeat is enhanced by the sweetness of the corn. For an Oriental accent, add grated ginger and garlic. No cheese, please.

Please keep in mind that risotto cannot be rushed. The cooking time is 20 to 25 minutes. The broth must be absorbed gradually and the right texture attained. Only Italian short-grain arborio rice will work for a genuine risotto. It holds a firm center while the outside produces the creamy sauce consistency of the broth.

## Procedure

Bring the chicken stock to a boil. Reduce the heat and hold at a simmer.

Warm the butter and olive oil in a large, high-sided sauté pan or a wide saucepan over low heat. Add the onion and cook until translucent and sweet, 5 to 10 minutes. Add the rice and cook, stirring to coat with butter, until opaque, 3 to 5 minutes.

Add 1 cup hot stock and cook, stirring constantly, until the stock is absorbed. Add 3 more cups stock, 1 cup at a time, stirring until each cup of the stock is absorbed. Then add the corn kernels and cook 1 to 2 minutes. Add the spinach and stir until wilted. Add the crabmeat and cook until heated through. Add the ginger or garlic, if using. Then add stock as needed until the rice is al dente in the center and creamy on the outside. Season to taste with salt and pepper.

*Variation:* For a Salmon, Corn, and Spinach Risotto, sauté cubes of salmon in a little oil or butter and add during the last 3 to 5 minutes of cooking.

## PORTUGUESE-INSPIRED DUCK AND SAUSAGE RISOTTO

◆ *Serves 6*

*1 duck, about 5 pounds, neck and wing tips removed, excess fat removed*

*Salt and freshly ground pepper*

*½ pound chorizo or linguiça*

*3 cups duck stock plus 3 cups Chicken Stock (page 119), or 6 cups chicken stock*

*6 tablespoons unsalted butter or olive oil*

*2 cups diced onions*

*2 cups arborio rice*

*1 cup julienned (1 inch long, ¼ inch wide) carrots*

*⅓ pound prosciutto, sliced ⅛ inch thick and julienned*

*2 tablespoons grated lemon zest*

*2 tablespoons chopped parsley*

The Portuguese prefer rice dishes baked in the oven. I tried to do this dish the "authentic" way, with duck pieces, sausage, ham, rice, carrots, and lemon, bound together with egg and baked in a casserole—a recipe from the town of Braga—but the result was too heavy for my taste. Because risotto is growing in popularity, I tried the more familiar Italian route and presented the Portuguese ingredients in the manner of a classic risotto. Yes!

### Procedure

Preheat the oven to 450 to 500 degrees. Place the duck on a rack in a shallow roasting pan. Sprinkle with salt and pepper and roast until tender, about 1 hour. Let stand until cool enough to handle. Then remove the meat from the bones and discard the skin (or eat it at your own risk). Tear the meat into bite-size pieces or cut into dice. (The duck may be cooked 1 day ahead and refrigerated.)

If the chorizo is in the casing, prick in a few places with a fork and bake at 400 degrees until cooked through, about 15 minutes. Cool and then cut into 1-inch chunks. If the sausage is in bulk, just crumble it into large chunks in a sauté pan or skillet and sauté in a little olive oil over medium heat to brown. Set aside.

Bring the stock to a boil. Reduce the heat and hold at a simmer.

Heat the butter or oil in a large sauté pan or heavy saucepan over low heat. Add the diced onions and cook until soft and translucent, 5 to 10 minutes. Add the rice and cook, stirring to coat with the butter or oil until opaque, 3 to 5 minutes. Add 1 cup hot stock and cook, stirring constantly, until the stock is absorbed. Add the carrots and then continue adding the stock, 1 cup at a time, stirring until the rice is almost cooked. Then add the duck meat, the sausage, the prosciutto, and the lemon zest. Continue adding stock and cooking until the rice is al dente in the center and creamy on the outside. Season to taste with salt and pepper. Serve at once, sprinkled with a little chopped parsley.

*Wine Notes:* A balanced and developed red wine is essential—try a local aged Dão, Bairrada, or Periquita, a Spanish Rioja, Italian Chianti, or American Pinot Noir.

## JAMBALAYA RISOTTO

**Risotto with Shrimp, Scallops, Ham, and Smoked Sausage**

◆ *Serves 6 to 8*

*1 pound spicy pork sausage, in casings*

*2 pounds medium or large shrimp*

*1 pound scallops, tough muscles removed*

*4 small bay leaves*

*10 fresh thyme sprigs*

*10 to 12 peppercorns*

*3 medium onions, chopped, trimmings saved for shrimp stock (see below)*

*2 celery ribs, chopped, trimmings saved for shrimp stock*

*½ cup combination ham drippings and fat from pancetta or bacon*

*2 green bell peppers, chopped*

*3 cups diced, peeled, fresh or canned tomatoes*

*2 tablespoons (or to taste) finely minced garlic*

*Salt and freshly ground pepper*

An American classic reinterpreted. I don't claim to cook authentic Cajun, but I do love those funky flavors. Why not combine two winners, Bayou cuisine and Italian risotto and see what happens? Make this for 6 to 8 or more as it is a good deal of work. But worth it.

### Procedure

Preheat the oven to 400 degrees. Prick the sausage in a few places with a fork and bake 15 minutes. Then, for additional funky flavor, if you have a smoker, you might like to smoke the cooked sausage on the low grill, covered, for 30 minutes. Let stand until cool enough to handle. Then cut into 1-inch pieces.

Peel and devein the shrimp, reserving the shells for stock. Refrigerate the shrimp along with the scallops. For the shrimp stock, put the reserved shells in a saucepan with water to cover. Add 2 of the bay leaves, 4 of the thyme sprigs, the peppercorns, and the reserved trimmings from the onions and celery. Bring to a boil, reduce the heat, and simmer 1 hour. Strain.

Melt the ham and pancetta or bacon drippings in a large sauté pan or skillet over medium heat. Add the onions, peppers, and celery and cook until tender, about 10 minutes. Add the remaining thyme and bay leaves, the tomato and garlic and cook 1 to 2 minutes. Season to taste with salt and pepper.

Combine the chicken and shrimp stocks in a saucepan and bring to a boil. Reduce the heat and hold the stocks at a simmer.

*4 cups Chicken Stock*
    *(page 119)*
*6 tablespoons olive oil or*
    *unsalted butter*
*2½ cups arborio rice*
*½ pound baked ham, drippings*
    *reserved, or ½ pound ham*
    *steak, diced (½ inch)*

Heat half the olive oil or butter in a large deep saucepan over low heat. Add the rice and cook, stirring to coat with the oil or butter, until opaque, 3 to 5 minutes.

Add 1 cup hot stock and cook, stirring constantly, until the stock is absorbed. Continue adding the stock, 1 cup at a time, stirring until each cup of the stock is absorbed. When the rice is about two thirds cooked, add the onion mixture, the sausage, and the ham. Then continue adding stock as needed until the risotto is almost completely cooked.

Meanwhile, quickly sauté the shrimp and scallops in the remaining olive oil over high heat in a large sauté pan or skillet. A minute or two before the rice is perfectly cooked, add the shellfish, season to taste with salt and pepper, and cook a few minutes longer until the rice is al dente in the center and creamy on the outside. Add more stock for a slightly soupy consistency, if you like. Serve in big bowls.

***Wine Notes:*** Opt for a red wine with spice: American Pinot Noir, French Rhône and provençal (Gigondas, Vacqueyras, and Côtes de Provence), California Zinfandel and Syrah, or those flavorful wines of Italy's south: Salice Salentino, Aglianico del Vulture, or Corvo from Sicily.

# RISOTTO WITH BUTTERNUT SQUASH, GREENS, AND PROSCIUTTO

♦ *Serves 6*

*Salt*

*1½ cups peeled, seeded, and cubed (½ inch) butternut squash*

*5 to 6 cups Chicken Stock (page 119)*

*8 tablespoons unsalted butter*

*2 cups diced onions*

*2 cups arborio rice*

*¾ cup diced prosciutto*

*¾ cup diced (½ inch) canned plum tomatoes (optional)*

*4 cups chiffonade of swiss chard (or another green such as escarole or kale)*

*Salt and freshly ground pepper*

*6 tablespoons grated Parmesan cheese*

This risotto would be at home in northern Italy, as well as in Portugal, where they combine these same ingredients but bake the rice in a casserole. The sweetness of the squash and the onion are a wonderful contrast with the salty prosciutto and tender greens. For another accent, you may want to add tomatoes, too; "sweet 100" cherry tomatoes or an equally sweet summer tomato would be best, but canned are acceptable.

## *Procedure*

Bring a small pot of lightly salted water to a boil. Add the squash cubes and cook until tender but not mushy, about 5 minutes. Drain and set aside.

Bring the chicken stock to a boil. Reduce the heat and hold at a simmer.

Melt the butter in a heavy-bottomed, high-sided sauté pan, or a wide saucepan over low heat. Add the onions and cook until translucent and sweet, 5 to 10 minutes. Add the rice and cook stirring to coat with the butter, until opaque, 3 to 5 minutes.

Add 1 cup hot stock and cook, stirring constantly, until it is absorbed. Add 3 more cups stock, 1 cup at a time, stirring until each cup of the stock is absorbed. Add the cooked squash, the prosciutto, and the tomatoes, if using, and cook 1 to 2 minutes. Add the greens and stir until wilted. Then add stock as needed until the rice is al dente in the center and creamy on the outside. Season to taste with salt and pepper. Sprinkle with grated Parmesan cheese.

**Wine Notes:** Ripe, sweet fruit is the key element here. For reds I'd choose Beaujolais, Burgundian passe-tout-grains (blend of Pinot Noir and Gamay), rich fragrant Pinot Noir from anywhere, and those current-vintage Dolcettos, bursting with berries and sweet citrus. For whites, I love Alsatian Riesling, Pinot Gris, and Gewürztraminer. American and Aussie Chardonnays, especially those that appear off-dry, are also well matched.

# PERSIAN-STYLE RICE

♦ *Serves 4 to 6*

*4 quarts water*

*2 tablespoons salt*

*2 cups basmati rice (see note)*

*6 tablespoons unsalted butter, melted*

*2 egg yolks*

*Salt and freshly ground pepper*

In most traditional recipes for Persian rice, the rice is cooked on top of the stove in a pot wrapped with towels. Timing is important to develop the chewy crust (called the *dig*) on the bottom of the pot. There seems to be a mystique about it. But I have developed a method of finishing the rice in the oven that produces a perfect crust. This is my usual accompaniment for shish-kebab and chicken brochettes.

## Procedure

Preheat the oven to 350 degrees.

Bring the water to a boil in a large pot. Add the salt and rice and simmer, uncovered, over medium heat until a kernel of rice tests done when you bite it, 10 to 12 minutes. Immediately drain the rice and rinse it under warm water. Drain well.

Coat a shallow baking pan, such as a lasagne pan, with some of the melted butter. Mix 1 cup of the cooked rice with the egg yolks, 2 tablespoons melted butter, and 1 tablespoon hot water. Spoon the mixture into the baking pan and press it down with your fingers, covering the pan completely in a thin layer. Spread the rest of the rice over the top. Season the remaining butter with salt and pepper to taste and drizzle it over the rice. Cover the pan with foil and bake 20 to 25 minutes.

Spoon the top layer of loose rice into another baking pan or heatproof bowl, cover with foil, and keep warm in a turned-off but still warm oven, or over hot water. Return the original baking pan to the oven and continue baking until the underside of the egg-rice mixture is a very pale, golden brown, and the rice is chewy, but not hard. Let stand on a cool surface for 5 minutes; it should be easy to remove this rice "crust" with a spatula. Transfer the loose rice to a serving bowl and place pieces of the rice "crust" on top.

*Note:* If you soak the rice for about 1 hour before cooking it will swell up more.

## CRACKED WHEAT OR BULGUR PILAF

♦ *Serves 6 to 8*

*3 cups Chicken Stock*
   *(page 119)*

*4 tablespoons unsalted butter or*
   *olive oil*

*1 onion, finely chopped (about*
   *1 cup)*

*1½ cups medium bulgur wheat*

*Salt*

*Chopped green onions or fresh*
   *mint or cilantro (optional)*

*Currants plumped in hot water*
   *and then drained (optional)*

*Chopped toasted almonds or*
   *pine nuts (optional)*

Most recipes have you cook bulgur as if it were rice, steaming it in stock to cover. More often than not, this results in a mixture that is heavy and soggy, with the grains sticking together. I prefer my pilaf light and dry, so I cook it as if it were risotto, then finish it in the oven for the final drying.

### Procedure

Preheat the oven to 350 degrees.

Bring the stock to a boil. Reduce the heat and hold at a simmer.

Melt the butter in a heavy sauté pan or skillet over medium heat. Add the onion and cook until tender and translucent, about 10 minutes. Reduce the heat to low, add the bulgur, and cook, stirring, until the grains are coated with butter. Add half the hot stock and cook, stirring constantly, until the stock is absorbed. Add the rest of the stock as needed and bring to a boil. Reduce the heat and simmer for about 15 minutes.

Turn the bulgur into a baking dish or a casserole and bake, uncovered, 15 to 20 minutes. Remove from the oven and stir; if the grains are still sticky, return the pan to the oven for about 10 more minutes, or until the grains are dry and separate. Fold in the green onions or herbs, the currants, or the nuts, if using, and serve.

**Note:** A few thyme sprigs or small bay leaves may be added to the bulgur while cooking.

# POLENTA

♦ *Serves 6 to 8*

*7 to 8 cups cold water*

*2 cups coarse cornmeal for*
  *polenta*

*¾ cup unsalted butter*
  *(optional)*

*1 cup freshly grated Parmesan*
  *cheese (optional)*

*Salt*

Polenta is easy to prepare (and lumpfree!) if you start with cold water. Parmesan or butter are optional enrichments. Polenta can be held in its soft state in a double boiler over hot water. Alternately, it can be poured onto a buttered or oiled baking sheet and chilled until firm, then cut into shapes for frying, grilling, or baking.

## Procedure

Stir 7 cups cold water and the polenta together in a large heavy saucepan. Cook over low heat, stirring often and scraping the bottom of the pot, until thick and it no longer feels grainy on your tongue, about 30 minutes. Add more water if the polenta thickens too much before it's cooked. Stir in the optional butter and Parmesan and season to taste with salt. Serve the polenta soft right out of the pot or pour it into a double boiler and keep it warm over simmering water, adding water or stock as needed.

Or spread the polenta on 1 or 2 buttered or oiled baking sheets and refrigerate until firm. Once it's cooled, cover it with plastic wrap. Cut the polenta into strips or triangles in the baking sheet.

To sauté, cook the polenta in clarified butter or olive oil in a cast-iron skillet over high heat until golden on both sides. To bake, place the pieces in buttered gratin dishes and sprinkle with Parmesan cheese. Bake at 400 degrees until hot and crusty. To deep fry, coat the pieces first with flour, then egg, then bread crumbs. Place the pieces on a wire rack and let the coating set. Deep fry a few at a time in peanut oil heated to 350 degrees.

# FISH AND SHELLFISH

SAUCES AND MARINADES FOR FISH AND BASIC FISH COOKING INSTRUCTIONS ◆ HERB-MARINATED GRILLED FISH ◆ SALMORIGLIO ◆ GRILLED FISH IN A YUCATECAN MARINADE ◆ PESCE IN SAOR ◆ PROVENÇAL ALMOND AND ANCHOVY FISH SAUCE ◆ FISH WITH MOROCCAN SWEET AND HOT TOMATO SAUCE ◆ ARMENIAN ROASTED PEPPER SAUCE FOR FISH ◆ SAMAK AL SAHARA ◆ SAMAK AL KAMMOUN ◆ MARTINI BUTTER FOR GRILLED FISH ◆ MIDDLE EASTERN TOMATO-RHUBARB SAUCE FOR FISH ◆ PICADILLO DE PESCADO ◆ FISH WITH ORANGE MINT SALSA VERDE ◆ ROAST SALMON WITH SPICED ONIONS AND CURRANTS ◆ POTLATCH

SALMON WITH JUNIPER MARINADE ◆ SALMON WITH ALMONDS, ONIONS, AND TOASTED BREAD CRUMBS ◆ SALMON CATALAN ◆ BAKED SALMON WITH PRUNE SAUCE ◆ GRILLED SALMON WITH PISTACHIOS, LEMON, AND OLIVE OIL ◆ SALMONE ALLA GIAPPONESE ◆ GRILLED SALMON WITH HUNGARIAN HORSERADISH ALMOND CREAM ◆ SAUTÉED TROUT OR FILLET OF SOLE WITH PINE NUTS, SOUR CREAM, AND DILL ◆ TROUT STUFFED WITH BREAD CRUMBS, PINE NUTS, AND CURRANTS ◆ BAKED ROCKFISH WITH INDONESIAN SAUCE ◆ SWORDFISH OR TUNA ORIENTALE ◆ GRILLED TUNA WITH WASABI, SAKE, AND LIME ◆ MARISCADA ◆ VATAPÀ ◆ CURRIED CRAB CAKES ◆ INDIAN FRITTO MISTO AL MARE ◆ GRILLED SHELLFISH IN A SCOTCH, SOY, AND GINGER MARINADE ◆ ROAST LOBSTER ◆

## THIRTEEN SAUCES AND MARINADES FOR FISH

When I shop for fish I often do so without a specific recipe or even a specific fish in mind. That way I can make quality and freshness my priority and I simply buy what looks best to me that day. With that in mind, I offer several tasty and versatile marinades and sauces that will work beautifully for a variety of fish fillets. Many can be easily assembled from basic ingredients in your larder. Some of the recipes call for a specific cooking technique, while others leave the choice up to you. To help you here, I am also including basic instructions for baking, grilling or broiling, and poaching any 6-ounce fish fillet.

## BASIC FISH COOKING INSTRUCTIONS

◆ *For 6-ounce skinless fish fillets*

TO BAKE

Preheat the oven to 450 degrees.

Sprinkle the fish with salt and pepper and place in an oiled baking dish. Bake until just cooked through, 8 to 10 minutes. Place on serving plates and spoon the sauce over.

TO GRILL OR BROIL

Heat the grill or broiler. Brush fish lightly with olive oil and sprinkle with salt and pepper. Grill or broil until just cooked through, 3 to 4 minutes per side. Place on serving plates and spoon the sauce over.

*(continued)*

TO POACH

Bring 2 to 3 inches poaching liquid (white wine, fish stock, or water) to a boil in a large deep sauté pan with high sides. Lower the heat to a bare simmer, add the fish fillets, and poach, uncovered until just cooked through, 6 to 7 minutes.

Carefully remove the fish from the poaching liquid with a slotted spoon or spatula. Drain or blot fish dry with a clean cloth towel. Place on serving plates and spoon the sauce over.

## HERB-MARINATED GRILLED FISH

◆ *Serves 4*

*⅔ to ¾ cup olive oil (you may use part mild and part virgin olive oil)*

*4 to 6 bay leaves*

*4 fresh thyme sprigs*

*2 tablespoons fresh rosemary needles, coarsely chopped*

*1 tablespoon finely chopped garlic*

*2 tablespoons grated orange zest (optional)*

*Salt and freshly ground pepper*

*4 fish fillets, about 6 ounces each*

Herbal marinades are a strong tradition in peasant cooking all over the Mediterranean where the cooks don't spend time worrying about innovation in cuisine. They use whatever fresh ingredients they have on hand. In Italy, France, Greece, Turkey, Spain, and North Africa, fish is rubbed with oil and fresh herbs and grilled over a wood fire. This is one of those idiotically simple "peasant" recipes, ideal for an outdoor barbecue where everything tastes better and more interesting. Must be the power of the sun to dazzle and stimulate the appetite. It's pretty spectacular prepared in your kitchen broiler too, in the middle of winter, when the sun is but a memory. I like this marinade best with tuna, swordfish, and sea bass. Serve it with roasted potatoes, green beans, and zucchini.

### Procedure

Simmer the olive oil with the herbs in a small saucepan over medium heat for a few minutes. Set aside and let cool slightly (the oil should still be warmer than room temperature). Then add the garlic, the orange zest, if using, and salt and pepper to taste. Let stand until completely cooled. Place the fish fillets in a shallow baking dish or bowl. Pour the herbed oil over the fish (see note) and let marinate 2 to 3 hours in the refrigerator.

Heat the grill or broiler. Remove the fish from the marinade; reserve the marinade. Sprinkle the fish with salt and pepper. Grill or broil the fish until just cooked through, 3 to 4 minutes each side. Brush with the marinade and garnish with lemon wedges.

*(continued)*

**Note:** Use just enough of the marinade to coat the fish; you may not need all of it. Extra marinade may be rubbed on potatoes before roasting and brushed on eggplant or zucchini while broiling.

**Wine Notes:** I like spicy full-bodied white wines, and those with bold flavor: earthy Chardonnays, Vernaccia, Loire Valley and California Sauvignon Blanc, and Oregon Pinot Gris top my list. Soft easy drinking red wine with peppery flavor is also very good. Try lighter styles of Zinfandel, southern Rhône wines, village-level Beaujolais, and Dolcetto. Much is dependent on the fish you choose to prepare.

## SALMORIGLIO
### *Garlic and Oregano Sauce for Fish*

♦ *Serves 4*

**Salmoriglio Sauce**

*2 tablespoons dried oregano*

*2 teaspoons finely minced garlic*

*¼ cup virgin olive oil*

*3 tablespoons fresh lemon juice*

*2 tablespoons chopped parsley*

*½ teaspoon salt*

*½ teaspoon freshly ground
  pepper*

*½ cup mild olive oil*

*2 tablespoons water* (optional)

*4 fish fillets, about 6 ounces
  each*

You've probably tasted this classic Sicilian sauce many times before. You just didn't know what it was called. It's usually drizzled on swordfish or tuna. Salmoriglio, also known as *salmorigano*, is also a good marinade for a roast pork loin. Rub the meat with a paste of garlic and oregano, baste with the sauce while cooking, and spoon a little on afterward. Great with broccoli with olives and toasted bread crumbs, and roast potatoes.

### *Procedure*

For the sauce, combine the oregano and garlic in a mortar or blender and grind with a pestle, or purée. Gradually add the virgin olive oil to make a paste. Add the lemon juice, parsley, salt, and pepper and mix well. Gradually beat or blend in the mild olive oil. Sicilians beat in the 2 tablespoons water and hold the sauce warm in a bain marie, but it works as well, without the water, at room temperature.

Pour half the sauce over the fish in a shallow, nonaluminum container and marinate 1 to 2 hours in the refrigerator. Then bake, grill, or broil (see Basic Fish Cooking Instructions, page 167) the fish until just cooked through. Spoon the remaining sauce over and serve.

**Wine Notes:** White wines of medium body and pronounced herbal green flavors are best: Verdicchio, Vernaccia, and Arneis from Italy, Sauvignon Blanc from France's Loire Valley or California's Sonoma County, and some of the steelier styles of Chardonnay from anywhere in the world. Delicate lacy reds that stress a similar herbal tone can work too.

## GRILLED FISH IN A YUCATECAN MARINADE

♦ *Serves 6 to 8*

*6 to 8 mild white fish fillets,*
*    about 6 ounces each,*
*    or 2¼ to 3 pounds shrimp or*
*    scallops*

*¼ cup olive oil*

*½ cup fresh orange juice*

*¼ cup fresh lime juice*

*2 teaspoons grated orange zest*

*1 teaspoon grated lime zest*

*1½ tablespoons finely minced*
*    garlic*

*1 teaspoon (or to taste) finely*
*    minced jalapeño pepper*

*¼ cup chili powder*

*1½ teaspoons ground coriander*

*¾ teaspoon ground allspice*

*¼ teaspoon (or to taste)*
*    cayenne pepper*

*¾ teaspoon freshly ground*
*    pepper, plus additional for*
*    the fish*

*Salt*

*Lime wedges, for garnish*

I wish more people were familiar with the cuisine of the Yucatán. What a pleasure to have seafood caught just hours before serving, marinated in a mixture of pungent citrus juices and chilies. While bitter orange is the traditional citrus, a combination of orange and lime will approximate its taste. Sometimes the fish is served with rice, beans, tortillas, or potatoes rubbed with some of the same marinade. This recipe makes enough marinade for 6 to 8 portions of fish (I like to use grouper, sea bass, flounder, cod, or halibut), shrimp, scallops, or lobster (page 209), depending upon how strong you like your flavors. Any extra marinade can be refrigerated for a few days. Serve with Black Beans (page 299), warm tortillas, and Avocado Salsa (page 351).

### Procedure

Place the fish fillets or the shellfish in a nonaluminum container. Combine the remaining ingredients and pour over the fish or shellfish. Let marinate 2 to 4 hours in the refrigerator.

Heat a grill or broiler. Thread the shrimp or scallops on 6 to 8 skewers, if using. Sprinkle the fish (or shellfish) with salt and grill or broil until just cooked through, about 3 minutes on each side. Serve hot with lime wedges.

***Wine Notes:*** Off-dry whites like German and American Riesling, young balanced Vouvray, or Montlouis are great, although a bright austere white like Muscadet or Pinot Bianco is very nice, too. In reds, a bit of tannin is okay—Pinot Noir, fragrant Merlot, and cru-level Beaujolais.

## PESCE IN SAOR

### Fish with Sweet and Sour Onions, Raisins, and Pine Nuts

♦ *Serves 4*

1/4 cup (or as needed) mild
    olive oil

8 cups sliced onions (about
    4 very large onions)

1/4 cup red wine vinegar

1/4 cup raisins, plumped in 1/2
    cup hot water and drained

1 tablespoon grated orange zest

2 teaspoons grated lemon zest

1 teaspoon salt, plus additional
    for the fish

1/2 teaspoon freshly ground
    pepper, plus additional for
    the fish

4 fish fillets, about 6 ounces
    each

1/4 cup pine nuts, toasted

In the traditional Venetian recipe, fillet of sole is sautéed, covered with the onion marinade, and served at room temperature, sort of an Italian escabeche. In this version, the sweet and sour onion mixture is served as a warm sauce over baked or sautéed sole, salmon, or flounder. For an interesting Turkish variation, add a little pomegranate juice to the onion mixture instead of vinegar and sprinkle the fish with pomegranate seeds before serving. Saffron rice and spinach are nice accompaniments to this dish.

### Procedure

Heat the oil in a large sauté pan or skillet over medium heat. Add the onions and cook until tender and translucent, about 20 minutes. (They will cook down to about 4 cups.) Add the vinegar, the raisins, and the grated zests and cook a few minutes longer. Stir in the salt and pepper. Taste and adjust seasonings. (The onions may be prepared several hours ahead.)

Preheat the oven to 450 degrees. Sprinkle the fish fillets with salt and pepper and place in a baking dish. Spread the onions over the fish and bake until just cooked through, about 7 minutes. Or sauté the fish in a little olive oil in a sauté pan or skillet over medium-high heat, adding the onions to the pan with the fish during the last few minutes of cooking. Or rewarm the onions separately.

To serve, place the fish on 4 serving plates. Top with the hot onion mixture and the toasted pine nuts and serve hot.

*(continued)*

***Wine Notes:*** The sweet/sour sauce calls for a bright, exuberant wine, either white or red, without tannin. Light-bodied whites with a touch of sweetness are fun: German kabinett Riesling or off-dry examples from America, or young northern Italian wines like Pinot Grigio, Sauvignon, or Tocai. For reds, a lively Barbera, Dolcetto, or even Grignolino from Italy are all lovely, and a juicy, tart Pinot Noir from California or Oregon would be well paired.

## PROVENÇAL ALMOND AND ANCHOVY FISH SAUCE

♦ *Serves 4 to 6*

**Almond Anchovy Sauce**

1 cup sliced almonds, toasted
   and lightly crushed

¾ teaspoon anchovy purée

¼ cup fresh lemon juice

1 teaspoon red wine vinegar

¾ cup mild olive oil

6 tablespoons chopped fresh
   mint

3 tablespoons chopped fennel
   fronds (see note)

½ teaspoon salt

¼ teaspoon freshly ground
   pepper

4 to 6 fish fillets, about
   6 ounces each

The food of Provence is aromatic, pungent, herbaceous, infused with the warmth of the sun. The classic salade niçoise—cooked tuna, potatoes, tomatoes, green beans, and hard-boiled eggs—is traditionally served with anchovy garlic vinaigrette. Why not try this sauce instead? Not only is it excellent with tuna, hot or cold, it works well with hot fish such as cod, sole, bass, and flounder. It is also an interesting dressing for avocado or for a salad of shrimp or smoked trout with avocado and orange sections.

### Procedure

For the almond anchovy sauce, combine all the ingredients in a bowl. Taste and adjust seasonings.

Bake, grill or broil, or poach the fish until just cooked through (see Basic Fish Cooking Instructions, page 167). Place on individual serving plates and top with sauce.

**Note:** If fresh fennel fronds are not available, substitute 1 teaspoon toasted ground fennel seed or a spoonful of Pernod.

**Wine Notes:** No surprise, but provençal wines are excellent! A fresh Cassis for white, a spicy and refreshing dry rosé, or a light herbal-scented red such as Bandol from France's southeast would all work well. Alternative whites stressing acidity and earthy nuances are fine: French and Italian Chardonnay, American or South American Sauvignon Blanc, and whites of Spain and northern Italy.

# FISH WITH MOROCCAN SWEET AND HOT TOMATO SAUCE

◆ *Serves 6*

*3 tablespoons olive oil or unsalted butter*

*1 large onion, grated in a food processor or blender (about 1 cup)*

*2 garlic cloves, finely minced*

*2 teaspoons cinnamon*

*1 teaspoon ground ginger*

*½ teaspoon (or to taste) cayenne pepper*

*1 teaspoon ground cumin*

*¼ cup honey or brown sugar*

*3 cups Basic Tomato Sauce (page 349)*

*¾ cup brown raisins, plumped in hot water to cover and then drained*

*½ cup sliced almonds, toasted*

*½ teaspoon salt, plus additional for the fish*

*¼ teaspoon freshly ground pepper, plus additional for the fish*

*6 fish fillets, about 6 ounces each*

This recipe is a composite of two Moroccan fish recipes. The sweet and spicy tomato sauce is excellent with swordfish, sea bass, tuna, rockfish, or flounder. You can grill or broil the fish and spoon the sauce on after cooking, or you can bake the fish covered with some of the sauce and spoon a little more sauce on after it emerges from the oven. I like to top the sauced fish with a small handful of deep-fried onions, as their sweetness plays nicely against the sauce and raisins. Couscous is the ideal accompaniment, as are grilled eggplant, peppers, or swiss chard.

## Procedure

Heat the oil or butter in a large saucepan over low heat. Add the grated onion and cook about 10 minutes. Add the garlic and cook 2 to 3 minutes longer. Then add the spices and cook for a few minutes. Finally, stir in honey or brown sugar and the tomato sauce and bring to a simmer. Add raisins, almonds, salt, and pepper. Taste and adjust seasonings.

Heat a grill or broiler. Brush the fish with olive oil and sprinkle with salt and pepper. Grill or broil the fish until just cooked through, 3 to 4 minutes each side. Spoon the sauce over the fish and top with crispy fried onions. (The fish may also be baked. Place it in a single layer in an oiled baking dish, sprinkle with salt and pepper, and cover with half the sauce. Bake at 450 degrees until just cooked through, about 8 minutes. Spoon the rest of the sauce over the fish and serve with the onions.)

*Olive oil for brushing the fish*
*Crispy Fried Onions (see below)*

**Wine Notes:** Off-dry white wines and off-dry rosés à la white Zinfandel or rosé of Cabernet Sauvignon are nice here. Clean light red wines, especially Pinot Noir, or a juicy Côtes du Rhône "nouveau" or "primeur," are also good choices.

### Crispy Fried Onions

*Peanut oil, for deep-frying, or*
*4 tablespoons butter plus*
*4 tablespoons oil for sautéing*
*3 large onions, cut in half and*
*sliced ¼-inch thick*

### Procedure

If deep-frying, heat 3 inches peanut oil to 350 degrees in a deep pan. Drop in onion slices and cook until dark golden brown, 4 to 5 minutes. Or sauté over medium-high heat, stirring occasionally, until brown. It is important that the onions fry until dark brown and slightly crisp. Do not let them get black or they will be bitter.

## ARMENIAN ROASTED PEPPER SAUCE FOR FISH

♦ *Serves 4*

*2 red bell peppers*

*2 red onions*

*Olive oil for roasting the onions*

*4 fish fillets, about 6 ounces*
*each*

*Salt and freshly ground pepper*

*¼ cup olive oil*

*1 teaspoon finely minced garlic*

*1 teaspoon ground allspice, plus*
*additional for the fish*
*(optional)*

*¼ teaspoon cayenne pepper,*
*plus additional for the fish*
*(optional)*

*¼ cup fresh basil, cut into*
*¼-inch strips*

I t's not really a sauce but a little vegetable stew placed on top of the fish; I serve it with tuna, swordfish, sturgeon, or rockfish. Use the cayenne judiciously so as not to overpower the sweetness of the peppers, onions, allspice, and basil. If red peppers are not available, use green. Serve with roasted potatoes or cracked wheat pilaf and grilled eggplant.

### Procedure

Char the peppers in a broiler or over direct flame, turning often with tongs, until they are blackened on all sides. Transfer to a plastic container with a lid, or a paper or plastic bag. Cover the container or close the bag and let steam for 15 to 20 minutes. Then peel off the skins with your fingers, scraping off any stubborn pieces of peel with a knife blade. Cut the peppers in half, remove the stems, seeds, and ribs, and cut the peppers into 1-inch strips. Set aside.

Preheat the oven to 400 degrees. Rub the onions with olive oil and roast in a baking dish until tender, but not mushy, 45 minutes to 1 hour. Peel the onions and cut into 1-inch strips. Set aside.

Raise the oven temperature to 450 degrees. Place the fish in a lightly oiled baking dish and sprinkle with salt and pepper and a little allspice and cayenne, if you like. Heat the oil in a medium sauté pan or skillet over low heat. Add the garlic, allspice, and cayenne and cook 1 to 2 minutes. Stir in the peppers and onions and half the basil. Pour over the fish and bake until the fish is just cooked through, 8 to 10 minutes, depending on the thickness. (The fish may also be grilled or broiled 3 to 4 minutes each side, depending on thickness.) Transfer to 4 serving plates and spoon the sauce over. Top with the remaining basil. Serve hot.

*Variation:* Roast 1 pound tomatoes at 450 degrees for 20 minutes. (Or, char on a griddle, over a flame, or under the broiler until the skins darken.) Remove the skin (or leave it on if not too blackened) and seeds and coarsely chop. Stir into the sauce along with the peppers, onions, and basil.

*Wine Notes:* For whites, pick up the smoky-sweet element of the peppers with barrel-fermented Chardonnays from France or California or with round rich Semillon from Australia. Ripe juicy reds, particularly Beaujolais Nouveau, are stellar, as are rosé wines from Provence and southern France.

# SAMAK AL SAHARA

### Fish with Tahini, Cilantro, and Cayenne

◆ *Serves 6*

*½ cup tahini, including some of its oil*

*2½ tablespoons fresh lemon juice*

*1 teaspoon finely minced garlic*

*½ teaspoon cayenne pepper*

*¼ teaspoon salt*

*½ cup tightly packed cilantro leaves*

*½ cup (or as needed) water*

*6 fish fillets, about 6 ounces each*

*S*amak is Arabic for "fish." This recipe is a variation on the traditional Middle Eastern samak bi tahini, in which the fish is covered with sesame paste flavored with garlic and lemon. To the basic sauce the Lebanese add a tingle of heat with the cayenne and chopped cilantro for accent. Snapper, swordfish, rockfish, and sea bass are particularly good with this sauce; the tahini crust on the fish keeps it moist throughout the baking process. You can garnish with olives or chopped walnuts along with more chopped cilantro. Serve with lemon wedges, rice, or cracked wheat pilaf. Spinach or zucchini counters the richness of the tahini.

### Procedure

For the sauce, combine all the ingredients except the fish in the container of a food processor or blender and pulse to blend. Add more water as needed to thin the sauce. Taste and adjust the salt and spiciness.

Preheat the oven to 450 degrees. Place the fish fillets in a lightly oiled baking dish and spread liberally with the sauce. Bake until the fish is just cooked through, 7 to 10 minutes, depending on the thickness of the fish. Transfer to serving plates. Serve hot.

*Wine Notes:* Racy young whites are called for with such a *rich* sauce: Austere mineral-scented Chardonnay, bright Pinot Grigio or similar northern Italian whites, and dry Riesling, at trocken levels or Fraconian, come to mind. Sparkling wines with a lot of Chardonnay could be an interesting twist.

## SAMAK AL KAMMOUN

### Fish with Cumin and Cilantro

♦ *Serves 6*

*6 tablespoons fresh lemon juice*

*2 tablespoons toasted cumin*
   *seed, ground*

*1½ tablespoons ground paprika*

*1 teaspoon finely minced garlic*

*½ teaspoon salt*

*½ teaspoon freshly ground*
   *pepper*

*½ cup olive oil*

*½ cup chopped fresh cilantro*

*6 fish fillets, about 6 ounces*
   *each*

The Moroccans have a similar dish called *hut b'camoun*, minus the cilantro and lemon juice that are integral parts of the Arab recipe. You can bake or grill the fish after marinating it in the sauce for about a half hour, then spoon a little extra sauce on top after cooking.

### Procedure

For the marinade, whisk together all the ingredients except the fish.

Place the fish in a nonaluminum container. Pour over about one third of the marinade and turn the fish to coat. Let marinate about ½ hour. Bake, grill, or broil the fish until just cooked through (see Basic Fish Cooking Instructions, page 167). Transfer to serving plates and spoon the remaining marinade over the fish. Serve with rice pilaf, roast potatoes, or cracked wheat pilaf, and spinach, zucchini, or eggplant.

**Wine Notes:** A Pouilly Fumé or Sancerre, a muscular varietal Graves, or most American and New Zealand Sauvignon Blancs are excellent. Pinot Blanc, either from Alsace or northern Italy, is tasty, as is lean Chablis-style Chardonnay from France or California. A light herbaceous red, like Chinon or slightly greener examples of Pinot Noir, is also a great match.

## MARTINI BUTTER FOR GRILLED FISH

*½ pound unsalted butter,*
*softened*

*¼ cup Seasoned Gin*
*(page 65)*

*1 tablespoon dry vermouth*

*¼ cup kalamata or niçoise*
*olives, pitted*

*Salt and freshly ground pepper*

I came up with this recipe last July Fourth. I wanted a sauce that was all-American; just why the martini came to mind I don't know. But the combination of juniper and olives is a natural for fish. The compound butter can be prepared well ahead. Try it on grilled swordfish or tuna.

### Procedure

Combine all the ingredients and salt and pepper to taste in the container of a food processor and process to blend. This butter may be well wrapped and frozen in a log shape and then sliced as needed. Use about 2 tablespoons for a 6- to 8-ounce piece of fish.

## MIDDLE EASTERN TOMATO-RHUBARB SAUCE FOR FISH

◆ *Serves 4*

*1½ pounds rhubarb, trimmed*

*½ cup water*

*2 tablespoons olive oil*

*1½ pounds fresh or canned*
*tomatoes, peeled, seeded, and*
*chopped (about 3 cups)*

*1 cup red wine*

*1 to 2 tablespoons honey*

*Juice and zest (optional) of*
*1 lemon*

*Salt and freshly ground pepper*

*Pinch of cinnamon (optional)*

*4 fish fillets, 6 to 8 ounces each*

I know this sounds weird, but trust me—it is a delicious sweet and sour sauce for fish. In Greece and Turkey, this recipe is traditional at Passover. In Greece there are two parts tomato to one part rhubarb; in Turkey, the proportions are reversed. To keep the peace, this version has equal amounts of tomato and rhubarb. While the sauce usually is served at room temperature, it's also delightful spooned warm over the cooked fish. Swordfish, sea bass, cod, flounder, and salmon are excellent choices for this preparation. Spinach is the most harmonious vegetable, but eggplant would work well, too.

### Procedure

To clean the rhubarb, pull off the thick strings, as you would do to string celery. Cut into 1½-inch chunks. Place in a medium saucepan and cover with the water. Bring to a boil, reduce the heat, and simmer until the rhubarb has wilted and is tender, about 8 minutes.

Warm the olive oil in a sauté pan or skillet over medium heat. Add the tomatoes and cook until reduced to a thick sauce. Stir in the wine, the honey, and the lemon juice and zest, if using. Stir in the rhubarb purée and mix well. Bring to a boil, reduce the heat, and simmer gently until the sauce is thick and rich, about 20 minutes. Season to taste with salt and pepper, and the cinnamon, if using. (Taste for a balance of sweet and sour; you may want to add a bit more honey.)

Bake, grill, or broil the fish (see Basic Fish Cooking Instructions, page 167). Spoon the sauce over the fish and serve hot.

*Wine Notes:* This melding of sweet and sour is a wine-friendly sauce. Spicy and dry white wines are nice here: Alsatian Gewürztraminer or Pinot Gris or northwestern examples of the same. Off-dry rosés, à la white Zinfandel or rosé of Cabernet Sauvignon, work for the same reasons. Once again, play with the clean light red wines, especially Pinot Noir with its similar complex flavor set. A juicy Côtes du Rhône "nouveau" or "primeur" also works well.

## PICADILLO DE PESCADO

### Fish in a Spicy Tomato Sauce

◆ *Serves 6*

2 tablespoons olive oil

1 large onion, diced (about
   1 cup)

1 teaspoon finely minced garlic

1 teaspoon (or to taste) finely
   minced jalapeño pepper

1 tablespoon chili powder

1 teaspoon ground cumin

1/2 teaspoon cinnamon

1/2 teaspoon ground coriander

1/2 teaspoon salt, plus additional
   for the fish

1/4 teaspoon freshly ground
   pepper, plus additional for
   the fish

2 cups Basic Tomato Sauce
   (page 349)

1/2 cup diced fresh or canned
   tomatoes

1/3 cup raisins, plumped in hot
   water to cover and drained

2 tablespoons capers, rinsed and
   coarsely chopped

**P**icadillo is a classic Latin American dish of ground meat, tomatoes, garlic, onions, spices, olives, raisins, and capers. This hash-like mixture is often stuffed into roast chicken, tortillas, chayote squash, and other such convenient containers. In Cuba it's served over rice and black beans. Without the meat, the mixture is still very exciting and makes a wonderful sauce for swordfish, cod, flounder, and tuna. You can grill the fish, then spoon the picadillo on top, or you can bake the fish with the sauce. Both versions are excellent. Serve with rice, black beans, and greens and grilled pineapple.

### Procedure

Warm the olive oil in a large sauté pan or skillet over medium heat. Add the onion and cook until tender, about 10 minutes. Add the garlic, jalapeño, spices, salt, and pepper and cook 2 to 3 minutes. Then add the tomato sauce, the diced tomato, the raisins, capers, and olives. Bring to a boil, reduce the heat, and simmer a few minutes. Taste and adjust seasonings.

Preheat the oven to 400 degrees. Sprinkle the fish fillets with salt and pepper. Place them in a lightly oiled baking pan and cover with the picadillo sauce. Bake until just cooked through, 12 to 15 minutes, depending upon the thickness of the fish fillets. Serve hot.

**Wine Notes:** White wines are really best here. Clean and perfumed wines like French Chablis, Macon Vil-

Small handful of green olives
    stuffed with pimiento or
    2 tablespoons pitted green
    olives, cut into chunks
6 fish fillets, about 6 ounces
    each

lages, or Sancerre are great. American alternatives would be lighter fruity examples of Chardonnay, Riesling, or Pinot Blanc. More classic regional alternatives would be white Rioja or Albarinho from Spain, or Vinho Verde from Portugal's Minho.

# FISH WITH ORANGE MINT SALSA VERDE

♦ *Serves 8*

### Orange Mint Salsa Verde

⅓ cup very finely diced onion

¾ cup mild olive oil

3 tablespoons grated orange zest

½ cup fresh orange juice

6 tablespoons fresh lemon juice

1 cup chopped fresh mint, or
    combination chopped fresh
    mint and basil

½ teaspoon salt

8 fish fillets, about 6 ounces
    each

Orange sections for garnish

Salsa verde is the classic Italian green sauce for cooked fish, meat, or vegetables. This lively orange and mint sauce is a versatile variation on the classic. Instead of lemon, orange juice and zest are added and mint replaces parsley. I usually serve this sauce at room temperature, spooned over hot fish. Salmon, sea bass, or tuna is best. It can also be used as a vinaigrette on cooked shrimp or scallops, or on cooked artichokes, asparagus, or green beans, for a summer salad.

## Procedure

For the sauce, whisk together all the ingredients in a bowl.

Bake, grill or broil, or poach the fish (see Basic Fish Cooking Instructions, page 167). Transfer to serving plates, top with salsa verde, and garnish with orange sections.

**Wine Notes:** To accent the citrus and fragrant mint, try a youthful Pinot Noir or Dolcetto, rich with bright fruit and good acidity. A dry Riesling or crisp Chardonnay with citrus undertones will also work.

# ROAST SALMON WITH SPICED ONIONS AND CURRANTS

♦ *Serves 4*

*½ cup currants*

*¼ cup Cognac*

*4 tablespoons olive oil or unsalted butter*

*4 large onions, sliced ¼ inch thick (about 6 cups)*

*½ teaspoon cinnamon*

*½ teaspoon freshly grated nutmeg*

*½ teaspoon salt, plus additional for the fish*

*¼ teaspoon freshly ground pepper, plus additional for the fish*

*4 salmon fillets, about 6 ounces each*

*½ cup Fish Fumet (page 202) or Chicken Stock (page 119)*

Here's another interpretation of the sweet and sour onion theme. This French-inspired recipe plumps the currants in Cognac and adds the perfume of cinnamon and nutmeg to the onions instead of citrus zest. It's especially good with a leafy green vegetable such as spinach.

Incidentally, this aromatic onion-currant mixture is great with sautéed calf's liver or chicken livers.

## Procedure

Soak the currants in the Cognac and ¼ cup water until softened and plump, about 30 minutes.

Heat the oil or butter in a large sauté pan or skillet over medium heat. Add the onions and cook until very tender and translucent, about 20 minutes. Stir in the spices, reduce the heat to low, and cook for just a few minutes to meld the flavors. Stir in the currants and the salt and pepper. Taste and adjust seasonings. Set aside.

Preheat the oven to 450 degrees. Divide the onion mixture into 4 piles in a baking dish. Place each salmon fillet on top of a pile of onions and sprinkle with salt and pepper. Spoon the fumet or stock over the salmon and bake until the fish is just cooked through, 7 to 12 minutes, depending on the thickness of the fillets.

***Variation:*** You may also poach or broil the salmon fillets and then serve the warm onion mixture on top as a sauce.

***Wine Notes:*** Both white and red wines can work here. For whites, look for a dry Alsatian wine rich with aromatic spice: Riesling, Muscat, or Tokay-

Pinot Gris. Chenin Blanc from the Loire, such as Savennières, is quite good, as are spicy Chardonnays from Europe or California. A light to medium-bodied red is also quite nice—a Pinot Noir, a soft Grenache-based wine from France's southern coast, or youthful Chianti or Bordeaux, for example.

## POTLATCH SALMON WITH JUNIPER MARINADE

♦ *Serves 6*

*6 tablespoons sugar*

*3 tablespoons kosher salt*

*3 tablespoons juniper berries, ground in a spice or coffee grinder*

*1 teaspoon freshly ground pepper*

*1 tablespoon grated orange zest (optional)*

*6 boneless and skinless salmon fillets, about 6 ounces each*

*Olive oil for brushing the fish*

*Lemon or orange wedges, for garnish*

Pacific Northwest Coast Indians used to celebrate the start of salmon season with a traditional feast known as a potlatch. At this festival, the host gave away everything he had to his guests, to impress them with his status and generosity. As part of the ceremony, the first of the season's salmon or halibut was served. The fish was nailed to a board, rubbed with a mixture of salt, sugar, and juniper, then smoked over wood fires. Of course fish is still prepared this way, festival or not. This is my home version. Share with your friends, too.

### Procedure

Mix the sugar, salt, juniper, pepper, and orange zest if using, and rub over both sides of the fillets. Cover and refrigerate for at least 4 hours, or up to 12 hours.

Heat the grill or broiler.

Bring the fish to room temperature. Brush the fish fillets with olive oil. Grill or broil until just cooked through, 2 to 3 minutes on each side. Garnish with a lemon or orange wedge.

**Wine Notes:** Rich white wines exploding with fruit—complex American or Australian Chardonnay, a textured Washington State Semillon, or a full-bodied Pinot Gris from Oregon or Alsace—come to mind. Racy young reds without tannin are nice, too.

# SALMON WITH ALMONDS, ONIONS, AND TOASTED BREAD CRUMBS

♦ *Serves 6*

*1½ cups sliced almonds*

*1 cup toasted bread crumbs*
  *(see page 189)*

*6 tablespoons unsalted butter*

*4 onions, cut into ½-inch dice*
  *(about 6 cups)*

*2 tablespoons chopped fresh*
  *sage*

*2 tablespoons grated lemon zest*

*Salt and freshly ground pepper*

*6 salmon fillets, about 6 ounces*
  *each*

*Lemon wedges, for garnish*

People in the northern Italian province of Lombardy love to cook with onions, rendered until they're sweet and tender. Bread crumbs are typical of a region that invented *alla Milanese,* the classic bread crumb crust. Combining them with toasted almonds adds extra crunch. Sage leaves appear in many traditional recipes; here I mixed them in with the onions, along with lemon zest, to brighten and lighten the mixture.

This dish is easy to prepare. As it can be assembled in a baking dish and heated at serving time, it is ideal for entertaining. Serve it with spinach, sautéed fennel, or fennel gratin. And don't forget the Chardonnay.

## Procedure

Preheat the oven to 350 degrees. Spread the almonds on a baking sheet and toast until pale gold and fragrant, about 7 minutes. Let cool slightly, then coarsely chop and combine with the toasted bread crumbs.

Melt the butter in a medium ovenproof sauté pan or skillet over medium heat. Add the onions and cook until tender and sweet, 15 to 20 minutes. Add the sage and lemon zest and season to taste with salt and pepper; set aside.

Raise the oven temperature to 450 degrees. Place onion mixture in baking dish or on sheet pan. Sprinkle the salmon with salt and pepper and place on top of the onion mixture. Top with the almond and bread crumb mixture. Bake until the salmon is just cooked through, 10 to 12 minutes. Serve hot with lemon wedges.

## Toasted Bread Crumbs

2 cups fresh Italian or French
    bread cubes, crusts removed
1 teaspoon salt
1 teaspoon freshly ground
    pepper
½ cup olive oil or melted
    unsalted butter

## Procedure

Preheat the oven to 350 degrees. Pulse the bread in a food processor to make coarse crumbs. Spread on a baking sheet. Stir the salt and pepper into the oil or butter and drizzle over the bread crumbs. Bake, stirring occasionally, until golden but not hard, 15 to 20 minutes.

**Wine Notes:** Clean and flowery whites are my preference: German Riesling (trocken or halbtrocken), northern Italian Tocai, non-oaked Chardonnay, and bright Sauvignon Blanc from the Loire (Quincy, Reuilly) or Chile. Verdicchio, Soave, and Oregon Pinot Gris are also very good.

# SALMON CATALAN

♦ *Serves 6*

*1 cup sliced almonds*

*1 cup olive oil*

*¼ cup sherry wine vinegar*

*½ cup fresh orange juice*

*2 tablespoons capers, drained, rinsed, and chopped medium fine*

*2 to 3 tablespoons grated orange zest*

*1 tablespoon puréed or finely chopped anchovies*

*Salt and freshly ground pepper*

*6 salmon fillets, about 6 ounces each*

*Olive oil for brushing the fish*

*3 avocados (optional)*

I love crunchy textures. One of my favorite Spanish salads, avocado Catalan, from the region of Catalonia, combines diced avocado with a chunky sauce of toasted almonds, orange zest, capers, anchovy, and sherry wine vinegar. The sauce is so tasty you will want to eat it with a spoon. Creamy avocado is a nice counterpoint for salmon. Why not serve the Catalan sauce on cooked salmon? And garnish with sautéed avocado if you like.

## Procedure

Preheat the oven to 350 degrees. Spread the almonds on a baking sheet and toast until fragrant and golden, about 7 minutes. Let stand until cool enough to handle and then coarsely chop. Whisk together the olive oil, vinegar, orange juice, capers, orange zest, and anchovies. Add the chopped almonds and season to taste with salt and pepper.

Heat the grill or broiler. Brush the salmon fillets with olive oil and sprinkle with salt and pepper. Grill or broil until the fish is just cooked through in the center, 3 to 4 minutes each side. (Or you may bake the salmon at 450 degrees for about 8 minutes.) Spoon the sauce over the fish and serve hot. If using the avocados, halve, pit, and seed and then slice them. Warm the slices in a skillet in a little oil over low heat. Place the avocado around the salmon and drizzle the sauce over all.

**Wine Notes:** Spicy full-bodied whites are ideal with this dish. The Spanish Albariño is particularly good. A full-bodied and dry rosé, say from the Loire Valley's Sancerre, or a vin gris from Burgundy, are also exquisite.

# BAKED SALMON WITH PRUNE SAUCE

♦ *Serves 6*

*1 tablespoon olive oil*

*4 large onions, diced (about 5 cups)*

*8 ounces (1½ cups) pitted prunes, soaked in hot water and then drained (reserve ⅔ cup of the liquid) and coarsely chopped*

*¼ teaspoon cayenne pepper*

*1½ tablespoons chopped fresh dill*

*1½ tablespoons chopped fresh cilantro*

*1½ tablespoons grated lemon zest*

*½ teaspoon salt, plus additional for the fish*

*¼ teaspoon freshly ground pepper, plus additional for the fish*

*6 salmon fillets, about 6 ounces each*

Most of us are used to combining prunes with meat and poultry, but the notion of serving prunes with fish may appear a bit unusual. This traditional Russian sauce is a variation of the classic sour plum sauce called Tkemali (page 237) and is reminiscent of a good tsimmes. I think you'll find the combination most harmonious with salmon, trout, and sole. Simple roast or boiled potatoes and spinach are fine accompaniments.

## Procedure

Warm the olive oil over medium heat in a large sauté pan or skillet. Add the onions and cook until tender, 10 to 15 minutes. Add the chopped prunes, cayenne, herbs, lemon zest, and reserved prune liquid. Bring to a boil, reduce the heat, and simmer for about 10 minutes. Taste and adjust seasonings.

Preheat the oven to 450 degrees. Arrange the fillets in a single layer in a large baking dish. Spoon some of the sauce over and bake until just cooked through, 5 to 8 minutes.

**Note:** If you prefer to use sole or trout, sauté the fish in a few tablespoons olive oil in a large sauté pan over medium-high heat, about 3 minutes each side. To serve, spoon the warm sauce on top.

**Wine Notes:** While salmon is actually more of a red wine fish than white, this prune sauce seals its ruby colored fate. A lesser Bordeaux or any other example of Cabernet Sauvignon is nice, especially if just slightly more mature. Ample juicy red wines are excellent: try lesser Rhônes, Pinot Noirs from California, Oregon, or lesser areas of France's Burgundy. Beaujolais is sublime as is a ripe and fruity Barbera.

# GRILLED SALMON WITH PISTACHIOS, LEMON, AND OLIVE OIL

◆ *Serves 4*

*½ cup shelled pistachios*

*2 tablespoons fresh lemon juice*

*⅓ cup olive oil*

*Salt and freshly ground pepper*

*Grated zest of 1 orange covered with ¼ cup fresh orange juice (optional)*

*4 salmon fillets, about 6 ounces each*

*Olive oil for brushing the fish*

*Lemon wedges, for garnish*

Nut-based sauces are a specialty of the Italian province of Liguria. This simple sauce for fish, using toasted pistachios, is a beautiful pale green and looks wonderful on the pink of the salmon. Tastes good, too. As a variation, try some orange juice or zest in the sauce in addition to the lemon. Serve with rice pilaf and asparagus, broccoli, or spinach.

## Procedure

Preheat the oven to 375 degrees. Spread the pistachios on a baking sheet and toast until fragrant, 8 to 10 minutes. Let stand until cool enough to handle. Then rub off the skins in a dishcloth and chop the nuts medium fine in a food processor. Process in the lemon juice, oil, salt and pepper to taste, and orange zest and juice, if using. Set aside. If not using orange juice, you may need a little water to thin the mixture.

Heat the grill or broiler. Brush the salmon fillets with olive oil and sprinkle with salt and pepper. Grill or broil until the fish is just cooked through, 3 to 4 minutes each side. (Or, bake the fish at 450 degrees for about 8 minutes.) Spoon the pistachio sauce over the fish and serve hot, with lemon wedges.

**Wine Notes:** The thick oily texture provided by nuts and the crisp refreshing acidity of lemon call for an austere Chardonnay, Pinot Grigio, or dry Riesling.

# SALMONE ALLA GIAPPONESE

### *Salmon with Soy, Ginger, and Sake*

♦ *Serves 6*

*¼ cup soy sauce*

*½ cup sake*

*1 cup Chicken Stock (page 119)*

*1 tablespoon (or to taste) grated fresh ginger*

*1 teaspoon finely minced garlic*

*3 tablespoons unsalted butter (optional)*

*6 salmon fillets, about 6 ounces each*

*Olive oil for brushing the fish*

*Freshly ground pepper*

The name of this dish is a little inside joke. When I was chef at the Chez Panisse Café, I was supposed to cook only French and Italian food. One day I had a craving for Japanese-style salmon with ginger and soy. To get around the geographical limitations of the menu, I wrote the name in Italian. Everyone loves the dish, and no one has ever questioned the lunacy of the label. Serve with green onion rice, spinach, snap peas, bok choy, or asparagus.

## Procedure

Combine the soy sauce, sake, stock, ginger and garlic in a medium saucepan. Bring to a boil, reduce the heat, and simmer until reduced by half, about ½ hour. Whisk in the butter, if using. (This sauce may be made several days ahead; it keeps well in the refrigerator.)

Heat a grill or broiler. Brush the salmon fillets with olive oil and sprinkle with pepper. Grill or broil until just cooked through, 3 to 4 minutes each side. (Or, bake the fish for about 8 minutes at 450 degrees, basting often with the sauce.) Transfer the fish to serving plates. Reheat the sauce, if necessary, and spoon over the fish.

*Wine Notes:* I like this dish with lots of different wines: crisp off-dry whites (German kabinett Riesling and light Chenin Blanc), light high acid whites (Sauvignon, Ribolla, and Tocai from northeastern Italy), and fresh spicy reds (Pinot Noir from the Côte Chalonnaise, like Rully and Givry). A delicate pilsner beer is also very nice!

# GRILLED SALMON WITH HUNGARIAN HORSERADISH ALMOND CREAM

♦ *Serves 6*

*¾ cup sliced almonds*

*5 slices 1-inch thick horseradish, peeled and puréed with 1 tablespoon white vinegar and 1 tablespoon water (approximately 3 tablespoons purée)*

*3 cups heavy cream*

*1 teaspoon salt, plus additional for the fish*

*½ teaspoon freshly ground pepper, plus additional for the fish*

*6 boneless salmon fillets, about 6 ounces each*

*Olive oil for brushing the fish*

*3 tablespoons chopped parsley or fresh dill*

The sweetness of toasted almonds and the zip of horseradish tempered with cream combine to make a wonderful sweet and hot sauce for salmon, trout, or halibut. In keeping with the Hungarian spirit, serve with potato pancakes, potato strudel, or little steamed or roast new potatoes. Sautéed cucumbers, zucchini and cucumbers combined, or spinach and broccoli also work well.

### Procedure

Preheat the oven to 350 degrees. Spread the almonds on a baking sheet and toast until fragrant and golden, about 7 minutes. Let stand until cool enough to handle and then coarsely chop. Combine the almonds, horseradish, cream, salt, and pepper in a small saucepan. Set aside.

Heat a grill or broiler. Brush the fish with olive oil and sprinkle with salt and pepper. Grill or broil until just cooked through in the center, 3 to 4 minutes each side. (Or, you may poach the fish in barely simmering wine, water, or fish stock, 6 to 8 minutes.)

Meanwhile bring the sauce to a boil, reduce the heat, and simmer for a few minutes until slightly reduced. Spoon sauce over the fish on serving plates and sprinkle with the parsley or dill. Serve hot.

**Wine Notes:** A French white Burgundy, or an American, French, or New Zealand Sauvignon Blanc, would be delicious. In red wines, try Pinot Noir from Burgundy, Oregon, and California's central coast; or an Italian Barbera, Nebbiolo, or Gattinara.

# SAUTÉED TROUT OR FILLET OF SOLE WITH PINE NUTS, SOUR CREAM, AND DILL

◆ *Serves 2*

*¼ cup pine nuts*

*2 boneless trout, heads removed,*
*about 8 ounces each, or 12*
*ounces sole fillets, or 2 salmon*
*fillets, about 6 ounces each*

*Salt and freshly ground pepper*

*½ cup dry bread crumbs*

*3 tablespoons unsalted butter*

*1 tablespoon olive oil*

*½ cup white wine*

*4 to 6 tablespoons sour cream,*
*at room temperature*

*2 tablespoons chopped fresh dill*
*or a combination of parsley*
*and dill*

Y ou want simple? Tasty? Fast? This Russian recipe is a winner. It's a classic, quick-sauté dish that can be prepared in minutes. To gild the lily, add a few shrimp to the sauce. Serve with boiled potatoes or rice and asparagus or green beans.

## Procedure

Preheat the oven to 350 degrees. Spread the pine nuts on a baking sheet and toast until fragrant and golden, about 7 minutes. Set aside.

Sprinkle the fish with salt and pepper and dip in bread crumbs. Melt the butter and olive oil in a large sauté pan or skillet over medium heat. Add the fish to the pan and sauté, turning once, until golden, 3 to 4 minutes each side for trout, 2 to 3 minutes per side for sole, and 4 minutes each side for salmon. Set aside on 2 warm plates. Deglaze the pan with the wine and reduce by half over high heat. Remove from the heat and stir in the sour cream. Season to taste with salt and pepper.

To serve, pour the sauce over the fish and sprinkle with the toasted pine nuts and dill.

*Variation:* Sauté the fish and remove from the pan. Then add ½ pound shelled and deveined shrimp to the pan and sauté just until pink, 2 to 3 minutes. Remove from the pan and keep warm. Deglaze the pan with the wine, and finish the sauce as in the original recipe. (You may also bake the fish at 450 degrees for 8 minutes while preparing the sauce.)

*Wine Notes:* While the fish is delicate, a wine that can hold its own with the sour cream is required. Exuberant Sauvignon Blanc is my preference, but a steely more austere Chardonnay is a viable alternative.

## TROUT STUFFED WITH BREAD CRUMBS, PINE NUTS, AND CURRANTS

◆ *Serves 6*

*3 tablespoons olive oil or*
*    unsalted butter*

*1 cup chopped onions*

*2 teaspoons ground coriander*

*1 teaspoon ground allspice or*
*    cinnamon (optional)*

*¼ cup pine nuts, toasted*

*¼ cup currants, soaked in hot*
*    water to cover and drained*

*2 tablespoons chopped parsley*

*1 tablespoon chopped fresh dill*

*2 cups fresh bread crumbs,*
*    lightly toasted in a skillet with*
*    3 tablespoons olive oil or*
*    unsalted butter*

*Salt and freshly ground pepper*

*6 boneless trout, coho salmon*
*    trout or small mackerel, heads*
*    removed, 8 to 10 ounces each*

*Olive oil for brushing the fish*

*Lemon wedges, for garnish*

The traditional Middle Eastern dolma, or grape leaf, filling can be used as a stuffing for fish as well as for vegetables. In Turkey this dish is most often prepared with mackerel; Americans seem to prefer the milder and sweeter trout or coho salmon trout. Serve with sautéed spinach or broiled eggplant and zucchini.

### Procedure

Heat the oil or butter in a small sauté pan or skillet over medium heat. Add the onions and cook until tender, about 7 minutes. Add the coriander and allspice or cinnamon, if using, and cook 1 to 2 minutes. Stir in the pine nuts, currants, parsley, dill, and toasted bread crumbs. Season to taste. Let cool.

Spoon the stuffing mixture into the cavities of the trout and sew the openings closed with a large sewing needle and cotton thread. (You may prepare the fish several hours in advance and refrigerate.) Heat a grill or broiler. Brush each fish with olive oil and sprinkle with salt and pepper. Grill or broil until just cooked through, about 4 minutes each side. (The trout may also be baked in a 375-degree oven for about 15 minutes; baste them occasionally with a little olive oil. Or if you are very careful, the fish may be sautéed in a large sauté pan or skillet over medium heat in butter or oil.) Serve hot with lemon wedges.

**Wine Notes:** Look for a simple Chardonnay, Sauvignon Blanc, or American Pinot Blanc. Cabernet Franc and dry fruity rosés are also well matched.

# BAKED ROCKFISH WITH INDONESIAN SAUCE

◆ *Serves 4*

*1 tablespoon very finely minced*
 *garlic*

*2 teaspoons salt*

*1 teaspoon freshly ground*
 *pepper*

*2 pounds rockfish fillet*
 *(see note)*

*½ cup soy sauce*

*3 tablespoons fresh lemon juice*

*2 tablespoons brown sugar*

*1 teaspoon dried red pepper*
 *flakes, crushed*

*4 to 6 tablespoons unsalted*
 *butter, melted, plus additional*
 *butter for the baking dish*

The recent wave of Southeast Asian immigrants to our shores, and the proliferation of Southeast Asian restaurants, have had a profound influence on our palates. We are now in love with their traditional flavor combinations of sweet, tart, and hot. This sauce of sweet soy, lemon, and hot pepper is a perfect example. You can make a large batch and keep it covered in the refrigerator for a week or so. It's nice to have on hand for an instant great meal. Serve the fish with rice garnished with finely chopped green onion and sautéed sugar-snap or snow peas.

## Procedure

Preheat the oven to 450 degrees. Work the garlic, salt, and black pepper into a paste in a mortar, or with the side of a large knife on a cutting board. Rub it over the fish fillets and place them in a buttered baking dish. Combine the remaining ingredients in a saucepan and bring to a boil. Taste for spiciness: if the sauce is too mild, add more pepper flakes. Pour half the sauce over the fish and bake until just cooked through, 6 to 8 minutes, depending on the thickness of the fillets. Transfer the fish to serving plates and spoon a little of the remaining warm sauce over. You may also grill or broil the fish, 3 to 4 minutes each side, basting occasionally with the sauce.

**Note:** This sauce is also delicious with halibut, salmon, and tuna fillets.

**Wine Notes:** Choose light-bodied juicy reds like Beaujolais, Pinot Noir, and Dolcetto d'Alba or off-dry whites, such as Riesling from Germany or Chenin Blanc from California.

## SWORDFISH OR TUNA ORIENTALE

♦ *Serves 6*

*3 tablespoons sesame seeds*

*2 garlic cloves*

*3 inches fresh ginger, peeled*

*1½ tablespoons Square One Hot*
  *Mustard (page 348) or Dijon*
  *(see note)*

*3 tablespoons soy sauce*

*⅓ cup rice or white wine*
  *vinegar*

*⅔ cup peanut oil, plus*
  *additional for brushing*
  *the fish*

*¼ cup sesame oil*

*6 pieces swordfish or tuna fillet,*
  *about 6 ounces each and*
  *¾ to 1 inch thick*

*Salt and freshly ground pepper*

*½ cup finely chopped green*
  *onions*

*¼ cup chopped fresh cilantro*
  *(optional)*

Everyone seems to love Chinese chicken salad. The tangy ginger dressing enlivens the blandness of the chicken, romaine lettuce, and cucumbers. I thought if such a dressing could make chicken interesting, it surely could do wonders for a simple fish. Serve with rice and sprinkle both with finely minced green onions. Chopped cilantro is optional but appropriate.

### Procedure

Toast the sesame seeds in a small dry pan over low heat until they pop. Set aside.

Combine the garlic, ginger, mustard, and soy sauce, and process in the container of a food processor or blender until blended. Process in the vinegar. Then gradually process in the oils, drop by drop at first and then more quickly, until all the oil has been used and the sauce is emulsified. Set aside.

Heat a grill or broiler. Brush the fish with oil and sprinkle with salt and pepper. Broil or grill until just cooked through, 3 to 4 minutes each side. Transfer to serving plates and spoon the sauce over. Sprinkle with the chopped green onions and sesame seeds, and cilantro, if using.

*Note:* Add 1 tablespoon sugar if using Dijon mustard.

*Wine Notes:* The recommendations for Salmone alla Giapponese (page 193) work equally well with this Chinese variation.

# GRILLED TUNA WITH WASABI, SAKE, AND LIME

♦ *Serves 4*

### Marinade

*2 tablespoons sake*

*2 tablespoons fresh lime juice*

*1 teaspoon grated lime zest*

*1 tablespoon soy sauce*

*2 tablespoons mild olive oil*

*4 pieces yellowfin tuna fillet,*
*    about 6 ounces each and*
*    ¾ to 1 inch thick*

### Wasabi Butter

*1 tablespoon wasabi powder*

*1 tablespoon sake*

*8 tablespoons unsalted butter,*
*    softened*

*Olive oil for brushing the fish*
*Salt and freshly ground pepper*

The Japanese have a knack with fish. Techniques are simple, sauces clean and vibrant. Here is one that takes moments to put together, and moments to consume, happily. Serve with rice and snap peas, spinach, or Japanese eggplant.

### Procedure

For the marinade, combine all the ingredients in a shallow nonaluminum container. Turn the tuna fillets in the marinade and let stand about 30 minutes.

For the wasabi butter, mix the wasabi with the sake to make a paste. Let rest 20 minutes and then beat the paste into the softened butter (see note). Season with salt and pepper.

Heat a grill or broiler. Brush the tuna lightly with oil, sprinkle with salt and pepper, and grill or broil to medium rare, 2 to 3 minutes each side. Transfer to serving plates and place 1 tablespoon wasabi butter on each piece of tuna. Serve hot.

**Note:** This butter freezes well so don't worry about leftovers.

**Wine Notes:** Clean perfumed whites, bold in young acidity but accented with citrusy undertones, are sublime. A more austere mineral-scented Chardonnay, bright Pinot Grigio or similar northern Italian whites, and dry Riesling, at trocken levels or Fraconian, are wines that come to mind. Play with sparkling wines, those ample in Chardonnay, as another twist. Red wines can work depending on how little you cook your tuna. The more raw the tuna, the more likely it will pair well with a simple but well-balanced red wine.

## MARISCADA
### Brazilian Shellfish Ragout

♦ *Serves 6*

*4 tablespoons unsalted butter*

*2 onions, chopped*

*2 green bell peppers, chopped*

*2 to 3 jalapeño or other hot*
*peppers, finely minced*

*4 garlic cloves, finely minced*

*1 tablespoon ground coriander*

*¼ teaspoon saffron filaments,*
*steeped for 10 minutes in*
*¼ cup warmed white wine*

*8 fresh or canned plum*
*tomatoes, cut into ½-inch dice*
*(1½ cups)*

*½ cup coconut cream (Coco*
*Lopez)*

*6 tablespoons chopped fresh*
*cilantro*

*4 cups Fish Fumet (page 202),*
*made with dried hot peppers,*
*2 bay leaves, 2 walnut-size*
*pieces fresh ginger, and the*
*zest of 1 lime, stripped off in*
*wide pieces*

*2 to 3 tablespoons fresh lemon*
*or lime juice*

*Salt and freshly ground pepper*

This recipe is a combination of three Brazilian fish and shellfish dishes: *moqueca de peixe*—sautéed fish with coconut, tomatoes, garlic, lemon juice, chopped cilantro, cayenne, and the inevitable dende oil; *lagosta com leite de coco*—a lobster sauté with coconut, tomatoes, and hot pepper; and *Mariscada*—a Brazilian bouillabaisse made with fish and shellfish, seasoned with coriander, onion, tomatoes, garlic, saffron, and cayenne. I took the most popular elements from each dish and put them together. It's a winner. Serve with rice.

### Procedure

Melt the butter in a wide deep pan over medium heat. Add the onions and cook until translucent, about 10 minutes. Add the green peppers, jalapeños, garlic, and coriander and cook 5 minutes. Add the saffron infusion, the tomatoes, coconut cream, cilantro, and fish fumet. Bring to a boil, reduce the heat, and simmer 3 minutes. Add the lemon or lime juice and salt and pepper to taste. Taste and adjust the balance of sweet and sour. Add the clams and the lobster or crab pieces, if using, and simmer, covered, for 2 minutes. Add the fish, mussels, and shrimp and simmer 2 minutes longer. Add the scallops and cook until the clams and mussels have opened, 3 to 4 minutes. Serve the ragout over rice and garnish with the chopped coconut and cilantro.

**Note:** Lobster and crab make a flashier presentation if served in the shell. However, they are messier to eat. If you prefer, remove meat from the shell. If

18 Manila clams, scrubbed

1 lobster, about 1½ pounds,
    cooked (see note), cut into
    chunks, or 1 crab, about
    2 pounds, cooked (see note),
    cut into chunks (optional)

1½ pounds combination of
    angler fish, snapper, rock cod,
    or flounder, cut into 3-inch
    chunks

18 mussels, scrubbed and
    bearded

18 large shrimp, shelled and
    deveined

18 sea scallops, tough muscles
    removed

2 tablespoons toasted coconut
    and 2 tablespoons chopped
    fresh cilantro, for garnish

using lobster, steam for 6 to 8 minutes, then chill, and cut into pieces. If using crab, steam 10 minutes, chill, and cut into pieces.

**Wine Notes:** This needs well-structured whites with a hint of sweetness to accent the coconut and foil the light heat. German and American Rieslings and Chenin Blancs from northern California and the Loire Valley are very good. Off-dry rosé wines are lovely, and a sparkling wine is also fun. In reds, I especially like those made from Gamay or Grenache, with characteristic low tannin and ripe fruit.

(continued)

## Fish Fumet

♦ *2 quarts*

6 to 8 pounds fish frames (*with
    heads and tails but gills
    removed*), preferably mild fish
    such as snapper, rockfish,
    halibut, or sea bass

2 tablespoons mild olive oil

2 quarts water or to cover

3 cups dry white wine

3 to 4 onions, coarsely chopped

5 celery ribs, coarsely chopped

4 strips lemon zest

5 parsley sprigs

2 thyme sprigs

10 peppercorns

4 whole coriander seeds

3 whole allspice

1 large bay leaf

1 walnut-size piece of ginger,
    peeled (*optional*)

1 dried red pepper (*optional*)

1 teaspoon fennel seeds
    (*optional*)

## Procedure

Rinse the fish frames well. Heat the olive oil in a large stockpot over medium heat. Add the fish frames and cook, stirring often, until the frames give off a little liquid, about 10 minutes. Add the remaining ingredients and bring to a boil. Reduce the heat and simmer uncovered for 30 minutes, skimming the scum from the surface as needed. Strain through a cheesecloth-lined strainer. Let cool to room temperature, then refrigerate or freeze.

# VATAPÀ

### Shrimp and Rockfish Brazilian Style

♦ *Serves 6*

*2 pounds medium shrimp, shelled and deveined, shells reserved for stock (page 204)*

*1 pound rockfish, flounder, snapper and/or sea bass fillets, cut into 1- by 3-inch pieces*

*½ cup peeled and sliced fresh ginger*

*1 tablespoon paprika*

*2 tablespoons fresh lemon juice*

*6 tablespoons mild olive oil*

*3 large onions, diced (about 6 cups)*

*6 garlic cloves, finely minced*

*3 hot peppers, finely minced, or 1 teaspoon cayenne pepper to taste*

*3 cups canned plum tomatoes, diced, plus ½ cup reserved tomato juice*

*½ cup (or to taste) canned coconut cream*

*½ cup dry-roasted peanuts and/or cashews, finely ground*

I t took a lot of experimenting to come up with this great version of the classic Bahian dish, rich with coconut, peanuts, shrimp, and chilies. We eliminated the traditional dende or palm oil (and that extra dose of saturated fat isn't missed); paprika acts as a substitute for its red color. And we replaced the dried shrimp—with its strong smell and odd (to Americans) taste—with a stock made from shrimp shells that provides that certain funky undertone the dried shrimp imparted.

### Procedure

Refrigerate the shrimp and fish until serving time.

For the fish soup base, combine the sliced ginger, the paprika, and lemon juice in the container of a blender or food processor and purée. Set aside. Heat 3 tablespoons of the oil in a large saucepan over low heat. Add the diced onions and cook until tender, about 10 minutes. Add the puréed ginger, the minced garlic, and hot peppers or cayenne and cook 2 to 3 minutes. Add half the diced tomatoes and all the reserved juice, and the coconut cream and cook 2 to 3 minutes. Add the ground nuts, the toasted coconut, and half the chopped cilantro and cook 2 to 3 minutes longer. Transfer to the container of a blender or food processor and purée. Return to the saucepan and add the remaining diced tomatoes and cilantro, and the shrimp stock. Bring to a boil, reduce the heat, and simmer until the sauce is rich and somewhat thickened. Season to taste with salt and pepper. Taste for a balance of sweet and sour (add more

(*continued*)

¼ cup toasted unsweetened
    coconut, pulsed in a food
    processor to chop
¼ cup chopped fresh cilantro
4 cups Shrimp Stock (see
    below), or fish or chicken
    stock (see note)
Salt and freshly ground pepper
Coarsely chopped dry-roasted
    peanuts and/or cashews,
    coconut, and fresh cilantro,
    for garnish

**Shrimp Stock**

♦ *4 to 5 cups*
Shells from 2 pounds shrimp
2 tablespoons mild olive oil
1½ quarts (or as needed) water
2 cups dry white wine
3 medium onions, coarsely
    chopped
3 celery ribs, coarsely chopped
3 strips lemon zest
3 parsley sprigs
2 thyme sprigs
8 to 10 peppercorns
3 whole coriander seeds
2 whole allspice
1 large bay leaf
1 walnut-size piece of fresh
    ginger, peeled (optional)
1 dried red pepper pod
    (optional)

coconut cream, if needed) and adjust the heat, if necessary.

Remove the fish and shrimp from the refrigerator and sprinkle with salt and pepper. Heat the remaining 3 tablespoons olive oil in a deep sauté pan or skillet over high heat. Add the shrimp and the fish and sauté until just cooked through, about 2 minutes. Reduce the heat to medium, add the sauce, and heat through. Serve over rice and garnish with the chopped nuts, coconut, and cilantro.

**Note:** For a more authentic Vatapà, grind ½ cup dried shrimp with the fresh ginger in a food processor and use along with 4 cups fish or chicken stock in place of the shrimp stock.

**Wine Notes:** I recommend the same wines suggested for the Mariscada (page 200).

**Procedure**

Rinse the shells well. Heat the olive oil in a large stockpot over medium heat. Add the shells and sauté, stirring often, about 10 minutes. Add the remaining ingredients, adding more water if needed to cover the shells. Bring to a boil, reduce the heat, and simmer uncovered for 1 hour, skimming the scum from the surface often. Strain through a cheesecloth-lined strainer into a large saucepan and reduce by half. If not using immediately, let cool to room temperature, then refrigerate or freeze.

# CURRIED CRAB CAKES

♦ *Serves 8*

*8 tablespoons unsalted butter*

*2 large onions, minced (about 2 cups)*

*6 celery ribs, minced (about ¾ cup)*

*2 tablespoons grated fresh ginger*

*1 teaspoon finely minced garlic*

*2 to 3 tablespoons curry powder*

*1 tablespoon ground cumin*

*2 teaspoons dry mustard*

*1 teaspoon ginger powder*

*½ to 1 teaspoon cayenne pepper*

*½ teaspoon ground cloves*

*½ teaspoon ground coriander*

*¼ teaspoon ground cardamom*

*2 pounds crabmeat, picked over for cartilage*

*2 teaspoons grated lemon zest*

*¾ cup fresh bread crumbs*

*½ cup (or as needed) Basic Mayonnaise (page 76)*

*2 eggs*

*Salt and freshly ground pepper to taste*

*1 cup dry bread crumbs*

*Peanut oil, for frying*

These could be served as part of the Indian Fritto Misto al Mare (page 206) or as a main dish with ginger aioli. Or a single crab cake could be paired with lettuces, avocado, and mango slices and dressed with a ginger-lime vinaigrette.

## Procedure

Melt the butter in a small saucepan over low heat. Add the onions and celery and cook until tender, about 8 minutes. Add the fresh ginger and the garlic and cook 1 to 2 minutes longer. Stir in the dried spices and cook 5 more minutes. Let cool.

Add all the remaining ingredients except the dry bread crumbs and peanut oil to the onion mixture and stir to combine. Shape into 16 patties, about ½ inch thick. Dredge each crab cake in the dry bread crumbs and refrigerate on a baking sheet lined with parchment or wax paper until serving time.

Heat ½ inch peanut oil in a large heavy skillet over medium-high heat. Add as many crab cakes as will comfortably fit and sauté until golden brown, about 3 minutes each side. Serve with mint or cilantro chutney, papaya or cantaloupe pickle, lemon lentils, coconut-cardamom rice, and sautéed spinach.

**Wine Notes:** An off-dry wine is best here, enhancing both the crabmeat's sweet flavor and contrasting the heat. Try a young kabinett or spätlese-level German Riesling or a Chenin Blanc from France or the United States. Finally, try refreshing young reds, ample in fruit and absent of tannin such as Beaujolais, Dolcetto, or Pinot Noir.

# INDIAN FRITTO MISTO AL MARE

♦ *Serves 4*

*2 eggs*

*2 tablespoons cold water*

*⅓ cup finely chopped green onions or fresh chives*

*2 cups all-purpose flour*

*¼ cup Masala Powder (page 207) or strong curry powder*

*16 medium shrimp (about 1 pound, in the shell), shelled and deveined*

*24 mussels or 28 clams, scrubbed, steamed open in white wine, and removed from the shells*

*1 pound squid, cleaned, cut into ½-inch rings, large tentacles halved (½ pound cleaned)*

*½ pound bay or sea scallops, tough muscles removed*

*½ pound sole fillets, cut into 3- by 1-inch strips (optional; cut back on shellfish if using)*

*4 Curried Crab Cakes (page 205), each about 3 ounces (optional)*

*Peanut oil, for deep-frying*

*Lemon or lime wedges, for serving*

An Indian variation on an Italian classic. This is wonderful served with saffron rice, lemon lentils (page 326), sautéed spinach, and a zippy cilantro or mint chutney (page 344). Allow seven to eight ounces of fish and shellfish per person (if you include clams or mussels, their weight is out of the shell).

### *Procedure*

Whisk together the eggs, cold water, and green onions or chives in a bowl. Combine the flour with the masala or curry powder in a second bowl. Working in batches, dip the shellfish and fish in the egg wash, and then dredge them in the flour mixture. Transfer to a strainer and shake off the excess flour.

Heat at least 3 inches peanut oil in a deep-fryer to 350 degrees. Add as many pieces of fish and shellfish as will comfortably fit and fry until golden. It will take only a few minutes. Do not overcook. Remove from the oil with a skimmer or strainer and drain on paper towels. Gently transfer to 4 warm plates and garnish with lemon or lime wedges. Serve with saffron rice, lemon lentils, sautéed spinach, and cilantro or mint chutney.

## Masala Powder

◆ *About ⅓ cup*

*2 tablespoons whole black
  peppercorns*

*1 tablespoon caraway seeds*

*1 tablespoon shelled cardamom
  seeds*

*1 tablespoon coriander seeds*

*1 teaspoon ground cloves*

*2 teaspoons cinnamon*

*1 teaspoon cayenne pepper*

*2 teaspoons salt*

## Procedure

Grind the whole spices in a spice mill or small coffee grinder. Add the ground cloves, cinnamon, cayenne, and the salt. Transfer to a jar; the mixture will keep for several months.

**Wine Notes:** I like sparkling wine with this fritto. Big Blanc de Noirs, strong cuvées based on Pinot Noir, or young bold rosés, all are well suited. Fresh light dry whites with citrus-scented fruit are also very good: Verdicchio, Sauvignon Blanc from Chile, and Pinot Blanc from Alsace are three good choices. And light juicy reds are excellent—try Beaujolais Nouveau or primeur Côtes du Rhône—and, of course, Pinot Noir is a natural.

## GRILLED SHELLFISH IN A SCOTCH, SOY, AND GINGER MARINADE

♦ *Serves 6*

*2 pounds large shrimp (shelled and deveined) or sea scallops (tough muscles removed), or a combination of the two*

*½ cup soy sauce*

*¼ cup scotch whisky*

*2 teaspoons grated fresh ginger*

*1 teaspoon finely minced garlic*

*2 tablespoons honey*

This recipe is a variation on a classic Chinese marinade. Instead of rice wine, sherry, or bourbon, which the Chinese love, I marinate the shellfish for an hour or two in scotch, soy, and ginger, grill them quickly, and serve them over lettuces tossed in a vinaigrette made from combining some of the marinade with olive oil and vinegar.

You don't have to serve them with greens as a warm salad as they are perfectly wonderful hot off the grill/broiler, or sautéed and served as a stir-fry with rice. Snap peas, snow peas, or spinach are lovely accompaniments.

### Procedure

Divide the shellfish into 6 portions and thread on skewers (for six 5-ounce portions).

Combine the remaining ingredients in a shallow nonaluminum container. Turn the skewered shellfish in the marinade and let marinate in the refrigerator for about 30 minutes.

Heat a grill or broiler. Grill the seafood until just cooked through, about 2 minutes each side. (Do not overcook or the seafood will be tough.) Serve on a bed of quickly sautéed greens, such as spinach, watercress, or bok choy, or on a bed of lettuces dressed with half the marinade whisked with 1 cup olive oil and 2 tablespoons each sesame oil and rice wine vinegar.

**Wine Notes:** In whites, full-bodied Chardonnay stressing spice and citrus, from California, France, or Australia are best. Richer but less grassy styles of Sauvignon Blanc are also ideal. For a change of pace, try a light Pinot Noir.

# ROAST LOBSTER

♦ *Serves 2*

*2 lobsters, about 1½ pounds
   each*

*Yucatecan Marinade (page
   172), or Charmoula
   Vinaigrette (page 241), or
   Basil or Indian Spiced Butter
   (page 211)*

I love to serve lobster for special occasions. The expense and preparation make it prohibitive to cook for a crowd, but it's great for two.

## *Procedure*

Bring a large pot of salted water to a boil. Plunge the lobsters into the water and cook 6 to 8 minutes. Remove from the pot and let stand at room temperature until cool enough to handle, or chill in an ice water bath, drain, and then refrigerate until you are ready to shell them.

To shell the lobsters, lay them on a work surface and cut in half lengthwise with a large knife. Remove the gravelly sac at the lobster's head. Twist the claws from the body and carefully remove all the claw and knuckle meat. (Lobster or nut crackers, a mallet, or a sharp pair of small kitchen shears or scissors work well for this task.) Remove the tail meat from the shells, cut into 2-inch pieces and return it to the shells, along with the claw and knuckle meat.

Preheat the oven to 350 degrees.

If using the Yucatecan marinade, drizzle liberal amounts over the lobster meat in a nonaluminum baking dish and marinate 30 minutes. Then bake in the same dish until heated through, 10 to 15 minutes. Serve with fried potatoes and Avocado Salsa, or black beans, warm tortillas, and Avocado Salsa.

If using the Moroccan charmoula, drizzle the lobster with the charmoula in a nonaluminum baking dish and marinate 30 minutes. Bake in the same dish until heated through, 10 to 15 minutes. Serve with

(*continued*)

Moroccan Spicy Fried Potatoes (page 336) and green beans with cumin spiced onions, toasted almonds, and lemon zest.

If using the basil butter, spread over the lobster meat and bake 10 to 15 minutes. Serve with fried potatoes and green beans. If using the Indian spiced butter, spread over the lobster, bake 10 to 15 minutes, and serve with saffron rice seasoned with a cinnamon stick, a few cloves, and a few cardamom seeds, a fruit chutney (pages 355–358), Crispy Fried Onions (page 177), spinach curry, and Indian Spicy Lentils (page 326).

## Basil Butter

◆ *Serves 2*

*⅓ cup basil pesto*

*5 tablespoons unsalted butter,*
  *softened*

*Salt and freshly ground pepper*

### Procedure

In a food processor blend the pesto into the butter.
Season to taste with salt and pepper.

## Indian Spiced Butter

◆ *Serves 2*

*½ cup unsalted butter, softened*

*2 tablespoons grated fresh*
  *ginger*

*2 tablespoons ground coriander*

*2 teaspoons finely minced garlic*

*1 teaspoon turmeric*

*1 teaspoon fennel seed, toasted*
  *and finely ground*

*½ teaspoon cayenne pepper*

*1 teaspoon fresh lemon juice*

*Salt and freshly ground pepper*
  *to taste*

### Procedure

Process all ingredients in a food processor until
blended. This butter keeps well in the freezer and is
also delicious on simple broiled fish or as a dip for
grilled shrimp.

**Wine Notes:** See Curried Crab Cakes (page 205) or
Indian Fritto Misto al Mare (page 206) for recommendations.

# POULTRY

CHICKEN WITH APRICOTS AND TOMATOES ◆ ROAST CHICKEN WITH CHERRIES AND SOUR CREAM ◆ MOROCCAN-STYLE ROAST CHICKEN WITH CORIANDER AND MINT ◆ POULARDE À LA RENNAIS ◆ TANDOORI-STYLE ROAST CHICKEN ◆ POLLA ALLA SALSA DELLE API ◆ GRILLED CHICKEN IN A SPICY ORIENTAL MARINADE ◆ JUJEH KABABE ◆ CHICKEN BROCHETTE EL BAGHDADI ◆ INDONESIAN CHICKEN SATÉ ◆ INDONESIAN PEANUT SAUCE ◆ CHICKEN WITH SOUR CREAM, ONIONS, TOMATOES, AND DILL ◆ SAUTÉED CHICKEN WITH CUCUMBERS, DILL, AND SOUR CREAM ◆ TABAKA AND TKEMALI ◆ CHICKEN FRICASSEE WITH

MEATBALLS ◆ CHICKEN WITH ROASTED CHILIES AND SPICED CREAM ◆ MOROCCAN CHICKEN SALAD ◆ CATALAN-STYLE QUAIL STUFFED IN ROASTED PEPPERS ◆ MUSHROOM-STUFFED QUAIL WRAPPED IN GRAPE LEAVES ◆ QUAGLIE ALLA MELAGRANA ◆ FESENJAN ◆ THREE RECIPES FOR ORIENTAL ROAST DUCK WITH FRUIT: ROAST DUCK WITH PEACHES, ALMONDS, AND GINGER ◆ ROAST DUCK WITH ORANGE, HONEY, AND SOY ◆ ROAST DUCK WITH PEARS, CHESTNUTS, AND GINGER ◆ INDONESIAN-STYLE ROAST DUCK WITH COCONUT ◆ ROAST CURRIED DUCK WITH ORANGE, LEMON, HONEY, AND GINGER ◆ GRILLED SQUAB WITH BOURBON, HONEY, AND SOY ◆ ROAST DUCK WITH A MEXICAN SAUCE OF SESAME AND CHILIES ◆

# CHICKEN WITH APRICOTS AND TOMATOES

◆ *Serves 6*

*3 tablespoons chicken fat or olive oil*

*4 cups chopped onions*

*1 tablespoon plus 1 teaspoon cinnamon*

*1 teaspoon ground cloves*

*3 cups diced Italian plum tomatoes, juices reserved*

*3½ cups dried apricots, soaked in warm water to cover, for about 1 hour*

*2 cups Chicken Stock (page 119), water or combination apricot soaking liquid, reserved tomato juices, and water to equal 2 cups*

*⅓ cup brown sugar*

*Salt and freshly ground pepper*

*6 poussins (young chickens) or Rock Cornish game hens, about 1 pound each*

Apricots originated in Persia, but good news and good food travel fast. I have seen variations of this recipe in various Middle Eastern and Indian cookbooks. The apricot sauce is sweet, tart, and aromatic, and adds a certain tang to simple Cornish hens or chicken. I often serve this dish as part of a Passover seder meal, but I need no such excuse to cook this family favorite all year long. Serve with rice or rice and wild rice combined, cracked wheat pilaf or couscous, accompanied by sautéed spinach or zucchini.

## Procedure

For the apricot sauce, heat the fat or oil in a large saucepan over low heat. Add the onions and cook 3 minutes. Add the 1 tablespoon of cinnamon and all of the clove and cook 3 more minutes. Stir in about ¼ cup reserved tomato juices. Bring to a boil, then reduce the heat to a simmer. Purée half the soaked apricots in a food processor and coarsely chop the remainder. Add the puréed apricots, the diced tomatoes, and 1 cup chicken stock to the onion mixture and simmer 5 minutes. Purée half the onion mixture in the food processor and then return to the pan. Add the chopped apricots, the brown sugar, and the remaining cup chicken stock and simmer 5 minutes longer. Add enough of the reserved tomato juices to make a medium-thick sauce. Season to taste with salt and pepper and set aside. (The sauce can be made several hours ahead and refrigerated.)

Preheat the oven to 450 degrees. Place the

*(continued)*

poussins or Cornish hens in a shallow roasting pan on a rack and sprinkle with salt, pepper, and the reserved teaspoon cinnamon. Roast until juices run clear when the leg is pierced with a skewer, about 40 minutes. Remove from the oven and let stand until cool enough to handle; cut into quarters. Bring the apricot sauce back to a simmer, add the quartered birds, and simmer until heated through. Place 4 poussin or Cornish hen quarters on each of 6 serving plates and top with the sauce.

*Note:* The birds may also be cut into quarters and baked: Spread half the apricot sauce over the bottom of a large baking dish. Brown the pieces in oil and set them in the baking dish. Spoon the remaining sauce over and bake at 350 degrees until done, about 30 minutes. Or, the sauce may be used with chicken pieces (breasts, thighs, or boneless breasts): Sauté the chicken in oil and remove from the pan. Deglaze the pan with a little chicken stock and then add the sauce. Return the chicken to the pan and simmer until cooked through, 15 to 20 minutes for breasts, about 25 minutes for thighs, and about 8 minutes for boneless breasts.

*Wine Notes:* Try a medium-bodied red with ample fruit and spice and soft tannins—a simple Côtes du Rhône, Côte du Ventoux, or Côteaux de Tricastin. A fresh Pinot Noir from just about anywhere would also be well suited. Off-dry whites can be fun, as are the rich-textured whites of Alsace, especially Muscat.

## ROAST CHICKEN WITH CHERRIES AND SOUR CREAM

♦ *Serves 6*

*6 poussins (young chickens) or*
  *Rock Cornish game hens,*
  *about 1 pound each*

*Salt and freshly ground pepper*

*1½ teaspoons paprika*

*2½ teaspoons cinnamon*

*3 tablespoons unsalted butter*

*2 large onions, diced (about*
  *3 cups)*

*1 cup Chicken Stock (page 119)*

*¾ cup marsala*

*1½ cups sour cherries, pitted, or*
  *¾ cup sun-dried cherries,*
  *soaked 1 hour in ½ cup*
  *marsala or sherry and ½ cup*
  *brandy*

*3 to 4 tablespoons sour cream*

*½ cup chopped walnuts*
  *(optional)*

This dish originated in Turkestan. It eventually migrated to Bulgaria, where it evolved into a traditional preparation for pheasant. Use fresh sour cherries when they're in season; they require no soaking, just pitting. But this dish is so tasty you'll probably crave it in January, in which case sun-dried cherries make a great substitute.

### *Procedure*

Preheat the oven to 425 to 450 degrees. Sprinkle the birds with salt, pepper, and ½ teaspoon each paprika and cinnamon. Place on a rack in a shallow roasting pan and roast until the juices run clear when a thigh is pierced with a skewer, about 45 minutes. Let stand until cool enough to handle, and then cut into quarters, discarding the backbones. Place the poussin or hen quarters in a pan, cover with foil, and keep warm in a low oven, or set in a warm place.

Melt the butter in a medium saucepan over medium heat. Add the onions, and cook until soft, 8 to 10 minutes. Add the remaining 1 teaspoon paprika and 2 teaspoons cinnamon and cook 3 to 5 minutes. Add the stock and marsala and cook over high heat for a few minutes until the sauce is reduced and thickened. Add the cherries and walnuts, if using, and heat through. (The sauce and poussins or hens may be prepared ahead up to this point.) Remove the sauce from the heat (or, if made ahead, rewarm poussins or hens in the sauce and then remove from heat) and swirl in the sour cream. Season to taste with salt and pepper. Pour the sauce over the warm

*(continued)*

poussins or hens on a serving platter. Serve with rice and wild rice pilaf or cracked wheat and sautéed spinach. (Instead of using the optional walnuts in the sauce, toss them in the sautéed spinach if you'd like some crunch.)

***Wine Notes:*** If ever a dish was created with Pinot Noir in mind, this may be the one; cherries used in cooking enhance the bold cherry flavors of so many Pinot Noirs, and examples from all over the globe would work well. Seek those with more ripe fruit and less tannin. Young Chianti, a supple and tasty Merlot from Washington State, or an Australian Shiraz-Cabernet blend are very good as well. A more delicate wine such as Italian Bardolino or a Pinot Noir from Alsace or Germany (spätburgunder) would also be excellent.

# MOROCCAN-STYLE ROAST CHICKEN WITH CORIANDER AND MINT

♦ *Serves 4*

### Spice Paste Marinade

*½ cup chopped fresh cilantro*

*½ cup chopped fresh mint*

*2 tablespoons finely minced garlic*

*½ teaspoon saffron, steeped in 2 tablespoons hot water*

*2 tablespoons paprika*

*1 tablespoon ground cumin*

*1 tablespoon freshly ground pepper*

*2 teaspoons salt*

*2 tablespoons olive oil*

*4 poussins (young chickens) or Rock Cornish game hens, about 1 pound each*

*2 tablespoons olive oil*

*2 onions, diced (about 2 cups)*

*1½ cups reduced Chicken Stock (page 119)*

*16 to 20 kalamata or ripe green olives*

*⅓ cup Preserved Lemon Peel (page 359)*

*Salt and freshly ground pepper*

Some people think they hate cilantro, yet they devour Mexican and North African sauces that are laced with this pungent green herb. This is a classic chicken recipe from North Africa, and those folks who claim they don't like cilantro will enjoy it and wonder what makes it so good.

### Procedure

Stir together all the marinade ingredients into a paste. Reserve half of it. Rub the remaining paste over the outsides and in the cavities of the poussins or Cornish hens.

Preheat the oven to 450 degrees. Place the birds on a rack in a shallow roasting pan and roast until the juices run clear when a thigh is pierced with a skewer, 35 to 40 minutes. Remove from the oven and let stand until cool enough to handle. Cut the birds into quarters and keep warm.

Meanwhile, heat the olive oil in a medium sauté pan or skillet over medium heat. Add the onions and cook until tender and translucent, about 10 minutes. Add the reserved spice paste and cook 2 to 3 minutes. Add ½ cup of the stock and purée in a blender or food processor. Return the purée to the pan and thin with the remaining cup of stock. Add the olives and lemon peel. Season to taste with salt and pepper. This can be made ahead of time.

Rewarm the sauce, if necessary. Distribute the cut birds on each of 4 serving plates. Spoon the hot sauce over the birds and serve with couscous.

**Wine Notes:** Supple red wines are best: Rhône reds, Barbera from Italy, Rhône-clones from California, and spicy Shiraz-Cabernet blends from Down Under.

## POULARDE À LA RENNAIS

### Roast Chicken Stuffed with Sausage and Prunes

◆ *Serves 4*

1¼ cups pitted prunes, cut in
  half

1 cup (or to taste) Armagnac

3 tablespoons unsalted butter

2 small onions, chopped medium
  fine (about 1½ cups)

4 celery ribs, chopped (about
  ½ cup)

8 garlic cloves, very finely
  minced

2 tablespoons olive oil

½ pound lean ground pork

2 teaspoons (or to taste)
  chopped fresh thyme

1 teaspoon (or to taste) grated
  nutmeg

Salt and freshly ground pepper

4 poussins (young chickens) or
  Rock Cornish game hens,
  about 1 pound each, or
  1 large (5½ to 6 pound)
  roasting chicken

This recipe for roast chicken with pork and prune stuffing is from Brittany. I borrowed the traditional prune and Armagnac combination from Gascony because I love how the stuffing tastes when perfumed by the Armagnac-soaked prunes. Roast potatoes are fine as an accompaniment. Green beans would be wonderful, too, but as their season is so brief, I've come to rely on the leafier greens such as Swiss chard or spinach.

### Procedure

For the stuffing, cover the prunes with the Armagnac in a small bowl and soak 1 hour. Melt the butter in a large sauté pan or skillet over medium heat. Add the onions and cook until translucent, about 8 minutes. Add the celery and garlic and cook 1 to 2 minutes longer. Set aside. Heat the olive oil in a sauté pan or skillet over medium heat. Add the ground pork and cook, stirring, until cooked through. Add the cooked vegetables, the prunes and Armagnac, the thyme, and the nutmeg. Season to taste with salt and pepper. Add a little more nutmeg, thyme, or Armagnac, if you like. The stuffing can be made a day ahead.

**Basting Butter**

*5 tablespoons unsalted butter*

*2 teaspoons minced garlic*

*1 teaspoon chopped fresh thyme*

*¼ teaspoon grated nutmeg*

*Salt and freshly ground pepper*

Preheat the oven to 500 degrees. For the basting butter, melt the butter and season with the garlic, thyme, nutmeg, and salt and pepper to taste. Set aside. Spoon the stuffing into the cavities of the birds or the roasting chicken. Place the chickens on a rack in a shallow roasting pan and roast for 10 to 15 minutes. Then lower the oven temperature to 400 degrees and cook, basting occasionally with the seasoned butter, until the juices run clear when a thigh is pierced with a skewer, 20 to 30 minutes longer, or 1 hour and 15 minutes longer for the roasting chicken. Cut the smaller birds in half or cut the roasting chicken into serving pieces and serve hot.

**Wine Notes:** Simple and fruity red wines with a "local" angle are best here: Bordeaux, Corbières, and Côtes de Roussillon. Young Rioja Crianza, American Merlot, and Australian Shiraz are also quite delicious, as is solid French cru Beaujolais.

# TANDOORI-STYLE ROAST CHICKEN

♦ *Serves 6*

*Marinade*

*1 onion, cut into chunks*

*2 garlic cloves, chopped*

*¼ cup fresh lime or lemon juice*

*1 tablespoon ground coriander*

*2 teaspoons paprika, plus additional for sprinkling*

*1 teaspoon ground ginger*

*½ teaspoon cayenne pepper*

*½ teaspoon turmeric*

*¼ teaspoon each ground cloves and ground cardamom*

*½ teaspoon salt*

*Freshly ground pepper to taste*

*2 cups plain yogurt*

*6 poussins (young chickens) or Rock Cornish game hens, about 1 pound each*

Pair yogurt with aromatic Indian spices and lemon or lime juice and you have a remarkably tasty classic recipe known as tandoori chicken. The tandoor is an Indian clay oven that cooks food at incredibly high temperatures. (Tandoors are also used in Turkey.) While most of us don't have a tandoor at our disposal, we do have broilers and ovens. And outdoor grills. Incidentally, yogurt marinades have a tenderizing effect, and this one works wonderfully on butterflied leg of lamb and lamb chops.

### Procedure

For the marinade, purée the onion with the garlic in a food processor. Process in the lime or lemon juice. Then add the spices and yogurt and process to blend.

Place the poussins in a nonaluminum container. Pour the marinade over and turn to coat. Cover and refrigerate, turning occasionally, overnight.

Bring the chickens to room temperature. Preheat the oven to 450 degrees. Remove excess marinade and transfer the birds to a rack in a shallow roasting pan. Roast until the juices run clear when a thigh is pierced with a skewer, 40 to 45 minutes. Sprinkle with a little paprika.

Or, if you plan to grill or broil the birds, first butterfly them by cutting down both sides of the backbones and removing them. Open out and flatten the birds with the palm of your hand. Then marinate. Broil or grill, cook 5 minutes on each side or until they test done. Serve with saffron rice, chutney of your choice, and curried spinach or broccoli.

*Note:* Whole baby chickens make a pretty presentation, but you may also use this marinade on regular-size chickens, cut into halves or pieces, and broil, grill, or bake them. You could also skewer skinless, boneless chicken pieces and grill or broil as a sort of tandoori brochette. (Chicken pieces for brochette need marinate only 4 to 8 hours.) Great for those on a low-fat diet.

*Wine Notes:* Try a spicy medium-bodied red—a Burgundian Mercurey, Santenay, or Monthélie, or the Shiraz wines of Australia. Honest flavorful Portuguese and Spanish reds and the bevy of selections from France's Midi and Provence—Palette, Bandol, Corbières, Minervois, etc.—would also be wonderful. A smoky aromatic white with body and spice, like dry Alsatian Muscat, Washington State Semillon, and simpler white wines from Burgundy are all very good choices.

## POLLO ALLA SALSA DELLE API

**Grilled Chicken with Honey and Mustard**

◆ *Serves 4*

*4 poussins (young chickens),*
    *about 1 pound each*
    *(see note)*

*6 tablespoons honey*

*¼ cup Dijon mustard*

*2 tablespoons Square One*
    *Hot Mustard (page 348)*

*¼ cup water*

*Salt and freshly ground pepper*

The name translates as "sauce from the bees." The marinade evolved from a traditional conserve, like mostarda di frutta, from Piemonte in the north of Italy. Chopped walnuts usually are included in the mixture. I thought it would make a great marinade and sauce for grilled chicken, minus walnuts (as they would burn on the grill). Soft polenta and sautéed pears or apples, cooked in cider and topped with relocated chopped walnuts, are a nice accompaniment to the grilled chicken. You could make a little extra honey mustard mixture and warm it as a sauce to pour over the cooked chicken or to stir into the apples or pears.

### Procedure

To butterfly the poussins, cut down both sides of the backbone with a heavy, sharp knife to remove it. Then pull open the sides of the poussin, turn it skin side up and press firmly on the breast with the heel of your hand to flatten it and break the breastbone. Remove the breastbone and attached cartilage, if you like. Fold the wings back against themselves so they lie flat.

For the marinade, heat the honey in a small saucepan over low heat, until liquid. Add the remaining ingredients and whisk to combine. Place the butterflied poussins in a shallow nonaluminum container. Pour the marinade over the chickens and toss to coat well. Cover and refrigerate overnight.

Bring the poussins to room temperature. Heat a grill or broiler. Remove the poussins from the marinade. Sprinkle the birds with salt and pepper and grill or broil, skin side away from the flame, 4 to 7 minutes, basting once or twice with the marinade. Turn and cook until the juices run clear when a thigh is pierced with a skewer, 4 to 7 more minutes. The poussins will be quite brown because of the honey. Serve with sweet soft polenta with sautéed apples and sautéed Swiss chard.

***Note:*** You may also use half-broilers for this dish.

***Wine Notes:*** Spanna, Barbera d'Alba, and a lively Dolcetto come to mind, but a firm young Chianti, a juicy Montepulciano d'Abruzzi, or simple Valtellina would also be very good. Beaune-style Pinot Noir from France, California, or Oregon, or a lighter Zinfandel, are also nice options. A rich full-bodied Chardonnay is a good white alternative, as is bright young Piemontese Arneis.

## GRILLED CHICKEN IN A SPICY ORIENTAL MARINADE

◆ *Serves 6*

### Marinade

*2 cups olive oil*

*3 to 4 tablespoons red pepper flakes*

*Zest of 3 large oranges or 4 tangerines*

*6 garlic cloves, smashed*

*6 pieces (2 inches thick) peeled fresh ginger, smashed*

*2 tablespoons Five-Spice Powder (see note 2)*

*2 tablespoons sesame oil*

*¼ cup fresh lemon juice*

*6 poussins (young chickens), about 1 pound each (see note 1)*

*Salt*

While the Chinese do not grill chicken, they do make very tasty stir-fried chicken seasoned with ginger, dried orange or tangerine peel, five-spice powder, and hot pepper flakes. As it turns out, these flavors also make a dynamite marinade for broiled birds: The chickens emerge from the grill smoky, spicy, and aromatic. They can marinate for one or two days, but no longer as the ginger is corrosive and this chicken will "cook" without cooking. You can make your own five-spice mixture or buy it at a market that carries Chinese condiments. (Don't confuse these five with the classic French "quatre épices.")

### Procedure

For the marinade, heat the olive oil in a medium saucepan over medium heat until very hot but not boiling. Test the temperature of the oil by dropping one or two pepper flakes into it. If they skip to the surface and bubble, the oil is the correct temperature and you may add the rest of the flakes. (If the pepper flakes brown, the oil is too hot; if they sink to the bottom, the oil is too cool.) Remove from heat and let cool about 10 minutes (the oil will actually still be quite warm). Then add the orange or tangerine zest, the garlic, and the ginger. Let stand 10 more minutes and then add the remaining ingredients. Let cool completely.

To butterfly the poussins, cut down both sides of the backbone with a heavy, sharp knife and remove. Then pull open the sides of the poussin, turn it skin side up and press firmly on the breast with the heel of your hand to flatten it and break the breastbone, remove the breastbone and attached cartilage, if you like. Fold the wings back against the body so they are flat. Place the poussins in a shallow nonaluminum container and pour over the marinade. Toss to coat and then cover and refrigerate overnight.

Bring the poussins to room temperature. Heat a grill or broiler. Remove the poussins from the marinade, sprinkle with salt, and grill or broil, basting occasionally with the marinade, until the juices run clear when a thigh is pierced with a skewer, 4 to 5 minutes each side. Serve with green onion rice and sautéed snap peas with shiitakes.

*Note 1:* This dish may also be made with half-broilers.

*Note 2:* To make your own Five-Spice Powder, combine equal parts (in weight) cinnamon sticks, star anise, cloves, fennel seed, and black peppercorns and grind to a powder in a spice mill. May be stored for a few months at room temperature in a tightly sealed jar.

*Wine Notes:* The strong flavors imparted by the grill and the marinade require a moderately full-bodied red wine. Rhônes like Hermitage and Côte Rôtie are very good, as well as American Syrah or less coarse Zinfandel and Italian wines like Barbaresco and Brunello di Montalcino. Fruity reds provide a nice foil here, too—Beaujolais, Dolcetto, Napa Gamay or Gamay Beaujolais, or even some of the lacier reds of the Loire Valley (Bourgueil and Gamay de Touraine).

## JUJEH KABABE
### Persian-Style Chicken Brochette

◆ *Serves 6*

*1 large onion, cut into chunks*
  *(about 1½ cups)*

*½ cup fresh lemon juice*

*1 tablespoon paprika*

*2 teaspoons finely minced garlic*

*2 tablespoons dried oregano*
  *(optional)*

*1 cup mild olive oil or enough to*
  *cover the chicken*

*18 boneless chicken thighs,*
  *excess fat trimmed (see note)*

*Salt and freshly ground pepper*

While this recipe was passed on to me by an Iranian friend, I have seen versions of this dish in cookbooks from the Caucasus. Some variations of this recipe use saffron instead of paprika; others use no herbs at all. Although most recipes for chicken kebabs specify boneless and skinless cubed chicken breasts, these are easily overcooked and toughened on the grill. I prefer to use boned chicken thighs with the skin on; they remain moist and juicy throughout the broiling or grilling process and the skin retains a wonderful flavor of the marinade. (And if you are on a low-fat regime, you can remove the skin after cooking.) Serve with Persian-Style Rice (page 160) and lemon wedges. Sautéed spinach or zucchini with chopped walnuts or toasted pine nuts would be a nice accompaniment, as would Spinach Borani (page 323).

### Procedure

Combine the onion, lemon juice, paprika, garlic, and oregano, if using, in the container of a blender or food processor and purée. Stir in the olive oil.

Place the chicken thighs in a nonaluminum container. Pour the marinade over the chicken and toss well to coat. Cover and refrigerate at least 6 hours or overnight.

Bring the chicken to room temperature. Heat a grill or broiler. Remove the chicken from the marinade and thread 3 thighs on each of 6 skewers. Sprinkle with salt and pepper and grill or broil, skin side away from the flame, about 4 minutes. Turn and cook until the juices run clear, about 4 minutes more.

*Note:* Boneless, skinless chicken breasts may be used in place of the thighs. Cut them into 2-inch pieces, then marinate and skewer them and grill or broil about 2 minutes on each side. But cook with care! Overcooked chicken breasts are very tough.

*Wine Notes:* Grenache-based reds from California, France's Rhône and Provence, and Australia are all sublime. A young Pinot Noir from Oregon's Willamette Valley or California's Russian River are also high on my list.

# CHICKEN BROCHETTE EL BAGHDADI

♦ *Serves 6*

*18 boneless chicken thighs,*
*excess fat trimmed (see note)*

*1 tablespoon ground cardamom*

*2 teaspoons ground allspice*

*1 teaspoon turmeric*

*1 teaspoon freshly ground*
*pepper*

*1 tablespoon finely minced garlic*

*¼ cup each fresh lemon and*
*lime juice*

*Grated zest of 1 lemon and*
*1 lime*

*1 cup olive oil or enough to*
*cover the chicken*

International events notwithstanding, this is a wonderful recipe, so you might want to depoliticize it and cook it—or change its name.

## Procedure

Place the chicken thighs in a nonaluminum container. Whisk together the spices, garlic, and lemon and lime juices in a bowl. Whisk in the grated zest and then the olive oil. Pour the marinade over the thighs, toss to coat, and cover and refrigerate overnight.

Bring the thighs to room temperature. Heat a grill or broiler. Remove the chicken from the marinade; reserve the marinade. Thread 3 thighs onto each of 6 skewers. Grill or broil, skin side away from the flame and baste occasionally with the reserved marinade, about 4 minutes. Turn and cook until the juices run clear, about 4 minutes more. Serve with rice pilaf with apricots and pistachio nuts, and sautéed spinach.

*Note:* You may use skinless chicken thighs or breasts if you like, but be careful not to overcook them—they will dry out faster without the skin.

*Wine Notes:* The suggestions for Jujeh Kababe (page 228) would work equally well here.

# INDONESIAN CHICKEN SATÉ

◆ *Serves 6*

## Marinade

*½ cup finely chopped onion*

*2 tablespoons finely minced garlic*

*1 tablespoon ground coriander*

*1½ teaspoons ground toasted caraway seed*

*1½ teaspoons turmeric*

*1½ teaspoons ground ginger*

*1¼ cups canned coconut cream (Coco Lopez is fine)*

*6 tablespoons fresh lemon juice*

*¼ cup packed brown sugar*

*Salt and freshly ground pepper to taste*

*18 boneless chicken thighs, excess fat trimmed (about 4 pounds)*

*Indonesian Peanut Sauce (page 232)*

*Crispy Fried Onions (page 177)*

Boneless chicken thighs are still my choice for a juicy brochette, even though cubed boneless chicken breasts are traditional for satés. If you opt for tradition, just be careful not to overcook—a minute too long and it's dry. Peanut sauce is good on almost anything, but it really sings in this dish. Add a little toasted coconut to your cooked rice, top the rice or chicken with Crispy Fried Onions (page 177), and you have a winner of a dinner.

## Procedure

For the marinade, combine all the ingredients in the container of a processor and pulse very quickly to combine.

Place the chicken thighs in a shallow nonaluminum container. Pour the marinade over and toss well to coat. Cover and refrigerate overnight.

Bring the chicken to room temperature. Heat a grill or broiler. Remove the chicken from the marinade and thread 3 thighs onto each of 6 skewers. Grill or broil, skin side away from the flame, about 4 minutes. Turn and cook until the juices run clear, about 4 more minutes. Do not be alarmed if the chicken blackens in spots—this caramelization of the brown sugar and the coconut will make the chicken taste delicious.

Spoon a generous amount of Indonesian Peanut Sauce on each of 6 serving plates. Remove the chicken thighs from the skewers and arrange 3 on each plate on top of the sauce. Top with deep-fried onions and serve with coconut rice and snow peas.

# INDONESIAN PEANUT SAUCE

♦ *About 3 cups*

*1 cup unsalted smooth peanut
   butter*

*⅓ cup finely chopped
   dry-roasted peanuts*

*1 tablespoon sugar*

*2 tablespoons fresh lemon juice*

*½ cup canned coconut cream
   (Coco Lopez is fine; see note)*

*⅓ cup soy sauce*

*⅔ cup chicken stock or water*

*½ teaspoon finely minced garlic*

*1½ teaspoons (or to taste) red
   pepper flakes*

*1 teaspoon ground cumin*

*1 teaspoon ground coriander*

This is my take on the classic Indonesian pea-nut sauce. It's wonderful with grilled chicken, flank steak, and lamb chops. We also eat it with a spoon.

### Procedure

Combine all the ingredients in a small saucepan and bring it gradually to a boil, stirring often. Reduce the heat and simmer 2 minutes to blend. Whisk constantly to prevent scorching. This sauce will keep refrigerated for about 1 week.

**Note:** You may use canned coconut milk in place of coconut cream, but add a few tablespoons more sugar.

**Wine Notes:** Ripe fruit is the key here—light-bodied reds (Beaujolais, Dolcetto, Bourgogne Rouge) and off-dry whites or an Italian Moscato d'Asti. A light perfumed Tocai Friulano is tasty as is a Savennières from France's Loire Valley. Try a Burgundian dry "vin gris" rosé for a change of pace.

# CHICKEN WITH SOUR CREAM, ONIONS, TOMATOES, AND DILL

♦ *Serves 4*

*4 whole chicken breasts, about*
  *1 pound each*

*½ cup olive oil*

*Salt and freshly ground pepper*

*2 cups diced onions*

*1 cup dry white wine*

*2 cups Chicken Stock*
  *(page 119)*

*1 cup diced tomatoes*

*2 teaspoons finely minced garlic*

*1 teaspoon lemon zest*

*¾ cup sour cream, at room*
  *temperature*

*¼ cup finely chopped fresh dill*

This is a fast, easy, and homey Russian recipe. Serve with kasha if you like it or buckwheat fettuccine if you like your buckwheat in noodle form. Rice is fine, too.

## Procedure

Remove the bones and skin from the chicken breasts and cut the flesh into 1½- to 2-inch chunks. Toss with a few tablespoons olive oil and sprinkle with salt and pepper.

Heat ¼ cup olive oil in one or two large skillets over high heat. Add the chicken and quickly brown on all sides, turning occasionally with tongs. Do not overcook; the chicken should still be somewhat rare in the center. Remove from the pan and set aside.

Heat 3 tablespoons olive oil in one of the skillets over medium heat. Add the diced onions and cook until translucent and tender, 7 to 10 minutes. Add the white wine and simmer until reduced by half. Add the stock and reduce by two thirds. Return the chicken to the pan along with the tomatoes, garlic, and lemon zest and simmer until the chicken is cooked through but still juicy, 1 to 2 minutes. Remove from the heat and stir in the sour cream. Add the chopped dill, and season to taste with salt and pepper.

Serve with buckwheat fettuccine with green beans and walnuts. Or with kasha and sautéed green beans with walnuts and garlic.

**Wine Notes:** A rich Sauvignon Blanc from the Graves, California, or New Zealand is perfect. Mineral-scented Chardonnay from the Mâconnais, Chablis, or Italy's Alto Adige are also excellent.

# SAUTÉED CHICKEN WITH CUCUMBERS, DILL, AND SOUR CREAM

♦ *Serves 4*

*4 whole chicken breasts, boned,*
*    skinned, and split*

*2 eggs*

*1½ cups milk*

*1 cup all-purpose flour*

*Salt and freshly ground pepper*

*2½ tablespoons each clarified*
*    butter and olive oil, or*
*    5 tablespoons clarified butter*

*⅔ cup diced, peeled cucumbers*

*¾ cup reduced Chicken Stock*
*    (page 119)*

*2 tablespoons chopped fresh dill*

*6 tablespoons sour cream*

*1 teaspoon grated lemon zest*

Although this is reminiscent of the preceding Russian recipe, this one is Hungarian in inspiration. The cucumber sauce works equally well on veal and even better on salmon. Poached shrimp is a nice addition to the sauce if you choose to serve it over fish.

### Procedure

Lightly pound the chicken breasts to an even thickness between sheets of plastic wrap. Whisk the eggs with the milk in a shallow bowl. Season the flour with salt and pepper on a large plate. Dip the chicken breasts in the egg and milk mixture, and then in the seasoned flour. Shake off excess flour.

Heat 4 tablespoons combined butter and oil, or butter, in a large sauté pan over medium heat. Working in batches, add as many chicken breasts to the pan as will fit without crowding and sauté until golden brown on both sides, about 3 minutes on each side. Set aside in a warm place.

For the sauce, heat the remaining tablespoon combined butter and oil or butter in a small saucepan over low heat. Add the cucumbers and cook until tender, 1 to 2 minutes. Add the chicken stock, dill, sour cream, and lemon zest. Bring to a boil and cook until slightly reduced. Season with salt and pepper.

Place 2 pieces of chicken on each of 4 serving plates. Top with the sauce and serve with noodles or boiled potatoes. (If you want to give this dish a Russian accent, serve with buckwheat noodles or potato pancakes.)

**Wine Notes:** See Chicken with Sour Cream, Onions, Tomatoes, and Dill (page 233).

## TABAKA AND TKEMALI

### Russian Fried Chicken with Prune Chutney

♦ *Serves 4*

*½ cup sour cream*

*1½ cups buttermilk*

*4 whole chicken breasts, boned, skinned, split, and lightly pounded (or see note)*

*1 cup all-purpose flour*

*Salt and freshly ground pepper*

*Grated nutmeg to taste*

*6 to 8 tablespoons clarified butter*

*Tkemali Sauce (page 237)*

Tabaka is flattened fried chicken from the part of Russia known as the Caucasus. It is related in cooking style to *pollo al mattone*, the Italian chicken that is cooked under the weight of a brick or some such heavy object. For those of us who don't have bricks for cooking, a cast-iron pan will work, or a few phone books piled into a sauté pan. The easy way out is to use boneless chicken breasts. Serve the chicken with the spicy prune condiment known as tkemali sauce.

### Procedure

Combine the sour cream and buttermilk in a bowl or deep baking dish. Add the chicken and marinate about 1 hour.

Season the flour with the salt, pepper, and nutmeg on a large plate. Remove the chicken from the marinade and wipe off excess. Then dip in the seasoned flour and shake off the excess. Heat half the clarified butter in a large skillet over medium high heat. Add half the chicken and cook, weighted with a cast-iron pan if you like, until just cooked through, about 2 minutes each side. Remove from the pan and cook the remaining chicken in the rest of the clarified butter in the same manner. (Or you may deep-fry the breasts in 3 inches peanut oil at 350 degrees until cooked through, 4 to 6 minutes.)

Serve with cracked wheat pilaf or kasha and a ramekin of tkemali sauce. Spinach and green beans with walnuts are both nice accompaniments.

(*continued*)

***Note:*** This recipe also works well with butterflied poussins: Cut down both sides of the backbone with a heavy, sharp knife and remove. Then pull open the sides of the poussin, turn it skin side up and press firmly on the breast with the heel of your hand to flatten it and break the breastbone. Remove the breastbone and attached cartilage, if you like. Fold the wings back against the body so they lie flat. Pound the poussins between sheets of plastic wrap to flatten, marinate, dredge in seasoned flour and fry, weighted under a brick or weighted pan, until done, about 8 minutes each side.

## Tkemali Sauce

♦ *Makes about 1½ cups*

8 ounces (1¼ cups) pitted
   prunes

2 tablespoons red wine vinegar

1 teaspoon grated lemon zest

1 tablespoon chopped fresh basil

1 teaspoon finely minced garlic

2 tablespoons chopped fresh
   cilantro

½ teaspoon cayenne pepper

2 tablespoons (or to taste) sugar

Salt and freshly ground pepper

## Procedure

Cover the prunes with 1½ cups water and the vinegar in a small saucepan and soak for 30 minutes. Bring to a simmer over low heat, cover, and cook the prunes until tender, about 30 minutes. Add the lemon zest during the last few minutes of cooking. Purée the prunes with the cooking liquid in a blender or food processor. Add the chopped basil, garlic, cilantro, and cayenne. Season to taste with sugar, salt, and pepper. Thin with water as necessary until the mixture is the thickness of a spoonable but thick ketchup. (The sauce will continue to thicken as it sits, so you will need to add a bit more water at serving time.) This sauce is also a traditional accompaniment for Shashlyk (page 263).

**Wine Notes:** With fried foods I like two types of wine: sparkling or crisp whites, clean and refreshing. As the chutney is rich and flavorful this dish calls for Pinot Noir-based cuvées in sparkling wine (Blanc de Noirs and Pinot Noir-based vintage or nonvintage cuvées) or aggressive zippy whites. Northern Italian whites from the Alto Adige and Friuli-Venezia-Giulia are excellent, as are Sauvignon Blancs with acidity and fruit. If you want a red wine, a light red with plummy nuance, such as Pinot Noir of Merlot, will work.

## CHICKEN FRICASSEE WITH MEATBALLS

◆ *Serves 4*

### Meatballs

*½ pound ground beef*

*1 small onion, grated (about
³⁄₄ cup)*

*1 clove garlic, finely minced*

*1 tablespoon each minced fresh
sage, marjoram, and parsley*

*½ teaspoon salt*

*¼ teaspoon freshly ground
pepper*

*³⁄₄ cup (or as needed) mild
olive oil*

*4 whole chicken breasts (about
1 pound each), boned,
skinned, split, and cut into
1½- to 2-inch chunks*

*Salt and freshly ground pepper*

*3 cups diced onions*

*5 cups sliced mushrooms (half
chanterelles, if possible)*

*1½ cups Chicken Stock
(page 119)*

*2 tablespoons chopped parsley*

*1 tablespoon chopped fresh
marjoram*

*1 tablespoon chopped fresh sage*

This is an old family recipe. The only time I've seen something like this in print was in Mimi Sheraton's *From My Mother's Kitchen*. It turns out that she and I grew up in the same neighborhood and even attended the same high school, although we didn't know each other. Given the similarities of the two recipes, I would venture a guess that our families probably came from a similar neighborhood in the old country.

When I was cooking at home for my family, I used to make this with chicken parts with bones and skin. However, as time is always of the essence, I now make this with boneless chicken breasts.

### Procedure

For the meatballs, place all the ingredients in a bowl and mix with your hands until blended, or briefly pulse in a food processor to blend. Form into 24 tiny meatballs. (These may be prepared ahead and refrigerated on a baking sheet until needed.)

Heat 3 tablespoons of the olive oil in a large sauté pan or skillet over high heat. Add the meatballs and sauté until well browned on all sides, about 5 minutes. Remove from the pan and set aside.

Sprinkle the chicken with salt and pepper. Heat 3 more tablespoons olive oil in the same large pan over high heat. Add as much chicken as will comfortably fit in the pan without crowding and cook until browned on all sides, about 8 minutes. Repeat with the remaining chicken, adding oil to the pan as necessary, until all of the chicken has been cooked. Remove from the pan and set aside.

Heat 2 more tablespoons oil in the same pan over medium heat. Add the diced onion and cook until tender and translucent, about 10 minutes. Set aside with the chicken.

Heat 2 more tablespoons oil over high heat in the same pan. Add the mushrooms and cook quickly until they are tender and release some of their juices, about 5 minutes. Return the chicken, onions, and meatballs to the pan. Add the stock, bring to a boil, reduce the heat, and simmer until all is heated through. Sprinkle with the chopped herbs and serve with rice, or better yet, risotto, or still better yet, risotto with peas. Even mashed potatoes are fine for sopping up the juices.

***Wine Notes:*** In whites, choose a Chardonnay rich in earthy and mineral-scented flavors, or a complex nongrassy Sauvignon Blanc. In reds, Pinot Noir is a no-miss selection, while Napa Gamay, Dolcetto d'Alba, or a villages-level and above Beaujolais will more than suffice. A dry, refreshing rosé wine makes a lovely accompaniment, too.

## CHICKEN WITH ROASTED CHILIES AND SPICED CREAM

♦ *Serves 2*

*2 whole chicken breasts*

*4 tablespoons olive oil*

*Salt and freshly ground pepper*

*1 cup cubed ( ½ inch) or half
rounds of zucchini*

*½ cup Chicken Stock
(page 119)*

*1 cup cauliflower florets
(1 inch), cooked until
tender-crisp and blanched*

*1 cup corn kernels*

*2 to 3 tablespoons diced,
roasted poblano chilies*

*½ teaspoon ground cinnamon*

*½ teaspoon ground cumin*

*1½ cups heavy cream*

*2 tablespoons each chopped
fresh mint and cilantro*

Not quite a Mexican fantasy, this little pan ragout is a combination of two recipes, one for chicken, the other for vegetables. While I can't accurately pinpoint my sources, what I do recall are all the happy sounds emanating from my guests whenever I serve this dish. A thank you to Diana Kennedy and Rick Bayless for general inspiration.

### Procedure

Remove the skin and bones from the breasts and cut each in half. Then cut the 4 halves into 1½- to 2-inch chunks. Heat 2 tablespoons of the olive oil in a large sauté pan or skillet over high heat. Working in batches, if necessary, add the chicken and cook until browned on all sides. Sprinkle with salt and pepper. Remove from the pan and set aside. Add the remaining 2 tablespoons oil to the pan. Stir in the zucchini, then add the chicken stock and cook 1 to 2 minutes. Add the cauliflower, corn, and chilies and cook for 1 minute more. Return the chicken to the pan, add the cinnamon and cumin, and then the cream. Bring to a boil and cook until slightly thickened. Season with salt and pepper. Sprinkle with the mint and cilantro and serve with rice, black beans, and, if you have time, a little quesadilla stuffed with Monterey Jack cheese and avocado.

***Wine Notes:*** White or red will work. For whites, try an un-oaky California Chardonnay, an Australian Chardonnay-Semillon blend, or a Gewürztraminer or dry Muscat from Alsace. Reds should have good fruit and minimal tannin . . . Pinot Noir, of course.

# MOROCCAN CHICKEN SALAD

♦ *Serves 4*

### Charmoula Vinaigrette

*1 tablespoon ground cumin*

*1 teaspoon paprika*

*½ teaspoon cayenne pepper*

*2 tablespoons finely minced garlic*

*½ cup (or to taste) fresh lemon juice, or combination lemon juice and red wine vinegar*

*½ cup chopped parsley*

*½ cup chopped fresh cilantro*

*1¼ cups olive oil*

*Salt and freshly ground pepper*

*8 boneless, skinless chicken breast halves*

*2 green or combined red and green bell peppers, seeded, cored, and thinly sliced*

*1 red onion, thinly sliced*

*16 to 20 Moroccan or niçoise olives*

Everyone loves chicken salad. Even real men who don't eat quiche eat chicken salad. Charmoula, the traditional Moroccan marinade for fish, makes a great vinaigrette for vegetables, shellfish, and tuna—and chicken salad.

### Procedure

Cook the chicken by any method you like: Brush with olive oil and grill or broil 3 to 4 minutes each side, sauté 4 to 5 minutes each side in olive oil over medium heat, or poach 8 to 10 minutes in simmering chicken stock. Do not overcook. Let stand until cool enough to handle. Then slice into ½-inch-wide strips.

For the Charmoula vinaigrette, combine the dry spices, the garlic, and some of the lemon juice or combination lemon juice and vinegar in a mortar, or whisk together in a medium bowl. Blend in the remaining lemon juice or combination lemon juice and vinegar, the chopped herbs, and the olive oil. Season to taste with salt and pepper and additional vinegar or lemon juice, if you like.

To serve, toss the chicken strips, peppers, and onions with the prepared vinaigrette in a serving bowl. Garnish with the olives.

**Wine Notes:** Warm Mediterranean reds are best: Grenache-accented Côtes du Rhône, Gigondas, and Châteauneuf-du-Pape in the Rhône, any firm red from the Midi, or a Spanish red from Catalonia. Fragrant perfumed whites are a nice foil: Riesling from Germany, New York, or the Pacific Northwest, or the wines of Alsace and the Loire Valley's Anjou and Touraine.

## CATALAN-STYLE QUAIL STUFFED IN ROASTED PEPPERS

♦ *Serves 6*

*12 red bell peppers*

*12 quail, preferably boned*

*2 tablespoons olive oil*

*Salt and freshly ground pepper*

**Sauce**

*3 large heads garlic*

*Olive oil, as needed, for roasting*

*Leaves from 3 fresh thyme sprigs*

*3 cups strong duck, quail,*
  *Chicken Stock (page 119)*
  *or brown veal stock*

*2 cups finely chopped toasted*
  *almonds*

*⅓ cup pitted, diced combination*
  *green and black olives*

*½ teaspoon freshly ground*
  *pepper*

Sort of a Spanish "quail in a blanket." For people who think that quail is just a mere mouthful and fear that they will be hungry moments after eating, don't worry—this dish is rich and satisfying. The flavors are complex and intense, and the sauce of roasted garlic, almonds, and olives combined with the roasted peppers adds a meaty quality to the little birds. Plan on two per person, and maybe grilled eggplant and sautéed green beans or asparagus as accompaniments. If you feel the need to add a starch, roast potatoes or plain rice will round out the plate. Grilled bread will do nicely, too— maybe better, to sop up the sauce. This is a very pretty dish and well worth the effort.

### Procedure

Char the peppers in a broiler or over direct flame, turning often with tongs, until they are blackened on all sides. Transfer to a plastic container with a lid, or a paper or plastic bag. Cover the container or close the bag and let the peppers steam for about 15 minutes. Then peel off the skins with your fingers, scraping off any stubborn pieces of peel with a knife blade. Do not wash the peppers, if possible.

Meanwhile, heat a grill or broiler. Brush the quail with olive oil and sprinkle with salt and pepper. Grill or broil just to mark and color the skin, about 2 minutes each side. Or, heat the oil in a large sauté pan or skillet over medium high heat. Add the quail and cook until browned, about 2 minutes each side.

Stem, core, and seed the peppers. Then cut them down one side so they will lie flat. Wrap a roasted pepper around each quail and secure with toothpicks if necessary. (The quail may be wrapped several hours ahead and refrigerated.)

For the sauce, preheat the oven to 375 degrees. Cut the tops from the garlic heads and rub the heads with oil. Place in a baking pan and sprinkle with thyme. Cover with foil and bake until the garlic is very soft, 1 to 1½ hours. Let stand until cool enough to handle and then squeeze the skins to press out the roasted garlic. Pass through a food mill or large-holed strainer to remove all the peel. (You should have about ¼ cup garlic purée.)

Combine the garlic purée and the stock in a medium saucepan and whisk until smooth over low heat. Bring to a simmer and whisk in the almonds and the diced olives. Simmer 10 minutes. (The sauce may be made several hours ahead.)

Preheat the oven to 450 degrees. Place the quail on a baking sheet and bake until warmed through, 10 to 15 minutes. Reheat the sauce. Place 2 quail on each serving plate and spoon the hot sauce over the birds. Serve at once with grilled eggplant and sautéed green beans or asparagus, and roasted potatoes or white rice, if you like.

*Wine Notes:* Most any medium-bodied red wine will suffice: Rioja and other Spanish reds (Navarra, La Mancha, Tierra del Barros), Tuscan Sangiovese-based wine with an emphasis on young ripe fruit, American Pinot Noir, or a flavorful Portuguese Dão. If you want white, a rich Semillon from Australia or Washington State would also be good.

## MUSHROOM-STUFFED QUAIL WRAPPED IN GRAPE LEAVES

◆ *Serves 6*

*6 tablespoons unsalted butter*

*2 large onions, diced (about 3 cups)*

*½ teaspoon salt*

*½ teaspoon freshly ground pepper*

*1 pound mushrooms, diced*

*2 tablespoons chopped fresh marjoram*

*12 boneless quail*

*24 bottled grape leaves, rinsed and dried*

*12 strips (⅛ inch thick) pancetta*

It's not just the Italians who have a penchant for the quail/polenta combination. So do the Romanians, who call polenta *mamaliga* and like to garnish the soft cornmeal mush with a medley of sweet and smoked cheeses. This recipe is from the southern part of Romania.

### Procedure

Melt 3 tablespoons butter in a small sauté pan or skillet over medium heat. Add the onions and cook until soft, about 10 minutes. Season with the salt and pepper and set aside. Melt the remaining 3 tablespoons butter in a second sauté pan or skillet over medium heat. Add the mushrooms and cook until they release some of their juices, about 5 minutes. Add the onions and the marjoram to the pan and cook 2 to 3 more minutes. Season the mixture with additional salt and pepper to taste. Let stand until completely cooled.

Spoon the cooled stuffing into the cavities of the quail. Wrap the quail in the grape leaves and then in pancetta. Secure with toothpicks.

Heat a grill or broiler. Grill or broil the quail until medium-rare to medium, about 4 minutes each side. Remove the toothpicks and place 2 quail on each of 6 serving plates. Serve with soft polenta sprinkled with smoked mozzarella and fresh ricotta or cream cheeses. Grilled peppers and eggplant make nice vegetable accompaniments.

**Wine Notes:** Merlot from California, Washington, or Long Island, or a red wine from Bordeaux with a high percentage of Merlot in the blend. Pinot Noir will go well, as will wines from the coastal Mediterranean, especially Provence (Bandol) and the Languedoc. Medium to full-bodied wines from the central part of Italy are also excellent choices.

## QUAGLIE ALLA MELAGRANA
### Quail with Pomegranate, Orange, and Marsala

• *Serves 4*

8 quail, preferably boneless (*see note 1*)

½ cup pomegranate syrup or ⅓ cup molasses (*see note 2*)

1 cup fresh orange juice

1 cup marsala

½ cup (*or to taste*) honey

2 cups reduced Chicken Stock (*page 119*)

2 tablespoons grated orange zest

Salt and freshly ground pepper

32 orange segments

½ cup pomegranate seeds

I recently ate a dish in Greece very similar to this one, described as Byzantine quail and implying ancient times, but this is a Renaissance recipe from the Veneto. The sauce would work well on squab or duck. During the fall and winter, the colorful garnish of orange segments is further enhanced with a sprinkling of ruby-red fresh pomegranate seeds. Serve with saffron risotto and sautéed spinach with pine nuts and you have a most elegant and dramatic plate that tastes as wonderful as it looks.

### Procedure

Place the quail side-by-side in a nonaluminum container. Whisk together the pomegranate syrup or molasses, the orange juice, marsala, and honey in a small bowl. Set aside ¾ cup of this mixture and pour the remainder over the quail. Cover and refrigerate the quail for at least 6 hours, or overnight.

Bring the quail to room temperature. Heat a grill or broiler. Remove the quail from the marinade; reserve the marinade for basting. Grill or broil the birds until medium rare, basting a few times with the reserved marinade, about 4 minutes each side.

For the sauce, combine the reserved ¾ cup pomegranate-orange mixture with the reduced

(*continued*)

chicken stock and orange zest in a small saucepan and bring to a boil. Season to taste with salt and pepper. Remove from the heat and add the orange segments.

Place 2 birds on each of 4 serving plates. Pour the sauce and orange segments over the birds and sprinkle with pomegranate seeds. Serve with saffron risotto and sautéed spinach.

*Note 1:* You may also prepare this dish with 4 butterflied squab or two 5 to 6 pound ducks. To butterfly the squab, cut down both sides of the backbone to separate it from the body. Remove the breastbone, the central cartilage, and ribs. Marinate and grill medium rare, as you would the quail, 4 minutes, each side. For the ducks, roast in a 500-degree oven, basting often with the marinade, until cooked through, about 1 hour. Use a reduced Duck Stock (page 248) rather than a chicken stock in the sauce.

*Note 2:* Pomegranate syrup is available at stores that specialize in Middle Eastern foodstuffs. It comes in two forms: a very thick dark "grenadine molasses" that is quite tart, and a syrup that is sweeter and thinner and is called a "concentrate."

*Wine Notes:* Merlot and Valpolicella from the Veneto are sure bets, as are other Italian wines like Barbera, Vino Nobile, and young fruity Chianti. A tame Petite Sirah from California, an American Barbera or ripe Zinfandel, or a youthful Spanish red would also be well matched. A very rich white wine, approaching off-dry, is a possibility, but not my first choice.

## FESENJAN

### *Duck with a Persian Sauce of Walnuts and Pomegranate*

♦ *Serves 4*

2 ducks, about 5 pounds each,
    necks, wing tips, and excess
    fat removed
Salt and freshly ground pepper
Cinnamon for duck, plus
    2 teaspoons for sauce
4 tablespoons unsalted butter
4 onions, chopped (about
    4 cups)
½ cup pomegranate molasses or
    ⅔ cup pomegranate syrup
    (see note, page 246)
⅔ cup Basic Tomato Sauce
    (page 319)
3½ cups of Duck Stock (page
    248) or Chicken Stock
    (page 119)
3 cups walnuts, toasted and
    chopped
Fresh lemon juice and sugar to
    taste (optional)

This is one of the most famous dishes of Persian cuisine, and deservedly so because it is so delicious. Fesenjan is usually served with chelo, Persian-Style Rice (page 160). Fresh pomegranate juice will work for this recipe, as will bottled pomegranate juice from the health food store. (Grenadine would not be right as it is much too bland and sweet.) Whichever pomegranate extract or juice you use, you will have to compensate for the sweetness or tartness, and cook the sauce until it is thick. I think the best results come with the molasses rather than the concentrate or the plain juice.

### *Procedure*

Preheat the oven to 450 to 500 degrees. Prick the ducks all over with a fork and rub them inside and out with a little salt, pepper, and cinnamon. Place the ducks on a rack in a large roasting pan and roast until cooked through, about 1 hour. Remove from the oven and let stand until cool enough to handle. Cut the ducks into quarters or eighths.

For the sauce, melt the butter in a large saucepan over low heat. Add the onions and cook until tender, about 15 minutes. Add the 2 teaspoons cinnamon and cook 1 to 2 minutes more. Add the pomegranate molasses or syrup, the tomato sauce, duck stock, and the walnuts and simmer until thickened, about 20 minutes. Season to taste with salt and pepper. Taste for balance and add lemon juice if the pomegranate syrup is too sweet, sugar if it is too tart.

Rewarm the ducks in the sauce and serve with Persian-Style Rice.

*(continued)*

## Duck Stock

♦ *Makes about 2 quarts*

*Carcasses, necks, wings, and
   feet of 4 ducks*

*2 onions, chopped*

*2 leeks, chopped*

*6 garlic cloves, smashed*

*12 black peppercorns, bruised*

*8 fresh parsley sprigs*

*3 fresh thyme sprigs*

*1 bay leaf*

### Procedure

Preheat the oven to 450 degrees. Break up the duck carcasses and place them with the necks, wings, and feet in a roasting pan. Roast until browned, about 30 minutes. Using a slotted spoon, transfer the duck parts to a stockpot, add enough cold water to cover, and heat to boiling. Skim the scum from the surface. Reduce the heat and simmer uncovered.

Meanwhile, pour off most of the fat in the roasting pan. Add the onions, leeks, and garlic to the pan and roast until browned, about 30 minutes. Add the vegetables to the pot. Pour ¼ to ½ cup water into the roasting pan, heat, scraping up the browned bits on the bottom, and add it to the pot. Add the peppercorns and herbs. Simmer uncovered 4 to 6 hours.

Strain the stock and chill, then remove the fat from the surface. Boil until reduced by about half. This stock can be stored in the refrigerator up to 1 week, or in the freezer up to 6 months.

**Wine Notes:** A less oaked Spanish red wine from Rioja or Valdepeñas; an exuberant young Pinot Noir from France, California, or Oregon; a juicy Côtes du Rhône or soft Zinfandel would all work. A steely white wine—Aligoté from Burgundy or tart Chardonnay from the New World, for example—are fine whites with this dish.

## THREE RECIPES FOR ORIENTAL ROAST DUCK WITH FRUIT

The classic combination of duck and fruit started in Renaissance Italy with duck in orange sauce, a recipe that French chefs embraced with fervor and have been serving to happy diners for years as *canard à l'orange.* Everybody loves a winner, so over time the fruit theme has been expanded to include cherries, grapefruit, mangoes, pears, figs, and peaches. Probably kiwis, too.

On the other side of the world, the Chinese embraced duck with equal fervor, and what follows are three Oriental inspired recipes for duck, one with peaches, almonds, and ginger, one with orange/tangerine and five spices, and one with pears, chestnuts, and ginger.

# ROAST DUCK WITH PEACHES, ALMONDS, AND GINGER

◆ *Serves 4*

**Spice Paste**

*1 tablespoon curry powder*

*2 tablespoons grated fresh ginger*

*1 tablespoon grated lemon zest*

*1 tablespoon grated orange zest*

*3 tablespoons fresh lemon juice*

*3 tablespoons fresh orange juice*

*2 ducks, about 5 pounds each, neck, wing tips, and excess fat removed*

**Sauce**

*½ cup reduced Duck Stock (page 248)*

*¼ cup fresh orange juice*

*2 tablespoons fresh lemon juice*

*1 tablespoon grated fresh ginger*

*¼ cup almonds, toasted and finely ground*

*2 tablespoons brown sugar*

*2 freestone peaches, peeled, pitted, and quartered (see note)*

## *Procedure*

For the spice paste, mix all the ingredients into a paste.

Preheat the oven to 500 degrees. Prick the ducks all over with a fork and rub inside and out with the spice paste. Place on a shallow rack in a roasting pan and roast until cooked through, about 1 hour. Let stand until cool enough to handle.

Meanwhile, for the sauce, combine all the ingredients except the peaches in a small saucepan. Set aside until serving time.

Cut the ducks into quarters or eighths and warm in a 450-degree oven for about 5 minutes. Bring the sauce to a simmer. Add the peach quarters and simmer until warmed through, about 5 minutes. Serve with rice or wild rice pilaf and sautéed spinach.

**Note:** White peaches would be elegant with this dish, although they are rarely freestone. They are worth the effort, however.

**Wine Notes:** A Rhône white (Condrieu), an Alsatian Pinot Gris, or a New World Chardonnay would be nice. You might also try an off-dry white such as a German kabinett from the Mosel or young Riesling from the Pacific Northwest. Gentle fruity reds à la Gamay (Beaujolais) are nice, too.

## ROAST DUCK WITH ORANGE, HONEY, AND SOY

◆ *Serves 4*

2 ducks, about 5 pounds each,
  necks, wing tips, and excess
  fat removed

**Spice Paste**

2 tablespoons grated fresh
  ginger

1 tablespoon grated orange or
  tangerine zest

2 teaspoons Chinese five-spice
  powder

1 teaspoon finely minced garlic

¼ cup soy sauce

¼ cup honey

**Sauce**

1 tablespoon grated fresh ginger

2 tablespoons peanut oil

1 teaspoon Chinese five-spice
  powder

½ cup reduced Duck Stock
  (*page 248*)

2 tablespoons soy sauce

1 teaspoon grated orange or
  tangerine zest

1 tablespoon (or to taste) honey

½ cup fresh orange or tangerine
  juice

Salt and freshly ground pepper

Orange sections (optional)

C lassic duck à l'orange with an Oriental twist. Orange segments and especially blood orange segments are a nice addition to the sauce. You can also make this with tangerines, tangelos, or—no pun intended—mandarin oranges.

**Procedure**

Preheat the oven to 450 to 500 degrees. Prick the ducks all over with a fork. Mix the grated ginger, orange or tangerine zest, five-spice powder, garlic, soy sauce, and honey into a paste. Rub the paste into the cavities of the ducks. Place on a rack in a shallow pan and sprinkle with salt and pepper. Roast until cooked through and tender, about 1 hour. Remove and let stand until cool enough to handle.

Meanwhile, prepare the sauce: Warm the grated ginger in oil in a small saucepan. Add the five-spice powder and cook 1 minute longer. Add the stock, soy sauce, and orange or tangerine zest and bring to a boil. Reduce heat and simmer 5 minutes. Add honey, orange or tangerine juice, and salt and pepper to taste.

Cut the ducks into quarters or eighths and warm in a 400-degree oven about 7 minutes. Bring the sauce to a simmer. Place the ducks on 4 serving plates and spoon the sauce over. Garnish with orange sections, if using. Serve with rice or sweet potatoes flavored with aniseed and ginger, or Sweet Potato Strudel (page 332) and sugar snap peas.

*Wine Notes:* Red wines work better than whites: Pinot Noir, Australian Shiraz, or Rhône styles from the south and California.

# ROAST DUCK WITH PEARS, CHESTNUTS, AND GINGER

♦ *Serves 4*

*2 ducks, about 5 pounds each, necks, wing tips, and excess fat removed*

**Paste**

*1 tablespoon grated fresh ginger*

*1 tablespoon grated lemon zest*

*½ teaspoon cinnamon*

*½ cup fresh lemon juice*

*¼ cup honey*

*Salt and freshly ground pepper*

**Sauce**

*20 fresh chestnuts*

*2 cups sugar*

*2 cups water*

*1 cinnamon stick*

*2 slices (½ inch thick) lemon*

*3 pieces (1 inch) fresh ginger, peeled and lightly smashed*

*3 whole cloves*

*2 Bosc or Comice pears, peeled, halved, cored, and stored in acidulated water*

*1 cup reduced Duck Stock (page 248) or use Chicken Stock (page 119)*

ere's a late autumn and winter duck recipe, when peaches are but a memory. I know this seems like a strange thing to say, but this duck dish is sexy. Something happens when the chestnuts poach in the ginger pear syrup and the two flavors intermingle. It's incredibly voluptuous, but this is not an X-rated duck. You can serve it to friends and family as well as lovers.

## Procedure

Preheat the oven to 450 to 500 degrees. Prick the ducks all over with a fork and place on a rack in a shallow roasting pan. Mix the grated ginger, lemon zest, and cinnamon into a paste and rub into the cavities of the ducks. Combine the lemon juice and honey and set aside. Sprinkle the ducks with salt and pepper and roast for about an hour until cooked through and tender, basting during the last half hour with the lemon-honey mixture. Remove the ducks from the oven and let stand until cool enough to handle.

Cut an X in the chestnuts with a small, sharp knife. Drop into a saucepan of boiling water and simmer 2 to 3 minutes to loosen the shells. Drain and peel while still hot, removing all the brown papery peel as well as the outer shell. The chestnuts should be firm and barely cooked. Set aside. (The chestnuts may be peeled a few days ahead.)

Combine the sugar, water, cinnamon stick, lemon slices, ginger, and cloves in a saucepan. Bring to a boil, reduce the heat, and simmer 5 minutes. Add the pears and poach gently until translucent but still

*1 tablespoon julienned blanched lemon zest (optional)*

*1 tablespoon julienned fresh ginger (optional)*

firm, about 25 minutes. Remove from the syrup with a slotted spoon and set aside. Add the reserved chestnuts to the syrup and poach until translucent and cooked through, about 15 minutes, depending on size. Remove from the syrup with a slotted spoon and set aside. Reserve the syrup. (The pears and chestnuts may be poached 1 day ahead.)

For the sauce, combine the duck stock and ½ cup of the reserved poaching syrup in a saucepan. Add the lemon zest and ginger julienne, if using. Cut each poached pear half into thirds and add to the sauce along with the poached chestnuts. Bring the sauce to a simmer and simmer until the pears and chestnuts are heated through.

Cut the ducks into quarters or eighths and warm in a 400-degree oven about 7 minutes. Place the duck pieces on 4 serving plates and spoon the sauce, pears, and chestnuts over. Serve with rice or wild rice pilaf with almonds, butternut squash gratin, and a sautéed green such as spinach, Swiss chard, or bok choy.

**Wine Notes:** See the selections for Roast Duck with Peaches, Almonds, and Ginger (page 250). Other good choices would be a round Sauvignon Blanc and dry Chenin Blanc from the Loire Valley. Young Pinots like those from smaller appellations in the Côte de Beaune (Santenay, Monthélie) and Côte Chalonnaise are sumptuous.

# INDONESIAN-STYLE ROAST DUCK WITH COCONUT

◆ *Serves 4*

*2 ducks, about 5 pounds each, necks, wing tips, and excess fat removed*

**Spice Paste**

*2 tablespoons grated fresh ginger*

*2 teaspoons finely minced garlic*

*2 teaspoons finely minced jalapeño peppers*

*¼ cup ground coriander*

*2 teaspoons ground cumin*

*2 teaspoons freshly ground pepper*

*2 teaspoons cinnamon*

*1 teaspoon turmeric*

*1 teaspoon ground cloves*

*2 tablespoons fresh lemon juice*

**Sauce**

*1 tablespoon grated fresh ginger*

*1 teaspoon finely minced garlic*

*½ teaspoon finely minced jalapeño peppers*

*1 teaspoon ground coriander*

*½ teaspoon cinnamon*

*½ teaspoon ground cumin*

In this Southeast Asian recipe the sauce for the duck has sweetness without fruit. Hot and pungent spices combine with the richness of coconut for a very tasty bird. I strongly recommend serving this with Indonesian Hot and Sweet Fruit Salad (page 29) to complement and cool the spices of the bird.

## Procedure

Preheat the oven to 450 to 500 degrees. Prick the ducks all over with a fork. For the paste, combine the spices, garlic, jalapeños, and the lemon juice and rub into the cavities of the ducks. Place the ducks on a rack in a shallow roasting pan and roast until cooked through, about 1 hour. Remove the ducks from the oven and set aside until cool enough to handle.

For the sauce, warm the ginger, garlic, jalapeños, and spices in the oil in a small saucepan over low heat. Add the stock, bring to a boil, reduce the heat, and simmer 10 minutes. Add the coconut cream and salt to taste. Taste for balance—you may want to bring up some of the spices, or add a drop of lemon juice for balance.

Cut the ducks into quarters or eighths and warm in a 400-degree oven about 7 minutes. Bring the sauce to a simmer. Place the ducks on 4 serving plates and spoon the sauce over. Serve with coconut rice, snap peas, and Indonesian Hot and Sweet Fruit Salad.

**Wine Notes:** The Indonesian variation of this duck can be treated as Roast Duck with Orange, Honey, and Soy (page 251), with a bit more emphasis on

*½ teaspoon freshly ground
    pepper*

*¼ teaspoon ground cloves*

*2 tablespoons olive oil*

*2 cups reduced Duck Stock
    (page 248)*

*½ cup coconut cream*

*Salt*

*Fresh lemon juice, as needed
    (optional)*

structure (the lemon and ginger crave tartness). Here, those headier reds of Syrah and Grenache are not as well married. Substitute wines of southwestern France (Languedoc, Aude and Gard) or a rustic red from Italy, such as Aglianico from the south.

# ROAST CURRIED DUCK WITH ORANGE, LEMON, HONEY, AND GINGER

◆ *Serves 4*

### Curry Citrus Sauce

*1 cup fresh orange juice*

*½ cup fresh lemon juice*

*¼ cup curry powder, dissolved in ¼ cup of the lemon juice*

*1½ teaspoons dried red pepper flakes, crushed*

*1 teaspoon ground cloves*

*¼ cup grated fresh ginger*

*½ to ¾ cup honey*

*¼ cup finely minced garlic*

*2 ducks, about 5 pounds each, necks and wing tips removed, excess fat removed*

*2 tablespoons curry powder*

*2 teaspoons finely chopped garlic*

*2 teaspoons dried red pepper flakes, crushed*

*2 tablespoons fresh lemon juice*

*Salt and freshly ground pepper*

I love combinations that are hot, sweet, and tart. The heat of the fresh ginger and red pepper, the pungency of the curry and cloves, the tartness of citrus, and the sweetness of honey combine in a balanced and complex sauce for duck. A piquant fruit-based chutney is a nice addition to the plate, but is not required for taste satisfaction.

### Procedure

For the sauce, combine all the ingredients in a small saucepan and bring to a boil. Remove from the heat. Set aside half for basting and reserve the remainder to serve as a sauce.

Preheat the oven to 450 to 500 degrees. Prick the ducks all over with a fork. Mix the curry powder, garlic, red pepper flakes, and lemon juice into a paste and rub it into the cavities of the ducks. Place the ducks on a rack in a shallow roasting pan and sprinkle with salt and pepper. Roast for half an hour, then start basting occasionally with half the basting sauce, until the ducks are cooked through, about 1 hour. Let stand until cool enough to handle.

Meanwhile, cook the reserved sauce until reduced by about half. Cut the ducks into quarters or eighths and place on 4 serving plates. Spoon the sauce over and serve with saffron rice, chutney (page 344), and spiced green beans or broccoli curry.

**Wine Notes:** Bold assertive whites like Gewürztraminer, off-dry but stated wines like Vouvray, or non-effervescent Moscato d'Asti are well matched with curry. Pinot Noir is quite nice as a red wine selection, and quality rosés with a hint of sugar—white Zinfandel, Rosé d'Anjou—work well.

## GRILLED SQUAB WITH BOURBON, HONEY, AND SOY

◆ *Serves 6*

*6 squab, about 1 pound each*
  *(see note)*

*1 cup soy sauce*

*½ cup bourbon*

*½ cup honey*

*3 to 4 garlic cloves, finely*
  *minced*

*1 tablespoon grated fresh ginger*

*Freshly ground pepper*

This is my favorite way to prepare and to eat squab. The traditional Chinese marinade produces a velvety-textured bird.

Unlike chicken, grilled squab are best served rare to medium-rare. The longer you grill them, the tougher and drier they become. Cooking them on a home broiler will take a bit longer than grilling over mesquite or charcoal. You should test for doneness rather than relying on times suggested in recipes; a discreet probe with a sharp knife will show you how far you have gone.

### Procedure

To butterfly the squab, cut down both sides of the backbone and remove. Then carefully remove the breastbone, the central cartilage, and ribs. Place the squab in a shallow nonaluminum container. Combine all the remaining ingredients except the pepper and pour over the squab. Cover and refrigerate overnight. (Do not marinate more than 24 hours or the ginger will cause the meat to break down and become mushy.)

Bring the squab to room temperature. Heat a grill or broiler. Remove the squab from the marinade and sprinkle with a bit of pepper. Grill or broil, skin side away from the flame, about 4 minutes. Then turn and cook 3 more minutes. (Do not worry if the squab are very brown—the honey will caramelize and give the squab a great flavor.) Transfer to 6 serving plates and serve with rice, sprinkled with chopped green onion, and stir-fried snow peas, grilled Japanese eggplant, or sautéed spinach.

*(continued)*

**Note:** For a change of pace, substitute 2 quail for each squab; quail pick up the marinade quite nicely but their texture is less voluptuous.

**Wine Notes:** For whites, choose off-dry wines—Riesling from Washington State or Germany, fresh Vouvray and Saumur from France, or very ripe/apparently sweet New World Chardonnay. In reds, my preference, go with lighter lively wines: Beaujolais, Dolcetto, less tannic styles of Zinfandel or Pinot Noir are all excellent.

# ROAST DUCK WITH A MEXICAN SAUCE OF SESAME AND CHILIES

◆ *Serves 4*

*2 ducks, about 5 pounds each, neck, wing tips, and excess fat removed*

**Spice Paste**

*¼ cup sesame seeds, toasted and ground in a spice mill*

*2 teaspoons finely minced garlic*

*2 teaspoons cinnamon*

*½ teaspoon ground cloves*

*1 teaspoon dried oregano*

*1 tablespoon each lemon zest and juice*

Again, the taste theme of sweet, hot, and tart, but in another language.

**Procedure**

Preheat the oven to 500 degrees.

Prick the ducks all over with a fork. Mix together all the ingredients for the spice paste and rub over the outsides and into the cavities of the ducks. Place the ducks on a rack in a shallow roasting pan and roast until fully cooked, about 1 hour. Let stand until cool enough to handle.

Meanwhile, prepare the sauce: Combine the sesame seeds, spices, garlic, peppers, vinegar, orange juice, zests, and salt and pepper in a small saucepan. Add the duck stock and bring to a simmer over medium heat. Taste and adjust seasonings—you may want to add a pinch or two of brown sugar to round out the flavor.

1 tablespoon each lime zest and
juice

1 tablespoon each orange zest
and juice

**Sauce**

1/3 cup sesame seeds, toasted
and ground in a spice mill

2 tablespoons chili powder blend

2 teaspoons cinnamon

1 teaspoon dried oregano

1/2 teaspoon cumin

Pinch of ground cloves or
allspice

1 tablespoon finely minced garlic

1 teaspoon finely minced
jalapeño peppers

2 tablespoons sherry wine
vinegar

1/2 cup orange juice

2 teaspoons lemon or lime zest

2 teaspoons orange zest

1 teaspoon salt

1/2 teaspoon freshly ground
pepper

1 1/2 cups reduced Duck Stock
(page 248) or Chicken Stock
(page 119)

2 tablespoons (or as needed)
brown sugar

Preheat the oven to 400 degrees. Cut the ducks into quarters or eighths and warm in the oven about 7 minutes. Return the sauce to a simmer. Transfer the ducks to serving plates and spoon the sauce over. Serve with black beans, a compote of mangoes, jalapeño, and lime, and rice or corn ragout with peppers and tomatoes.

**Note:** The spice paste will also work very well on pork tenderloin, cut into cubes, and skewered and grilled, or on a roast loin of pork.

**Wine Notes:** Even better than beer are spicy, fruity medium-bodied reds: Côtes du Ventoux from the Rhône Valley, Côtes de Provence, Corbières, and Fitou. Reliable Pinot Noirs of substance are fine: Côte de Nuits, California and Oregon. Tart lively whites are surprisingly good here: northeastern Italian Pinot Grigio or Sauvignon, Alsatian Pinot Blanc or Sylvaner, or a lean lemon-scented Chardonnay from Chablis or America.

# M E A T S

Shashlyk ◆ Grilled Lamb Loin with Honey, Mustard, Sherry, and Mint ◆ Roast Leg of Lamb alla Perugina ◆ Lamb with Moroccan Mint Mechoui ◆ Yogurtlu Kebab ◆ Grilled Lamb in an Uzbek Marinade ◆ Lamb in an Indian Marinade ◆ Afghani Lamb Sausages ◆ Moroccan Tagine of Lamb with Prunes and Honey ◆ Tfina Djerbaliya ◆ Do Piaza ◆ Pork Loin Marinated in Garlic and Paprika ◆ Roasted Pork Loin with Five-Onion Sauce ◆ Arista di Maiale alla Fiorentina ◆ Apples in Spiced Red Wine ◆ Rojoes Cominho ◆ Roast Pork Loin Braziliana with Chilies

AND GINGER ◆ ROAST PORK LOIN WITH POMEGRANATE AND ORANGE ◆ ROAST LOIN OF PORK IN GINGER MARINADE ◆ GYPSY GOULASH ◆ PORK SCALOPPINE WITH PAPRIKA, WALNUTS, SAGE, AND CREAM ◆ SARTIZZU ◆ CHOUCROUTE ◆ BURGUNDIAN SAUSAGE ◆ CHURRASCO: BRAZILIAN MIXED GRILL ◆ BARBECUE MARINADES FOR STEAKS: BARBECUE MARINADE ◆ MUSTARD, SOY, AND BROWN SUGAR MARINADE ◆ BASTURMA ◆ GRILLED RIB-EYE STEAK WITH MUSTARD, ONIONS, AND CARAWAY ◆ GEORGIAN TOMATO SAUCE FOR BEEF OR VEAL ◆ BEEF À LA STROGANOFF REVISITED ◆ PEPPERED FILLET OF BEEF WITH COGNAC MUSTARD CREAM ◆ GRILLED STEAK WITH ARMAGNAC, RAISINS, AND BLACK PEPPER ◆ HUNGARIAN BANDIT'S STEAK ◆ BRAISED BRISKET OF BEEF ◆ GEORGIAN BEEF RAGOUT ◆ CATALAN BEEF RAGOUT ◆ VEAL ROLLATINI WITH GORGONZOLA AND WALNUTS ◆ BRACIOLETTINE DI VITELLO ALLA MESSINESE ◆

# SHASHLYK
### *Russian Grilled Lamb Kebab*

♦ *Serves 6*

*3 pounds boneless leg of lamb, trimmed of excess fat and connective tissue and cut into 2-inch cubes, or 3 pounds well-trimmed loin of lamb, 12 large loin lamb chops, or 18 to 24 baby rib chops*

### *Marinade*

*¾ cup pomegranate syrup (see note, page 246)*

*¼ cup red wine*

*1 large onion, grated or puréed in a food processor*

*3 tablespoons fresh lemon juice*

*2 tablespoons chopped fresh cilantro*

*2 teaspoons freshly ground pepper*

*½ cup mild olive oil*

*1 teaspoon salt*

*2 red onions, cut into cubes*

*Olive oil for brushing*

*Salt and freshly ground pepper*

*1 teaspoon ground cloves*

When I was a little girl my mother would get misty-eyed whenever she talked about shashlyk (aka shish kebab). In those days waiters would come to the table brandishing them on flaming swords.

Traditionally shashlyk is a brochette of cubed lamb. Using leg of lamb for brochettes creates lots of leftovers, which is wonderful if you are planning to make ground lamb patties or moussaka or lamb sauce for pasta. If that is the case, get the leg, bone it, cube the choice part, and grind the rest. However, lamb loin takes the marinade beautifully, as do lamb chops or racks, with no waste at all. Less work for the same delicious flavor. Serve this with a cracked wheat pilaf with cilantro and green onions, spicy prune or plum Tkemali Sauce (page 237), grilled onions that have been marinated in the shashlyk marinade, grilled eggplant, or Spinach Borani.

### *Procedure*

Place the lamb in a shallow, nonaluminum container. Combine marinade ingredients and pour over meat. Cover and refrigerate overnight, or up to 2 days.

Bring the lamb to room temperature. Heat the grill or broiler. Remove the lamb from the marinade; reserve the marinade. Thread the meat onto 6 skewers, alternating with the red onion chunks. Brush with olive oil and sprinkle with salt and pepper and the ground cloves. Broil or grill, basting occasionally with the marinade and turning to brown evenly, 8 to 12 minutes for medium-rare.

## GRILLED LAMB LOIN WITH HONEY, MUSTARD, SHERRY, AND MINT

♦ *Serves 4*

**Marinade**

*¼ cup honey*

*¼ cup dry sherry*

*½ cup olive oil*

*¼ cup chopped fresh mint*

*1 tablespoon whole cumin,
     toasted and ground in a
     spice mill*

*3 tablespoons combination part
     Dijon and Square One Hot
     Mustard (page 348)*

*2 pounds lamb loin trimmed of
     excess fat and connective
     tissue*

**Sauce**

*½ cup dry sherry reduced to
     ⅓ cup*

*1 cup strong Lamb Stock (page
     265) or reduced Chicken
     Stock (page 119)*

*1 teaspoon ground cumin*

*¼ cup chopped fresh mint*

*2 tablespoons prepared mustard*

*1 tablespoon honey*

*Salt and freshly ground pepper
     to taste*

While this is not a traditional Spanish recipe, the aura of Spain permeates this dish. This is what happens when you take some signature flavors from a country's cuisine and combine them to create a new but traditionally inspired dish.

### Procedure

For the marinade, warm the sherry, honey, and olive oil in a small pan over low heat. Remove from the heat, add the chopped mint, and let infuse 20 minutes. When cool, whisk in the remaining marinade ingredients and pour over the lamb in a nonaluminum container. Cover and refrigerate overnight or up to 48 hours.

Combine the ingredients for the sauce in a small saucepan. Bring to a simmer over medium heat and cook 5 minutes; set aside.

Bring the lamb to room temperature. Heat a grill or broiler. Remove the lamb from the marinade and grill or broil until rare or medium-rare, 3 to 4 minutes each side. Slice and arrange on 4 serving plates. Return the sauce to a simmer and spoon over the meat. Serve with fried potatoes and carrots, green beans, or asparagus.

**Wine Notes:** You will have a harder time finding a red wine that does not work than one that does! A Cabernet, be it from Bordeaux, Washington, Long Island, or California, would be splendid; Pinot Noirs shine with this dish. Spanish reds, especially those from the Ribera del Duero, are excellent.

## Lamb Stock

♦ *Makes 5 to 6 quarts*

*6 pounds lamb shanks and any
 meat trimmings*

*2 medium onions, coarsely
 chopped*

*3 carrots, coarsely chopped*

*1 celery rib, coarsely chopped*

*6 fresh parsley sprigs*

*2 fresh thyme sprigs*

*3 garlic cloves, smashed*

*2 small bay leaves*

*2 cloves*

*10 peppercorns*

*3 ripe tomatoes, sliced*

## Procedure

Preheat the oven to 450 degrees. Place the bones and any trimmings in a large roasting pan and roast until well browned, about 1½ hours. Transfer to a large stockpot and cover with cold water (reserve the roasting pan). Bring to a boil and skim the scum from the surface. Reduce the heat and simmer uncovered 1 hour, skimming frequently the first half hour.

Meanwhile, pour off most of the fat in the roasting pan. Add the onions, carrots, and celery; cook on top of the stove or in the oven until tender and browned. Transfer the vegetables to the stockpot. Pour a half inch or so of water into the roasting pan and boil, scraping up the browned bits on the bottom with a wooden spoon or whisk. Add to the stockpot with the remaining ingredients. Simmer uncovered 4 to 6 hours.

Remove the solids from the stock with a slotted spoon or large skimmer. Strain the stock through a cheesecloth-lined strainer and let cool to room temperature. Refrigerate until cold, then remove the fat from the top. Reduce the stock if you want a more intense lamb flavor.

## ROAST LEG OF LAMB ALLA PERUGINA

♦ *Serves 6 to 7*

*1 cup chopped niçoise or
    kalamata olives, pitted*

*2 tablespoons grated orange zest*

*2 tablespoons chopped fresh
    sage*

*2 tablespoons finely minced
    garlic*

*2 tablespoons finely chopped
    anchovies*

*½ teaspoon freshly ground
    pepper*

*1 leg of lamb, about 6 pounds,
    boned and butterflied for
    stuffing*

*3 garlic cloves, slivered
    (optional)*

Perugia is a fabulous medieval hill town in Umbria, where I spent a few months of pure bliss, roaming the stepped streets and hills, smelling the most wonderful aromas wafting out of windows. Sage, garlic, and anchovy are traditional Umbrian seasonings, just right for leg of lamb. To these I added the olives with orange zest that are a classic snack food of the region.

For this recipe you will need a leg of lamb, about 6 pounds. Have the butcher remove the bone, or if you are in the mood, debone it yourself. Flatten the leg, remove excess fat and gristle, and spread the leg with the aromatic paste, then roll and tie. If you don't want to go to all this work, you can cut pockets in large loin lamb chops and put the stuffing inside, but it's not the same.

Incidentally, don't let the anchovy scare you. It adds a subtle saltiness that is better than salt and really picks up the other flavors.

### Procedure

Combine the olives, orange zest, sage, garlic, anchovies, and pepper and mix to a paste. Spread over the interior of the boned lamb and roll and tie at 2-inch intervals. If you like, make a few shallow incisions in the leg and insert a garlic sliver into each one. (You can never have too much of a good thing!)

Preheat the oven to 400 degrees. Place the tied leg of lamb on a rack in a roasting pan and roast until a meat thermometer registers 120 degrees for rare, 45 to 60 minutes. Let rest 10 minutes before carving. Then slice the leg and serve with mashed potatoes, green beans, Swiss chard, or carrots.

***Note:*** If you like, reserve about 3 tablespoons of the stuffing paste and simmer 10 minutes with 1 cup lamb stock to make a quick sauce.

***Wine Notes:*** An Umbrian Torgiano is sublime, as are similar styles such as Chianti Classico, Rosso di Montalcino, and Montepulciano d'Abruzzi. A Spanish Rioja or Navarra would work beautifully; so would a cru bourgeois Bordeaux, a spicy Washington State Merlot, or a Chilean Cabernet Sauvignon.

# LAMB WITH MOROCCAN MINT MECHOUI

◆ *Serves 6*

*1 leg of lamb, about 6 pounds, boned and butterflied*

*Marinade*

*1 cup chopped fresh mint*

*Juice of 2 lemons (about ¼ cup)*

*1 tablespoon finely minced garlic*

*2 tablespoons ground coriander*

*1 teaspoon cayenne pepper*

*2 teaspoons paprika*

*2 teaspoons ground cumin*

*2 teaspoons freshly ground pepper*

*¼ cup olive oil*

*½ cup orange juice (optional)*

*2 tablespoons chopped fresh mint (optional)*

Americans love lamb with mint. Most prefer sweet mint jelly, but a few enjoy the sharper English malt vinegar mint sauce. With this recipe they can have their mint in a savory way, with the romance of Morocco as an added bonus. This marinade is good on a butterflied leg of lamb, on cubed lamb brochettes, and on lamb chops. Serve with couscous and the North African-Style Beets and Carrots (page 324).

## Procedure

Place the lamb in a nonaluminum container. Combine all the ingredients for the marinade and rub over the meat. Cover and refrigerate overnight or let stand 2 to 3 hours at room temperature.

Bring the lamb to room temperature, if refrigerated. Heat a grill or broiler. Remove the lamb from the marinade and sprinkle with salt. Grill until a meat thermometer registers 120 degrees for rare, about 15 minutes. Let rest 10 minutes before carving. Then slice the leg and arrange on 6 serving plates. Sprinkle with a little chopped mint before serving, if you like.

*Wine Notes:* Robust and full-flavored reds are the call: hearty Piemontese Gattinara or Barbaresco, Rhône reds such as Cornas, Côte Rôtie, and Châteauneuf-du-Pape, Australian Shiraz-Cabernet blends, and those super Tuscans that combine Cabernet Sauvignon with the native Sangiovese.

# YOGURTLU KEBAB

♦ *Serves 4*

*½ cup white wine*

*14 garlic cloves*

*1 medium onion, chopped*

*4 tablespoons chopped fresh or
    2 tablespoons dried oregano*

*2 boneless loins of lamb, well
    trimmed, about 1 pound each,
    or 2 pounds boneless leg of
    lamb, well trimmed and cut
    into 1½-inch cubes for
    brochettes*

*1 tablespoon olive oil or
    unsalted butter*

*1 cup plain yogurt*

*Salt and freshly ground pepper*

*4 large rounds pita bread*

*1 cup Basic Tomato Sauce
    (page 349) seasoned with
    2 teaspoons ground cumin*

Most of us have eaten shish kebab served with pilaf. This classic Turkish kebab is served on top a bed of warm pita bread, then drizzled with a cumin-flavored tomato sauce and one with yogurt and garlic. It's a really wonderful combination, the textures very complex and the flavors quite rich. You may come to prefer this to the more restrained conventional kebab. As a summer variation, try adding fresh peeled and diced tomatoes, sprinkled with cumin, to the yogurt sauce and omit the cooked cumin tomato sauce entirely.

## Procedure

Combine the wine, 12 of the garlic cloves, the onion, and oregano in the container of a food processor or blender and pulse to purée. Pour over the lamb in a nonaluminum container. Cover and refrigerate overnight, or let stand at room temperature for a few hours.

Finely mince the remaining 2 garlic cloves. Heat the oil or butter in a small skillet over low heat. Add the garlic and cook a few minutes to soften. Scrape into a bowl with the yogurt, season with salt and pepper, and refrigerate until serving time.

Bring the lamb to room temperature, if necessary. Heat a grill or broiler.

Wrap the pita bread in foil and warm in a 375-degree oven, or in the top of a double boiler or steamer. Or place directly on the grill to warm for a minute or two on each side. Bring the tomato sauce to a simmer and keep warm. Bring the yogurt sauce to room temperature.

*(continued)*

Remove the lamb from the marinade, and, if making brochettes, thread the cubes onto 4 skewers. Sprinkle with salt and pepper and grill 4 to 5 minutes on each side, until rare, for loins, or 8 to 12 minutes total for brochettes. Slice the loin meat across the grain or remove the lamb cubes from the skewers.

Cut the warmed pita breads into quarters and place on 4 hot serving plates. Top with the lamb slices or cubes. Drizzle with tomato sauce and then the yogurt sauce. Serve with grilled eggplant and/or zucchini.

**Wine Notes:** This is as much a beer dish as it is wine. Wine fans will find Côtes du Rhône, Gigondas, or Saint-Joseph will work with this robust dish.

# GRILLED LAMB IN AN UZBEK MARINADE

♦ *Serves 4*

*Marinade*

*1 large onion*

*10 to 12 garlic cloves, finely minced*

*3 to 4 plum tomatoes*

*¼ cup chopped parsley*

*¼ cup chopped fresh cilantro*

*1 tablespoon ground coriander*

*2 teaspoons ground toasted cumin*

*1 tablespoon sweet paprika*

*1 teaspoon cayenne pepper*

*½ cup olive oil*

*8 loin lamb chops, about 1½ inches thick, or 12 baby rib chops, or 2 pounds boneless leg of lamb, well trimmed and cut into 1½-inch cubes for brochettes*

*Olive oil for grilling*

*Salt and freshly ground black pepper*

After all those years of thinking of Russia as one large unified country, it's fascinating to discover the ethnic differences in cuisine from the diverse regions that made up the former U.S.S.R. Here's a vibrant-flavored lamb marinade from the province of Uzbekistan. Lots of garlic, combined with pungent spices and a little tomato, infuses the meat with intense flavor.

## Procedure

For the marinade, place the onion, garlic, and tomatoes in the container of a blender or food processor and pulse to purée. Add the herbs, spices, and oil and pour over the lamb in a nonaluminum container. Cover and refrigerate overnight or let stand at room temperature for a few hours.

Bring the lamb to room temperature, if necessary. Heat a grill or broiler. Remove the lamb from the marinade and, if making brochettes, thread the cubes onto 4 skewers. Brush the meat with oil and sprinkle with salt and pepper. Grill, turning occasionally for even browning, 3 to 4 minutes on each side for rare to medium-rare. Serve with roasted potatoes with sour cream and sautéed carrots with diced onion, cumin, and paprika.

**Wine Notes:** See the suggestions for Afghani Lamb Sausages (page 273). Northeastern Italian reds, like Friulian Merlot, are also very good.

## LAMB IN AN INDIAN MARINADE

◆ *Serves 6*

*12 loin lamb chops, about 1½ inches thick, or 3 lamb loins, about 1 pound each, well trimmed, or 3 pounds leg of lamb, well trimmed and cut into 1½-inch cubes for brochettes*

### Marinade

*1 cup white wine*

*½ cup olive oil*

*Zest of 1 small lemon, cut into strips*

*4 garlic cloves, finely minced*

*2 teaspoons ground coriander*

*1 teaspoon ground ginger*

*1 teaspoon turmeric*

*1 teaspoon cinnamon*

*½ teaspoon ground cloves*

*2 teaspoons freshly ground pepper*

*½ teaspoon cayenne pepper*

For those who love Indian cuisine. Allow enough time for the marinade to penetrate the meat—preferably overnight, although 4 hours at room temperature would suffice. Serve with spicy mint chutney (page 344) or one of the fruit chutneys (pages 355–358).

### Procedure

Place the lamb in a nonaluminum container. Whisk together the marinade ingredients and pour over the lamb. Cover and refrigerate overnight.

Bring the meat to room temperature. Heat a grill or broiler. Remove the lamb from the marinade and, if making brochettes, thread the cubes onto 6 skewers. Then grill or broil the lamb 3 to 4 minutes each side for medium-rare, or 8 to 12 minutes total for brochettes. Serve with chutney, saffron rice seasoned with cloves, cinnamon and cardamom, spicy lentils (page 326), eggplant curry, or the vegetable curry of your choice.

**Wine Notes:** Because of the heat of this dish, I want light, refreshing, and fruity reds here: a good bottle of Beaujolais that I can throw on ice, or a lively Dolcetto or simple American Pinot Noir. Try chilling down a Côtes du Rhône or Chinon if you want something a bit weightier.

# AFGHANI LAMB SAUSAGES

♦ *Makes 4 4-inch sausages or*
   *4 patties*

*1 pound lean ground lamb*

*1 medium onion, puréed in a*
   *food processor or grated*

*1 teaspoon finely minced garlic*

*1 teaspoon curry powder*

*¼ teaspoon cinnamon*

*¼ teaspoon grated nutmeg*

*3 tablespoons dry bread crumbs*

*2 tablespoons finely chopped*
   *parsley*

*Salt and freshly ground pepper*
   *to taste*

*1½ feet hog casing (optional)*

*Olive oil*

Here's something to do with those lamb scraps you've accumulated from using the leg meat for brochettes: a simple but succulent lamb burger. You can grill these as patties, or fry as burgers. These are best dipped in bread crumbs before frying. I like to garnish these with Dried Apricot Chutney (page 358), but Raita (page 344) would be a good choice as well. They make a nice casual supper served with pilaf and a green vegetable.

### Procedure

Combine all the ingredients except the casing and the olive oil in a bowl and mix well with your hands. Fry a small ball as a test; taste and adjust.

Using the sausage attachment on a heavy duty mixer, stuff the casings with the lamb mixture and twist and tie to make 3- to 4-inch links. Or shape into 4 patties.

Heat a grill or broiler. If the sausages are in casings, prick all over with a fork. Brush with a little oil and grill or broil, turning occasionally to brown evenly, 8 minutes until cooked through. For patties, brush with a little oil and grill or broil 3 minutes each side until cooked through. (The sausages may also be sautéed in a little oil in a skillet; dip the patties first in bread crumbs to coat and then sauté.)

Serve with a cracked wheat or rice pilaf, and spinach pairs well with apricots or yogurt raita.

**Wine Notes:** A medium-bodied red wine marries well: a Valpolicella or Barbera, Shiraz or lighter-style blend from Australia, or a red from southern France such a Bergerac, Corbières, Côteaux de Languedoc, or Bandol. Earthy, spicy Pinot Noir is once again a sure bet.

## MOROCCAN TAGINE OF LAMB WITH PRUNES AND HONEY

♦ *Serves 6 to 8*

*1 pound pitted prunes*

*¼ cup (or as needed) mild olive or vegetable oil*

*4 tablespoons (or as needed) unsalted butter*

*4 pounds boneless lamb shoulder, trimmed well and cut into 1½-inch cubes*

*2 medium onions, chopped (about 2 cups)*

*2 teaspoons ground coriander*

*1½ teaspoons cinnamon*

*1 teaspoon ground ginger*

*Pinch of saffron*

*2 to 3 cups (or as needed) Lamb Stock (page 265)*

*¼ to ⅓ cup honey*

*Salt and freshly ground pepper*

*2 to 3 tablespoons sesame seeds, toasted*

You'll understand what the term "sweet-meat" means after tasting this North African ragout. It is very rich and needs little in the way of embellishment other than some couscous. Follow this with a simple salad.

### Procedure

Cover the prunes with warm water in a small bowl and let soak until needed.

Heat 2 tablespoons oil and 2 tablespoons butter in a heavy sauté pan or skillet over high heat. Add as many lamb cubes as will fit without crowding and brown on all sides. Transfer to a deep casserole. Repeat with the remaining lamb cubes, adding a little oil and butter to the pan as needed.

Heat the remaining 2 tablespoons oil and 2 tablespoons butter in the same pan over medium heat. Add the onion and cook until translucent, about 10 minutes. Add the spices and cook 3 minutes. Transfer the onion mixture to the casserole with the lamb, and add enough stock or water to barely cover the meat. Bring to a boil, reduce the heat, and simmer, covered, about 45 minutes. Drain the prunes and add to the stew. Continue cooking until the lamb is very tender, about 20 more minutes. Add the honey and salt and pepper to taste. Sprinkle with the sesame seeds, and serve with couscous.

**Wine Notes:** Fairly robust and ripe fruity reds are what we are looking for with this dish, such as Australian Shiraz, Rhône Valley reds like Gigondas and Crozes-Hermitage, California Zinfandel, Syrah or Petite Sirah and more rustic reds like Madiran and Cahors from southwestern France.

# TFINA DJERBALIYA

♦ *Serves 6 to 8*

*½ cup dried chick-peas*

*½ cup dried apricots, soaked in hot water to cover for a few hours*

*½ cup pitted prunes, soaked in hot water to cover for a few hours*

*¼ cup (or as needed) mild olive or vegetable oil*

*3 to 4 pounds boneless lamb shoulder, trimmed of excess fat and cut into 2-inch cubes*

*2 to 3 onions, diced (about 4 cups)*

*1 large green bell pepper, diced*

*4 garlic cloves, finely minced*

*1 teaspoon ground cumin*

*½ teaspoon ground allspice or cinnamon*

*½ teaspoon cayenne pepper*

*1 teaspoon freshly ground pepper*

*2 cups Lamb Stock (page 265) or water*

*Salt to taste*

*1 cup raisins (optional)*

This very rich and filling Moroccan Jewish sabbath dish is related to the traditional cholent, or stew, which cooks in the oven overnight. You can make this with beef as well as lamb. Or both. Serve with couscous.

## Procedure

Rinse the chick-peas and soak overnight in 2 cups cold water in the refrigerator. Drain and rinse again. Put the chick-peas in a saucepan with fresh cold water. Bring to a boil, reduce heat, and simmer covered, until tender, about 1 hour. Drain and set aside.

Drain and chop the soaked fruits. Set aside.

Heat the oil in a large sauté pan or skillet over high heat. Add as many lamb cubes as will fit without crowding and brown on all sides. Transfer to a deep casserole with a slotted spoon. Repeat with the remaining cubes, adding oil to the pan, if necessary.

Add the onions, green pepper, and garlic to the oil remaining in the pan and cook until softened, about 10 minutes. Add the spices and cook 5 minutes longer. Add the vegetable mixture to the casserole with the meat and then add the water or stock. Bring to a boil, reduce the heat, and cook, covered, for about 1 hour. Add the dried fruits and the raisins if using, and the chick-peas and cook until the meat is tender, about 30 minutes longer. Season to taste with salt. Serve with couscous.

***Wine Notes:*** Look for full-bodied whites with an edge of sweetness: Gewürztraminer, Muscat, American Chardonnays, and the like. Soft reds are nice too.

# DO PIAZA

**Lamb Curry with Onions, Cilantro, and Mint**

♦ *Serves 6 to 8*

*¼ cup (or as needed) olive oil*

*4 pounds boneless lamb shoulder, trimmed well and cut into 1-inch cubes*

*4 tablespoons unsalted butter*

*5 large onions, diced*

*1 tablespoon (or to taste) grated fresh ginger*

*1 tablespoon minced garlic*

*2 teaspoons turmeric*

*1 to 2 teaspoons cayenne pepper*

*2 to 3 cups (or as needed) Lamb Stock (page 265) or water*

*1 cup coarsely chopped fresh mint*

*1 cup coarsely chopped fresh cilantro*

*1 to 2 jalapeño peppers, coarsely chopped*

*3 to 4 tablespoons fresh lemon juice*

*Salt and freshly ground pepper*

Not only do the Americans, Italians, and Spaniards love mint with lamb, but so do the Indians. You can make this lamb curry as hot as you like. Just don't forget the raita to refresh your palate. *Do piaza* means two onions, or twice as many onions as meat. I don't use quite that many, but you can increase the amount if you like literal translations.

## Procedure

Heat the oil in a heavy sauté pan or skillet over high heat. Add as many lamb cubes as will comfortably fit without crowding and brown on all sides. Remove from the pan and set aside. Repeat with the remaining lamb cubes, adding a little oil to the pan as needed.

Melt the butter in a heavy casserole over medium heat. Add the onions and cook until tender and sweet, about 10 minutes. Add the ginger, garlic, turmeric, and cayenne and cook 1 to 2 minutes. Add enough lamb stock or water to barely cover the meat. Bring to a boil, reduce the heat, cover the pan, and simmer gently until the meat is tender, about 1½ hours.

Combine the mint, cilantro, and chopped jalapeños in a blender. Add the lemon juice and about 1 cup cooking liquid from the stew. Purée and then add to the casserole with the lamb. Simmer 1 to 2 minutes. Season to taste with salt and pepper, and adjust seasonings as needed—you may wish to add more lemon juice, ginger, or cayenne.

Serve with saffron rice, Indian Spicy Lentils (page 326), carrots with dill, and your favorite curry condiments.

*Wine Notes:* A medium-bodied amber beer is fantastic with this, but if wine is what you crave, muscular reds are fine: Côtes du Rhône, Nebbiolo d'Alba, more substantive cru-Beaujolais-like Morgon and Moulin à Vent, a medium-bodied Pinot Noir from California or Oregon, or Merlot.

## PORK LOIN MARINATED IN GARLIC AND PAPRIKA

◆ *Serves 4 to 6*

*1½ tablespoons finely minced garlic*

*1 tablespoon dried oregano*

*6 tablespoons olive oil*

*3 tablespoons paprika*

*1½ tablespoons ground cumin*

*1 teaspoon salt, plus additional for the meat*

*½ teaspoon freshly ground pepper, plus additional for the meat*

*2 pounds pork tenderloins or a boneless pork loin, well trimmed*

A special Spanish dinner had been planned and I was excited that a guest chef from Madrid was coming to work in my kitchen. Tomas Herranz arrived dressed in a dramatic black suit, billowy coat, and a stylish ponytail. He was young, energetic, and well organized. Like many talented cooks, Tomas didn't measure anything nor did he work from a written recipe. As everyone loved the pork he prepared, I wanted to re-create the dish. This recipe is my educated guess based on taste memory and a little research. It's a traditional recipe called *lomo de cerdo adobado,* with the garlic and paprika marinade enhanced by cumin and oregano. Tomas served this with eggplant purée enriched by aioli. But I like it with simple grilled eggplant and the aioli or the classic Romescu Sauce on the side. You can try it both ways and see which you prefer.

### Procedure

Warm the garlic and oregano with half the olive oil in a small sauté pan or skillet over low heat for 2 to 3 minutes, to release the aromas. Whisk in the paprika, cumin, the 1 teaspoon salt and ½ teaspoon pepper, and then the remaining oil, and cook 1 to 2

(*continued*)

minutes longer. Let cool to room temperature and then pour over the pork in a shallow, nonaluminum container. Rub the marinade into the meat and then cover and refrigerate overnight or up to 3 days.

Heat a grill or broiler. Remove the pork from the marinade and sprinkle lightly with salt and pepper. Grill or broil until cooked through, turning the meat occasionally, 8 to 10 minutes for the tenderloins, 15 to 18 minutes for the loin. Slice the meat and serve with Romescu (page 347) or aioli (note, page 76), fried potatoes, and grilled eggplant. Asparagus is also a nice accompaniment.

***Wine Notes:*** Spanish Rioja, red wines of the Penedès and La Mancha, Portuguese Periquita, Bucelas, or Colares are wonderful, as are Pinot Noirs from any-where, simple reds from Bordeaux, or Chianti-like Italian variations. Whites are delicious, too: a spicy Italian Vernaccia, a Spanish white from Catalonia, or a lean Chardonnay. And don't overlook dry rosés!

# ROASTED PORK LOIN WITH FIVE-ONION SAUCE

◆ *Serves 6*

*1 pork loin roast on the bone,*
  *4 to 5 pounds*

*4 large garlic cloves, cut into*
  *slivers*

*Salt and freshly ground pepper*

*3 to 4 cups Chicken Stock*
  *(page 119)*

### *Sauce*

*6 tablespoons unsalted butter*

*2 cups yellow onions, diced*

*2 cups red onions, diced*

*2 cups leeks (white part only),*
  *well washed and sliced*

*½ cup thinly sliced shallots*

*¼ teaspoon freshly grated*
  *nutmeg*

*Salt and freshly ground pepper*

*¼ cup chopped fresh chives*

One of my favorite soups is a French-inspired purée of five onions (page 110). After the onions cook for a long while they develop a wonderful sweetness. I thought a variation of this soup would make a great sauce. Potato pancakes are a great accompaniment; if time is tight, pan-fried or roast potatoes will do nicely.

### *Procedure*

Preheat the oven to 400 degrees. Cut shallow incisions in the loin between the meat and the bones and insert a garlic sliver into each one. Sprinkle meat with salt and pepper and place on a rack in a shallow roasting pan. Roast the pork until a meat thermometer registers 140 degrees for medium-rare, about 1 hour. Remove the meat in one piece from the bones and wrap in foil and keep warm. Reserve the bones for stock.

Roughly chop the reserved bones with a heavy knife or cleaver. Pour off the fat from the roasting pan. Add the bones to the pan along with enough chicken stock to cover, bring to a boil, reduce the heat, and simmer 30 minutes. Strain and reduce over high heat until you have 1 cup. (If you want to omit this step, you may use 1 cup chicken stock for the sauce.)

For the sauce, melt 3 tablespoons of the butter in a large sauté pan or skillet over low heat. Add the yellow and red onions and cook very slowly until meltingly tender and sweet, 30 to 50 minutes. Melt the remaining butter in a second sauté pan or skillet over low heat. Add the leeks and cook, covered, until tender, about 20 minutes. Add the shallots and cook

(*continued*)

10 minutes longer. Transfer the onion mixture to a blender or food processor and purée. Add the nutmeg and thin with the reserved pork stock. Season to taste with salt and pepper.

Preheat the oven to 400 degrees. Warm the foil-wrapped roast in the oven a few minutes until heated through. Then cut into slices. (Or, better yet, slice the pork and rewarm the slices gently in the warm sauce.) Arrange on 6 serving plates and top with the sauce. Sprinkle with the chopped chives. Serve with potato strudel, potato pancakes, pan-fried or roasted potatoes, and Apples in Spiced Red Wine (page 282).

**Note:** This five-onion sauce, made with chicken stock, is also excellent on poached salmon.

**Wine Notes:** Both whites and reds work equally well, although I lean to full-bodied and complex whites—local choices from Alsace or California, or Australian Chardonnays, and rich whites from the Graves. Spicy Pinot Noir, a true Merlot, and a cru-level Beaujolais would pair nicely as well.

# ARISTA DI MAIALE ALLA FIORENTINA

**Pork Loin with Rosemary, Garlic, Cloves, and Lemon**

◆ *Serves 6*

*1 pork loin roast on the bone, 4 to 5 pounds*

*4 to 6 garlic cloves, peeled and cut into slivers*

*3 tablespoons fresh rosemary leaves, plus 1 tablespoon for the sauce*

*Salt and freshly ground pepper*

*2 to 3 cups Chicken Stock (page 119)*

*¼ cup fresh lemon juice*

*½ teaspoon ground cloves*

I n Italy the pork is so sweet and tender that this classic Florentine roast vibrates with intense flavor. Because American pork is fatter and less sweet, I've accented the roast with a pinch of cloves and a little lemon juice. Simple oven-roast potatoes and bitter greens such as Swiss chard, dandelion, or broccoli rabe are ideal accompaniments to balance the richness of the pork.

### Procedure

Preheat the oven to 400 degrees. Cut shallow incisions in the roast between the meat and the bones and on the top of the roast and insert a garlic sliver and a few rosemary leaves into each one. Place the pork on a rack in a shallow roasting pan and sprinkle with salt, pepper, and a little rosemary. Roast until a meat thermometer registers 140 degrees, about an hour. Let the roast stand until cool enough to handle (about 15 minutes), and then remove the meat in one piece from the bones; reserve the bones. Wrap the meat in foil and set aside.

For the sauce, roughly chop the reserved bones. Pour off the fat from the roasting pan. Add the bones and the chicken stock to the pan, bring to a boil, reduce the heat, and simmer 30 minutes. Strain and add the lemon juice, the cloves, and the remaining 1 tablespoon rosemary, finely chopped. Return to the pan and simmer 5 minutes longer, to meld the flavors. (If you like you may add a bit more finely minced garlic to the sauce.) Season to taste with salt and pepper.

Preheat the oven to 400 degrees. Warm the foil-wrapped pork in the oven for a few minutes until

(continued)

heated through. Then slice and arrange on 6 serving plates. Return the sauce to a simmer and spoon over the meat. (Or you can pre-slice the meat and then, at serving time, heat the sauce in a large pan and warm the slices very gently in the sauce, for about 1 minute. Do not boil or the meat will toughen.) Serve at once.

**Wine Notes:** Full-flavored whites, herbal and slightly off-dry, are my first choice: German spätlese Riesling, Washington State Riesling, or even a Savennières from the Loire Valley. In reds, look for soft and fruity: Pinot Noir, Dolcetto, and lighter styles of Barbera, Chianti, and Rosso di Montalcino are all tasty accompaniments.

## APPLES IN SPICED RED WINE

♦ *Serves 6*

*3 firm apples, such as Granny Smith or Pippins, peeled, cored, and cut into quarters*

*1 bottle Pinot Noir or other red wine*

*1 cinnamon stick*

*3 whole cloves*

*3 allspice berries*

*4 tablespoons sugar*

If you are looking for a wonderful addition to your winter holiday dinner repertoire, try these apples. They are aromatic, spicy, and colorful, and an ideal accompaniment for roast pork or roast chicken.

### Procedure

Combine the wine and the spices and sugar in a large saucepan and bring to a boil. Reduce the heat, add the apples, and simmer, uncovered, until the apples are tender and translucent, about 35 minutes. Remove the apples from the syrup with a slotted spoon and set aside. Boil the syrup until reduced to 2 cups and then cool in an ice bath. Pour the cooled syrup over the apples, and, if possible, refrigerate overnight before serving. Bring to room temperature or warm slightly before serving.

# ROJOES COMINHO

**Portuguese Pork Roast with Cumin, Lemon, and Cilantro**

♦ *Serves 6*

*1 pork loin roast on the bone, 4 to 5 pounds*

*6 garlic cloves, cut into slivers*

**Spice Paste**

*3 tablespoons ground cumin*

*2 tablespoons finely minced garlic*

*1 teaspoon salt*

*1 tablespoon freshly ground pepper*

*¼ cup chopped fresh cilantro*

*3 tablespoons fresh lemon juice*

**Sauce**

*3 cups Chicken Stock (page 119)*

*1 teaspoon ground cumin*

*½ to 1 teaspoon grated lemon zest*

*½ teaspoon salt*

*1 teaspoon freshly ground pepper*

*3 tablespoons chopped fresh cilantro*

Portuguese cuisine is not very spicy, unless it includes piri piri hot sauce made with incendiary African chilies. This traditional pork roast is subtly flavored with cumin, lemon, and cilantro. I like to serve it with orange segments mixed with olives, roast or fried potatoes that have been sprinkled with cumin and chopped cilantro, and sautéed greens with toasted bread crumbs, a traditional Portuguese vegetable.

*Procedure*

Preheat the oven to 400 degrees. Cut shallow incisions in the roast between the meat and the bones and insert a garlic sliver into each. For the spice paste, mix the cumin, garlic, salt, pepper, cilantro, and lemon juice and rub over the roast. Place the roast on a rack in a shallow roasting pan and roast until a meat thermometer registers 140 degrees, about 1 hour. Let stand until cool enough to handle and then remove the meat in one piece from the bones; reserve the bones. Wrap the meat in foil and set aside.

For the sauce, roughly chop the bones with a large knife or cleaver. Pour off the fat from the roasting pan and add the bones to the pan along with the chicken stock. Bring to a boil, reduce the heat, and simmer until the stock is reduced by half. Remove the bones. Add the cumin, lemon zest, salt, pepper, and cilantro. Taste and adjust seasonings. (Or, for a simpler sauce, deglaze the roasting pan with the chicken stock and simmer until reduced by half. Then add the cumin, lemon zest, cilantro, and salt and pepper to taste.)

*(continued)*

Preheat the oven to 400 degrees. Warm the pork roast in the oven for a few minutes until heated through. Then slice and arrange on 6 serving plates. Return the sauce to a simmer and spoon over the pork.

***Wine Notes:*** Portuguese Dão or Bairrada, something Spanish from the Ribera del Duero, or even a Rhône Valley red wine with lots of Grenache are all well suited. A big but not necessarily complex white would hold up fine, too, such as an earthy style of Chardonnay or a Vernaccia.

# ROAST PORK LOIN BRAZILIANA WITH CHILIES AND GINGER

♦ *Serves 6*

*1 pork loin roast on the bone,*
    *4 to 5 pounds*

*4 large garlic cloves, cut into*
    *slivers*

*¼ cup grated fresh ginger*

*1 tablespoon finely minced garlic*

*2 teaspoons finely minced*
    *jalapeño peppers*

*3 tablespoons fresh lemon juice*

*3 tablespoons chopped parsley*

*¼ cup olive oil*

*Salt and freshly ground pepper*

*3 to 4 cups Chicken Stock*
    *(page 119)*

You'll definitely want to keep this spicy and aromatic pork dish in your repertoire. To follow through on the tropical theme, serve with rice mixed with toasted coconut and raisins, bitter greens like kale or chard cut into fine strips and braised with onions, garlic, and a pinch of hot pepper, and grilled pineapple or fried bananas.

## Procedure

Preheat the oven to 400 degrees. Cut shallow incisions in the roast between the meat and the bones and insert a garlic sliver into each one. Mix the ginger, minced garlic, jalapeños, lemon juice, parsley, and olive oil into a paste and rub over the pork roast. Place on a rack in a shallow roasting pan and sprinkle with salt and pepper. Roast until a meat thermometer registers 140 degrees, about 1 hour. Let stand until cool enough to handle and then remove the meat in one piece from the bones; reserve the bones. Wrap the meat in foil and set aside.

For the sauce, roughly chop the bones with a large knife or cleaver. Pour off the fat from the roasting pan. Add the bones to the pan along with the chicken stock. Bring to a boil, reduce the heat, and simmer until the sauce tastes of pork and the paste, about ½ hour. Strain.

Slice the pork. Return the sauce to a simmer and add the pork; warm gently until heated through. Arrange the pork slices on 6 plates and spoon the sauce over.

**Wine Notes:** It's reds all the way: Merlot, medium weight and intensity Bordeaux, Pinot Noir from California or France, as well as softer Rhône reds à la Crozes-Hermitage, Saint-Joseph, and Gigondas.

# ROAST PORK LOIN WITH POMEGRANATE AND ORANGE

♦ *Serves 6*

*1 pork loin roast on the bone, 4 to 5 pounds*

*4 large garlic cloves, cut into slivers*

**Spice Paste**

*2 tablespoons finely minced garlic*

*2 teaspoons grated nutmeg*

*2 tablespoons chopped fresh thyme*

*2 teaspoons grated fresh ginger*

*2 teaspoons salt*

*1 teaspoon freshly ground pepper*

**Basting Mixture**

*1 cup fresh orange juice*

*¼ cup honey*

*¼ cup pomegranate syrup (see note, page 246)*

*2 to 3 cups Chicken Stock (page 119)*

This pork recipe has evolved into a cross-cultural mélange with bittersweet flavors of the Middle East and the Orient. It started with a grenadine-glazed pork from Roy de Groot's *Feast for All Seasons;* the sauce was a variation on the classic port, citrus, and mustard Cumberland sauce the English like to serve with game. I found the pomegranate-based grenadine too sweet and substituted pomegranate syrup, which gives the dish a decidedly Middle Eastern accent. Then I replaced the port with the less sweet and more herbaceous vermouth. The ginger and mustard are Oriental in inspiration and add a zing that plays nicely off the sweet and tart aspects of the pomegranate and orange. I know this recipe would work well with duck, squab, and even lamb. But start with pork and go from there.

## Procedure

Preheat the oven to 400 degrees. Cut shallow incisions in the roast between the meat and the bone and insert slivers of garlic into each one. For the spice paste, mix the garlic, nutmeg, thyme, ginger, salt, and pepper to a paste and rub it over the pork. Mix together the orange juice, honey and pomegranate syrup for the basting mixture and set aside. Set the pork on a rack, in a shallow roasting pan and roast, basting occasionally with the basting mixture, until a meat thermometer registers 140 degrees, about 1 hour. Let stand until cool enough to handle and then remove the meat in one piece from the bones; reserve the bones. Wrap the meat in foil and set aside in a warm place while you make the sauce.

### Sauce

*2 tablespoons unsalted butter*

*¼ cup finely minced shallots*

*¼ cup pomegranate syrup
    (see note, page 246)*

*1 cup fresh orange juice*

*2 tablespoons Square One Hot
    Mustard (page 348)*

*2 tablespoons grated fresh
    ginger*

*½ teaspoon cayenne pepper*

*⅓ cup sweet vermouth*

*2 tablespoons orange zest*

*¾ cup pork jus (see recipe) or
    Chicken Stock (page 119)*

*2 tablespoons honey*

*Salt and freshly ground pepper*

For the pork jus, roughly chop the bones with a large knife or cleaver. Pour off the fat from the roasting pan. Add the bones to the pan along with the chicken stock. Bring to a boil, reduce the heat, and simmer until the stock has a nice rich pork flavor, about 30 minutes. Strain. You should have about 1 cup pork jus.

For the sauce, melt the butter in a small saucepan over low heat. Add the shallots and cook until soft, about 5 minutes. Whisk together the pomegranate syrup, orange juice, and mustard and add to the pan. Then add the ginger, cayenne, sweet vermouth, orange zest, and pork jus or chicken stock and simmer 1 to 2 minutes. Add the honey and salt and pepper to taste.

Preheat the oven to 400 degrees. Warm the pork roast in the oven for a few minutes until heated through. Then slice and arrange on 6 serving plates. Return the sauce to a simmer and spoon over the pork. Serve with Sweet Potato Strudel (page 332) or sweet potato and apple gratin and sautéed greens or brussels sprouts.

***Wine Notes:*** I like both well-structured off-dry white wines (German Rieslings, French Vouvray, Montlouis, and some American Riesling) as well as fruity young reds such as any Grenache-based wine from California, the Rhône, or Spain. In addition, youthful Carignan-based wines from France's Midi, Gamay wines from California or Beaujolais, and supple Italian reds all fit the bill.

# ROAST LOIN OF PORK IN GINGER MARINADE

◆ *Serves 4*

### Marinade

1 garlic clove

1 3- to 4-inch piece fresh ginger, peeled and sliced across the grain

2 tablespoons soy sauce

2 tablespoons tomato purée

1 tablespoon wine vinegar

¼ cup firmly packed brown sugar

½ cup chicken or beef broth

1 boneless pork loin, or
   2 to 3 pork tenderloins,
   2 to 2½ pounds, well trimmed

I have been cooking this pork roast recipe, with one variation or another, for many years, and it's always a crowd pleaser. You can use two or three little boneless tenderloins or a larger boneless roast. Don't forget to serve it with a chutney (page 344) or Square One Hot Mustard (page 348) and wait for compliments. Ginger pork is great for picnics, too. Cold (I really mean room temperature) roast pork makes a great sandwich with chutney or hot mustard smeared on the bread, and also goes well with Curried Rice Salad (page 44).

### Procedure

Combine all the marinade ingredients in the container of a food processor or blender and process to blend. Pour over the pork in a nonaluminum container. Cover and refrigerate overnight.

Bring the pork to room temperature. Preheat the oven to 350 degrees. Remove the pork from the marinade; reserve the marinade. Transfer the pork to a rack in a shallow roasting pan and roast, basting occasionally with the marinade, until a meat thermometer registers 140 degrees, about 1 hour for the pork loin, or 35 to 40 minutes for the tenderloins. Or, grill or broil the pork until cooked through, 20 to 25 minutes for the loin, 10 to 12 minutes for the tenderloins. Let the pork rest 10 minutes and then cut in thin slices. Serve warm or at room temperature.

**Wine Notes:** Both red and whites work well. I like German spätlese Riesling, spicy Chardonnays, and richer Rhône Valley whites like Condrieu. For reds, Pinot Noir, Italian Barbera, and Spanish Rioja are excellent.

# GYPSY GOULASH

♦ *Serves 6 to 8*

*1 tablespoon paprika*

*2 tablespoons finely minced garlic*

*1 teaspoon freshly ground pepper*

*2 pounds boneless pork shoulder, well trimmed and cut into 2-inch cubes*

*2½ pounds veal, well trimmed, cut into 2-inch cubes*

*3 tablespoons (or as needed) olive oil*

*½ cup diced pancetta or bacon*

*4 cups diced onions (2 to 3 onions)*

*2 cups diced green bell peppers (2 to 3 bell peppers)*

*2 tablespoons paprika*

*1½ cups diced fresh or canned plum tomatoes*

*2 cups (or as needed) strong veal or Chicken Stock (page 119)*

*Salt and freshly ground pepper*

I don't really know too many gypsies but the name struck me as romantic and dramatic at the same time. Even without a gypsy violinist circulating in the dining room, this robust winter dish received sighs of pleasure from my Hungarian friends. Some said it tasted like their Grandma's goulash. You can prepare this well ahead and, like most stews, it reheats beautifully. Instead of the traditional lard I used pancetta; you can also use bacon for a smokier effect. Lamb, pork, or veal, or a combination, are all good choices for the meat.

This hearty stew does not pretend to be a low-fat dish. It should be treated with nostalgic respect. And eaten with noodles and delight.

### Procedure

Mix together the paprika, 1 tablespoon of the garlic, and the pepper and rub over the pork and veal in a nonaluminum container. Cover and refrigerate overnight.

Heat the 3 tablespoons olive oil in a large skillet over medium-high heat. Add as many meat cubes as will fit without crowding and brown on all sides. Transfer to a large casserole. Repeat to brown all of the meat. Then add the pancetta and the onions and cook over low heat in the fat remaining in the pan until the onions are translucent, about 15 minutes. Add the diced peppers, remaining tablespoon garlic and the paprika and cook 10 minutes longer. Transfer to the casserole with the meat. Add the tomatoes and stock to cover. Season to taste with salt and

*(continued)*

pepper. Bring to a boil, reduce the heat, and simmer, covered, over low heat until the meat is tender, about 1½ hours. Taste, and adjust seasonings. Serve with buttered noodles flavored with caraway and toasted bread crumbs, and beets with sour cream and dill.

*Wine Notes:* Stick to mature medium-weight reds: Chianti, Rioja, American Cabernet Sauvignon (velvety and soft), or Merlot, developed Bordeaux, and any mellowed Pinot Noir are all sublime.

# PORK SCALOPPINE WITH PAPRIKA, WALNUTS, SAGE, AND CREAM

♦ *Serves 6*

### Brine

*6 tablespoons salt*

*10 tablespoons sugar*

*6 juniper berries, crushed*

*4 to 6 whole white or black*
   *peppercorns*

*2 whole cloves*

*3 bay leaves*

*Scant teaspoon dried or*
   *2 teaspoons fresh thyme*

*1 boneless pork loin, 2 to 2½*
   *pounds, well trimmed*

*1½ cups walnuts*

*½ to ⅔ cup olive oil*

*1½ cups Chicken Stock*
   *(page 119)*

*2 tablespoons paprika*

*2 tablespoons chopped fresh*
   *sage*

*2 cups heavy cream*

*1 tablespoon lemon zest*

*Salt and freshly ground pepper*

**W**hen you read a lot of cookbooks and talk to many people about family food, as I do, the origins of recipes begin to blur. I forget when or how I got the inspiration for this recipe. My intentions are honorable even if my memory is at an impasse, so if I've slighted my sources, I sincerely apologize. However, all is not lost. By analyzing the combination of ingredients, I recognize the flavors of Hungary and northern Italy. Who knows when this recipe crossed the border, or how many times. The paprika seems Austro-Hungarian, although it is used in the Trentino and Friuli regions of Italy as well. The walnuts and sage are more commonly combined in northern Italian cuisine. Just cook and enjoy and say thank you to whomever.

### Procedure

For the brine, combine the salt and sugar in a non-aluminum container. Add enough warm water to dissolve, and stir well. Add the remaining brine ingredients and the pork loin and enough cold water to just cover the meat. Cover and refrigerate overnight or up to 2 days.

Remove the pork from the brine; discard the brine. Cut the loin into eighteen ½-inch-thick slices. Pound lightly, about ¼ inch thick, between sheets of plastic wrap.

Preheat the oven to 350 degrees. Place the walnuts on a baking sheet and toast until fragrant, about 7 minutes. Let cool and then coarsely chop and set aside.

*(continued)*

Heat half of the oil in a large sauté pan or skillet over medium heat. Add as many pork slices as will comfortably fit in the pan and brown 2 to 3 minutes each side. Set aside to keep warm and repeat with the remaining pork slices, adding 1 to 2 tablespoons oil to the pan as needed for each batch. Pour off the fat in the pan, add the chicken stock, and deglaze, scraping up the browned bits on the bottom of the pan. Add the paprika and boil until reduced to about a cup. Then add the sage, cream, lemon zest, and half the walnuts and boil until reduced by half. Season to taste with salt and pepper. Place 3 pork slices on each of 6 serving plates and pour the sauce over. Top with the remaining chopped walnuts. Serve with pappardelle and sautéed beets, or with potato pancakes.

*Variation:* This sauce is very nice with grated orange zest instead of the lemon. Reduce the paprika to 1 tablespoon to bring out the marriage of sage, walnuts, and orange. You may also make this dish with boneless chicken breasts or veal scaloppine.

*Wine Notes:* Play to the richness of the cream and walnuts. Green and earthy Sancerre and Pouilly Fumé from the Loire Valley, Vernaccia and young Greco di Tufo from Italy, or a lean Chardonnay or robust Sauvignon Blanc from California are excellent choices among the whites. A spicy Pinot Noir, Italian Barbera, or any other high-acid red will also do the dish justice.

## SARTIZZU

**Sardinian Pork Sausage with Fennel and Cinnamon**

♦ *Makes 8 3- to 4-inch sausages or patties*

*2 pounds ground pork (⅓ the weight in fat)*

*2 teaspoons cinnamon*

*1 tablespoon fennel seed, toasted and ground*

*1 tablespoon freshly ground pepper*

*½ cup white wine*

*1½ teaspoons salt*

*2½ feet hog casing (optional)*

*Olive Oil (optional)*

Most of the prepared Italian sausages we buy are of the pungent and hot variety. In doing research for a Sardinian dinner, I came across a description of this sausage, seasoned with sweet spices and black pepper. It's a great change of pace. I like this in a pasta with onions, peppers, and greens. You can also sauté the meat in patties and serve with a little pan ragout of artichokes, peas, and potatoes.

### Procedure

Combine all of the ingredients except the casings and the olive oil in a bowl and mix well with your hands. Fry or poach a small ball of the mixture as a test; taste and adjust seasonings.

Using the sausage attachment on a heavy-duty mixer, stuff the casings with the sausage mixture and twist and tie to make 3- to 4-inch links. Or shape into 8 patties.

Prick cased sausage with a fork and grill or broil 7 to 8 minutes. For the patties, sauté in a little olive oil in a large skillet until cooked through, about 3 to 4 minutes on each side.

*Note:* If you like the taste of smoked sausages, heat a smoker or covered grill. Prick the sausages all over with a fork and smoke over low heat, according to the manufacturer's instructions, 15 to 20 minutes.

*Wine Notes:* A generous red wine is called for: Slightly older Barolo, Barbaresco, or Brunello di Montalcino, an herbal-scented Pinot Noir, or plain country reds from France's southwest or Tuscany are all very good. California Barbera, Syrah, and Zinfandel would also marry well.

## CHOUCROUTE

### Braised Spiced Sauerkraut with Pork and Sausage

◆ *Serves 8*

**Brine**

*6 tablespoons salt*

*12 tablespoons sugar*

*12 juniper berries, crushed*

*12 peppercorns, crushed*

*4 whole cloves*

*6 allspice berries*

*6 coriander seeds*

*4 bay leaves*

*3 thyme sprigs*

*1 boneless pork loin, 2½ to 3 pounds, well trimmed*

*1½ cups diced pancetta*

*1 large onion, thinly sliced (about 1 cup)*

*2½ pounds prepared sauerkraut, drained, and well rinsed, and drained again*

*4 to 5 cups (or as needed) Riesling or other slightly sweet white wine*

*1 teaspoon coarsely ground pepper*

*1 tablespoon ground juniper berries*

The classic Alsatian dish reinterpreted. Despite spirited debates with my French friends, I have chosen to roast the potatoes instead of boiling them because I think they taste better that way. The pork is cured in a brine and just one kind of sausage is added. I buy a good brand of sauerkraut at a reputable German grocer. If you use bottled or canned sauerkraut, drain it, rinse it well, cover it with an Alsatian or German or American Riesling, then simmer it with spices, pancetta, and onions.

### Procedure

Two days before assembling the choucroute, prepare the brine: Dissolve the salt and sugar in a little warm water in a nonaluminum container. Add the remaining ingredients, the pork loin, and enough cold water to just cover. Cover and refrigerate 2 days.

Sauté the pancetta in a heavy saucepan over medium heat until almost cooked through but not crisp. Add the onion and cook 10 minutes. Add the drained sauerkraut and enough Reisling to cover. Bring to a boil and then reduce the heat. Stir in the spices and currants and simmer, partially covered, 1 hour. (The sauerkraut may be cooked a day or so ahead and reheated at serving time.)

Preheat the oven to 400 degrees. Place the pork on a rack in a shallow roasting pan and roast until a meat thermometer registers 140 degrees, about 40 minutes. (Or, brush with oil and grill or broil the pork, turning occasionally, 15 to 20 minutes.) Set aside. Prick the sausages all over with a fork and

½ cup currants, soaked 30
minutes in hot water to cover,
and drained

16 to 24 small new potatoes

2 to 3 tablespoons olive oil

Salt and freshly ground pepper

8 to 16 Burgundian Sausages
(page 296)

bake at 400 degrees on a rack in a shallow baking dish until cooked through but not dry, 15 to 20 minutes.

Place the potatoes in a small baking dish. Rub lightly with oil and sprinkle with salt and pepper. Roast until cooked through but still firm, about 25 minutes.

Bring the sauerkraut to a simmer. Cut the pork into thick slices and add to the sauerkraut along with the cooked sausages. Simmer briefly to heat through. Serve with a ramekin of Dijon mustard and the roasted potatoes.

**Wine Notes:** I have found no better match for this classic dish than the wines of the Alsace—Riesling and Gewürztraminer. Try light and fruity reds, too, either the local Pinot Noir, Spätburgunder from Germany, or a delicate red from Burgundy (Santenay, Monthélie). A fragrant and flavorful dry rosé is also quite tasty.

# BURGUNDIAN SAUSAGE

♦ *Makes 8 3- to 4-inch*
*sausages or patties*

*2 pounds ground pork*

*½ pound pork fat*

*1 tablespoon freshly grated*
*nutmeg*

*1 teaspoon ground allspice*

*½ teaspoon ground cloves*

*2 tablespoons chopped parsley*

*2 teaspoons chopped fresh*
*thyme*

*1½ teaspoons salt*

*½ teaspoon freshly ground*
*pepper*

*½ cup Armagnac or Cognac*

*2½ feet hog casings*

*Olive oil*

This is one of my favorite sausages. I serve it grilled, accompanied by Dijon mustard and potato gratin, or as part of a choucroute plate. Each sausage is about a quarter pound, so allow two per portion for the grill. For Choucroute, I serve one sausage per person, so cut the recipe in half or eat sausage two days in a row (you won't mind).

### Procedure

Combine all ingredients except the casings and the olive oil in a bowl and mix well with your hands. Fry a small ball of the mixture as a test; taste and adjust seasonings.

Using the sausage attachment on a heavy-duty mixer, stuff the casings with the pork mixture and twist and tie to make 3- to 4-inch links, or shape into 8 patties.

Heat a grill or broiler. If the sausages are in casings, prick all over with a fork, brush with olive oil, and grill or broil turning occasionally to brown evenly, until cooked through, 10 to 12 minutes. For patties, brush with oil and grill or broil 4 minutes each side until cooked through.

*Wine Notes:* The "local" wines are excellent, especially those of the Côte de Nuits (Morey-Saint-Denis, Nuits-Saint-Georges) and the Côte Chalonnaise (Mercurey, Givry, and the reds of Rully). Spanish wines are excellent; try a Valdepeñas, a Rioja, or red from the Extramadura.

# CHURRASCO: BRAZILIAN MIXED GRILL

♦ *Serves 6*

### Flank Steak

*3 large onions coarsely chopped*

*12 large garlic cloves, coarsely chopped*

*1 cup fresh lemon juice*

*1½ teaspoons salt*

*2 tablespoons freshly ground pepper*

*2 flank steaks, about 2½ pounds total*

### Pork Loin

*¼ cup salt*

*½ cup sugar*

*6 juniper berries, bruised*

*4 white peppercorns, cracked*

*3 black peppercorns, cracked*

*2 coriander seeds, bruised*

*2 whole cloves*

*3 bay leaves*

*1 teaspoon dried thyme*

*1 boneless pork loin, about 2 pounds, well trimmed*

*6 Brazilian-Inspired Pork Sausages (page 298)*

*Sautéed Greens (page 298)*

*Baked Rice (page 299)*

The churrasco is a great alternative to an American barbecue. It has all the elements of success: beef, pork, sausage, and salsa. In Brazil there are restaurants called churrascarias, devoted entirely to barbecue or grill cookery. The meat will sometimes be presented strung on long skewers at the table. There are an assortment of salsas and hot sauces, and the beer flows freely. Of course you don't have to go the whole churrasco and grill all three meats. Flank steak is worthy of solo attention. And any leftover beef or pork makes a great sandwich, paired with avocado slices and Salsa Mayonnaise (page 80).

## Procedure

For the flank steaks, quickly pulse the onions and garlic in a food processor to chop. Add the lemon juice and pulse to blend. (The mixture should be chunky.) Add the salt and pepper. Pour over the flank steaks in a nonaluminum container. Cover and let stand 1 to 2 hours, turning the steaks once or twice in the marinade.

For the pork loin, dissolve the salt and sugar in a little warm water in a nonaluminum container. Add the spices and herbs. Add the pork loin and enough cold water to cover. Cover and refrigerate 1 to 2 days.

Heat a grill or broiler. Bring the pork loin to room temperature; remove from the marinade. Brush the pork with olive oil and grill or broil, turning occasionally, until cooked through, 8 to 10 minutes. Grill or broil the sausages or sausage patties until cooked through and well browned, about 8 to 10 minutes.

*(continued)*

Brazilian Black Beans
  (page 299)
Salsa (page 300)
Olive oil for grilling

## Brazilian-Inspired Pork Sausage

♦ *Makes 6 4-inch sausages*
1½ pounds ground pork, about
  ⅓ the weight in fat
¼ cup chopped fresh cilantro
2 tablespoons finely minced
  garlic
1 tablespoon dried red pepper
  flakes
1 teaspoon salt
1 tablespoon black pepper
2 feet hog casings

## Sautéed Greens

♦ *Serves 6*
½ cup rendered bacon fat
2 onions, finely chopped
4 garlic cloves, finely minced
6 bunches Swiss chard or kale,
  cut into fine (⅛ inch) strips,
  well washed and drained
Salt and freshly ground pepper

Grill or broil the flank steaks until rare, about 3 minutes each side.

Cut the steaks and the pork across the grain into thin slices. Arrange a few slices of each on 6 serving plates. Place a sausage on each plate, along with a spoonful each of the Sautéed Greens, Baked Rice, and the Brazilian Black Beans. Serve with the Salsa.

### Procedure

Combine all the ingredients except the hog casings in a bowl and mix with your hands. Add a little water to facilitate stuffing. Fry a small ball of the mixture as a test; taste and adjust seasonings to taste. Using the sausage attachment on a heavy-duty mixer, stuff the casings with the pork mixture and twist and tie to make 4-inch sausages. Or shape into 6 finger-shaped patties.

### Procedure

Melt the bacon fat in a large sauté pan or skillet over medium heat. Add the onions and cook until translucent, about 10 minutes. Add the garlic and stir. Then add the greens by handfuls, stirring after each handful until wilted. (If necessary, add a few tablespoons water to the pan.) Season to taste with salt and pepper.

## Baked Rice

◆ *Serves 6*

*Salt*

*3 cups white rice, preferably basmati*

*4 quarts water*

*8 tablespoons unsalted butter, melted and seasoned with salt and freshly ground pepper*

### Procedure

Preheat the oven to 350 degrees. Bring a large saucepan of salted water to a boil. Add the rice all at once and simmer until cooked through but still firm, 10 to 12 minutes. (Bite a kernel to test for doneness.) Drain in a colander and rinse with warm water. Place in a baking dish and pour the seasoned, melted butter over. Cover and bake 25 minutes.

## Brazilian Black Beans

◆ *Serves 6*

*2 cups dried black beans*

*2 onions, chopped*

*4 to 6 garlic cloves, minced*

*¼ small cinnamon stick*

*1 whole clove*

*Prosciutto or ham bone, or small piece of prosciutto or ham (optional)*

*Salt and freshly ground pepper*

### Procedure

Soak the beans overnight in cold water to cover in the refrigerator. (Or, combine with 6 cups water in a saucepan; bring to a boil and boil 1 minute. Let stand 1 hour.) Drain and transfer to a large saucepan. Add the onions, garlic, prosciutto or ham bone, if using, the cinnamon stick, clove, and water. Bring to a boil, reduce the heat, and simmer until beans are tender, about 1 hour. Remove the bone, cinnamon stick, and clove, and season to taste with salt and pepper.

*Variation:* Combine the soaked beans and the bone, if using, in a large saucepan. Add the water, bring to a boil, and reduce the heat to a simmer. Heat 1 tablespoon olive oil in a medium sauté pan over low heat. Add the onions, garlic, 1 teaspoon ground cinnamon and ¼ teaspoon cloves and cook 2 to 3 minutes. Scrape into the pan with the beans, and simmer until the beans are tender. Remove the bone and season to taste with salt and pepper.

(*continued*)

## Salsa

♦ *Serves 6*

*½ cup fresh lemon juice*

*4 garlic cloves, finely minced*

*4 jalapeño peppers, finely
   minced*

## Procedure

Combine all of the ingredients in a small bowl.

**Wine Notes:** In Brazil, this dish is consumed with either a crisp light pilsner beer or a near lethal concoction of rum and lime. The wine options are directly affected by the heat of the salsa you have with it. Sturdy and assertive reds are best—young tannic Pinot Noir from France, California, or Oregon, a Syrah-based young Rhône (Cornas, Côte Rôtie, or Hermitage), or a blended Australian Shiraz.

## BARBECUE MARINADES FOR STEAKS

Although people all over the world cook food on open wood fires, can anything seem more all-American than the barbecue? Everything seems to taste better when you eat outdoors, and a wood fire certainly imparts a special scent and smokiness to the food. What follows are two quick and easy marinades for outdoor summer grilling. However, with fewer and fewer of us having time or space for the outdoor barbecue, there's no reason you can't cook these in your broiler in the dead of winter and enjoy the food even more.

## BARBECUE MARINADE

♦ *Serves 4 to 6*

*½ cup Worcestershire sauce*

*¼ cup bourbon*

*2 finely minced garlic cloves (about 1 tablespoon)*

*2 tablespoons sugar*

*2 tablespoons grated fresh ginger*

*1½ teaspoons freshly ground pepper*

*2 flank steaks, about 2½ pounds total, or 1 beef tenderloin, well trimmed, about 3 pounds total (see note)*

### *Procedure*

Combine all the marinade ingredients and pour over the meat in a nonaluminum container. Cover and let stand 2 hours at room temperature for the steaks, or 4 to 6 hours for the tenderloin. (Do not over marinate—the ginger will eventually begin to break down the meat.)

Heat a grill or broiler. Remove the meat from the marinade and grill or broil until rare, about 3 minutes each side for the flank steak or 15 to 18 minutes for the tenderloin. Cut the meat into slices and serve hot.

**Note:** If you prefer to cook individual tenderloin steaks, cut the tenderloin into 8-ounce pieces, marinate 2 hours and then grill or broil 3 minutes each side.

**Wine Notes:** Try a bigger style California Pinot Noir, a less refined Pinot from France's Côte de Nuits such as Morey-Saint-Denis, a Shiraz from Australia, or a fresh young Cabernet from Chile.

## MUSTARD, SOY, AND BROWN SUGAR MARINADE

♦ *Serves 4 to 6*

*½ cup Square One Hot Mustard
(page 348)*

*¼ cup soy sauce*

*3 tablespoons sherry*

*¼ cup firmly packed brown
sugar*

*2 flank steaks, about 2½ pounds
total*

This barbecue sauce recipe is sort of a cross between the Orient and California. But it's not new and trendy: Soy-based marinades have been with us since the Chinese came to America. The sugar and mustard give the meat a nice crust, and the balance of sweet, hot, and tangy makes for a good foil for the beef taste. Serve with rice and snap peas for an Oriental accent. Deep-fried sweet potato chips and greens, asparagus, or green beans would work well, too.

### Procedure

Combine the mustard, soy sauce, sherry, and sugar and pour over the steaks in a shallow nonaluminum container. Cover and let stand 2 hours at room temperature.

Heat a grill or broiler. Remove the steaks from the marinade; reserve the marinade. Grill or broil the steaks, basting occasionally with the marinade, until rare to medium-rare, about 3 minutes each side.

Slice the meat across the grain on a slight diagonal and serve with green onion rice and sugar snap peas.

**Wine Notes:** Look for red wines like those for the Churrasco (page 297), but with slightly more fruit. American Cabernet Sauvignon, especially the lighter styles from Long Island, a simple Piemontese Nebbiolo d'Alba or Barbera, and Carignan-based wine from France's Côte de Roussillon are fine accompaniments. A dark beer, such as an ale or even a stout, is also sublime.

## BASTURMA
### Grilled Flank Steak in Onion, Basil, and Vinegar

◆ *Serves 4 to 6*

*1 small onion, cut into chunks*

*1 tablespoon finely minced garlic*

*¼ cup chopped fresh basil*

*1 teaspoon salt, plus additional for the steak*

*2 teaspoons freshly ground pepper, plus additional for the steak*

*¼ cup red wine vinegar*

*2 flank steaks, about 2½ pounds total*

**R**ussia and Armenia both claim this recipe. Let's call it the Caucasus as a compromise. The lively vinaigrette traditionally is used on cubes of beef, sort of a beef shashlyk—kebab. I find it works well on flank steak, as the meat absorbs the flavors quickly. In a nontraditional mood? Try it on a full-flavored fish such as tuna.

### Procedure

Purée the onion in a blender or food processor. Add the garlic, basil, salt, and pepper and pulse a few times to combine. Process in the vinegar. Pour the marinade over the flank steaks in a nonaluminum container; rub the marinade into the meat. Cover and let stand 2 to 3 hours at room temperature.

Heat a grill or broiler. Sprinkle the steaks lightly with salt and pepper and grill or broil until rare to medium-rare, about 3 minutes each side. Slice across the grain on a slight diagonal and serve with kasha or white and wild rice pilaf seasoned with chopped green onions and cilantro, and with grilled eggplant or sautéed green beans with onions and chopped toasted walnuts.

**Wine Notes:** The key elements are ample acidity and ripe fruit. Pinot Noirs from Oregon and France are best. Italian reds also work well—like Chianti, Taurasi from Campania, and even Barbaresco.

## GRILLED RIB-EYE STEAK WITH MUSTARD, ONIONS, AND CARAWAY

♦ *Serves 6*

*4 tablespoons unsalted butter*

*4 large onions, sliced ¼ inch thick (about 6 cups)*

*3 tablespoons Square One Hot Mustard (page 348)*

*2 teaspoons caraway seeds, toasted*

*½ teaspoon salt, plus additional for the steaks*

*½ teaspoon freshly ground pepper, plus additional for the steaks*

*6 rib-eye steaks, about ½ pound each*

*2 tablespoons olive oil*

Here's a dish that could be Hungarian or from the north of Italy at the Austro-Hungarian border, but surprisingly, the recipe that inspired it was found in a Russian cookbook. Mustard seems to be a key for enlivening the flavor of a good piece of meat no matter what the province. The caraway adds another dimension to the cooked onions that makes me want to serve potato pancakes or strudel with the steak. But, mashed potatoes would work just as well.

### Procedure

Melt the butter in a large sauté pan or skillet over medium heat. Add the onions and cook slowly until very soft and tender, about 15 minutes. Stir in the mustard, caraway seeds, salt, and pepper and keep warm.

Heat the grill or broiler. Brush the steaks with oil and sprinkle with salt and pepper and grill or broil 3 minutes on each side for medium-rare, 4 minutes on each side for medium. Make a bed of onions on each plate and top with the steak, or just pile the onions on top of the steaks.

***Wine Notes:*** A robust red is called for. From France, look for a firm red from Cornas, Gigondas, or Hermitage. Red Bordeaux is a natural, those with more Cabernet Sauvignon than Merlot, as is a sturdy California Cabernet Sauvignon. Italian reds such as Barolo or Brunello di Montalcino are very happy here, too.

## GEORGIAN TOMATO SAUCE FOR BEEF OR VEAL

♦ *Serves 6*

**Georgian Tomato Sauce**

*2 tablespoons olive oil*

*2 teaspoons finely minced garlic*

*1 tablespoon curry powder*

*2 teaspoons ground coriander*

*¼ teaspoon (or to taste)*
  *cayenne pepper*

*1½ cups Basic Tomato Sauce*
  *(page 349)*

*¼ teaspoon salt*

*¼ teaspoon freshly ground*
  *pepper*

*Pinch of sugar (optional)*


*6 veal loin chops, ¾ to 1 pound*
  *each and about 1 inch thick*
  *or 6 rib-eye steaks, about*
  *½ pound each*

*2 tablespoons olive oil*

*Salt and freshly ground pepper*

Not from the Deep South—this Georgia is in Russia, and the flavor influences are somewhat Afghani. The robust curry-flavored tomato sauce goes well with meat, but it can brighten up a simple fish such as bass, swordfish, or cod. Serve with cracked wheat pilaf, rice, or potatoes. Grilled eggplant is nice with the meat, and spinach curry is a good balance for the fish.

### Procedure

For the sauce, warm the oil in a small saucepan over low heat. Add the garlic and cook 1 to 2 minutes. Add the spices, and cook, stirring, 1 to 2 minutes. Add the Tomato Sauce and bring to a simmer. Season with the salt and pepper and if the tomato sauce is acidic and/or the blend of curry powder is tart, add sugar to round out the flavor.

Heat a grill or broiler. Brush the chops or steaks with oil and sprinkle lightly with salt and pepper. Grill or broil until medium-rare, 5 to 6 minutes a side for the veal, 3 to 4 minutes a side for the steaks. Spoon the sauce over the meat and serve.

**Wine Notes:** You'll need an earthy, spicy, medium-bodied red wine from the Côtes du Rhône such as Châteauneuf-du-Pape, or a California Rhône-clone, Grenache or Barbera.

# BEEF À LA STROGANOFF REVISITED

♦ *Serves 4*

*6 tablespoons unsalted butter*

*2 cups sliced onions*

*1 tablespoon paprika*

*3 cups sliced (¼ inch) cultivated mushrooms*

*2 cups sliced (¼ inch) wild mushrooms, such as chanterelles or morels (morels may be cut in halves or quartered)*

*⅔ cup Beef Stock (page 309)*

*1 teaspoon grated lemon zest*

*½ cup sour cream, at room temperature*

*Salt and freshly ground pepper*

*4 tenderloin steaks, about 7 ounces each*

I've never been a fan of beef à la stroganoff, which always surprised me since I love the basic ingredients. It finally dawned on me that twice-cooked fillet was not my idea of great beef. Why not cook the fillet simply and just use the other ingredients as a sauce? And instead of serving the beef with rice, why not great potato pancakes or potato strudel? No reason. I love the result.

### Procedure

Melt 2 tablespoons of the butter in a medium saucepan over medium heat. Add the onions and cook until tender and translucent, about 10 minutes. Add the paprika and cook 3 minutes longer. Set aside.

Melt the remaining 4 tablespoons butter in a very large sauté pan or skillet over high heat. Add the sliced mushrooms and sauté until tender, 5 to 7 minutes. They will give off some liquid and shrink down considerably. Add the cooked onions, the beef stock, and lemon zest. Bring to a boil and reduce heat to a simmer. Remove from heat and stir in the sour cream and simmer 1 to 2 minutes. Season to taste with salt and pepper.

Heat a grill or broiler. Sprinkle the steaks with salt and pepper and grill or broil 3 to 4 minutes each side for medium-rare. Return the sauce to a simmer. Transfer the steaks to serving plates and top with the sauce. Serve at once with the potato delight of your choice.

**Wine Notes:** Medium-bodied, elegant reds work best. Pinot Noir and Merlot are good choices. A cru Beaujolais would also be lovely, as would a Rioja or Portuguese Dão.

## PEPPERED FILLET OF BEEF WITH COGNAC MUSTARD CREAM

◆ *Serves 4*

*1½ cups Cognac*

*2 cups heavy cream*

*2 tablespoons Dijon mustard*

*2 tablespoons Square One Hot Mustard (page 348) or Dijon mustard*

*½ teaspoon salt, plus additional for the beef*

*4 beef tenderloin steaks, about 2 inches thick, about 8 ounces each, or 2 pounds whole beef tenderloin, well trimmed*

*4 to 6 tablespoons coarsely cracked peppercorns*

*2 to 3 tablespoons olive oil*

I thought everybody would know this old French classic by heart by now. But that is not the case. People still ask for the recipe, proving that when a dish is a true classic, the taste memory lingers on and with it the desire to re-create the flavors.

### Procedure

Reduce the Cognac in a small saucepan over medium heat to about ¾ cup. (The alcohol will flame as it reduces, so step back.)

Reduce the cream in a second saucepan over high heat to about 1 cup. Whisk in the mustards and then the Cognac. Add the salt; taste and adjust seasonings. Set aside.

Dip the steaks or roll the whole tenderloin in the cracked peppercorns to coat and gently press into the beef with the heel of your hand.

For the tenderloin steaks, heat a grill or broiler. Brush the steaks with oil, sprinkle with salt, and grill or broil 3 to 4 minutes each side for medium-rare. For the whole tenderloin, preheat the oven to 400 degrees. Heat a little oil in a cast-iron pan over very high heat; add the meat and brown on all sides. Transfer to a rack in a shallow roasting pan, sprinkle with salt, and roast until a meat thermometer registers 110 degrees for rare, about 15 minutes. Let stand for a few minutes before slicing.

Rewarm the sauce over medium heat. Place a steak or a few slices of the tenderloin on each serving plate and spoon the sauce over.

**Wine Notes:** Noble red Bordeaux from the Left Bank and the Graves, California Cabernet Sauvignon, and even a harmonious Barolo are excellent choices.

# GRILLED STEAK WITH ARMAGNAC, RAISINS, AND BLACK PEPPER

♦ *Serves 6*

*¼ cup raisins*

*6 tablespoons (or to taste) Armagnac*

*2 cups Beef Stock (page 309)*

*½ teaspoon salt, plus additional for steaks*

*1 teaspoon freshly ground pepper, plus additional for the steaks*

*6 tenderloin or rib-eye steaks, about ½ pound each*

Everyone loves beef with pepper since the French introduced us to steak au poivre, but Roger Vergé's idea of adding raisins and Armagnac intrigued me. Vergé coats the steaks with cracked pepper and deglazes the pan with the Armagnac, then adds yellow raisins and butter and beef stock. I prefer brown raisins, and I find that by puréeing some of the Armagnac-soaked raisins and adding pepper to the beef stock, I wind up with a very rich hot and sweet sauce. This may sound strange, but try it once—I think you'll find it's an interesting pick-me-up for plain, mild-flavored fillet, and a good contrast for the richness of rib-eye steak as well.

## Procedure

Soak the raisins in the Armagnac for 1 hour. Strain, and reserve the Armagnac. Transfer all but 1 tablespoon of the soaked raisins to the container of a food processor and process until finely chopped; set aside.

Combine the beef stock, the chopped raisins, and the reserved Armagnac in a medium saucepan. Bring to a boil and cook until reduced to 1½ cups. Add the salt and pepper and the reserved whole raisins. Taste and adjust seasonings.

Heat a grill or broiler. Sprinkle the steaks with salt and pepper and grill or broil until rare, about 3 minutes each side (or you may sauté the steaks in a little oil in a large sauté pan over medium-high heat).

Return the sauce to a simmer. Transfer the steaks to 6 serving plates and spoon the sauce over. Serve with potato gratin and sautéed spinach.

## Beef Stock

♦ *Makes 4 to 5 quarts*

*6 pounds meaty beef shanks,
  cracked*

*1 marrow bone, cracked*

*Beef trimmings from steaks or
  roasts (optional)*

*2 medium onions, coarsely
  chopped*

*1 leek, coarsely chopped
  (optional)*

*2 medium carrots, coarsely
  chopped*

*1 celery rib, coarsely chopped*

*2 tomatoes, halved*

*Mushroom stems (optional)*

*6 garlic cloves*

*5 parsley sprigs*

*8 peppercorns*

*3 thyme sprigs*

*2 small bay leaves*

*2 cloves*

## Procedure

Preheat the oven to 450 degrees. Place the beef shanks and marrow bone in a large roasting pan and roast, turning the pieces occasionally, until browned but not scorched, about 1½ hours. Transfer the bones to a large stockpot (reserve the roasting pan) and cover with cold water. Add meat scraps if you have them. Bring to a boil, reduce the heat, and simmer uncovered 1 to 2 hours. Add more water as needed to keep the bones well covered and skim the scum from the surface occasionally.

Meanwhile, place the roasting pan on top of the stove and brown the onions, leek, carrots, and celery in the fat in the pan. They should be nicely caramelized; stir often so that they don't scorch. Transfer the vegetables to the stockpot. Pour a little water into the pan and simmer, scraping up the browned bits on the bottom. Pour the pan juices into the stock and add the remaining ingredients.

Simmer the stock uncovered over very low heat all day, or at least 6 hours.

Remove the solids with a slotted spoon or Chinese skimmer. Pour the stock through a strainer, then line the strainer with cheesecloth and strain the stock again. Let cool, then refrigerate until cold. Remove the layer of fat from the top.

For a richer stock, gently boil uncovered until reduced by half. Let cool and refrigerate or freeze.

***Wine Notes:*** Young pedigreed red Bordeaux, American Cabernet Sauvignon, Australian Shiraz-Cabernet blends, and those luscious Merlots from Washington State are superb.

# HUNGARIAN BANDIT'S STEAK

◆ *Serves 2*

*12 ounces beef tenderloin, well trimmed, cut into 6 2-ounce slices*

*2 tablespoons sweet paprika*

*½ teaspoon cayenne pepper or hot paprika*

*1 tablespoon finely minced garlic*

*1 tablespoon freshly ground pepper*

*6 thin slices pancetta*

*1 tablespoon olive oil*

*½ cup Beef Stock (page 309)*

*Salt, as needed*

I'm the bandit in this case because this is not my creation. I read about this steak in two Hungarian cookbooks—George Lang's definitive opus and Paprikas Weiss's work—where it is called "gypsy steak." As most of us seem to broil or grill steaks, I thought it would be nice to have a sautéed steak in the repertoire. While fillet is the prestige cut, I find it can be the least flavorful. This recipe gives the beef some character. Serve with fried polenta rounds topped with fried or grilled onions and with green beans or asparagus.

### Procedure

Pound the beef slices to about ⅓ inch thick between sheets of plastic wrap, very gently so as not to break the flesh. (A strong tap with the palm of your hand should do it.) Combine the sweet paprika, cayenne or hot paprika, garlic, and black pepper and massage into the sliced beef. Roll each beef slice into a cylinder and wrap with pancetta. Secure with a toothpick, if you like; the steak rolls should actually hold pretty well without assistance, if you turn them with tongs carefully during cooking.

Heat the olive oil in large sauté pan or skillet over high heat. Add the meat rolls and cook, turning a few times, until evenly browned. Do not overcook. Transfer to a warm platter and remove the toothpicks. Pour off the fat in the pan, add the beef stock, and cook over high heat to deglaze, scraping up all the browned bits on the bottom of the pan. Taste for salt—the sauce may not need any at all.

Pour the sauce over the meat on the platter and serve with polenta rounds, or mashed potatoes, grilled or fried onions, and green beans or asparagus. **Wine Notes:** See the selections for Beef à la Stroganoff Revisited (page 306).

# BRAISED BRISKET OF BEEF

♦ *Serves 12 to 14*

*6 to 8 pounds first-cut brisket of beef, trimmed well*

*1 teaspoon salt, plus additional for seasoning*

*2 tablespoons freshly ground pepper, plus additional for seasoning*

*1 tablespoon paprika*

*6 tablespoons chicken fat or unsalted butter*

*7 large onions, cut into medium dice*

*3 cups tomato purée*

*12 large carrots, cut into large chunks*

*2 pounds mushrooms, trimmed and halved, if large*

*Hot prepared mustard, for serving*

e sure to get brisket of beef for this traditional Jewish-style pot roast. Only this cut has sufficient fat marbling to keep the meat moist and tender during the long, slow braising process. No additional stock is needed, as the meat and the onions release the most wonderful juices. The brisket is excellent served cold, with devilishly hot mustard, but of course it can be reheated easily with its pan juices.

## Procedure

Sprinkle the brisket with the salt, pepper, and paprika. Melt 3 tablespoons of the fat or butter in a large heavy saucepan over high heat. Add the meat and brown all sides; set aside. Melt the remaining 3 tablespoons fat or butter in a heavy Dutch oven or kettle over medium heat. Add the onions and cook until very tender and pale gold, about 20 minutes. Place the brisket on top of the onions. Reduce the heat and simmer, covered, over low heat 1 hour. (The meat will give off quite a bit of juice.) Add the tomato purée and simmer, covered, 15 to 20 more minutes. Add the carrots and simmer, covered, until tender and easily pierced with a fork, but not falling apart, about 30 minutes. Add the mushrooms during the last 10 minutes of cooking time.

Remove the meat from the pan to a carving board

*(continued)*

and cover to keep warm. Remove the carrots and mushrooms with a slotted spoon and arrange on a platter or in a serving bowl. Season the pan juices to taste with salt and pepper and transfer to a gravy pitcher. Slice the brisket across the grain and serve with the vegetables, the pan juices, hot mustard, and of course, potato latkes. Some people like applesauce with this. The choice is yours.

***Wine Notes:*** Find a very fruity red wine, be it a Beaujolais (at villages or simple cru level), a youthful Pinot Noir, or Australian Shiraz. A white wine is not out of the question if it is full-bodied, fresh, and generous with ripe fruit—a California Chardonnay or simple French white Burgundy.

# GEORGIAN BEEF RAGOUT

♦ *Serves 6 to 8*

*1 teaspoon finely minced garlic*

*2 teaspoons paprika*

*1 teaspoon ground coriander*

*3 pounds beef chuck or other*
*stewing beef, cut into 1½-inch*
*cubes*

*2 to 3 tablespoons (or as*
*needed) olive oil*

*3 large onions, diced (about 4*
*cups)*

*1 tablespoon minced garlic*

*2 teaspoons paprika*

*1 teaspoon ground coriander*

*1½ cups diced, canned tomatoes*

*1½ cups water or Beef Stock*
*(page 309)*

*2 cups pitted prunes (about*
*12 ounces)*

*1 cup chopped walnuts, toasted*

*1 tablespoon grated lemon zest*

*3 tablespoons chopped fresh*
*cilantro*

*1½ teaspoons chopped fresh*
*tarragon*

*1 teaspoon (or to taste) salt*

*½ teaspoon (or to taste) freshly*
*ground pepper*

The theme of prunes and meat is a recurring one in the cuisines of North Africa and the Middle East, but also in France, Scandinavia, Germany, and Hungary. The clues that this dish is from Russia are the additions of cilantro, lemon zest, and walnuts—sort of tkemali sauce with crunch! I like to rub the meat with a dry marinade and let it absorb the spices overnight. This stew can be prepared 1 to 2 days ahead and reheated over a low flame or in a 350-degree oven before serving.

### Procedure

Combine the garlic, paprika, and coriander and rub into the beef cubes. Cover and refrigerate overnight.

Heat 2 tablespoons olive oil in a large sauté pan or skillet over medium heat. Add as many beef cubes as will comfortably fit without crowding and brown on all sides; transfer to a deep kettle or stew pot. Repeat to brown the remaining beef cubes, adding oil to the pan as needed for each batch. Add the onions to the sauté pan and cook 15 minutes. Add the garlic, paprika, and coriander and cook 5 more minutes. Scrape the onion mixture into the pot with the beef and then add the tomatoes and stock. Bring to a boil, reduce the heat, and simmer, covered, until the meat is tender, 2½ to 3 hours. Add the prunes, walnuts, lemon zest, cilantro, and tarragon during the last 30 minutes of cooking time. Season to taste and serve with noodles, kasha, or potatoes.

**Wine Notes:** I enjoy this most with Cabernet Sauvignon. Merlots are also enjoyable.

## CATALAN BEEF RAGOUT

◆ *Serves 6*

**Marinade**

*1 teaspoon cinnamon*

*½ teaspoon ground cloves*

*1 teaspoon dried oregano*

*½ teaspoon ground toasted
    fennel seed*

*1 teaspoon freshly ground
    pepper*

*2 cups full-bodied red wine (Lar
    de Barros Reserva, Zinfandel,
    Sangre de Toro, Côtes du
    Rhône)*

*3 pounds beef chuck or other
    marbled stewing beef, trimmed
    well and cut into 2-inch cubes*

*½ cup (or as needed) olive oil*

*¼ pound pancetta, cut into
    ¼-inch dice*

*6 cups diced onions*

*2 tablespoons finely minced
    garlic*

*1 teaspoon dried oregano*

*1 teaspoon cinnamon*

*1 teaspoon freshly ground
    pepper*

*½ teaspoon ground cloves*

*½ teaspoon ground, toasted
    fennel seed*

Three Catalan recipes—one inspired by Colman Andrews, one from Paula Wolfert, and another from Penelope Casas's Spanish cookbook—are combined here. I've played with the combinations and have varied the vegetable additions from time to time. I'm sure you'll make your own version of this stew as soon as you feel comfortable with the recipe.

### Procedure

Combine the marinade ingredients and pour over the beef in a nonaluminum container. Cover and refrigerate overnight.

Bring the meat to room temperature. Drain and pat dry with paper towels. Reserve marinade. Heat ¼ cup olive oil in a large sauté pan or skillet over high heat. Add as many meat cubes as will comfortably fit without crowding and brown on all sides. Remove with a slotted spoon and set aside. Repeat to brown all the meat, adding 1 to 2 tablespoons oil to the pan as needed for each batch.

Heat the remaining ¼ cup olive oil in a deep casserole over medium heat. Add the pancetta and cook until lightly browned. Then add the onions and cook until tender and translucent, about 10 minutes. Add the garlic, the spices, the crumbled bay leaves, the orange zest, the stock, the red wine, any remaining marinade, and the browned meat. Bring to a boil, reduce the heat and simmer, covered, until the meat is tender but not falling apart, 2 to 3 hours. Skim the fat. Add the Elysium or sherry, the chocolate, if using, the cooked vegetables, and the cooked sausage

4 bay leaves, crumbled

1 tablespoon grated orange zest

½ cup veal or Beef Stock
(page 309)

2 cups full-bodied red wine
(see above)

4 tablespoons Quady Elysium or
sweet sherry

1 teaspoon grated bitter
chocolate (optional)

24 small new potatoes, roasted
at 400 degrees for about 25
minutes or boiled until cooked
through

24 baby carrots or carrot
chunks, peeled and blanched
until cooked through

24 pearl onions, peeled and
blanched until cooked through

4 Spanish sausages, cooked and
sliced (optional)

24 green or black olives
(optional)

Salt and freshly ground pepper

6 tablespoons chopped parsley

and olives, if using. Simmer 15 more minutes. Season to taste with salt and pepper and adjust seasonings, if necessary; you may want to add more orange zest, sherry, or pepper. Sprinkle with chopped parsley and serve hot.

This stew, without the vegetables, may be made several days ahead and refrigerated. To serve, prepare the vegetables separately, add to the stew, and rewarm over low heat or in a 350-degree oven until heated through, about 20 minutes.

**Wine Notes:** A fine red Rioja, Cabernet-based wines from Catalonia, or other related reds from Valdepeñas, La Mancha, and the Ribera del Duero are excellent with this dish. A Portuguese red, simple red Burgundy (Givry, Rully) are also good choices, as are easy-drinking reds from Bordeaux and California such as Merlot and Cabernet.

## VEAL ROLLATINI WITH GORGONZOLA AND WALNUTS

◆ *Serves 4*

*1½ pounds veal tenderloin or
    leg, cut into 12 ½-inch-thick
    slices, about 2 ounces each*

*2 eggs*

*½ cup milk*

*1½ cups all-purpose flour*

*3 cups dry bread crumbs*

*1½ cups crumbled Gorgonzola
    cheese*

*¾ cup walnuts, toasted and
    coarsely chopped*

*2 tablespoons (or as needed)
    unsalted butter*

*2 tablespoons (or as needed)
    olive oil*

*⅔ cup brandy*

*2 cups veal or Chicken Stock
    (page 119)*

*Salt and freshly ground pepper*

Rollatini—sometimes called uccelletti, or little birds—are little stuffed scallops of veal that can be rolled and sautéed or placed on skewers and grilled. Because of the bread crumb coating I prefer to sauté the veal rolls, to accentuate the crunch.

### Procedure

Lightly pound the veal slices to about ¼ inch thick between sheets of plastic wrap. Whisk together the eggs and milk in a bowl. Place the flour on a large plate and the bread crumbs on a second plate; set aside.

Spoon 2 tablespoons Gorgonzola and 1 tablespoon chopped walnuts over the center third of each veal slice. Roll the slices up and dip first in the flour, then in the egg mixture and finally in the bread crumbs. Set the veal rolls aside on a baking sheet lined with parchment paper. (These breaded veal rolls will keep nicely, refrigerated, for several hours or even overnight.)

Bring the veal rolls to room temperature, if refrigerated. Heat the butter and oil in a large sauté pan or skillet over high heat. Add as many veal rolls as will comfortably fit without crowding and cook, turning a few times, until evenly browned. Remove to a warm platter and cover to keep warm. Repeat to cook the remaining veal rolls, adding oil to the pan as necessary, for each batch.

Pour off the fat, add the brandy to the pan and cook over medium-high heat to deglaze, scraping up all the browned bits on the bottom of the pan. Add the stock and boil to reduce by half. Season to taste with salt and pepper. Pour over the veal and serve at once with mashed or roasted potatoes, and sautéed green beans, or asparagus. If figs are in season, cut them in half, wrap in prosciutto, broil until warm and golden, and serve with the veal rollantine for an added treat.

***Wine Notes:*** Sometimes the regional roots are so powerful, you can't ignore them. Italian reds of medium to full body, autumnal and earthy flavors are best: a truffly Nebbiolo-based wine from Piedmont, a Chianti, Rosso di Montalcino, or Vino Nobile from Tuscany, and a flavorful Torgiano from Umbria. Non-Italophiles will find happiness in Pinot Noir, lighter Syrah wines from France (Saint-Joseph and Crozes-Hermitage) and California, and the country wines of Spain.

## BRACIOLETTINE DI VITELLO ALLA MESSINESE
### *Sicilian-Stuffed Veal Brochette*

♦ *Serves 2*

12 ounces veal tenderloin or leg,
  cut into 6 ½-inch-thick slices,
  about 2 ounces each

2 tablespoons olive oil

½ cup fresh bread crumbs

⅓ cup grated Cacciocavallo
  cheese

¼ cup pine nuts, toasted

¼ cup raisins, plumped
  15 minutes in warm water
  and drained

6 bay leaves

8 slices red onion

Olive oil for brushing

Salt and freshly ground pepper

Braciole usually means a chop, but in some regions of Italy it is a rolled stuffed piece of veal or beef. (Braciolettine means little rolls.) This recipe is popular in the Sicilian town of Messina, where the veal rolls are grilled on skewers along with bay leaves and onion slices. Occasionally these are served with tomato sauce. However they're pretty savory in their own right. If you don't feel like heating the broiler or making a fire, you can tie these with string and sauté them in olive oil or butter. (Just remember that the depth of flavor that comes from the grill, the charred onions, and aromatic bay leaves will be lost.) Cacciocavallo cheese (which means "to chase a horse") is a mild, golden melting cheese when fresh. If you can't find it at your specialty cheese shop, substitute Monterey Jack or a mild creamy Cheddar—just not Velveeta.

### Procedure

Lightly pound the veal slices to about ¼ inch thick between sheets of plastic wrap. Set aside.

Heat the olive oil in a small sauté pan or skillet over high heat. Add the bread crumbs, and sauté, stirring, until golden, about 5 minutes. Remove from the heat and let cool slightly. Then stir in the cheese, pine nuts, and raisins. Spoon the mixture over the center third of the veal slices and roll them up. Thread a slice of onion onto a skewer, followed by a bay leaf, and then a veal roll. Repeat twice more, to use 3 veal rolls, and ending with a slice of onion. Thread a second skewer with the remaining ingredients in the same manner.

Heat a grill or broiler. Brush the brochettes with olive oil and sprinkle with salt and pepper. Grill or broil, turning occasionally, until evenly browned, 3 to 4 minutes each side. Serve with Cazzilli (page 337), a wonderful Sicilian potato croquette, or mashed potatoes. Tomato sauce is optional.

*Wine Notes:* For local color, the red wines of Sicily such as Corvo are nice, but any red wine of medium body, moderate tannin, and good rustic flavor is appropriate. An Aglianico-based red wine from Campania or Basilicata is lovely, as would be a Chianti or any similar red from Tuscany, the Abruzzi, Friuli, or the Veneto. In American wines, try a Barbera or Merlot. Hard to go wrong here—the dish is very wine friendly.

# VEGETABLES

PERSIAN-STYLE SPINACH WITH MINT AND WALNUTS ◆ SPINACH BORANI ◆ NORTH AFRICAN-STYLE BEETS AND CARROTS ◆ INDONESIAN VEGETABLE RAGOUT ◆ INDIAN SPICY LENTILS ◆ CURRIED EGGPLANT ◆ CURRIED POTATO PANCAKES ◆ CURRIED CAULIFLOWER ◆ SKORDALIA ◆ SCURDALIA ◆ SWEET POTATO STRUDEL ◆ POTATO STRUDEL ◆ MOROCCAN SPICY FRIED POTATOES ◆ CAZZILLI ◆ POTATOES AND ASPARAGUS ALL'ERICINA ◆ POTATOES À LA GRECQUE ◆ FENNEL GRATIN ◆ CORN PUDDING

## PERSIAN-STYLE SPINACH WITH MINT AND WALNUTS

♦ *Serves 6*

*2 pounds fresh spinach*

*3 tablespoons mild olive oil or unsalted butter*

*1 large onion, chopped (about 1½ cups)*

*6 garlic cloves, finely minced*

*6 tablespoons chopped fresh mint*

*Salt and freshly ground pepper*

*6 tablespoons chopped walnuts, toasted*

Traditionally, this cooked spinach is served as a salad at room temperature, but there's no reason you can't serve it hot as a vegetable.

### Procedure

Trim the tough stems from the spinach. Coarsely chop the leaves and wash carefully in 2 or 3 changes of water to remove all sand. Drain.

Heat the oil or butter in a very large sauté pan or skillet over medium heat. Add the onion and cook 5 minutes. Add the garlic and the spinach leaves and cook in their own moisture, stirring often, until the spinach wilts, about 4 minutes. Add the mint and mix well. Season to taste with salt and pepper. Transfer to a serving bowl and top with the chopped walnuts.

**Variation:** To serve as a salad, cook the onions and spinach in olive oil, chill the cooked spinach mixture completely, chop well, and then fold in 2 cups plain yogurt. Top with the chopped walnuts and mint.

# SPINACH BORANI

♦ *Serves 4*

*1 pound fresh spinach, tough
    stems trimmed*

*¼ cup olive oil or unsalted
    butter*

*3 onions, chopped (about
    4 cups)*

*4 garlic cloves, finely minced*

*3 tablespoons chopped fresh
    basil*

*2 tablespoons chopped fresh
    cilantro*

*1 tablespoon chopped fresh
    thyme (optional)*

*Salt and freshly ground pepper*

*2 cups plain yogurt*

*½ teaspoon cinnamon*

*½ teaspoon turmeric*

*Fresh pomegranate seeds for
    garnish (optional)*

The origin of this dish lies somewhere in the Caucasus: Armenia, Afghanistan, Turkestan, Iran. Borani dishes are topped with yogurt; some are enriched with egg and baked. I've left the eggs out of this version of spinach with a borani topping for a lighter result. It is a wonderful accompaniment for Shashlyk (page 263) or for Persian and Turkish lamb stews, and for Chicken with Apricots and Tomatoes (page 215). It could even work well as part of an Indian menu.

## Procedure

Wash the spinach carefully in 2 to 3 changes of water; drain well. Tear any very large leaves into smaller pieces or cut into wide strips. Heat the oil or butter in a large sauté pan or skillet over low to medium heat. Add the onions and cook until tender and translucent, about 15 minutes. Add the garlic and cook 2 to 3 minutes. Add the herbs and cook a few minutes longer. Add the spinach, a few handfuls at a time, and cook stirring, until wilted. Season to taste with salt and pepper and transfer to a serving bowl.

Stir together the yogurt, cinnamon, and turmeric and spoon over the spinach. Sprinkle with a few pomegranate seeds, if using, and serve hot.

## NORTH AFRICAN-STYLE BEETS AND CARROTS

♦ *Serves 4*

*8 very small beets*

*8 medium carrots*

*3 to 4 tablespoons unsalted butter*

*½ cup raisins, plumped 15 minutes in hot water to cover and drained, soaking liquid reserved*

*1 tablespoon lemon zest*

*1 tablespoon fresh lemon juice*

*½ teaspoon cinnamon*

*2 tablespoons brown sugar*

*3 tablespoons chopped fresh mint*

*Salt and freshly ground pepper*

*6 cups tightly packed beet greens, Swiss chard or escarole, cut into thin strips (optional)*

This isn't a traditional Moroccan vegetable dish, but the seasonings are North African in inspiration. I love serving it because it is so pretty.

### Procedure

Trim the beets, leaving 1 to 2 inches of stem attached. Cover the beets with cold water in a saucepan and bring to a boil. Reduce the heat and simmer until tender. (Cooking time will vary according to the size of the beets; start testing with a small knife after 40 minutes.) Drain and cover the beets with warm water. Let stand until cool enough to handle and then peel. Cut the beets into chunks or wedges; you should have 1½ to 2 cups (see note).

Peel the carrots and cut into chunks about the same size as the beets. You will need about 1½ cups carrots, or about the same volume as beets. Cook the carrots in a saucepan of boiling salted water until tender but not mushy, about 8 minutes. Drain and refresh under cold running water.

Melt the butter in a large sauté pan or skillet over medium heat. Add the beets and carrots and cook, stirring, 1 to 2 minutes. Add the raisins and about ¼ cup reserved soaking liquid, the lemon zest and juice, the cinnamon, and sugar and simmer 1 to 2 minutes. Add the greens, escarole, or Swiss chard, if using, and cook, stirring, until wilted. Stir in the mint and season to taste with salt and pepper.

***Note:*** The beets may also be baked in a foil-covered baking dish at 350 degrees until tender. Remove from the oven, let stand until cool enough to handle, and then peel and cut into chunks or wedges.

# INDONESIAN VEGETABLE RAGOUT

♦ *Serves 6 to 8*

*3 tablespoons peanut or olive oil*

*2 onions, thinly sliced*

*1 tablespoon ground cumin*

*1 teaspoon paprika*

*2 teaspoons crushed, dried chili peppers or dried red pepper flakes*

*1 tablespoon finely chopped garlic*

*1 tablespoon grated fresh ginger*

*1 cup green beans*

*1 cup sliced (⅛ inch) carrots*

*1 small head green cabbage, cored and thinly sliced*

*1½ cups coconut milk*

*2 teaspoons brown sugar*

*2 teaspoons grated lemon zest*

*2 tablespoons chopped fresh Thai basil or mint (optional)*

*Salt and freshly ground pepper*

*2 tablespoons shredded coconut, toasted*

*2 tablespoons peanuts, toasted and chopped*

J ust the vegetable dish to serve with Indonesian Chicken Saté (page 231), Indonesian-Style Roast Duck with Coconut (page 254), or any time you feel like eating a tasty vegetable assortment.

## Procedure

Heat the oil in a large sauté pan or skillet over medium heat. Add the onions and cook 5 minutes. Add the spices, garlic, and ginger and cook 2 to 3 minutes. Then add the beans and carrots and place the cabbage on top. Stir in the coconut milk, sugar, and lemon zest and steam, covered, until the vegetables are tender, 5 to 8 minutes. Stir in the basil or mint, if using, and season to taste with salt and pepper. Transfer to a serving bowl and sprinkle with coconut and peanuts. Serve hot.

# INDIAN SPICY LENTILS

♦ *Serves 4 to 6*

*2 cups green, brown, or red*
*lentils*

*6 tablespoons unsalted butter or*
*olive oil*

*3½ cups diced onions*

*½ teaspoon cinnamon*

*1 to 2 tablespoons grated fresh*
*ginger*

*¼ teaspoon (or to taste)*
*cayenne pepper*

*2 teaspoons finely minced garlic*

*2 to 3 teaspoons (or to taste)*
*minced jalapeño peppers*

*Zest of 1 large lemon*

*1 bay leaf*

*3 tablespoons (or to taste) fresh*
*lemon juice*

*1 small bunch fresh cilantro,*
*chopped*

*Salt and freshly ground black*
*pepper*

Indian cuisine is vegetable heaven. A culture that has so many vegetarians has of course created some of the very best vegetable recipes. Two or three of the dishes in this chapter, combined with some saffron rice, make an exciting and satisfying meal.

You can use one of several kinds of lentils in this recipe. The more expensive French green variety retain their firm contours, yet absorb the spices well. Brown lentils or Indian red lentils cook very quickly but lose their shape. Aesthetics may be the only deciding factor.

### Procedure

Cover the lentils (by about 2 inches) with water and cook until just tender and still slightly al dente, 30 to 40 minutes for green lentils, 15 to 20 minutes for brown and red. Do not overcook. Set aside.

Heat the butter or oil in a large sauté or skillet pan over medium heat. Add the onions and cook until tender and sweet, about 10 minutes. Add the cinnamon, ginger, cayenne, garlic, jalapeños, lemon zest, and bay leaf and cook 5 minutes. Fold in the lentils, add lemon juice to taste, and cook 2 to 3 minutes. You may need to add a little water. Then add the cilantro and salt and pepper to taste. Remove the bay leaf before serving.

# CURRIED EGGPLANT

♦ *Serves 4 to 6*

*2 to 3 medium eggplants, about*
  *1 pound each*

*4 to 6 tablespoons unsalted*
  *butter or olive oil*

*2 cups chopped onions*

*1 tablespoon minced garlic*

*¼ cup grated fresh ginger*

*2 teaspoons ground coriander*

*2 teaspoons ground cumin*

*1 teaspoon turmeric*

*¼ teaspoon (or to taste)*
  *cayenne pepper*

*Salt and freshly ground black*
  *pepper*

*Lemon juice to taste*

*Plain yogurt (optional)*

*1 cup diced tomatoes (optional)*

*2 to 3 tablespoons chopped fresh*
  *cilantro (optional)*

This dish is creamy and rich with a little kick. If it is too hot, stir in a little yogurt to temper the spices.

## Procedure

Preheat the oven to 450 degrees. Place the eggplants in a baking pan and prick in a few places with a fork. Bake until very tender, about 45 minutes. Set aside in a colander until cool enough to handle. Then peel carefully and transfer the pulp to drain in a strainer for 15 minutes. Coarsely chop the eggplant or pulse quickly in a food processor.

Heat the butter or olive oil in a medium sauté pan or skillet over medium heat. Add the onions and cook until translucent, about 10 minutes. Add the garlic, ginger, and spices and cook 5 minutes. Add the drained eggplant and season to taste with salt, pepper, and lemon juice. Add a little yogurt if the flavor needs smoothing out a bit. Stir in chopped tomatoes and cilantro, if using.

*Variation:* For those on low-fat diets, steam the onions and spices in a little vegetable stock or water rather than sautéing. Use nonfat yogurt and eat as much as you like!

# CURRIED POTATO PANCAKES

• *Makes about 18 medium or
   12 large pancakes*

*1 medium onion, diced (about
   1¼ cups)*

*1 egg*

*3 large russet potatoes, peeled
   and finely diced (about
   4 cups)*

*5 to 7 tablespoons all-purpose
   flour*

*1 tablespoon (or to taste) strong
   curry powder*

*Salt and freshly ground pepper*

*Vegetable shortening, for frying*

When is a latke not quite a latke? When it is curried and served with raita instead of cream and applesauce.

## Procedure

Process the onion and egg in a blender (see note) until puréed. Add about a third of the potato cubes and process just until smooth. Add the remaining potato cubes and process quickly just until smooth but not more than a minute. (You may have to do this in batches.) Pour the purée into a bowl and add the 5 tablespoons flour, the curry powder, and salt and pepper to taste. (The amount of flour needed will depend on the wetness of the potatoes—if the batter seems very wet and thin, add the remaining 2 tablespoons flour. If the batter is still wet after all the flour has been added, press a paper towel over the top to absorb the water.)

Heat ½ inch shortening in a heavy, deep sauté pan or cast-iron skillet over medium heat until very hot (about 350 degrees). Drop as many large spoonfuls of the batter into the hot fat as will comfortably fit without crowding and brown on one side, 2 to 3 minutes. Then turn carefully with a spatula and brown the other side. (Step back when turning the pancakes so that you don't splash yourself with hot oil.) Drain the pancakes on paper towels and serve immediately with Raita (page 344). If you need to make these in batches, hold the finished pancakes in a warm oven (no more than 5 minutes or the pancakes with get soggy).

*Note:* If you don't have a blender, grate the onions and potatoes by hand and stir in the egg. A food processor will produce a somewhat lumpy batter, but you can purée the onion and egg in the processor and fold in the grated potatoes.

# CURRIED CAULIFLOWER

◆ *Serves 6*

*3 small heads cauliflower, cut into florets (about 6 cups)*

*4 to 6 tablespoons unsalted butter or olive oil*

*2 cups chopped onions*

*2 tablespoons (or to taste) grated fresh ginger*

*1 teaspoon ground turmeric*

*2 teaspoons ground cumin*

*1 tablespoon black mustard seeds*

*2 jalapeño peppers, minced*

*2 cups diced fresh or canned plum tomatoes with their juices*

*Salt*

*¼ cup chopped fresh cilantro*

A colorful dish that goes well with curried lentils or eggplant. Add peas if you like.

## Procedure

Cook the cauliflower in a large pot of boiling water until just tender, 5 to 7 minutes. Drain.

Heat the butter or olive oil in a large sauté pan or skillet over medium heat. Add the onions and cook until translucent, about 10 minutes. Add the ginger, spices, and jalapeños and cook 5 minutes. Then add the drained cauliflower and the tomatoes with their juices and simmer 2 to 3 minutes to blend the flavors. Season to taste with salt and sprinkle with the cilantro. Serve hot.

# SKORDALIA

### Mashed Potatoes with Garlic and Olive Oil

♦ *Serves 6*

*6 large russet potatoes, about 10*
*    ounces each*

*Salt*

*6 tablespoons (or more to taste)*
*    finely minced garlic*

*2 egg yolks*

*⅓ cup fresh lemon juice or red*
*    wine vinegar*

*2 cups olive oil*

*Freshly ground pepper*

*⅓ cup finely ground toasted*
*    almonds, or ⅓ cup finely*
*    chopped kalamata olives*
*    (optional)*

Skordalia is a traditional Greek sauce to accompany vegetables or cooked fish. It is essentially glorified mashed potatoes enriched with garlic and olive oil but minus butter and cream. I like it thicker than it is traditionally made and often serve it as a potato dish with grilled fish sauced with tomato and seasoned with oregano or dill, or with fish baked on a bed of onions and tomatoes. Occasionally I like to add a texture and another flavor component, such as the sweetness of toasted almonds, the nuttiness of toasted walnuts, or the tang of chopped kalamata olives. Instead of just lemon juice, you can use vinegar for a slightly sharper flavor accent.

To turn this into the traditional Greek dipping sauce, thin with water or part vinegar and part water to taste.

### Procedure

Preheat the oven to 400 degrees. Place the potatoes on a baking sheet and prick in a few places with the point of a small knife. Bake until tender, about 1 hour. Let stand until cool enough to handle, then cut them in half and scoop out the pulp. Put the pulp through a ricer and set aside in a bowl.

Sprinkle about 1 teaspoon salt over the garlic in a mortar or on a cutting board and mash to a fine paste with the pestle or with the flat side of a large knife. Set aside.

Combine the egg yolks and a little of the lemon juice or vinegar in the container of a food processor or blender and process in the olive oil in a slow, steady stream to emulsify. (Or make the mayonnaise by hand with a whisk.) Add the mayonnaise and the garlic purée to the warm potato pulp and mix well. Season to taste with the remaining lemon juice or vinegar and salt and pepper. Stir in the almonds or olives. Serve hot.

## SCURDALIA
### Sicilian Spiced Potato Sauce

♦ *Serves 4*

*2 large russet potatoes*

*1 teaspoon salt*

*6 garlic cloves, finely minced*

*¼ cup almonds, toasted and finely chopped*

*1 teaspoon poppy seeds*

*½ teaspoon dried red pepper flakes, or ¼ teaspoon cayenne pepper*

*2 tablespoons finely chopped parsley*

*1½ tablespoons white wine vinegar*

*½ cup olive oil*

Many years ago the Greeks passed through Sicily, leaving fabulous temples, sculptures, and some pretty good recipes. Over time, this dish evolved. It's a really interesting variation on the classic lemon and garlic potato purée. The poppy seeds and hot pepper add richness to the sauce, which usually is served as a condiment for cooked fish, shellfish, and vegetables.

### Procedure

Preheat the oven to 400 degrees. Place the potatoes on a baking sheet and prick in a few places with the point of a small knife. Bake until tender, about 1 hour. Let stand until until cool enough to handle. Then cut in half and scoop out the pulp. Put the pulp through a ricer or mash very thoroughly with a potato masher. Measure about 2 cups.

Sprinkle the salt over the garlic in a mortar or on a cutting board, and mash to to a smooth paste with a pestle or with the flat side of a large knife. Transfer to the container of a food processor along with the almonds, poppy seeds, red pepper flakes or cayenne, parsley, and a little of the vinegar. (Or, if you're not a perfectionist, don't bother mashing the garlic—just put it and the salt in the food processor along with the other ingredients.) Add the potatoes and pulse

(*continued*)

quickly to combine. (Do not over-process or the potatoes will be gluey.) Quickly pulse in the olive oil. Taste and adjust seasonings. If too thick, thin with water.

**Note:** Scurdalia can be made a few hours ahead, but if it sits more than 3 or 4 hours the garlic may get too strong. You may also serve Scurdalia as very flavorful mashed potatoes: just use more potatoes or less oil.

# SWEET POTATO STRUDEL

♦ *Serves 4*

*6 medium sweet potatoes or yams, about 1½ pounds*

*4 teaspoons grated orange zest*

*¼ teaspoon freshly grated nutmeg*

*1 teaspoon salt*

*¼ teaspoon freshly ground pepper*

*¼ cup chopped pistachios, toasted (optional)*

*6 sheets filo dough*

*¼ pound unsalted butter, melted*

I like this as an accompaniment for roast duck with a citrus glaze or with roast turkey or pork loin. It can be assembled ahead and refrigerated, loosely covered with a foil tent. If you don't want to serve this in a roll, you can put layers of filo in a baking dish or deep pie pan, add the potatoes, then top with more filo and bake. In Greece they do a variation of this filo pie with butternut squash, and sprinkle a little cinnamon sugar in between the filo layers (page 95).

## Procedure

For the filling, preheat the oven to 400 degrees. Place the sweet potatoes on a baking sheet and bake until soft, about 1 hour. Let stand until cool enough to handle, and then cut in half and scoop out the pulp. Put the pulp through a ricer or mash with a potato masher. (If the potatoes are very watery, it is best to drain them overnight in a strainer placed over a bowl in the refrigerator. Or, if you don't have the time, bake the strudel on a rack to prevent the bottom from becoming soggy.) Measure 2½ cups pulp and stir in the orange zest, nutmeg, salt, and pepper. Fold in the pistachios, if using.

Brush a baking sheet with butter or set a rack large enough to hold the strudel on a baking sheet. Place a sheet of filo on a clean work surface with the long side at the bottom and brush with melted butter. Place another sheet of filo on top and brush with butter. Repeat with the remaining 4 filo sheets to make 6 layers. Spread a wide strip of filling over the filo, about 1 inch in from the bottom edge and 2 inches in from each side. Fold in the sides and bottom and roll up the strudel like a jelly roll, brushing the top with butter as you roll. The strudel may be covered loosely with foil and refrigerated overnight.

Preheat the oven to 350 degrees. Place the strudel seam side down on the buttered baking sheet or on the rack on the baking sheet and brush the top and sides again with melted butter. Bake until golden brown, about 25 minutes. Let rest a few minutes, then cut into thick slices with a serrated knife.

# POTATO STRUDEL

♦ *Serves 8*

*6 large russet potatoes*

*¼ pound plus 3 tablespoons*
*    unsalted butter, melted*

*½ cup pancetta, sliced ¼ inch*
*    thick and diced*

*1 large onion, diced*

*1 cup ricotta cheese*

*1 egg*

*2 tablespoons chopped parsley*

*2 teaspoons salt*

*1 teaspoon freshly ground*
*    pepper*

*Grated nutmeg (optional)*

*12 sheets filo dough*

This is a great accompaniment for Beef à la Stroganoff Revisited (page 306), Grilled Rib-Eye Steak with Mustard, Onions, and Caraway (page 304), Pork Scaloppine with Paprika, Walnuts, Sage, and Cream (page 291), or Roasted Pork Loin with Five-Onion Sauce (page 279), as well as Baked Salmon with Prune Sauce (page 191) or Grilled Salmon with Hungarian Horseradish Almond Cream (page 194). You may omit the pancetta.

## Procedure

Preheat the oven to 400 degrees.

Bake the potatoes for about 1 hour, until they test done. Cool until you are able to handle them easily. Cut in half lengthwise and remove the pulp. Put the potato pulp through a ricer or food mill. Set aside.

Melt the 3 tablespoons butter in a large sauté pan or skillet over medium heat, Add the pancetta and onion and cook until the onion is tender and golden, about 10 minutes. Scrape into the bowl with the potato pulp. Add the cheese, egg, parsley, salt, pepper, and nutmeg, if using, and mix until blended. Let cool.

Lay a sheet of filo on a work surface with one long side facing you. Brush with melted butter. Lay a second sheet on top of the first and brush with melted butter. Repeat with 4 more sheets of filo to make 6 layers.

Shape half the potato mixture into a 2-inch-thick log on one long side of the filo, leaving 2-inch borders. Fold in the sides of the filo and roll up like a jelly roll, brushing with butter as you roll. Place the strudel, seam side down, on a buttered baking sheet. Repeat with the remaining filo dough and potato mixture. The strudels may be refrigerated for up to 2 days or frozen.

Preheat the oven to 400 degrees. Bake the strudel until golden brown, 25 to 30 minutes. Let rest a few minutes, then cut into thick slices with a serrated knife.

# MOROCCAN SPICY FRIED POTATOES

◆ *Serves 4 to 5*

*2 pounds new potatoes*

*½ cup plus 2 tablespoons*
*olive oil*

*Salt and freshly ground pepper*

**Moroccan Spice Mix**

*1 cup chopped fresh cilantro*

*2 tablespoons ground cumin*

*1½ tablespoons paprika*

*1 teaspoon cayenne pepper*

*2 teaspoons salt*

*½ teaspoon freshly ground*
*pepper*

Consider this an alternative to couscous when you're having Moroccan food. The seasonings are inspired by a North African potato salad. I think this amount of heat works harmoniously with the mild potato flavor.

## Procedure

Preheat the oven to 350 degrees. Rub the potatoes with 2 to 3 tablespoons olive oil in a baking dish. Sprinkle with salt and pepper and roast until tender but not mushy when tested with a fork or skewer, 25 to 30 minutes. Let stand until cool enough to handle, and then cut the potatoes into halves or quarters depending on size.

Combine all the ingredients for the spice mix in a small bowl and set aside.

Heat the remaining olive oil in a deep sauté pan or skillet over medium-high heat. Add the potatoes and sauté until browned and crusty. While still warm, sprinkle with the spice mix and serve with grilled chicken, fish or shellfish, or Roast Lobster with Charmoula (page 209).

**Variation:** Deep-fry the potatoes in 4 inches of peanut or vegetable oil heated to 325 degrees. Sprinkle with the Moroccan spice mix and serve.

## CAZZILLI
### Sicilian Potato Croquettes

◆ *About 32 1½-inch*
*croquettes*

*4 russet potatoes*

*¼ cup pine nuts, toasted*

*1 cup grated pecorino cheese*

*2 egg yolks*

*2 tablespoons finely chopped*
*parsley*

*¼ teaspoon freshly ground*
*pepper*

*1½ cups fine dry bread crumbs*

*Peanut or vegetable oil, for*
*deep-frying*

These are wonderful with steak or lamb chops, but they would make a tasty little hot hors d'oeuvre. The pecorino cheese is salty, so I doubt you will need additional salt.

### Procedure

Preheat the oven to 400 degrees. Place the potatoes on a baking sheet and prick in a few places with the point of a small knife. Bake until tender, about 1 hour. Let stand until cool enough to handle, then cut the potatoes in half, and scoop out the pulp. Put the pulp through a ricer or mash with a fork—a ricer gives a nicer texture. Fold in all the remaining ingredients except the bread crumbs and oil and taste and adjust seasonings. Chill for about 1 hour, then form into 1½-inch balls and roll in the bread crumbs to coat. The croquettes may be made a day ahead and refrigerated.

Preheat the oven to 300 degrees. Heat at least 3 inches oil in a deep-fryer or heavy, deep saucepan over medium-high heat to 350 degrees. Add as many croquettes as will comfortably fit without crowding and fry, turning occasionally, until golden brown, about 5 minutes. Drain on paper towels and keep warm in the oven while frying the remaining croquettes. Serve hot.

## POTATOES AND ASPARAGUS ALL'ERICINA

♦ *Serves 2*

*4 small new potatoes*

*3 tablespoons olive oil or*

> *2 tablespoons olive oil plus*

> *1 tablespoon unsalted butter*

*8 asparagus stalks*

*Salt and freshly ground pepper*

*½ cup Chicken Stock*

> *(page 119)*

*2 tablespoons chopped fresh*

> *basil*

*2 tablespoons almonds, toasted*

E rice is an exquisite hill town in western Sicily. What I remember most vividly about it is that the streets were paved with a stone pattern that looked as if a giant pebble carpet had been thrown over the city. Magic. I can think of nothing better than sitting in a little café in Erice, sipping the local Marsala or Malvasia and smelling the sea. This recipe for potatoes and asparagus, like Erice, is simple but magic.

### Procedure

Preheat the oven to 350 degrees. Rub the potatoes with 1 tablespoon olive oil in a baking dish. Sprinkle with salt and pepper and bake until tender but not mushy, 25 to 30 minutes. Let stand until cool enough to handle and then cut into halves or quarters, depending on size.

Bring a large saucepan of lightly salted water to a boil. Add the asparagus and cook until just tender, 4 to 8 minutes, depending on thickness. Drain and refresh under cold running water. Cut into 2-inch lengths and set aside.

Warm the remaining 2 tablespoons olive oil or combination oil and butter in a medium sauté pan or skillet over medium heat. Add the potatoes and sauté 2 to 3 minutes. Add the asparagus and chicken stock and simmer until the stock has reduced and thickened. Add the basil and almonds and cook until warmed through. Season to taste with salt and pepper and serve at once.

## POTATOES À LA GRECQUE

◆ *Serves 2*

*8 small new potatoes*

*4 to 5 tablespoons olive oil*

*Salt and freshly ground pepper*

*1 red onion, cut into ¼-inch*
*    rounds*

*½ cup crumbled feta cheese*

*4 kalamata olives, pitted and*
*    coarsely chopped*

*2 teaspoons chopped fresh*
*    oregano (optional), or*
*    1 teaspoon dried*

It may not be a truly authentic Greek recipe but it captures some of the traditional flavors. Great with lamb or chicken.

### Procedure

Preheat the oven to 350 degrees. Rub the potatoes with 2 tablespoons olive oil in a baking dish. Sprinkle with salt and pepper and bake until tender but not mushy, 25 to 30 minutes. Let stand until cool enough to handle, then cut into halves or quarters, depending on size. Set aside.

Preheat a grill or broiler. Brush the onion slices with oil, sprinkle with salt and pepper, and grill or broil until tender and browned, 5 to 10 minutes. Or, heat 2 to 3 tablespoons oil in a sauté pan or griddle over medium-high heat. Add the onions and sauté until golden brown, 15 to 20 minutes. Sprinkle with salt and pepper. Set aside.

Heat 2 tablespoons olive oil in a sauté pan or skillet over high heat. Add the potatoes and sauté until lightly browned, about 6 minutes. Add the cooked onions and sauté until warmed through. Sprinkle with the cheese and olives and the oregano, if using. Serve hot.

*Note:* It is probably more convenient to sauté the onions than to grill them, but on a night when you are using the broiler or grill anyway, do try grilling the onions.

# FENNEL GRATIN

◆ *Serves 6*

*6 tablespoons unsalted butter,*
*  plus 2 tablespoons, melted,*
*  for drizzling*

*6 large fennel bulbs, trimmed,*
*  cored, and sliced, tough pieces*
*  removed*

*½ cup Chicken Stock*
*  (page 119)*

*½ teaspoon salt*

*¼ teaspoon freshly ground*
*  pepper*

*Grated nutmeg to taste*
*  (optional)*

*¼ cup grated Parmesan cheese*

*¼ cup Toasted Bread Crumbs*
*  (page 189)*

I first ate this in the dining car on a train between Florence and Venice. Talk about a surprise— good food on a train and a recipe I wanted to reproduce.

### Procedure

Melt the butter in a large sauté pan or skillet over medium heat until foamy. Add the sliced fennel and sauté, stirring often, until golden, about 10 minutes. Add the Chicken Stock, reduce the heat and simmer until tender, about 10 minutes. Season with salt and pepper and the nutmeg, if using.

Preheat the oven to 450 degrees. Transfer the fennel to 6 individual or one large gratin dish. Sprinkle with the Parmesan and bread crumbs. Drizzle with the melted butter and bake until crusty on top, about 10 minutes. Serve hot with fish, chicken, or meat.

# CORN PUDDING

◆ *Serves 6*

*4 cups corn kernels (cut from*
*about 8 ears corn)*

*2 tablespoons all-purpose flour*

*2 teaspoons salt*

*½ teaspoon freshly ground*
*pepper*

*¼ to ½ teaspoon cayenne*
*pepper*

*¼ teaspoon (or more to taste)*
*freshly grated nutmeg*

*½ cup milk*

*1 cup half-and-half or light*
*cream*

*3 eggs*

*6 tablespoons unsalted butter,*
*melted*

*1 roasted and peeled poblano*
*chili, cut into strips then*
*diced, about ¼ cup (optional)*

*¾ to 1 cup Monterey Jack*
*cheese (optional)*

An American classic that I like to make often when corn is in season. If you want to give this a Mexican tang, add some chopped roasted poblano chilies and top with grated Monterey Jack cheese during the last 5 minutes of baking. It's delicious with fried chicken or Mexican-style leg of lamb rubbed with cumin, oregano, chilies, and garlic. I have also eaten this and a salad as dinner, and have been supremely happy.

## Procedure

Preheat the oven to 350 degrees. Butter a shallow 2-quart Pyrex, ceramic, or metal baking dish.

Toss the corn kernels with the flour, salt, pepper, cayenne, and nutmeg in a large mixing bowl. Set aside.

Warm the milk and cream slightly in a small saucepan over medium heat. Whisk with the eggs and add to the bowl with the corn. Add the melted butter and mix well. Taste and adjust seasonings and then pour into the prepared baking dish. Place in a larger pan and pour hot water into the larger pan to come about halfway up the sides of the baking dish. Bake until the pudding is pale gold on top and the custard is almost firm, about 1 hour.

*Variation:* For a Mexican flavor, add 2 large poblano peppers, charred over a flame, peeled, and cut into small dice, to the corn mixture. Pour into the prepared baking dish and sprinkle 1½ cups grated Monterey Jack cheese over the top during the last 5 minutes of baking.

# SAUCES AND CONDIMENTS

Fresh Cilantro or Mint Chutney ◆ Raita ◆ Russian Walnut and Cilantro Sauce ◆ Tunisian Harissa ◆ Romescu ◆ Square One Hot Mustard ◆ Basic Vinaigrette for Green Salads ◆ Basic Tomato Sauce ◆ Salsa ◆ Avocado Salsa ◆ Moroccan-Inspired Sweet and Hot Cherry Tomato Jam ◆ Tangerine Jam ◆ Middle Eastern Rosewater Orange Marmalade ◆ Spiced Fig Jam ◆ Pear Chutney ◆ Apricot Chutney ◆ Apple Chutney ◆ Dried Apricot Chutney ◆ Rosemary Spiced Pears ◆ Moroccan Spiced Olives ◆ Moroccan Preserved Lemon Peel ◆

## FRESH CILANTRO OR MINT CHUTNEY

♦ *Makes about 1½ cups*

*2 cups tightly packed cilantro or*
*    mint leaves (3 to 4 bunches)*

*1 onion, diced (about ¾ cup)*

*2 to 3 walnut-size pieces fresh*
*    ginger*

*1 tablespoon minced garlic*

*3 to 4 jalapeño peppers, diced*

*½ cup fresh lemon juice*

*¼ cup (or as needed) water*

*½ teaspoon salt*

*1 teaspoon sugar*

A spicy and refreshing chutney that works well with almost any curry. I especially love it with Curried Crab Cakes (page 205), the Indian Fritto Misto al Mare (page 206), or grilled or baked fish in a tandoori marinade (page 222).

### Procedure

Combine all the ingredients in a blender and process to a smooth purée. Add water, if necessary, to thin to desired consistency. Transfer to a serving bowl and refrigerate until serving time. This chutney keeps well for about 1 day, and then the color begins to fade. (It still tastes good, though!)

## RAITA

♦ *Makes 3½ to 4 cups*

*1 pint plain yogurt*

*1 cup peeled, seeded, and finely*
*    diced cucumber (see note)*

*1 cup peeled, seeded, and diced*
*    tomato*

*2 to 3 tablespoons grated onion*
*    (optional)*

*Salt and freshly ground pepper*

*2 tablespoons cumin seeds,*
*    toasted (optional)*

*3 to 4 tablespoons chopped fresh*
*    mint or cilantro (optional)*

A refreshing relish to serve with Indian food. Good with lamb chops (page 272), too. You can assemble this in minutes.

### Procedure

Combine all the ingredients and mix well.

*Variation:* Omit the tomato and cumin seeds and add 2 tablespoons minced jalapeño peppers and 1 tablespoon minced garlic.

*Note:* English cucumbers need not be peeled.

# RUSSIAN WALNUT AND CILANTRO SAUCE

◆ *Makes 5 cups*

*1 cup walnuts, toasted and finely chopped*

*2 cups finely minced white onions*

*¾ cup chopped fresh cilantro*

*4 garlic cloves, finely minced*

*¼ cup wine vinegar (red or white)*

*1 cup olive oil*

*½ cup walnut oil*

*Salt and freshly ground pepper*

Cilantro in Russia? As surprising as it may seem, the herb is widely used in the Caucasus. This sauce is reminiscent of walnut pesto and would be good on most mild-flavored fish and grilled eggplant, zucchini, or peppers. Or as a dressing for rice salad, avocado salad, or chicken salad.

## Procedure

Whisk all the ingredients together in a bowl. This will keep well for a day or two in the refrigerator but the color may fade.

# TUNISIAN HARISSA

◆ *Makes 1 scant cup*

*4 large red bell peppers or*
   *pimientos, cored and seeded*

*2 large garlic cloves, finely*
   *minced*

*1 tablespoon ground coriander*

*1 tablespoon ground toasted*
   *caraway seed*

*1½ to 2 teaspoons (or to taste)*
   *cayenne pepper (see note)*

*¾ teaspoon salt*

*Pinch of ground cloves*

A few years ago we were fortunate to have a guest chef from Tunisia spend a few days in our kitchen. Baroui Karoui arrived with his own special spice mixture, some frozen ouarka leaves, dates, books, and a special giant restaurant-size couscousière. What is most important, he brought great energy and enthusiasm, and an open mind. We traded recipes and stories over beer and pizza. This recipe is his version of harissa, that zippy hot condiment served in North Africa as a sort of salsa.

### Procedure

Put the bell peppers through a meat grinder or pulse very quickly in a food processor to purée. Strain excess water. Measure ¾ cup purée, add the remaining ingredients, and mix to blend.

*Note:* You may use a finely minced fresh hot pepper such as a jalapeño or serrano chili in the harissa in place of, or in addition to, the cayenne.

# ROMESCU

### Spicy Tomato-Almond Aioli

◆ *Makes 2½ to 3 cups*

1 tablespoon finely chopped
   garlic

2 egg yolks

3 to 4 tablespoons fresh lemon
   juice

2 cups mild olive oil

Salt

1 cup sliced almonds, toasted
   and coarsely chopped

¾ cup drained, seeded, and
   finely chopped Italian plum
   tomatoes

½ to 1 teaspoon (or more, to
   taste) cayenne pepper

3 to 4 tablespoons red wine
   vinegar

2 tablespoons tomato purée

Freshly ground black pepper

This is my version of the classic Catalan romescu sauce that is great stirred into a fish stew, or spooned over grilled shrimp or scallops or cold-poached fish, grilled eggplant, and leeks. It's also delightful with fried potatoes.

### Procedure

Mash the garlic to a paste in a mortar; set aside. Place the egg yolks in the container of a blender or food processor or in a bowl with a little of the lemon juice and process or whisk to blend. Gradually process or whisk in the olive oil, a few drops at a time and then in a steady stream, until a thick emulsion is formed. Add the remaining lemon juice, garlic, and salt to taste. If the mayonnaise is too thick, thin with a little water. (You'll find that the mayonnaise is a little lighter made by hand than in the processor or in the blender.) Add the remaining ingredients. Taste and adjust seasonings; the sauce should be tart and hot, with a noticeable crunch of almond.

## SQUARE ONE HOT MUSTARD

◆ *Makes 3½ cups*

*8 ounces dry mustard*

*½ cup distilled white vinegar*

*½ cup water*

*2 tablespoons salt*

*⅓ to ½ cup sugar*

*2 eggs*

*2 cups light olive oil, such*
   *as Sasso*

This is hot, sweet, and tart. It makes a wonderful addition to sauces and vinaigrettes and will enliven the stodgiest sandwich. It keeps for a few months; just stir before using if it has separated or settled a bit. You can make this in the food processor or with an electric mixer.

### Procedure

Whisk the mustard with the vinegar, ¼ cup of the water, the sugar, and the salt. Add the eggs one at a time, whisking well after each addition. Then add the oil, gradually at first and then in a steady stream, as for a mayonnaise. Taste and adjust the balance of sugar, salt, and vinegar, and then thin with the remaining water. Cover and refrigerate. (If the sauce separates, just whisk for a minute or two and it will come together.)

## BASIC VINAIGRETTE FOR GREEN SALADS

◆ *About 1¼ cups*

*⅓ cup virgin olive oil*

*⅔ cup mild, pure olive oil, such*
   *as Sasso*

*3 tablespoons red wine vinegar*

*1 tablespoon balsamic vinegar*

*1 teaspoon Dijon mustard*

*Salt and freshly ground pepper*
   *to taste*

Your middle-of-the-road vinaigrette. Good for most lettuces. The balsamic vinegar adds a smoothness and depth of flavor that cuts the tart acid of the regular wine vinegar.

### Procedure

Whisk or process together all the ingredients in a bowl or blender. You may add chopped herbs or a minced clove of garlic, if you like. Season with salt and pepper to taste.

## BASIC TOMATO SAUCE

◆ *About 3 quarts*

*5 pounds canned Italian-style
plum tomatoes with their
juices*

*2 cups very rich tomato purée*

*Salt and freshly ground pepper*

*4 to 6 tablespoons unsalted
butter, cut into small pieces
(optional)*

*or*

*2 to 3 tablespoons good olive oil
(optional)*

*Pinch of sugar (optional)*

A good basic tomato sauce to have in your repertoire. It keeps about four days in the refrigerator. This makes enough for 12 to 14 portions of pasta.

### *Procedure*

Process the tomatoes with their juices in a food processor until finely chopped but not puréed. Transfer to a heavy saucepan and stir in the tomato purée. Simmer over low heat, stirring often, until the sauce is hot and slightly thickened. Season to taste with salt and pepper. If the tomatoes are sour, stir in the butter or olive oil, or add a pinch of sugar.

# SALSA

◆ *About 1 cup*

*½ cup fresh lemon or lime juice,*
*    or combination of both*

*1 teaspoon (or to taste) minced*
*    jalapeño peppers*

*1 teaspoon finely minced garlic*

*2 tablespoons chopped fresh*
*    cilantro*

*2 tablespoons finely chopped red*
*    onion*

*3 tablespoons chopped tomatoes*
*    (optional)*

*3 tablespoons fresh orange juice*
*    (optional)*

*3 tablespoons olive oil*

*Salt and freshly ground pepper*
*    to taste*

An excellent accompaniment for grilled meats, fish, and scallops and a great vinaigrette for shellfish and avocado salad.

## *Procedure*

Combine all the ingredients in a bowl.

**Note:** For seviche, cut ¾ pound raw fish or scallops into thin slices. Add the lemon or lime juice and let stand until the fish turns white, about 1 hour. Add the rest of the salsa ingredients and some thinly sliced peppers. Serve with fried tortillas and guacamole. You may increase the onions and tomatoes, if you like.

# AVOCADO SALSA

◆ *About 1 cup*

*1 large ripe avocado, cut into
    ½-inch dice*

*2 plum tomatoes, peeled, seeded,
    cut into ½-inch dice, fresh or
    canned*

*2 tablespoons finely chopped
    green pepper (optional)*

*1 teaspoon finely minced
    jalapeño pepper (including
    seeds)*

*1 tablespoon chopped cilantro*

*¼ cup olive oil*

*2 tablespoons red wine vinegar
    or lime or lemon juice*

*1 teaspoon salt*

*Freshly ground pepper to taste*

It's not really guacamole but close. This is an ideal dip for fried potatoes, and a dollop of this will perk up grilled fish, flank steak, or black bean soup.

### Procedure

Combine all of the ingredients in a bowl and mix carefully with a spoon. You don't want to mash the avocado too much.

# MOROCCAN-INSPIRED SWEET AND HOT CHERRY TOMATO JAM

♦ *Makes 6 pints*

*8 ounces fresh ginger, peeled*
*and thinly sliced across the*
*grain*

*1 cup cider vinegar*

*2 quarts cherry tomatoes,*
*washed and stemmed*

*2 cups brown sugar*

*2 cups white sugar*

*2 lemons, cut in half lengthwise*
*and sliced paper thin*

*1 cup water*

*1 tablespoon ground cinnamon*

*1 tablespoon ground cumin*

*1 teaspoon ground cloves*

*1 teaspoon cayenne pepper*

*Salt and freshly ground black*
*pepper*

This is great with cooked chicken or lamb, or drizzled on grilled eggplant. Minus the cumin and cayenne it makes a nice alternative to ketchup for steak.

## Procedure

Combine the ginger and the vinegar in the container of a food processor or blender and process until the ginger is finely ground. Transfer to a deep, heavy saucepan, preferably enamel-covered cast iron. Add the cherry tomatoes, the sugars, the sliced lemons, and the water. Cover and cook 15 minutes over medium to high heat. Add the spices, reduce the heat and simmer, stirring often to prevent scorching, until thickened, about 1 hour. Season to taste with salt and pepper. Pour into sterilized canning jars and seal. Reheat to serve warm or serve at room temperature.

# TANGERINE JAM

♦ *About 4 to 5 ½-pint jars*

*2 pounds tangerines*

*2 pounds sugar*

*Pinch of cinnamon*

Ever since reading Claudia Roden's *Book of Middle Eastern Food*, I have been in love with her tangerine jam. It's wonderful on toast, and I love it warmed and served as a sauce over ice cream. Add five-spice powder for an Oriental accent.

### Procedure

Cut the tangerines in half and squeeze the juice; strain and reserve the juice. Place the rinds in a saucepan and add water to cover. Bring to a boil, reduce the heat, and simmer 10 minutes. Drain. Cover with fresh water and soak overnight, changing the water 2 to 3 times. Drain, and then chop or mince the rinds.

Place the tangerine juice in a deep stainless steel or enameled cast-iron kettle. Add the sugar, the chopped rinds, and the cinnamon. Bring to a boil, reduce the heat, and simmer, stirring often, until thickened. This may take up to ½ hour. (Test the thickness by spooning a small amount onto a china plate that has been stored in the freezer. If the jam thickens on the plate and doesn't run when the plate is tilted, the jam is ready.) Ladle into sterilized canning jars and seal.

*Variation:* You may also make this jam with lemons, oranges, or blood oranges.

## MIDDLE EASTERN ROSEWATER ORANGE MARMALADE

♦ *8 to 10 ½-pint jars*

*5 pounds blood or regular oranges (about 12)*

*5 pounds sugar*

*2 teaspoons cinnamon, or*

 *1½ teaspoons cinnamon plus*

 *½ teaspoon ground cardamom*

*2 cups rosewater*

*3 cups rosé wine, or combination water and wine*

Try this on ice cream or spooned over rice pudding. Terrific.

### Procedure

Cut the oranges into very thin slices and seed them. Arrange a layer of slices over the bottom of a stainless steel or enameled cast-iron kettle. Sprinkle with sugar and cinnamon. Then make another layer of oranges slices and sprinkle again with sugar and cinnamon. Repeat to use all the orange slices, sugar, and cinnamon. Add the rosewater and wine and water as needed to cover the oranges. Simmer very gently 1 hour. Then remove from the heat and let stand a few hours or overnight to allow the oranges to plump. Bring to a boil, reduce the heat, and simmer slowly until the mixture is syrupy and thick, between 30 and 60 minutes depending on the diameter of the cooking vessel. Pack into sterilized jars and seal.

## SPICED FIG JAM

♦ *Makes 12 ½-pint jars*

*6 pounds ripe black Mission figs*

*1 lemon, cut into chunks, seeds removed*

*1 large orange, cut into chunks, seeds removed*

*8 ounces fresh ginger, peeled and thinly sliced across the grain*

I realize that not everyone has access to fresh figs, but if you can find them at the market, or have a tree that produces fruit before the birds eat it all, you will love this recipe. Fig conserve is wonderful spread on walnut or white toast. It will remind you of summer all winter long.

### Procedure

Peel the figs, cut them into chunks, and put them into a large heavy canning pot. (I prefer enameled cast iron.) Set aside. Peeling figs takes a little time so

*Juice of 2 oranges (about*
 *⅔ cup)*

*7 cups sugar*

*2 teaspoons cinnamon*

*Juice of 2 lemons (about ½ cup)*

if you can get someone to help you it won't seem so long or lonely. Combine the lemon and orange chunks, the ginger, and orange juice in a blender and purée. Pour over the figs, add the sugar and cinnamon, and stir well. Bring to a boil over medium heat, stirring often to prevent scorching and sticking. Then reduce the heat and simmer, stirring often, until the jam is thick, 20 to 30 minutes. Add the lemon juice to taste during the last 5 minutes of cooking time. Pack into sterilized canning jars and seal.

# PEAR CHUTNEY

♦ *Makes 8 to 9 pints*

*10 ounces preserved ginger or*
 *8 ounces fresh ginger*

*2 large onions, diced*

*4 oranges, cut into chunks,*
 *seeds removed*

*3 cups cider vinegar*

*16 cups sliced, peeled Anjou or*
 *Comice pears, firm and not*
 *too ripe*

*2 pounds light brown sugar*

*2 teaspoons ground cloves*

*2 teaspoons cinnamon*

*1 teaspoon salt*

*1 teaspoon cayenne pepper*

*3 to 4 cups golden raisins*

A s apricots and peaches have a brief season, and pears are around most of the year, this is a nice recipe to have in your repertoire when you have eaten all the summer-fruit chutney in your larder.

### Procedure

Combine the ginger, onions, oranges, and some of the vinegar in the container of a food processor or blender and purée. Transfer to a deep stainless steel or enameled cast-iron kettle and add all the other ingredients except the raisins. Bring to a boil, reduce the heat, and simmer until thickened, about 1 hour, stirring occasionally. Add the raisins during the last 20 minutes of cooking time. Pack into sterilized canning jars and seal, or refrigerate.

# APRICOT CHUTNEY

◆ *Makes 7 pints*

*1 lime*

*2 large onions, diced*

*3 garlic cloves*

*3 ounces fresh ginger, peeled and coarsely chopped*

*1 teaspoon ground cloves*

*1 teaspoon ground allspice*

*1 teaspoon ground ginger*

*1 tablespoon cinnamon*

*2 teaspoons salt*

*1 teaspoon cayenne pepper*

*3 cups cider vinegar*

*4 pounds apricots, seeded and cut into quarters (about 8 cups)*

*1½ pounds (or as needed) brown sugar*

*2 cups raisins*

Although you can buy chutney, it is never as good as the one you make. Most commercial brands are stiff and dry, the fruit pieces too large, and the spices impersonal and bland. You can store homemade chutney for at least two years, so why not make a big batch when the fruit is in season? A jar of it makes a wonderful gift.

This one is fine with curry, pork roasts, or chicken.

## Procedure

Grate the zest of the lime and squeeze the juice. Place in the container of a food processor or blender along with the onions, garlic, ginger, and spices. Add some of the vinegar and purée. Pour into a deep stainless steel or enameled cast-iron kettle. Add the apricots, sugar, and the remaining vinegar and bring to a boil. Reduce the heat and simmer for about 1 hour, stirring often to prevent sticking and scorching. Add the raisins during the last 15 minutes of cooking time. Taste and adjust for a good sweet/tart balance; the vinegar will die down after a few weeks so don't worry if the chutney seems acidic. Pack into sterilized canning jars, seal, and process in a hot-water bath for 10 minutes.

# APPLE CHUTNEY

◆ *Makes 10 pints*

*2 cups chopped onions*

*3 garlic cloves, minced*

*2 tablespoons ground ginger, or*
*6 tablespoons fresh ginger,*
*puréed*

*4 cups cider vinegar*

*2 red bell peppers, seeded and*
*chopped*

*12 cups peeled, cored and*
*chopped apples (Pippins or*
*Granny Smiths)*

*4 cups brown sugar*

*¼ cup mustard seeds*

*2 teaspoons ground allspice*

*1 to 2 teaspoons cayenne pepper*

*2 pounds raisins*

*2 teaspoons salt*

Another winter chutney. This is good with baked ham or pork chops. And it adds a little zip to Thanksgiving turkey.

## Procedure

Combine the onions, garlic, ginger, and some of the vinegar in the container of a food processor and purée. Transfer to a deep stainless steel or enameled cast-iron kettle and add all the remaining ingredients except the raisins. Bring to a boil, reduce the heat, and simmer until thickened, about 45 minutes. Add the raisins during the last 10 minutes of cooking time. Pack into sterilized canning jars and seal.

*Variation:* Omit the red bell peppers and increase the onions to 3 cups. Or simply substitute 2 cups cranberries for the peppers.

# DRIED APRICOT CHUTNEY

♦ *Makes 9 to 10 pint jars*

*4 pounds dried apricots, soaked*
  *in hot water to cover until soft*

*8 jalapeño peppers*

*½ cup water*

*1 quart plus ¼ cup (or to taste)*
  *white vinegar*

*4½ cups (or to taste) sugar*

*4 teaspoons ground cumin*

*¼ cup ground ginger*

*3 teaspoons (or to taste) salt*

I like this with Afghani lamb sausage or curries, but there's no reason it wouldn't make a lamb chop or leg of lamb or even a simple roast chicken happy. It's also perfect for cream cheese and chutney sandwiches.

### Procedure

Drain the apricots and pulse in a food processor to chop. Transfer to a deep stainless steel or enameled cast-iron saucepan. Purée the jalapeños with the water in a food processor and add to the pan with the apricots. Add all the remaining ingredients, bring to a boil, reduce the heat, and simmer until the apricots become puréed. Taste and adjust the sweet/sour/salt ratio. Pack into sterilized canning jars and seal.

# ROSEMARY SPICED PEARS

♦ *Serves 8*

*1 cup cider vinegar*

*½ cup water*

*1 cup sugar*

*2 teaspoons dried red pepper*
  *flakes*

*3 large fresh rosemary sprigs*

*4 Anjou or Bartlett pears,*
  *peeled, halved, and cored*

This is not a trendy dessert but a fine accompaniment for lamb chops and chicken, especially those with rosemary in the marinade.

### Procedure

Combine the vinegar, water, and sugar in a medium saucepan and bring to a boil over medium heat. Add the red pepper flakes and the rosemary sprigs and boil 5 minutes. Then add the pear halves, reduce the heat, and simmer until a skewer easily penetrates the pears, about 25 minutes. Remove from the heat and let cool in the syrup.

## MOROCCAN SPICED OLIVES AND PRESERVED LEMON PEEL

For the perfect martini. These keep well in the refrigerator so make as much as you think you'd like to have on hand.

### MOROCCAN SPICED OLIVES

*1 pound pitted (see note) green niçoise or other olives (niçoise are best for martinis)*

*1 teaspoon paprika*

*½ teaspoon cayenne pepper*

*½ teaspoon ground cumin*

*½ teaspoon salt*

*4 garlic cloves, crushed*

*3 tablespoons olive oil*

### *Procedure*

Combine all the ingredients in a bowl and let stand at least 1 day.

**Note:** If the olives have pits, pound lightly with a meat pounder to crack the skin so that the spices will penetrate.

### MOROCCAN PRESERVED LEMON PEEL

*¼ cup sugar*

*1 tablespoon kosher salt*

*2 lemons*

This is a fast way to get Moroccan lemon flavor without putting up the whole lemon.

### *Procedure*

Combine the sugar and salt and set aside. Remove the lemon zest in strips with a peeler and cut into pieces about 2 inches long and ¼ inch wide. Cover with water in a saucepan and bring to a boil. Boil 5 minutes, then drain in a colander and pat dry. Transfer to a nonaluminum container and cover with the sugar mixture. Cover and refrigerate; will keep several weeks in the refrigerator. Rinse before using.

# DESSERTS

PESCHE ALLE MANDORLE ◆ ORANGES WITH ORANGE ZEST AND HONEY ◆ PERSIMMON PUDDING ◆ NECTARINE CRISP ◆ SCOTCH CRÈME BRÛLÉE ◆ TARTUFO AL TRE SCALINI ◆ TARTUFO DI PARADISO ◆ CHOCOLATE SORBET ◆ TIRAMISÙ ◆ SACRIPANTINA ◆ CANNOLI DEI SOGNI ◆ MASCARPONE CUSTARD AND BERRY TART ◆ GREEK HONEY CHEESECAKE ◆ TARTA ALHAMBRA ◆ PÂTE SUCRÉE ◆ AURORA TART ◆ GÂTEAU ROLLA ◆ ALMOND CAKE ◆ CHOCOLATE MOUSSE TORTE WITH MOCHA GANACHE ◆ CHOCOLATE CHESTNUT TORTE WITH COGNAC ◆ WALNUT TORTE WITH CARAMEL CUSTARD AND MOCHA BUTTERCREAM ◆ SUSAN'S PASSOVER SPONGE CAKE ◆ COCONUT MACAROONS ◆ ROLLED HOLIDAY SHORTBREAD COOKIES ◆ BACI DI DAMA ◆ PECAN COOKIES ◆

## PESCHE ALLE MANDORLE

### *Peaches Stuffed with Almonds*

♦ *Serves 6*

*6 ripe freestone peaches*

*12 amaretti cookies*

*½ cup sliced almonds, toasted*

*¼ cup sugar*

*1 teaspoon ground ginger*

*8 tablespoons unsalted butter,*
  *cut into 8 pieces*

*½ cup sweet Marsala, white*
  *wine, or orange juice*
  *(optional)*

These always remind me of Italy, especially if I serve them with zabaglione. Wait for the perfect aromatic peaches of late summer for this dish; freestones are the easiest to work with as you need a pretty good-size cavity to get in the maximum amount of filling. The peaches can be stuffed ahead and refrigerated for up to 6 hours before baking.

### *Procedure*

Lightly butter a baking dish. Preheat the oven to 375 degrees.

Bring a saucepan of water to a boil. Drop in the peaches and then remove with a slotted spoon to a bowl of ice water. The skins should slip off easily. If not, return the peaches to the boiling water for a few seconds and cool again in the ice water. Cut the peaches in half and remove the pits. Place the peach halves, cut sides up, in the prepared baking dish.

Combine the amaretti, the almonds, ginger, and sugar in the container of a food processor and pulse a few times until crumbled. Add the butter and pulse to make a paste. Mound into the centers of the peach halves and bake 25 minutes, basting with a little Marsala, white wine, or orange juice, if you like. Serve warm, with peach, almond, or vanilla ice cream, or with chilled zabaglione.

*Wine Notes:* Many dessert wine options here. A young German or American late-harvested Riesling is a refreshing accompaniment, as are Sauternes and late-harvested Semillon-based wines. As an accent to the almonds, you might also enjoy a nutty cream sherry, Amaretto, or a younger tawny port.

# ORANGES WITH ORANGE ZEST AND HONEY

● *Serves 6*

*6 large oranges*

*½ cup water*

*1¼ cups sugar*

*¼ cup honey*

*¼ cup Grand Marnier or*
*2 tablespoons orange flower*
*water (optional)*

*2 tablespoons chopped fresh*
*mint (optional)*

*¼ cup chopped pistachios or*
*almonds, toasted (optional)*

This refreshing orange compote is one of my favorite desserts as it is so refreshing. It has a Middle Eastern aura about it because of the honey; to accentuate this characteristic you might want to add toasted pistachios or almonds, and a little orange flower water. Chopped mint would add an element of North Africa. Grand Marnier or another orange liqueur adds yet another dimension.

## Procedure

Remove the bright orange zest of the oranges with a potato peeler (try not to get the bitter white pith) and cut into thin julienne strips. Bring a saucepan of water to a boil, add the julienne, and blanch 2 to 3 minutes. Drain and refresh in cold water. Set aside.

Cut off all the white pith from the oranges with a small knife. Then remove the segments by cutting between the membranes. Place the peeled orange segments in a bowl and set aside.

Combine the water, sugar, and honey in a saucepan and cook over high heat, stirring, until the sugar has dissolved. Continue cooking until the syrup thickens and measures about 230 degrees on a candy thermometer. Let the syrup cool for a few minutes, stir in the blanched zest and pour over the orange segments. Add the Grand Marnier or orange flower water, the mint, or nuts, if you like. Serve at room temperature.

**Wine Notes:** This is a dessert first, wine afterward situation. Try a light Muscat, a drier Bual Madeira, an auslese-level German Riesling, or an extra-dry Champagne. I also like a slightly chilled Cointreau or Grand Marnier.

## PERSIMMON PUDDING

♦ *Makes 2 9- by 6- by 3-inch
loaves, or 1 8- to 9-cup
pudding mold*

*2½ cups sugar*

*½ pound plus 4 tablespoons
unsalted butter, melted*

*2½ cups all-purpose flour, sifted*

*¾ teaspoon salt*

*2½ teaspoons cinnamon or
Chinese five-spice powder*

*4 cups persimmon purée (about
6 persimmons)*

*5 teaspoons baking soda
dissolved in 5 tablespoons hot
water*

*5 tablespoons brandy*

*1 tablespoon vanilla extract*

*1 tablespoon fresh lemon juice*

*5 large eggs, lightly beaten*

*1 cup raisins or currants, or
combination of the two*

*¾ cup chopped walnuts*

G rowing up in Brooklyn, I never saw persimmons in our fruitstands. When I first started shopping in San Francisco markets, I was dazzled by the color and shape of this fruit and arranged bowls of them as dining table centerpieces. Finally I learned what you could do with them besides eat them out of hand when they become soft and ripe.

This is a traditional holiday dessert at my Thanksgiving and Christmas dinners, a variation on the English plum pudding. I used to serve hard sauce with it, but now I think whipped cream will do nicely, or some eggnog or vanilla ice cream.

### Procedure

Preheat the oven to 350 degrees. Butter two 9- by 6- by 3-inch loaf pans or a 6-cup pudding mold. Sift the flour with the salt and cinnamon. Cream together the sugar and butter in a mixing bowl. Set aside. Beat in the eggs, the persimmon purée, the soda, brandy, vanilla, and lemon juice and mix until smooth. Fold in the flour, salt, and cinnamon and beat into the batter. Add the raisins and/or currants and walnuts and mix just until blended. (Do not overbeat.)

Pour into the prepared loaf pans or mold and smooth the top(s). Place the pans or mold in a large baking pan and add enough hot water to come halfway up the sides of the pans or mold. Cover the pan with foil and bake until the pudding springs back when touched and pulls away from the side of the pan(s), about 2 hours for the loaf pans, or 2½ hours for the 6-cup mold. (Or place the covered pans over low heat on top of the stove and steam the pud-ding(s) in barely simmering water until done. Serve warm, with brandy-flavored whipped cream or hard sauce.

*Wine Notes:* I like this with late-harvested Australian wines (Muscat, Semillon) and with less syrupy Sauternes-style wine: Cerons, Cadillac Loupiac. A luscious German Beerenauslese or spicy Spanish Muscat sherry would also be good.

# NECTARINE CRISP

♦ *Serves 4*

**Streusel Topping**

⅓ pound unsalted butter

5 tablespoons brown sugar

7 tablespoons white sugar

1 cup plus 5 tablespoons
    all-purpose flour

¼ teaspoon baking powder

½ teaspoon cinnamon

Scant ⅞ cup chopped walnuts,
    lightly toasted

**Filling**

1 cup brown sugar

⅓ cup all-purpose flour

Pinch of salt

6 cups sliced, unpeeled
    nectarines

1 tablespoon vanilla extract

1 tablespoon kirsch

1 tablespoon lemon or
    orange zest

A classic summer dessert. Peaches, apricots, plums, and berries will work as well. Serve with cream or ice cream.

## Procedure

For the topping, beat the butter and sugars in the bowl of an electric mixer until light and fluffy. Add the flour, baking powder, and cinnamon and mix well. Add walnuts and mix to combine. Loosely pack the streusel mixture into a shallow container and freeze until firm.

Meanwhile for the filling lightly butter a 9- by 9- by 3-inch baking dish. Mix together the sugar, flour, and salt. Toss with the nectarines, vanilla, kirsch, and zest, and spread evenly over the bottom of the prepared baking dish.

Preheat the oven to 350 degrees. Transfer the frozen streusel topping to the container of a food processor and process to the size of small pebbles. Crumble over the nectarine filling and bake the crisp until the top is golden and bubbles appear at the sides, about 35 minutes. Serve warm with vanilla ice cream.

**Wine Notes:** Late-harvested Riesling, Semillon, or Sauvignon Blanc are best. Also try late-harvested dessert wines from the Loire Valley (Coteaux de Layon, Chaume, and Quart de Chaume). For plum or berry crisps, try young ruby ports, and late-harvested Zinfandels.

## SCOTCH CRÈME BRÛLÉE

◆ *Serves 6*

*Grated zest of 2 large oranges*
  *(about 2 tablespoons)*

*2 cups whipping cream*

*6 tablespoons sugar*

*1 tablespoon honey*

*7 large egg yolks*

*4½ tablespoons scotch whiskey*

*12 tablespoons sugar for*
  *caramelizing*

Y ou may be wondering about this title. No, this isn't a classic dessert from Scotland. It's just a new twist on an old favorite.

### Procedure

Combine the zest, cream, 6 tablespoons sugar, and the honey in a small saucepan. Bring to a simmer over medium heat. Remove from the heat, cover, and let steep 30 minutes.

Preheat the oven to 250 degrees. Place six 4-ounce ramekins in a shallow baking dish. Lightly whisk the egg yolks in a bowl and then whisk in the warm cream. Add the scotch and strain. Pour the mixture into the ramekins. Fill the baking dish with warm water to about halfway up the side of the ramekins. Cover the pan with foil, place in the oven, and bake until the custards are just set, 45 minutes to 1 hour. Remove the custards from the water bath and chill.

To serve, preheat the broiler. Sprinkle 2 tablespoons sugar on top of each custard and broil until the tops are golden brown. (Or a propane torch works beautifully to caramelize the sugar.)

**Wine Notes:** Try this with cream sherry, a less ripe French Sauternes, or similar-styled late-harvested wine from France, California, or Washington State. Hungarian Tokajii Aszu is also quite lovely.

## TARTUFO AL TRE SCALINI

◆ *Serves 6*

*6 ounces bittersweet chocolate*

*4 tablespoons unsalted butter*

*4 large egg yolks*

*1 tablespoon sugar*

*2 large egg whites*

*1 tablespoon heavy cream, sour cream, or mascarpone*

*½ teaspoon vanilla extract*

*½ teaspoon kirsch*

*12 Brandied Cherries (page 369)*

*1 cup chocolate jimmies or curls*

Many years ago, sitting in the Piazza Navona sipping my espresso, I noticed people eating a small brown oval slathered in whipped cream . . . and smiling. "What is it?" "Tartufo!" "A truffle?" Not the kind that pigs seek under oak trees but the kind that we sweets lovers devour and remember for years and years. I can remember the taste of my first tartufo at Tre Scalini. Still great. These can be made ahead and kept in the freezer, so why not make a batch and smile a lot.

### Procedure

Melt the chocolate with the butter in the top of a double boiler set over hot water. Beat the egg yolks with the sugar with a whisk in the bowl of an electric mixer until doubled in volume and very thick. Add the chocolate mixture to the yolks and mix well to blend. Beat the egg whites until they hold a medium-soft peak, and fold into the chocolate mixture. Then fold in the cream, vanilla, and kirsch. Transfer to a shallow container and freeze until firm but still malleable.

Using a number 36 ice cream scoop or your hands, form 12 2-inch balls of the chilled mixture and press a brandied cherry into the center of each. Roll in chocolate curls or jimmies and freeze until firm. Serve garnished with whipped cream and remaining brandied cherries, if you like.

## Brandied Cherries

*24 cherries, pitted*

*¼ cup sugar*

*¼ cup kirsch*

### Procedure

Combine all the ingredients in a saucepan and bring to a boil over medium heat. Let cool, transfer to a covered container, and let macerate 3 days at room temperature.

***Wine Notes:*** I like full-bodied and aggressively flavored port with chocolate; toward the vintage or late-bottled vintage as opposed to a young or aged tawny style. Rich orange Muscat from California or a southwestern French Banyuls are two other options.

# TARTUFO DI PARADISO

### Chocolate Truffle Mousse

♦ *Serves 8*

*12 ounces very bittersweet
chocolate, finely chopped*

*½ cup milk*

*½ cup heavy cream*

*¼ pound unsalted butter, cut
into bits*

*2 eggs*

*⅓ cup sugar*

*2 teaspoons vanilla extract*

*Pinch of salt*

*Whipped cream, for garnish*

This is an incredibly rich dessert and certainly not for the faint of heart or clogged of artery. Success depends on using the best high-cocoa solid chocolate, such as Valrhona Guanaja. The color should be almost black, hence the tartufo, or black truffle, name. You can form these into large truffle round mounds or pour into a loaf pan, and unmold and slice like a terrine. Somehow the mounds seem more voluptuous. You decide.

Serve with dollops of whipped cream and wait for groans.

### Procedure

Lightly butter and line the bottoms of 8 5-ounce ramekins or custard cups, or 1 9- by 4½- by 3-inch loaf pan with baker's parchment. Place the chocolate in the bowl of an electric mixer. Set aside. Combine the milk, cream, and butter in a medium saucepan and bring to a boil over high heat. Pour over the chocolate and beat on low speed with the whisk attachment until the chocolate melts. Increase the speed to medium and gradually beat in the eggs, sugar, vanilla, and salt. Beat until the mixture comes together, about 2 minutes. Don't overbeat or the texture will be coarse. Pour into the prepared ramekins or custard cups, or loaf pan and smooth the tops. Cover with plastic wrap and refrigerate 8 hours or overnight, until firm. To serve, dip the ramekins, custard cups, or loaf pan in very hot water to unmold. Turn out onto serving plates. Cut into slices with a knife dipped in hot water if you have used the loaf pan. Garnish with whipped cream.

**Wine Notes:** Port, port, port.

# CHOCOLATE SORBET

♦ *Serves 4 to 6*

*1 cup dark French cocoa, such*
*  as Valrhona*

*¾ cup (or to taste) sugar*

*2½ cups water*

*1 teaspoon vanilla extract*

*½ teaspoon salt*

Chocolate ice cream is well loved but is devastatingly rich. This French-inspired sorbet gives you the chocolate fix without cream or egg yolks. Light and satisfying, it can be garnished with fresh berries.

## Procedure

Combine the cocoa, sugar, and water in a medium saucepan and bring to a boil over medium heat, stirring often so that the cocoa doesn't burn. Add the vanilla and salt and whisk to blend. Strain through a fine sieve and refrigerate until cold. Taste and adjust sweetness, and then freeze in an ice cream maker according to the manufacturer's instructions.

**Wine Notes:** A young ruby port would be lovely. Remember that this is sorbet, not ice cream, and will be easily overwhelmed by a dessert wine that is both too rich and too generous.

## TIRAMISÙ

**Mascarpone, Espresso, and Ladyfinger Dessert**

♦ *Serves 8*

*5 large eggs, separated*

*⅓ cup sugar*

*1 pound mascarpone cheese*

*1 tablespoon dark rum or
   Marsala*

*1 teaspoon vanilla extract*

*Grated zest of 1 lemon or
   orange (optional)*

*¾ cup strong espresso coffee*

*30 to 40 Ladyfingers (page 373)*

*Cocoa for dusting or chocolate
   shavings for garnish*

This Venetian dessert needs no introduction. By now there is not an Italian restaurant in Italy or the United States that hasn't served tiramisù. The name means "pick-me-up." It will. It is also surprisingly easy to make; you can serve it at home and not ever have to order it again. Or, if you do, compare the restaurant version to yours and smile that knowing smile.

### Procedure

Whisk the egg yolks with half the sugar in the bowl of an electric mixer. Then set the bowl over a pan of barely simmering water and whisk until warm. Remove from the heat and beat on high speed about 8 to 10 minutes, until the mixture holds a 3-second dissolving ribbon when the beater is lifted. Whisk the mascarpone until smooth and fold into the beaten yolks. Then fold in the rum or Marsala, vanilla, and zest, if using.

In a second mixer bowl, beat the whites until foamy and then gradually beat in the remaining sugar. Continue beating until soft peaks form, about 1 minute longer. Do not overbeat. Carefully fold into the mascarpone mixture.

Dip about half the ladyfingers in the espresso and use them to line a 2-quart bowl. Spoon in half the mascarpone mixture and smooth the top. Arrange the remaining ladyfingers in a single layer on top, and cover with the remaining mascarpone mixture. (You may also make the tiramisù in individual parfait glasses.) Cover and refrigerate overnight. To serve, dust with cocoa or sprinkle with chocolate shavings.

## Ladyfingers

◆ *Makes 30 to 40 ladyfingers*
*5 large eggs, separated*
*Zest of 1 orange*
*1 teaspoon vanilla extract*
*1½ cups sugar*
*2 cups pastry flour, sifted*
*Confectioner's sugar*

### Procedure

Preheat the oven to 350 degrees. Line baking sheets with baker's parchment.

Combine the egg yolks, orange zest, vanilla, and ¾ cup of the sugar in the bowl of an electric mixer and beat on high speed until the mixture holds a 3-second dissolving ribbon on the batter when the beater is lifted, about 10 minutes.

In a second mixer bowl, beat the egg whites until foamy. Add the remaining ¾ cup sugar and continue to beat to medium-stiff peaks. Fold the yolk mixture into the beaten whites. Sift one third of the flour over the batter and fold in gently. Repeat twice more until all the flour has been incorporated. Do not overwork the batter; it should be very light and thick.

Spoon the batter into a pastry bag fitted with a #7 round tip and pipe 3-inch-long strips on the prepared baking sheets. Bake until set and golden brown, 8 to 10 minutes. Transfer to a wire rack and dust with confectioner's sugar while still hot. Let cool completely.

**Wine Notes:** For a classic Italian food and wine pairing, go with a Vin Santo from Tuscany, but the espresso accent here lends itself well to playful espresso/liqueur beverage combinations.

## SACRIPANTINA
### Marsala Zabaglione Cake

♦ *Serves 10 to 12*

**Génoise**

6 large eggs

1 cup sugar

1 teaspoon vanilla extract

1 teaspoon finely minced
  lemon zest

1 cup cake flour, sifted

6 tablespoons unsalted butter,
  melted

**Marsala Zabaglione Filling**

7 large egg yolks

6 tablespoons sugar

1 cup dry Marsala

1 cup heavy cream

**Icing**

2 cups heavy cream

¼ cup sugar

1 tablespoon Marsala

Berries, for garnish (optional)

For as long as I've been living in San Francisco, sacripantina has been a popular dessert. *Sacripante* in Italian means blusterer or bully and also is the name of a character in *Orlando Furioso*, a poem-play that is performed in Sicily with life-size puppets. Nick Malgieri believes that the origin of this cake is Liguria, but his recipe has chocolate buttercream filling. I suspect that the cake I know as sacripantina is Sicilian in inspiration because of the zabaglione filling. This is our interpretation of this San Francisco classic.

### Procedure

For the génoise, preheat the oven to 350 degrees. Lightly butter a 9-inch by 3-inch-high round cake pan and line with parchment paper.

Whisk the eggs and sugar together in the bowl of an electric mixer. Set it over hot water and whisk by hand until warm. Then remove from the heat and beat on high speed until the mixture holds a 3-second dissolving ribbon when the beater is lifted. Beat in the vanilla and lemon zest. Then, sift half the flour over the mixture and fold in. Fold in the melted butter, and then sift and fold in the remaining flour. Pour into the prepared cake pan and smooth the top. Bake until a toothpick inserted in the center of the cake comes out clean, and the cake springs back when touched, 30 to 35 minutes. Let cool for 5 minutes in the pan and then turn out onto a rack.

For the filling, whisk the egg yolks in a bowl until blended, whisk in the sugar and Marsala and strain into a shallow heatproof bowl. Set the bowl over boiling water and whisk constantly until the mixture is light and airy and forms a slowly dissolving ribbon on the mixture when the whisk is lifted, 10 to 15 minutes. Chill in a bowl of ice water.

Beat the cream until stiff peaks form. Fold into the cooled Marsala custard.

................................................................................

To assemble the cake, slice the génoise horizontally into 3 rounds. Place the bottom génoise round on a serving plate and spread with about half the filling. Top with a second génoise round and spread with the remaining filling. Cover with the third génoise round. Wrap and refrigerate overnight.

Just before serving, prepare the icing: Beat the cream with the sugar and Marsala until stiff peaks form. Spread over the top and sides of the cake. Garnish with strawberries, or raspberries if you like.

**Wine Notes:** A late-harvested Marsala from Sicily couldn't be more perfect. Other "ethnic" wines such as Vin Santo from Tuscany and Hungarian Tokajii are also recommended. Don't overlook liqueurs like Frangelico with or after desserts.

# CANNOLI DEI SOGNI

### Cannoli of Dreams

♦ *Makes 25 cannoli*

### Cannoli Shells

*2 cups all-purpose flour*

*⅛ teaspoon ground cloves*

*1½ teaspoons cinnamon*

*Pinch of salt*

*1 tablespoon vegetable*
    *shortening*

*1 tablespoon honey*

*¼ cup Marsala*

*1 large egg*

*1½ quarts peanut oil for frying*

### Cannoli Filling

*1 pound ricotta cheese*

*1 pound mascarpone cheese*

*½ cup sugar*

*½ cup Marsala*

*1 cup diced (medium) semisweet*
    *chocolate*

*¼ cup diced (medium) candied*
    *tangerine or orange peel*

*¼ cup diced (medium) candied*
    *lemon peel*

*1½ teaspoons cinnamon*

*1 cup pitted and coarsely*
    *chopped fresh apricots*
    *(optional)*

The first cannoli I ever tasted was bought in an Italian bakery in Brooklyn. I next tried one from a small shop in Manhattan's Little Italy. Eventually I ate one in Palermo and knew that I was hooked on cannoli for life.

You can use the traditional dried candied fruit and peel in the filling; I prefer to use fresh apricots and bing cherries when they are in season. I know that this recipe sounds like a lot of work. You have to love cannoli with a passion, and you have to believe that there is a real difference between a flavorful, delicate, freshly made cannoli shell and the ones you'll find in the average bakery. The dough is very elastic, much like a noodle dough, so I've taken to rolling it out through the pasta machine, but you can still do it the old-fashioned way, by hand. If you have a fear of frying, you can use this filling for little cream puff shells (though the effect is not the same).

### Procedure

For the cannoli shells, mix the dry ingredients together in the bowl of an electric mixer with the paddle or in the food processor. Beat or process in the shortening. Beat or process in the honey, Marsala, and the egg and then continue beating or processing until the dough comes together in a soft ball. Add a bit more Marsala if necessary. Flatten the dough into a disk, wrap in plastic, and let rest, covered, at room temperature for 1 hour.

Roll out the dough by hand on a lightly floured work surface until very thin, and then cut into 5-inch-wide strips. Or, roll the dough into 5-inch

*1 cup pitted and coarsely chopped bing cherries (optional)*

strips through a pasta machine, proceeding through all the settings until it has been rolled through the thinnest setting. Cut the dough into rounds with a 4-inch cookie cutter. Place the dough rounds on parchment-lined baking sheets and cover with plastic wrap until ready to cook.

Generously oil 6 cannoli tubes. Heat the oil in a deep-fryer or wok to 375 degrees. Roll 6 dough rounds into ovals with a rolling pin and roll up lengthwise around the cannoli tubes. Seal the edges with a dab of water.

Add as many cannoli-wrapped tubes to the oil as will comfortably fit without crowding and cook until lightly browned. Drain on paper towels and carefully remove from the tubes while still warm. Repeat to make all of the cannoli.

For the filling, pass the ricotta through a sieve if at all lumpy. Mix with the mascarpone in a medium bowl, set aside. Combine the sugar and Marsala in a small saucepan and reduce over medium heat until syrupy. Let cool, and then add to the cheeses along with the remaining ingredients. Stir to combine.

Within 30 minutes of serving time, spoon the filling into a pastry bag fitted with a large, plain tip and fill the cannoli shells with the filling. (After 30 minutes the filled cannoli will begin to get soggy.)

**Wine Notes:** As this dessert is not overly sweet, think Muscat. An Italian Moscato is a wonderful choice. French examples from Beaumes de Venise and Frontignan are exquisite, too, as are auslese-level German Rieslings, extra-dry Champagnes, or sparkling wines and a more regional Recioto di Soave.

# MASCARPONE CUSTARD AND BERRY TART

◆ *Serves 8*

### Pastry

*1¼ cups all-purpose flour*

*¼ cup sugar*

*¼ pound chilled unsalted butter,*
  *cut into bits*

*1 large egg yolk*

*3 tablespoons heavy cream*

*1 teaspoon Frangelico*

*1 tablespoon grated orange zest*

*¼ cup toasted and skinned*
  *chopped hazelnuts*

### Custard Filling

*1 cup mascarpone cheese*

*⅓ cup sugar*

*1 large egg*

*3 large egg yolks*

*Finely minced zest of 1 orange*

*1 tablespoon Frangelico*

*½ pint raspberries or*
  *blackberries*

It's not your classic New York cheesecake, but this Italian-inspired version is equally addictive. We all love berry-topped cheesecakes; in this recipe the berries are on the bottom. Serve warm for maximum sensual effect.

### Procedure

For the pastry, mix the flour and sugar in the bowl of an electric mixer or food processor. Cut or process in the butter with short pulses until the mixture resembles cornmeal. Whisk together the yolk, cream, Frangelico, and zest in a small bowl. Add to the dough mixture and mix or process in with short pulses until the dough just comes together. Gather the dough into a ball, flatten into a disk, wrap and chill 1 hour. Roll out the dough to an 11-inch circle on a well-floured surface. Ease into a 9-inch tart pan with a removable bottom. Roll the rolling pin over the top to remove excess pastry. Press the chopped hazelnuts over the bottom and sides of the tart shell. Freeze until set.

Preheat the oven to 400 degrees. Line the tart shell with aluminum foil and fill with pie weights or dried beans. Bake 15 minutes, then remove the pie weights and aluminum foil. Turn the oven down to 350 degrees and continue baking until the crust is golden brown, 10 to 15 minutes longer.

For the filling, whisk together all the ingredients until just combined.

Preheat the oven to 325 degrees. Arrange the berries in the prebaked crust. Pour in the filling and bake until the custard is just set, 25 to 30 minutes. Serve warm or at room temperature.

***Wine Notes:*** The cheese is more flavorful than sweet and requires a wine of medium body and pronounced acidity—German Rieslings and late-harvested Chenin Blancs from France's Loire Valley are sublime if you choose to have this without fruit. However, the intensity of berry flavor will require a more perfumed wine such as black Muscat or ruby port.

# GREEK HONEY CHEESECAKE

♦ *Serves 10 to 12*

### Crust

2 cups walnuts, toasted and
   cooled to room temperature

¼ cup sugar

½ teaspoon cinnamon

### Cheese Filling

2 pounds all-natural cream
   cheese

½ cup sour cream

¾ cup flavorful honey (Greek
   hymettus would be nice)

1 tablespoon sugar

4 large eggs

Grated zest of 1 lemon (about
   1 teaspoon)

Grated zest of 1 orange (about
   2 teaspoons)

1 teaspoon vanilla extract

This recipe is not traditionally Greek but it is the result of eating a fabulous Greek creamy cheese called manouri with some dried figs seasoned with bay leaves and black pepper. The combined flavors were so magical together I decided to use them as inspiration for this cheesecake. If you can find manouri cheese you may use that in combination with the cream cheese. If you can't find dried Mission figs, use the Greek imported calimyrna figs for the accompanying compote.

### Procedure

Butter a 9-inch cake pan and line with baker's parchment.

For the crust, combine the toasted walnuts, sugar, and cinnamon in the bowl of a food processor. Process until finely ground. Press over the bottom of the prepared cake pan.

Preheat the oven to 350 degrees.

For the filling, bring all the ingredients to room temperature. Combine the cream cheese and sour cream in the bowl of an electric mixer. Beat at medium speed with the paddle attachment, scraping the sides of the bowl and the paddle often, until smooth. Add the honey and sugar and continue beating until there are no lumps. Add the eggs 1 at a time. Then add zests and vanilla and mix well. Pour over the crust in the prepared pan. (Do not scrape the sides of the bowl as this would add lumps.) Put the cake pan in a large baking pan and add enough water to come halfway up the side of the cake pan. Bake until just barely set, about 25 minutes.

Turn the oven off and leave the cake in the oven with the door ajar for 1 to 2 hours to prevent the cake from splitting on top. Wrap the cake in the plastic wrap and refrigerate overnight to allow the cake to firm up.

To remove the cheesecake from the pan, first line a baking sheet with plastic wrap. Then dip the pan in a hot-water bath and turn the cake out onto the prepared baking sheet. Then invert onto a serving plate. The cake should be just barely set in the center.

Serve at room temperature with warm Spiced Fig Compote (see below).

### Spiced Fig Compote

*1 pound dried black Mission figs*

*¼ cup honey*

*½ cup red wine, orange juice, or water*

*2 bay leaves*

*2 cinnamon sticks*

*2 pieces star anise*

*Peel of 1 orange, removed in strips with a vegetable peeler*

*Peel of 1 lemon, removed in strips with a vegetable peeler*

*Pinch of freshly ground pepper*

### Procedure

Rinse the figs in warm water. Remove the stems and blossom ends of the figs. Cut the figs into quarters and place them in a medium saucepan with the remaining ingredients. Cook over low heat, stirring occasionally, until the figs are soft and perfumed with the spices, about 15 minutes.

**Wine Notes:** The primary flavors of fig and nuts cry out for dessert wines that amplify their sweet flavors: tawny port, cream sherry, and Bual Madeira are excellent fortified choices. For those who prefer less weighty wines, try late-harvested Semillon from California or Washington, Vin Santo from Italy, or a vanilla-scented Tokay Essencia from Hungary.

# TARTA ALHAMBRA

♦ *Serves 12*

*10 ounces prepared puff pastry*

*3 blood or regular oranges*

*2 tablespoons apricot jam*

*Candied violets for garnish*

  *(optional)*

### Chewy Caramel

*¾ cup heavy cream*

*½ cup sugar*

*1 tablespoon unsalted butter*

### Pastry Cream

*1 cup milk*

*Grated zest of 2 oranges*

*2 large egg yolks*

*¼ cup sugar*

*1 tablespoon cornstarch*

*1½ tablespoons unsalted butter*

*2 teaspoons Grand Marnier*

Years ago there was a bakery in New York that made a custard pie topped with sliced oranges and jelly glaze. To prevent the crust from getting soggy, the bottom of the tart shell was painted with a thin layer of crisp caramel. I always liked the idea of caramel under a custard, and when blood oranges became readily available in California, I decided to give this combination a try. First I used the conventional Pâte Sucrée or tart shell (page 385), a thin layer of caramel, a custard flavored with Grand Marnier, blood orange slices, and a thin currant jelly glaze. The tart was very, very good, but hard to serve. The orange slices slid off the custard and the caramel made the crust difficult to cut.

Undaunted, because it was so delicious, I kept playing with the recipe. Over time the caramel layer became a "sexier" chewy caramel, rather than a crisp one. To make slicing foolproof, I latched onto the notion of a puff pastry strip. While many of you will not make your own puff pastry, it is readily available in freezer cases at the market and many bakeries will sell it to you by the pound. If you do choose to make it yourself, refer to your favorite and most trusted baking book for instructions. No need for us to reinvent the wheel and repeat what others have done so well.

### Procedure

Roll out the puff pastry to 2 4- by 8-inch rectangles on a lightly floured surface. Transfer to a baking sheet. Use the point of a small knife to score a line along both long sides of each rectangle, about 1 inch in from each edge. Cover and freeze at least 45 minutes or overnight.

......................................................................................

For the caramel, bring the cream to a boil in a small saucepan and keep warm. Place the sugar in a heavy-bottomed saucepan and cook over high heat until the sugar starts to melt. Then stir to dissolve and continue cooking until the sugar caramelizes to an amber color. Slowly and carefully whisk in the warm cream. Stir in the butter. Cook over medium heat until the caramel has reduced by one quarter, about 10 minutes. Let cool at room temperature.

......................................................................................

For the pastry cream, combine the milk and orange zest in a small saucepan and bring to a boil over medium heat. Remove from the heat and let steep 10 minutes. Whisk the egg yolks, sugar, and cornstarch together in a bowl. Whisk in a bit of the warm milk (this is called tempering), and then whisk in the remainder all at once. Strain into a small, heavy-bottomed saucepan. Bring the cream to a boil over medium heat, stirring constantly to prevent scorching and boil until thickened to the consistency of sour cream, about 1 minute. Remove the pan from the heat and transfer the cream to a bowl. Whisk in butter and Grand Marnier. Place a piece of plastic wrap directly over the surface of the pastry cream to prevent a skin from forming and chill until cold.

Remove the peel and all of the white pith from the oranges with a small knife. Thinly slice the oranges and remove any seeds. Set aside.

Preheat the oven to 400 degrees.

(*continued*)

Bake the chilled puff pastry rectangles 5 minutes, then lower the heat to 350 degrees and bake until the pastry is golden brown, 8 to 12 minutes longer. Let cool completely on a wire rack.

Using a sharp paring knife, remove the under-cooked central portion of the pastry strips and discard. If the pastry strips are not light and crisp, bake 3 to 4 minutes longer.

To assemble, warm the jam in a small saucepan over low heat until liquid; keep warm. Spread a thin layer of caramel over the center of each pastry strip, between the raised borders. Then spread with the pastry cream. Carefully slice each strip crosswise into 6 equal pieces. Overlap 3 to 4 orange slices on top of each piece. Glaze the oranges with the warmed apricot jam. Garnish with candied violets, if you like.

*Variation:* This tart may also be made in a conventional 9-inch round tart pan. Line the tart pan with Pâte Sucrée (page 385) and double the pastry cream. Arrange the orange slices on top of the tart in an overlapping, circular pattern.

*Wine Notes:* A dessert sherry is a good choice, as is a dessert Muscat wine made in the town of Sitges. Orange Muscat wines from America, a Recioto di Soave from Italy, or an Australian Muscat port are three other good choices. If you want to accentuate the caramel, refer to suggestions for Aurora Tart on page 386.

# PÂTE SUCRÉE

♦ *Makes 1 9-inch tart shell*

*1¼ cups all-purpose flour*

*¼ cup sugar*

*¼ pound chilled unsalted butter,*
*cut into slivers*

*1 large egg yolk*

*3 tablespoons heavy cream*

*½ teaspoon vanilla extract*

## *Procedure*

Mix the flour and the sugar in the bowl of an electric mixer or food processor. Cut or process in the butter with short pulses until the mixture resembles cornmeal. Whisk together the yolk, cream, and vanilla in a small bowl and add to the dough mixture. Mix or process in with short pulses until the dough just comes together. Gather the dough into a ball, flatten into a disk, and wrap in plastic wrap. Refrigerate 1 hour.

Preheat the oven to 375 degrees. Roll out the dough to ¼-inch thickness on a lightly floured surface. Carefully drape the dough over the rolling pin and ease into a 9-inch tart pan with a removable bottom. Freeze 1 hour. Then line the tart shell with aluminum foil and fill with pie weights or dried beans. Bake 15 minutes. Remove the foil and weights and continue baking until the pastry is golden brown and baked through, about 15 minutes longer.

# AURORA TART

♦ *Serves 12*

### Pastry

1¾ *cups all-purpose flour*

⅓ *cup sugar*

12 *tablespoons cold unsalted*
  *butter, cut into bits*

2 *large egg yolks*

1 *tablespoon heavy cream*

½ *teaspoon vanilla extract*

### Caramel Custard Filling

1 *large egg*

4 *large egg yolks*

3 *cups heavy cream*

1¾ *cups sugar*

3 *tablespoons unsalted butter,*
  *cut into cubes*

### Glaze

1 *ounce bittersweet chocolate*

2 *tablespoons heavy cream*

1 *teaspoon vanilla extract*

### Praline Cream

2 *tablespoons unsalted butter*

1 *cup sugar*

½ *cup almonds or hazelnuts,*
  *lightly toasted*

1 *cup whipping cream*

Pastry chef Jennifer Millar adapted a recipe to create this variation of a French custard tart. When the pie is sliced, the graduated colors of the layers reminded us of dawn breaking on the horizon, hence the aurora designation. Everyone loves this tart and asks for the recipe. Those who have baking skills will triumph, of course. The rest of us will have to have patience and try to have fun with it!

### Procedure

For the pastry, mix the flour and sugar in the bowl of an electric mixer or food processor. Cut or process in the butter with short pulses until the mixture resembles cornmeal. Whisk together the yolks, cream, and vanilla in a small bowl and add to the dough mixture. Mix or process in with short pulses until the dough comes together. Gather the dough into a ball, flatten into a disk, and wrap in plastic wrap. Refrigerate overnight.

Place a 10½- by 2-inch flan ring or springform pan on an absolutely flat baking sheet that has been lined with baker's parchment; set aside. Roll out the dough to a 14-inch circle on a lightly floured surface, turning with each roll to prevent the dough from sticking. Carefully drape the dough over the rolling pin and ease into the flan ring or springform pan. Roll the rolling pin over the top to remove excess pastry. Chill the ring in the freezer for 1 hour or overnight.

Preheat the oven to 375 degrees. Line the tart shell with foil and fill with pie weights or dried beans. Bake until the pastry is set, 30 to 40 minutes. Remove the foil and weights and continue to bake until the pastry is golden brown, 2 to 5 minutes longer.

For the filling, preheat the oven to 300 degrees. Whisk together the whole egg and egg yolks in a heatproof bowl; set aside. Bring the cream to a boil in a medium saucepan and keep warm. Place the sugar in a heavy-bottomed 2-quart saucepan and cook over medium-high heat until the sugar starts to melt and color. Then stir until all the sugar dissolves. Continue cooking, stirring occasionally, until the sugar caramelizes to a dark amber color, 8 to 10 minutes.

Remove from the heat and carefully pour in the hot cream, whisking continuously. Be careful—the mixture will bubble up. If the caramel seizes and hardens, stir over low heat to redissolve the sugar. Stir in the butter off the heat. Let cool slightly. Slowly at first, and then in a steady stream, whisk the caramel mixture into the eggs. Strain.

Pour the custard into the prebaked tart shell and bake, rotating the pan occasionally for even cooking, until the custard is set, 20 to 25 minutes. The custard should jiggle slightly in the center when shaken. Let cool at room temperature. Then chill completely in the refrigerator or freezer.

For the glaze, melt the chocolate with the cream in a double boiler over barely simmering water. Stir in the vanilla. Spread a thin layer of the warm glaze over the chilled custard. Chill the tart again.

For the praline cream, brush the butter over the bot-
(*continued*)

tom of a jelly roll pan. Place the sugar in a small saucepan and cook over medium-high heat until it starts to melt and color. Then stir to dissolve and continue cooking, until the sugar caramelizes to a dark amber color. Stir in the nuts and continue stirring over heat until the mixture loosens. Pour onto the prepared jelly roll pan and spread to a thin layer with a metal spatula. Let cool completely and then grind to a fine powder in a food processor. (Praline powder may be made ahead and stored in a jar at room temperature or frozen in an airtight container.) Whip the cream until stiff peaks form. Fold in ½ cup of the praline powder and spread over the chilled tart. Top with the remaining cup of praline powder and refrigerate until set. Serve chilled.

*Note:* After all that work aren't you glad to hear that the Aurora Tart can be frozen and then warmed to room temperature at serving time. So make two!

*Wine Notes:* The nutty and caramel elements lend themselves to cream sherry, Madeira, Sauternes, and oak-influenced American and Australian wines based on Sauvignon Blanc and Semillon. An age-worthy Muscat from the southwest of France or a Muscat sherry from Spain would also be quite harmonious.

# GÂTEAU ROLLA

◆ *Serves 12*

**Meringues**

5 large egg whites

Pinch of salt

1 cup sugar

1 teaspoon vanilla extract

¾ cup finely ground almonds

**Chocolate Filling**

6 ounces sweet chocolate

2 tablespoons cocoa powder

3 large egg whites

¾ cup sugar

¾ pound unsalted butter,
   softened

This is an ideal party cake because it is best made the day before. And it uses up all the egg whites that seem to multiply in the refrigerator after an orgy of aioli and custard-making. While gâteau rolla resembles a French dacquoise, the absence of an egg yolk buttercream tells me that this could be Italian. I have made this cake for weddings; sometimes the memory of the cake lasts longer than the marriage.

### Procedure

For the meringues, preheat the oven to 250 degrees. Oil or butter two large baking sheets. Cut 4 10-inch squares of baker's parchment and trace a 9-inch circle onto each. Turn the paper squares over (tracing sides down) and place 2 on each baking sheet. Oil the papers lightly.

Whisk the egg whites with a pinch of salt and ¾ cup sugar in the bowl of an electric mixer over simmering water until warm. Remove from the heat and beat on high speed until stiff peaks form. Beat in the vanilla and the remaining ¼ cup of sugar on low speed. Fold in the almonds. Spoon the meringue into a pastry bag fitted with a large plain tip and completely fill in each circle with piped meringue. (Or, spread the meringue about ¼ inch thick over the traced circles with a spatula.) Bake until set, about 1 hour. Let the meringues cool completely on the parchment on a wire rack. Then peel off the parchment. Don't worry if one of the meringues breaks or cracks; it can be patched with the filling.

(*continued*)

For the filling, melt the chocolate with the cocoa in the top of a double boiler over barely simmering water; set aside. Place the egg whites and sugar in a heatproof bowl and beat over hot water until foamy. Remove from the heat and beat on high speed. Gradually beat in the softened butter, a bit at a time, and finally the melted chocolate. Beat until smooth. Chill until firm.

To assemble the cake, place 1 meringue round on a serving plate and thinly spread with the chocolate filling. Top with a second meringue round and spread with the filling. Repeat with the third meringue round and top with the remaining meringue. Cover the top and sides of the cake with the remaining filling. Cover loosely and refrigerate overnight. Bring to room temperature before serving. Cut into small slices with a warm serrated knife.

**Wine Notes:** A sweet Vin Santo, a rich cream sherry, or a semisweet Banyuls from the French Pyrenées go nicely with this dessert.

# ALMOND CAKE

◆ *Serves 8 to 10*

*12 tablespoons unsalted butter*

*¾ cup sugar*

*12 ounces almond paste*

*Grated zest of 1 orange*

*Grated zest of 1 lemon*

*1 teaspoon kirsch*

*1 teaspoon vanilla extract*

*½ teaspoon almond extract*

*5 large eggs*

*½ cup all-purpose flour*

*1 teaspoon baking powder*

*2 tablespoons apricot jam*

*¼ cup sliced almonds, toasted*

When you want a little sweet something—not a cookie, but a piece of cake that is simple, satisfying, and not covered with rich frosting—this is the one. You might have it with some berries or peaches, but frankly it doesn't need anything because it is so good by itself. I love this with my afternoon cup of tea or espresso.

## Procedure

Preheat the oven to 325 degrees. Lightly butter a 9-inch round cake pan and line it with baker's parchment.

Beat the butter with the sugar in the bowl of an electric mixer until light and fluffy. Add the almond paste, zests, kirsch, and vanilla and almond extracts. Beat until blended. Add the eggs and mix until combined. Beat in the flour and baking powder. Pour the batter into the prepared pan and smooth the top. Bake until cake shrinks back from the sides of the pan and springs back when touched, about 45 minutes. Let the cake cool completely in the pan and then turn it out onto a serving plate. Melt the jam in a small saucepan over low heat with 1 tablespoon water. Brush over the top of the cake and sprinkle with toasted almonds.

**Wine Notes:** Choose a simple, fragrant glass of Moscato from Italy's Piemonte, California, the south of France, or North Africa. A spätlese- to auslese-level German Riesling or equivalent from any other country is a lovely accent to the soft flavors of this cake.

## CHOCOLATE MOUSSE TORTE WITH MOCHA GANACHE

◆ *Serves 10 to 12*

**Cake**

16 ounces bittersweet chocolate

⅓ cup strong espresso coffee

¼ cup dark rum

1 cup heavy cream

7 large eggs, separated

½ cup sugar

2 tablespoons all-purpose flour

½ teaspoon vanilla extract

¼ teaspoon almond extract

**Mocha Chocolate Ganache**

2½ cups heavy cream

7 ounces bittersweet chocolate, finely chopped, or

7 ounces semisweet chocolate plus 2 tablespoons instant espresso powder

1 teaspoon vanilla extract

**Glaze**

8 ounces bittersweet chocolate

¼ cup heavy cream

¼ cup water

3 tablespoons unsalted butter

1 tablespoon instant espresso powder

It looks like a derby. It tastes like a dream. Practice makes perfect for getting a round cake, a smoothly curved dome, and a glistening glaze. Even if your first efforts are homely, this cake will taste so great you'll forgive yourself.

### Procedure

For the cake, preheat the oven to 350 degrees. Lightly butter a 9-inch cake pan and line with baker's parchment. Melt the chocolates with the espresso, rum, and cream in a double boiler over barely simmering water; set aside. Whisk the egg yolks with ¼ cup of the sugar in a mixer bowl and set it over barely simmering water. Whisk by hand until warm. Then remove from the heat and beat with an electric mixer until the mixture holds a dissolving 3-second ribbon when the beater is lifted. Whisk the flour and almond and vanilla extracts into the melted chocolate mixture and then fold into the beaten yolks.

In a second mixer bowl, beat the egg whites until foamy. Then gradually beat in the remaining ¼ cup sugar and continue to beat to soft peaks. Fold into the chocolate mixture. Pour the batter into the prepared cake pan and smooth the top. Cover with plastic wrap and place the pan in a larger baking pan. Pour hot water into the baking pan to come halfway up the sides of the cake pan. Cover the baking pan with foil and bake until a toothpick inserted into the center of the cake comes out with moist crumbs clinging, about 40 minutes. Let the cake cool completely in the pan on a wire rack.

For the ganache, bring the heavy cream to a boil in a saucepan and pour over the chopped chocolate in a heatproof bowl. Stir until the chocolate is dissolved. Stir in the vanilla. Strain the mixture and chill overnight.

For the glaze, combine the chocolate, cream, and water in a double boiler over simmering water and heat gently until the chocolate melts. Remove from the heat and stir in the butter and espresso. Strain.

To assemble the torte, knock the cake out of the pan onto a 9-inch cardboard circle. Trim with a knife, if necessary. Beat the chilled ganache in the bowl of an electric mixer to stiff peaks. Do not overwhip or the cream will break. Spread the ganache over the top of the cake with a spatula dipped in hot water to form a smooth dome. Chill. Warm the glaze over low heat until it leaves a faint trail when poured back on itself. Ladle the warm glaze over the cake, turning the cake back and forth until it is covered evenly. Prick any air bubbles with a toothpick before the glaze hardens. Refrigerate until serving time.

**Wine Notes:** See the recommendations for Tartufo di Paradiso (page 370).

# CHOCOLATE CHESTNUT TORTE WITH COGNAC

◆ *Serves 8 to 10*

### Chocolate Chestnut Torte

*5 ounces extra bittersweet*
*   chocolate, chopped*
*¼ pound unsalted butter*
*8 ounces unsweetened chestnut*
*   purée, sieved*
*¾ cup finely ground almonds*
*1 tablespoon all-purpose flour*
*6 large eggs, separated and*
*   brought to room temperature*
*¾ cup sugar*

### Mocha-Cognac Buttercream

*9 ounces bittersweet chocolate*
*¼ cup strong coffee*
*4 large egg yolks*
*1 cup sugar*
*⅓ cup water*
*¾ pound unsalted butter*
*2 tablespoons Cognac*

*12 whole glacéed chestnuts*
*Chocolate curls*

O ne of the classic perfect food marriages is chocolate and chestnuts. This French-inspired cake is very rich, and a little slice goes a long way.

### *Procedure*

For the torte, preheat the oven to 350 degrees. Lightly butter a 9-inch round cake pan and line it with baker's parchment.

Melt the chocolate with the butter in the top of a double boiler over barely simmering water. Add the chestnut purée and stir until smooth; set aside. Combine the almonds and the flour and set aside. Whisk the egg yolks and sugar together in the bowl of an electric mixer. Set it over hot water and whisk by hand until warm. Then remove from the heat and beat on high speed until the mixture forms a 3-second dissolving ribbon when the beater is lifted. Fold in the chocolate mixture. Fold in the almond and flour mixture.

In a second mixer bowl, beat the egg whites with the whisk to soft peaks. Fold into the chocolate mixture. Pour the batter into the prepared pan and smooth the top. Bake until a toothpick inserted into the cake comes out with moist crumbs attached, 35 to 40 minutes. (The cake should still be soft in the center.) Cool in the pan on a wire rack and then turn out onto a serving platter.

For the buttercream, melt the chocolate with the coffee in the top of a double boiler over barely simmering water. Set aside and keep warm.

Place the yolks in the bowl of an electric mixer set over warm water and whisk by hand until warm to the touch. Then beat on high speed until thick and pale. Meanwhile, combine the sugar and water in a small saucepan and bring to a boil over high heat, stirring until the sugar has dissolved. Boil rapidly without stirring until the syrup reaches the soft ball stage (240 degrees on a candy thermometer). Gradually beat the syrup into the beaten egg yolks on low speed. Beat in the warm chocolate. Beat in the butter, a little at a time, and then the Cognac. Chill until thick enough to spread.

To assemble the torte, spread the cake with the buttercream and top with whole glacéed chestnuts and chocolate curls. The torte may be made a day ahead and refrigerated, but bring it to room temperature before serving.

*Wine Notes:* Port is a perfect choice—see the recommendations for Tartufo al Tre Scalini (page 368). As an interesting foil, try a sweet orange or black Muscat wine from either America or Australia.

## WALNUT TORTE WITH CARAMEL CUSTARD AND MOCHA BUTTERCREAM

♦ *Serves 12 to 14*

### Walnut Génoise

10 tablespoons sifted cake flour

6 tablespoons finely ground
  walnuts

6 large eggs

1 cup sugar

2 teaspoons grated orange zest

1 teaspoon vanilla extract

6 tablespoons unsalted butter,
  melted

### Caramel Custard Filling

2 cups heavy cream

1 vanilla bean, or 1 teaspoon
  vanilla extract

¾ cup sugar

6 large egg yolks

Ever since Carème worked for the Czar, the Russians have loved rich French desserts. This fabulous cake is a combination of three classic recipes, a walnut génoise, a mocha buttercream, and a caramel custard filling, all rich enough for the nobility but definitely satisfying to the masses. Enjoy!

### Procedure

For the génoise, preheat the oven to 350 degrees. Lightly butter a 9-inch round cake pan and line with baker's parchment.

Combine the flour and nuts and set aside. Whisk the eggs, sugar, and orange zest together in a mixer bowl and set it over barely simmering water. Whisk by hand until the mixture is warm and the sugar is completely dissolved. Then remove from the heat and beat on high speed with the whisk attachment of an electric mixer until the mixture holds a 3-second dissolving ribbon when the beater is lifted. Add the vanilla and mix to blend. Then fold in the flour and nut mixture in three batches, alternating with the butter, beginning and ending with the flour mixture. Pour into the prepared pan and smooth the top. Bake until a toothpick inserted in the center comes out clean and the cake springs back when touched, 30 to 35 minutes. Remove from the oven and let the cake cool 5 minutes on a wire rack. Then turn the cake out onto the rack and let cool completely.

For the custard, preheat the oven to 300 degrees. Pour the cream into a heavy saucepan. If using the vanilla bean, cut it open, scrape the seeds into the

### Mocha Buttercream

*3 ounces bittersweet chocolate*

*½ cup strong coffee*

*1 pound unsalted butter, softened*

*1 cup sugar*

*1 tablespoon light corn syrup*

*6 tablespoons water*

*6 large egg whites*

### Caramel Sauce

*1 cup heavy cream*

*2 cups sugar*

*Juice of ½ lemon*

*¼ pound unsalted butter*


*¼ cup apricot jam*

*Orange slices, for garnish*

cream, and add the bean too. Bring to a simmer and keep warm.

Place the sugar in a heavy saucepan and cook over medium-high heat until the sugar starts to melt and color. Then stir until all the sugar dissolves. Continue cooking, stirring occasionally, until the sugar caramelizes to a golden brown color. Immediately remove from the heat and gradually and carefully pour in the warm cream, whisking constantly. Be very careful—the caramel will bubble up. Gently, so as not to make big bubbles, break up the yolks with a fork in a mixing bowl. Gradually stir in the hot caramel cream and then strain the mixture into a second bowl. Add the vanilla extract, if using, and mix to blend. Gently pour into a 1-quart Pyrex or soufflé dish. Put the dish into a baking pan and pour hot water in the pan to come halfway up the sides of the dish.

Cover the pan with foil and bake until the custard is firm, 45 to 60 minutes. Remove the pan of custard from the oven and let cool to room temperature. Cover and refrigerate until you wish to assemble the cake.

..............................................................................

For the buttercream, combine the chocolate and coffee in the top of a double boiler and heat over barely simmering water until the chocolate is melted. Set aside. Beat the butter in the bowl of an electric mixer until light and fluffy; set aside. Combine the sugar, corn syrup, and water in a small saucepan and cook over high heat, stirring, until the sugar has dissolved.

*(continued)*

Then bring to a boil without stirring, brushing the sides of the pan occasionally with a wet brush to dissolve any sugar crystals that form there. Cook the syrup to the soft ball stage (240 degrees on a candy thermometer). Beat the egg whites in the bowl of an electric mixer until foamy. Stop the mixer, and slowly add about one third of the sugar syrup into the center of the bowl. Beat about 1 minute and then stop the mixer again. Add another third of the syrup and beat 1 more minute. Stop the mixer, add the remaining syrup, and beat at high speed until the meringue is completely cool. Slowly beat in the butter until smooth. Beat in the chocolate mixture. Set aside at room temperature if you plan to assemble the cake soon. If not, refrigerate and bring back to room temperature before assembling the cake.

For the caramel sauce, bring the cream to a bare simmer and keep warm. Combine the sugar and lemon juice in a small, heavy saucepan and stir until the sugar is moistened. Then stir over medium-high heat to dissolve the sugar. Turn the heat to high and cook, stirring occasionally, until the sugar caramelizes to a golden brown color. Immediately remove from the heat and gradually pour in the hot cream, whisking constantly. Be careful—the caramel will bubble up. Bring to a boil, stirring constantly, then remove from heat. Add the butter and stir until smooth. Pour into a heatproof bowl and set aside.

To assemble the torte, melt the apricot jam in a small saucepan over low heat. Slice the cake horizontally into 4 rounds and brush each with the warm jam. Place the bottom cake round on a serving plate and use a spoon to spread with one third of the custard. (The custard should be about ⅛ inch thick.) Place a second cake round on top and spread with another third of the custard. Repeat to make a third layer and top with the remaining cake round, glazed side up. Spread the buttercream smoothly over the top and sides of the cake. Serve with the caramel sauce and garnish with orange slices. Walnut ice cream would be gilding the lily, but why not!

**Wine Notes:** A velvety wood port, a vanilla-scented cream sherry, or a sweeter-style Marsala would provide just the right decadence. A zesty fresh dessert wine of Riesling or Sauvignon Blanc would also be a nice foil.

## SUSAN'S PASSOVER SPONGE CAKE

◆ *Serves 10*

*10 large eggs, separated*

*1 cup sugar*

*Zest and juice of 1 orange*

*Zest and juice of 1 lemon*

*½ cup plus 2 tablespoons*
  *Passover cake meal, sifted*

*1 tablespoon plus 2 teaspoons*
  *potato starch*

*Pinch of salt*

*1 teaspoon vanilla extract*

When I was growing up, our neighbor Mrs. Weinstein, a fabulous cook, used to make the best Passover sponge cake. With the holidays approaching, Susan in our pastry department made this simple cake to serve with berries or dried fruit compotes and it is a ringer for Mrs. Weinstein's. Another happy taste memory brought back to the present. As she would say, "Enjoy."

### Procedure

Combine the egg yolks, ½ cup of the sugar and the orange and lemon zest and juice in the bowl of an electric mixer and beat until the mixture holds a slowly dissolving 3-second ribbon on the batter when the beater is lifted. In a second mixer bowl, beat the whites until foamy. Gradually beat in the remaining ½ cup sugar, and continue beating to stiff peaks. Fold in the egg yolk mixture. Then fold in the sifted cake meal, the potato starch, salt, and vanilla. Pour the batter into an ungreased 10-inch tube pan and smooth the top. Put it into a cold oven. Turn the oven to 325 degrees and bake until a toothpick comes out clean when inserted into the center of the cake, about 45 minutes. Invert onto a wire rack and let cool completely. Remove from the pan and cut into slices. Serve with fruit, if desired.

# COCONUT MACAROONS

♦ *Makes 4 to 5 dozen*
  *macaroons*

*5 large egg whites*

*1⅓ cups sugar*

*5 cups long-shred unsweetened*
  *coconut, toasted*

*½ tablespoon vanilla extract*

*8 ounces bittersweet chocolate*

J erry Tewell in our pastry department knows that these are my weakness. They remind me of a Mounds Bar, only better. This is the ideal cookie to serve with coconut ice cream and hot fudge sauce. Bet you can't eat just one.

## Procedure

Preheat the oven to 275 degrees. Line baking sheets with baker's parchment.

Whisk the egg whites and sugar in a bowl over simmering water until warm. Remove from the heat and beat on high speed until stiff peaks form. Then fold in the coconut and vanilla.

Spoon the macaroon mixture into a pastry bag fitted with a #8 round tip and pipe out 1-inch mounds, about 2 inches apart, on the prepared baking sheets. (Or, you may use #70 ice cream scoop, or a tablespoon and your finger.) Bake until the macaroons are set, but not colored, and still moist inside, about 20 minutes. Transfer to a rack and let cool.

Melt the chocolate in a double boiler over barely simmering water. Dip the bottom of each cookie in melted chocolate and let dry.

# ROLLED HOLIDAY SHORTBREAD COOKIES

♦ *Makes 3 to 4 dozen cookies*

*¾ pound unsalted butter, at*
   *room temperature*

*1 cup sifted confectioner's sugar*

*1 teaspoon vanilla extract*

*3 cups sifted all-purpose flour*

*Pinch of salt*

These rolled cookies are easy to make and you may commemorate any event by cutting the shape of cookie appropriate to the occasion. For Hanukkah, pastry chef Jennifer Millar selects dreidels (tops) and kiddush cups. But reindeer and stars would work well too.

### *Procedure*

Beat the softened butter with the confectioner's sugar in the bowl of an electric mixer fitted with the paddle attachment until light and fluffy. Add the vanilla and then the flour and salt and mix on low speed until blended. Wrap and refrigerate 1 hour or overnight.

Preheat the oven to 325 degrees. Line a baking sheet with baker's parchment. Roll out the dough to ⅛-inch thickness on a lightly floured surface and cut into desired shapes with cookie cutters. Transfer to the baking sheets and bake until very lightly browned, 8 to 10 minutes.

## BACI DI DAMA
### *Ladies' Kisses*

♦ *About 7 dozen tiny cookies*

*½ cup blanched almonds*

*12 tablespoons unsalted butter,*
*    at room temperature*

*½ cup sugar*

*1 large egg yolk*

*½ teaspoon almond extract*

*½ teaspoon vanilla extract*

*2 tablespoons Amaretto*

*½ cup plus 2 tablespoons*
*    all-purpose flour*

*½ cup plus 2 tablespoons cake*
*    flour*

*3 ounces bittersweet chocolate*

*Confectioner's sugar*

One of our favorite cookie recipes. Italian, of course.

### Procedure

Preheat the oven to 325 degrees. Line a baking sheet with baker's parchment.

Grind the almonds to a powder in a nut grinder. (Do not use a food processor.) Beat the butter and the sugar in the bowl of an electric mixer until light and fluffy. Beat in the egg yolk and flavorings and then mix in flours and ground almonds until blended. Using a hand-held cookie press fitted with the rosette attachment, pipe the mixture onto the prepared baking sheet and bake until very lightly browned, 8 to 10 minutes. Transfer to a wire rack and let cool.

Melt the chocolate in a double boiler over barely simmering water. Spread the flat sides of half the cookie rosettes with the melted chocolate and top each with a second cookie rosette, flat sides to the chocolate. Dust with confectioner's sugar.

# PECAN COOKIES

◆ *Makes 6 to 7 dozen*
  *1½-inch cookies*

*½ pound pecans*

*¾ cup plus 2 tablespoons*
  *all-purpose flour*

*½ pound unsalted butter,*
  *softened*

*1¾ cups sugar*

*1½ tablespoons candied orange*
  *peel, finely chopped*

*1 large egg yolk*

*½ teaspoon salt*

*1½ teaspoons vanilla extract*

*2 tablespoons bourbon*

A variation on "walnut clouds" but with pecans and orange zest.

## Procedure

Preheat the oven to 350 degrees. Place the pecans on a baking sheet and toast until fragrant, about 10 minutes. Remove from the oven and let cool completely.

Combine the cooled pecans and the flour in the container of a food processor and process until finely ground; set aside. Beat the butter and sugar in the bowl of an electric mixer until light and fluffy. Add the orange peel, the egg yolk, the salt, vanilla, and bourbon, and beat until smooth. Add the nuts and flour and mix just until blended. Shape the dough into a log about 1½ inches in diameter. Wrap in plastic and chill until firm.

Preheat the oven to 325 degrees. Line a baking sheet with baker's parchment. Cut the dough into ¼-inch-thick slices. Place on the prepared baking sheet and bake until golden, 10 to 12 minutes.

# I N D E X

Afghani:
> Georgian tomato sauce for beef or veal, 305
> lamb sausages, 273
> Persian ravioli with leeks and two sauces, 150–152
> spinach borani, 232

African, *see* North African

Aioli, spicy tomato-almond, 347

Ajiaco bogotano, 124

Albanian leek and goat cheese pie, 92–93

Almond(s):
> and anchovy fish sauce, Provençal, 175
> aurora tart, 386–388
> baci di dama, 403
> cake, 391
> Catalan chick-pea and spinach soup with shrimp, garlic and, 128–129
> Catalan-style quail stuffed in roasted peppers, 242–243
> Circassian chicken fettuccine with spiced onions, nuts, and cream, 144–145
> horseradish cream, Hungarian, grilled salmon with, 194
> peaches stuffed with, 362
> roast duck with peaches, ginger and, 250
> salmon Catalan, 190
> salmon with onions, toasted bread crumbs and, 188–189
> tomato aioli, spicy, 347

Appetizers, 53–69
> Albanian leek and goat cheese pie, 92–93
> deep-fried stuffed olives, 69
> duck liver pâté with juniper and allspice, 66

gefilte fish for Passover, 60–62

hard-boiled eggs with tapenade, 67

huevos haminados, 68

Oriental "gravlax," 64–65

pickled salmon, 57

polenta with smoked fish and crème fraîche, 58–59

scotch gravlax, 63–64

smoked trout, carrots, and cucumbers, 55

smoked trout pâté, 62

smoked trout with horseradish apple cream, 56

tonno tonnato, 53–54

wines with, 16

*see also* Salad

Apple(s):
> carrot, and red cabbage salad, 33
> chutney, 357
> horseradish cream, smoked trout with, 56
> in spiced red wine, 282

Apricot(s):
> cannoli dei sogni, 376–377
> chicken with tomatoes and, 215–216
> chutney, 356
> dried, chutney, 358

Arista di maiale alla fiorentina, 281–282

Armenian:
> basturma, 303
> roasted pepper sauce for fish, 178–179
> spinach borani, 323

Artichokes:
> carrots, and zucchini with lemon and dill, 40
> pasta with prosciutto, peas and, 148–149

Arugula:
> basil, and mint salad with

sun-dried tomato vinaigrette, 35

linguine with tuna, potatoes and, 142–143

Ashe maste, 121–122

Asian:
> Thai-inspired shrimp salad with spicy peanut vinaigrette, 45
> *see also* Afghani; Indian; Indonesian; Persian; Turkish; Russian

Asparagus:
> pasta with artichokes, prosciutto and, 148–149
> and potatoes all'ericina, 338

Aushak, 150–152

Avocado:
> cream of potato soup with chicken, corn and, 124
> salsa, 351
> and shrimp "cocktail," 46–47
> and shrimp salad with tomato ginger vinaigrette, 48
> soup, 116

Baci di dama, 403

Balkan:
> Albanian leek and goat cheese pie, 92–93
> crab salad with walnut and lemon mayonnaise, 50–51
> *see also* Bulgarian; Greek; Romanian; Turkish

Basil:
> arugula, and mint salad with sun-dried tomato vinaigrette, 35
> butter, 211
> grilled flank steak in onion, vinegar and, 303